D1144451

Śrī Caitanya-caritāmṛta

BOOKS by
His Divine Grace A.C. Bhaktivedanta Swami Prabhupāda

Bhagavad-gītā As It Is
Śrīmad-Bhāgavatam, Cantos 1-4 (13 Vols.)
Śrī Caitanya-caritāmṛta (4 Vols.)
Teachings of Lord Caitanya
The Nectar of Devotion
Śrī Īśopaniṣad
Easy Journey to Other Planets
Kṛṣṇa Consciousness: The Topmost Yoga System
Kṛṣṇa, The Supreme Personality of Godhead (3 Vols.)
Transcendental Teachings of Prahlād Mahārāja
Kṛṣṇa, the Reservoir of Pleasure
The Perfection of Yoga
Beyond Birth and Death
On the Way to Kṛṣṇa
Rāja-vidyā: The King of Knowledge
Elevation to Kṛṣṇa Consciousness
Kṛṣṇa Consciousness: The Matchless Gift
Back to Godhead Magazine (Founder)

A complete catalogue is available upon request.

International Society for Krishna Consciousness
3764 Watseka Avenue
Los Angeles, California 90034

Please address all Correspondence To:
Bhaktivedanta Book Trust,
Croome Court, Severn Stoke,
Nr. Worcester, WR8 9DW
Great Britain

All Glory to Śrī Guru and Gaurāṅga

ŚRĪ CAITANYA-CARITĀMṚTA

of Kṛṣṇadāsa Kavirāja Gosvāmī

Madhya-Līlā
Volume One

"The Ecstatic Manifestations of Lord Caitanya Mahāprabhu"

with the original Bengali text, Roman transliterations, synonyms, translation and elaborate purports

by

HIS DIVINE GRACE

A.C. Bhaktivedanta Swami Prabhupāda

Founder-Ācārya of the International Society for Krishna Consciousness

THE BHAKTIVEDANTA BOOK TRUST
New York · Los Angeles · London · Bombay

Readers interested in the subject matter of this book
are invited by the International Society for Krishna Consciousness
to correspond with its Secretary.

International Society for Krishna Consciousness
3764 Watseka Avenue
Los Angeles, California 90034

Please address all Correspondence To:
Bhaktivedanta Book Trust,
Croome Court, Severn Stoke,
Nr. Worcester, WR8 9DW
Great Britain

©1975 Bhaktivedanta Book Trust

All Rights Reserved

Library of Congress Catalogue Card Number: 73-93206
International Standard Book Number: 0-912776-63-3

Printed in the United States of America

Contents

Introduction

"HARE KṚṢṆA" has become a household phrase in cities, towns and villages throughout the world, fulfilling a prophecy made almost five hundred years ago by Lord Śrī Caitanya Mahāprabhu. From Los Angeles to London, from Bombay to Buenos Aires, from Pittsburgh and Melbourne to Paris and even Moscow, people of all ages, colors, creeds and faiths are feeling the bliss of the dynamic *yoga* system called "Kṛṣṇa consciousness."

This Kṛṣṇa consciousness movement began in full force some five hundred years ago, when Lord Śrī Caitanya Mahāprabhu, an incarnation of Kṛṣṇa (God), flooded the subcontinent of India with the chanting of the *mantra* Hare Kṛṣṇa, Hare Kṛṣṇa, Kṛṣṇa Kṛṣṇa, Hare Hare/ Hare Rāma, Hare Rāma, Rāma Rāma, Hare Hare. To reveal the secret of what real love is, Kṛṣṇa came to earth five hundred years ago in the guise of His own devotee—as Lord Caitanya Mahāprabhu. With His chief associates— Nityānanda, Advaita, Gadādhara and Śrīvāsa—He taught how to develop love of Godhead simply by chanting Hare Kṛṣṇa and dancing in ecstasy.

Śrī Caitanya-caritāmṛta, which was written by the great saint Kṛṣṇadāsa Kavirāja Gosvāmī shortly after Lord Caitanya's disappearance, vividly describes Lord Caitanya's blissful pastimes and probes deeply into His profound spiritual philosophy.

The translations and purports, the explanations of the verses, are the work of His Divine Grace A. C. Bhaktivedanta Swami Prabhupāda, the author of *Bhagavad-gītā As It is; The Nectar of Devotion; Kṛṣṇa, the Supreme Personality of Godhead* (first published in 1970 with the kind help of Mr. George Harrison); and numerous other books about *yoga* and self-realization.

Although this is the fourth volume of *Śrī Caitanya-caritāmṛta,* one need not have read the previous volumes to understand and appreciate this book. Śrīla Prabhupāda remarks that such a spiritual work is like sugar, for wherever you begin tasting it you will surely enjoy its sweetness.

His Divine Grace
A.C. BHAKTIVEDANTA SWAMI PRABHUPĀDA
Founder-Ācārya of the International Society for Krishna Consciousness

ŚRĪLA BHAKTISIDDHĀNTA SARASVATĪ GOSVĀMĪ MAHĀRĀJA
the spiritual master of
His Divine Grace A.C. Bhaktivedanta Swami Prabhupāda
and foremost scholar and devotee in the recent age.

Śrī Pañca-tattva

Lord Kṛṣṇa Caitanya surrounded (from left to right) by His avatāra *(Advaita Ācārya), His expansion (Lord Nityānanda), His manifest internal energy (Śrī Gadādhara), and His perfect devotee (Śrī Śrīvāsa).*

The great temple at Jagannātha Purī, where Lord Caitanya displayed many of His transcendental pastimes.

The samādhis *(tombs) of Śrīla Rūpa Gosvāmī (left) and Śrīla Raghunātha dāsa Gosvāmī (right), the spiritual masters of Kṛṣṇadāsa Kavirāja Gosvāmī (the author of Śrī Caitanya-caritāmṛta).*

The ISKCON world headquarters at Śrīdhāma Māyapura, the birthplace of Lord Caitanya Mahāprabhu.

Simple living and high thinking. *Members of the ISKCON world center depend on the Supreme Lord for the necessities of life.*

Following in the footsteps of Lord Caitanya, the devotees of the International Society for Krishna Consciousness distribute prasāda *(food offered to Kṛṣṇa) at the ISKCON center in Māyāpura, West Bengal.*

Every town and village. *Members of the Hare Kṛṣṇa movement performing* saṅkīrtana *(congregational chanting of the holy names of the Lord) in West Germany.*

Plate 1 *"Glory to the all-merciful Rādhā and Madana-mohana! I am lame and ill-advised, yet They are my directors, and Their lotus feet are everything to me."* (p. 3)

Plate 2 *"May Gopīnāthajī, who attracts all the* gopīs *with the song of His flute, be merciful upon us."* *(p. 4)*

Plate 3 *The six Gosvāmīs studied various Vedic literatures and picked up the essence of them, the devotional service of the Lord.* *(p. 17)*

Plate 4 *While Lord Caitanya was in an ecstatic state after reading the verse, Śrīla Rūpa Gosvāmī came and immediately fell down on the floor like a rod.* *(p. 46)*

Plate 5 *When Nṛsiṁhānanda Brahmacārī heard that Lord Caitanya Mahāprabhu would go to Vṛndāvana, he became very pleased and mentally began decorating the way there.* (p. 94)

Plate 6 "O Kṛṣṇa, the player of the flute, the sweetness of Your early age is wonderful within these three worlds." (p. 209)

Plate 7 *When two or four pieces of the thrown rice touched His body, Advaita Ācārya began to dance in various ways with the rice still stuck to His body. (p. 290)*

CHAPTER 1

The Later Pastimes of Lord Śrī Caitanya Mahāprabhu

In this chapter there is a summary description of all the pastimes performed by Śrī Caitanya Mahāprabhu during the middle period of His activities as well as the six years at the end of His activities. All of these are described in brief. There is also a description of Śrī Caitanya Mahāprabhu's ecstasy that occurred when He recited the verse beginning *yaḥ kaumāra-haraḥ*, and there is also an explanation of that ecstasy given in the verse *priyaḥ so 'yaṁ kṛṣṇaḥ* by Śrīla Rūpa Gosvāmī. Because he wrote that verse, Śrīla Rūpa Gosvāmī was specifically blessed by the Lord. There is also a description of the many books written by Śrīla Rūpa Gosvāmī, Śrīla Sanātana Gosvāmī and Śrīla Jīva Gosvāmī. There is also a description of the meeting between Śrī Caitanya Mahāprabhu, Śrīla Rūpa Gosvāmī and Śrīla Sanātana Gosvāmī in the village known as Rāmakeli.

TEXT 1

যস্য প্রসাদাদজ্ঞোঽপি সদ্যঃ সর্বজ্ঞতাং ব্রজেৎ ।
স শ্রীচৈতন্যদেবো মে ভগবান্ সংপ্রসীদতু ॥ ১ ॥

yasya prasādād ajño 'pi
sadyaḥ sarva-jñatāṁ vrajet
sa śrī-caitanya-devo me
bhagavān samprasīdatu

SYNONYMS

yasya—of whom; *prasādāt*—by the mercy; *ajñaḥ api*—even a person who has no knowledge; *sadyaḥ*—immediately; *sarva-jñatām*—all knowledge; *vrajet*—can achieve; *saḥ*—that; *śrī-caitanya-devaḥ*—Lord Śrī Caitanya Mahāprabhu; *me*—on me; *bhagavān*—the Supreme Personality of Godhead; *samprasīdatu*—may He bestow His causeless mercy.

TRANSLATION

Even a person with no knowledge can immediately acquire all knowledge simply by the benediction of Śrī Caitanya Mahāprabhu. Therefore I am praying to the Lord for His causeless mercy upon me.

TEXT 2

বন্দে শ্রীকৃষ্ণচৈতন্য-নিত্যানন্দৌ সহোদিতৌ।
গৌড়োদয়ে পুষ্পবন্তৌ চিত্রৌ শন্দৌ তমোনুদৌ ॥২॥

vande śrī-kṛṣṇa-caitanya-
nityānandau sahoditau
gauḍodaye puṣpavantau
citrau śandau tamo-nudau

SYNONYMS

vande—I offer respectful obeisances; *śrī-kṛṣṇa-caitanya*—to Lord Śrī Kṛṣṇa Caitanya; *nityānandau*—and to Lord Nityānanda; *saha-uditau*—simultaneously arisen; *gauḍa-udaye*—on the eastern horizon of Gauḍa; *puṣpavantau*—the sun and moon together; *citrau*—wonderful; *śam-dau*—bestowing benediction; *tamaḥ-nudau*—dissipating darkness.

TRANSLATION

I offer my respectful obeisances unto Śrī Kṛṣṇa Caitanya and Lord Nityānanda, who are like the sun and moon. They have arisen simultaneously on the horizon of Gauḍa to dissipate the darkness of ignorance and thus wonderfully bestow benediction upon all.

TEXT 3

জয়তাং সুরতৌ পঙ্গোর্মম মন্দমতের্গতী।
মৎসর্বস্বপদাম্ভোজৌ রাধামদনমোহনৌ ॥ ৩ ॥

jayatāṁ suratau paṅgor
mama manda-mater gatī
mat-sarvasva-padāmbhojau
rādhā-madana-mohanau

SYNONYMS

jayatām—all glory to; *su-ratau*—most merciful, or attached in conjugal love; *paṅgoḥ*—of one who is lame; *mama*—of me; *manda-mateḥ*—foolish; *gatī*—refuge; *mat*—my; *sarva-sva*—everything; *pada-ambhojau*—whose lotus feet; *rādhā-madana-mohanau*—Rādhārāṇī and Madana-mohana.

TRANSLATION

Glory to the all-merciful Rādhā and Madana-mohana! I am lame and ill-advised, yet They are my directors, and Their lotus feet are everything to me.

TEXT 4

দীব্যদ্বৃন্দারণ্যকল্পদ্রুমাধঃ-
শ্রীমদ্রত্নাগারসিংহাসনস্থৌ ।
শ্রীমদ্রাধাশ্রীলগোবিন্দদেবৌ
প্রেষ্ঠালীভিঃ সেব্যমানৌ স্মরামি ॥ ৪ ॥

dīvyad-vṛndāraṇya-kalpa-drumādhaḥ-
śrīmad-ratnāgāra-siṁhāsana-sthau
śrīmad-rādhā-śrīla-govinda-devau
preṣṭhālībhiḥ sevyamānau smarāmi

SYNONYMS

dīvyat—shining; *vṛndā-araṇya*—in the forest of Vṛndāvana; *kalpa-druma*—desire tree; *adhaḥ*—beneath; *śrīmat*—most beautiful; *ratna-āgāra*—in a temple of jewels; *siṁha-āsana-sthau*—sitting on a throne; *śrīmat*—very beautiful; *rādhā*—Śrīmatī Rādhārāṇī; *śrīla-govinda-devau*—and Śrī Govindadeva; *preṣṭha-ālībhiḥ*—by most confidential associates; *sevyamānau*—being served; *smarāmi*—I remember.

TRANSLATION

In a temple of jewels in Vṛndāvana, underneath a desire tree, Śrī Śrī Rādhā-Govinda, served by Their most confidential associates, sit upon an effulgent throne. I offer my humble obeisances unto Them.

TEXT 5

শ্রীমান্‌রাসরসারম্ভী বংশীবটতটস্থিতঃ।
কর্ষন্‌ বেণুস্বনৈর্গোপীর্গোপীনাথঃ শ্রিয়েঽস্তু নঃ ॥ ৫ ॥

śrīmān rāsa-rasārambhī
vaṁśīvaṭa-taṭa-sthitaḥ
karṣan veṇu-svanair gopīr
gopī-nāthaḥ śriye 'stu naḥ

SYNONYMS

śrīmān—the most beautiful form; *rāsa*—of the *rāsa* dance; *rasa-ārambhī*—the initiator of the mellow; *vaṁśī-vaṭa*—the celebrated place named Vaṁśīvaṭa; *taṭa*—on the bank of Yamunā; *sthitaḥ*—being situated; *karṣan*—attracting; *veṇu-svanaiḥ*—by the sounds of the flute; *gopīḥ*—all the *gopīs*; *gopī-nāthaḥ*—the master of all the *gopīs*; *śriye*—the opulence of love and affection; *astu*—let there be; *naḥ*—upon us.

TRANSLATION

May Gopīnāthajī, who attracts all the gopīs with the song of His flute and who has begun the most melodious rāsa dance on the bank of the Yamunā in Vaṁśīvaṭa, be merciful upon us.

TEXT 6

জয় জয় গৌরচন্দ্র জয় কৃপাসিন্ধু।
জয় জয় শচীসুত জয় দীনবন্ধু ॥ ৬ ॥

jaya jaya gauracandra jaya kṛpā-sindhu
jaya jaya śacī-suta jaya dīna-bandhu

SYNONYMS

jaya jaya—all glories; *gauracandra*—to Śrī Caitanya Mahāprabhu; *jaya*—all glories; *kṛpā-sindhu*—to the ocean of mercy; *jaya jaya*—all glories unto You; *śacī-suta*—the son of Śacī; *jaya*—all glories unto You; *dīna-bandhu*—the friend of the fallen.

TRANSLATION

All glories unto Śrī Gaurahari, who is an ocean of mercy! All glories unto You, the son of Śacīdevī, for You are the only friend of all fallen souls!

TEXT 7

জয় জয় নিত্যানন্দ জয়াদ্বৈতচন্দ্র ।
জয় শ্রীবাসাদি জয় গৌরভক্তবৃন্দ ॥ ৭ ॥

jaya jaya nityānanda jayādvaita-candra
jaya śrīvāsādi jaya gaura-bhakta-vṛnda

SYNONYMS

jaya jaya—all glories; *nityānanda*—to Lord Nityānanda; *jaya advaita-candra*—all glories to Advaita Prabhu; *jaya*—all glories; *śrīvāsa-ādi*—to all the devotees, headed by Śrīvāsa Ṭhākura; *jaya gaura-bhakta-vṛnda*—all glories unto the devotees of Lord Gaurasundara.

TRANSLATION

All glories unto Lord Nityānanda and Advaita Prabhu, and all glories unto all the devotees of Lord Caitanya, headed by Śrīvāsa Ṭhākura!

TEXT 8

পূর্বে কহিলুঁ আদিলীলার সূত্রগণ ।
যাহা বিস্তারিয়াছেন দাস-বৃন্দাবন ॥ ৮ ॥

pūrve kahiluṅ ādi-līlāra sūtra-gaṇa
yāhā vistāriyāchena dāsa-vṛndāvana

SYNONYMS

pūrve—previously; *kahiluṅ*—I have described; *ādi-līlāra*—of the *ādi-līlā*; *sūtra-gaṇa*—the synopsis; *yāhā*—which; *vistāriyāchena*—has elaborately explained; *dāsa-vṛndāvana*—Vṛndāvana dāsa Ṭhākura.

TRANSLATION

I have previously described in synopsis the ādi-līlā [initial pastimes], which have already been fully described by Vṛndāvana dāsa Ṭhākura.

TEXT 9

অতএব তার আমি সূত্রমাত্র কৈলুঁ ।
যে কিছু বিশেষ, সূত্রমধ্যেই কহিলুঁ ॥ ৯ ॥

ataeva tāra āmi sūtra-mātra kailuṅ
ye kichu viśeṣa, sūtra-madhyei kahiluṅ

SYNONYMS

ataeva—therefore; *tāra*—of that; *āmi*—I; *sūtra-mātra*—only the synopsis; *kailuṅ*—did; *ye kichu*—whatever; *viśeṣa*—specifics; *sūtra-madhyei kahiluṅ*—I have already stated within the synopsis.

TRANSLATION

I have therefore given only a synopsis of those incidents, and whatever specifics were to be related have already been given in that synopsis.

TEXT 10

এবে কহি শেষলীলার মুখ্য সূত্রগণ ।
প্রভুর অশেষ লীলা না যায় বর্ণন ॥ ১০ ॥

ebe kahi śeṣa-līlāra mukhya sūtra-gaṇa
prabhura aśeṣa līlā nā yāya varṇana

SYNONYMS

ebe—now; *kahi*—I describe; *śeṣa-līlāra*—of the pastimes at the end; *mukhya*—chief; *sūtra-gaṇa*—synopsis; *prabhura*—of Lord Caitanya Mahāprabhu; *aśeṣa*—unlimited; *līlā*—pastimes; *nā yāya varṇana*—it is not possible to describe.

TRANSLATION

To describe the unlimited pastimes of Śrī Caitanya Mahāprabhu is not possible, but I now wish to relate the chief incidents and give a synopsis of those pastimes occurring at the end.

TEXTS 11-12

তার মধ্যে যেই ভাগ দাস-বৃন্দাবন ।
'চৈতন্যমঙ্গলে' বিস্তারি' করিলা বর্ণন ॥ ১১ ॥

সেই ভাগের ইহাঁ সূত্রমাত্র লিখিব ।
তাহাঁ যে বিশেষ কিছু, ইহাঁ বিস্তারিব ॥ ১২ ॥

tāra madhye yei bhāga dāsa-vṛndāvana
'caitanya-maṅgale' vistāri' karilā varṇana

sei bhāgera ihāṅ sūtra-mātra likhiba
tāhāṅ ye viśeṣa kichu, ihāṅ vistāriba

SYNONYMS

tāra madhye—amongst them; *yei*—which; *bhāga*—portion; *dāsa-vṛndāvana*—Śrīla Vṛndāvana dāsa Ṭhākura; *caitanya-maṅgale*—in his book *Caitanya-maṅgala*; *vistāri'*—elaborating; *karilā varṇana*—has described; *sei bhāgera*—of that portion; *ihāṅ*—here in this book; *sūtra-mātra*—the synopsis only; *likhiba*—I shall write; *tāhāṅ*—there; *ye*—whatever; *viśeṣa*—special details; *kichu*—something; *ihāṅ vistāriba*—I shall describe elaborately.

TRANSLATION

I shall describe only in synopsis that portion which Vṛndāvana dāsa Ṭhākura has described very elaborately in his book Caitanya-maṅgala. Whatever incidents are outstanding, however, I shall later elaborate.

TEXT 13

চৈতন্যলীলার ব্যাস—দাস বৃন্দাবন ।
তাঁর আজ্ঞায় করোঁ তাঁর উচ্ছিষ্ট চর্বণ ॥ ১৩ ॥

caitanya-līlāra vyāsa—dāsa vṛndāvana
tāṅra ājñāya karoṅ tāṅra ucchiṣṭa carvaṇa

SYNONYMS

caitanya-līlāra vyāsa—the Vyāsadeva, or compiler of the pastimes, of Lord Caitanya Mahāprabhu; *dāsa vṛndāvana*—Vṛndāvana dāsa Ṭhākura; *tāṅra*—of him; *ājñāya*—upon the order; *karoṅ*—I do; *tāṅra*—his; *ucchiṣṭa*—of the remnants of foodstuff; *carvaṇa*—chewing.

TRANSLATION

Actually the authorized compiler of the pastimes of Śrī Caitanya Mahāprabhu is Śrīla dāsa Vṛndāvana, the incarnation of Vyāsadeva. Only upon his orders am I trying to chew the remnants of food that he has left.

TEXT 14

ভক্তি করি' শিরে ধরি তাঁহার চরণ ।
শেষলীলার সূত্রগণ করিয়ে বর্ণন ॥ ১৪ ॥

bhakti kari' śire dhari tāṅhāra caraṇa
śeṣa-līlāra sūtra-gaṇa kariye varṇana

SYNONYMS

bhakti kari'—with great devotion; *śire*—on my head; *dhari*—I hold; *tāṅhāra*—his; *caraṇa*—lotus feet; *śeṣa-līlāra*—of the pastimes at the end; *sūtra-gaṇa*—the synopsis; *kariye*—I do; *varṇana*—describe.

TRANSLATION

Placing his lotus feet upon my head in great devotion, I shall now describe in summary the Lord's final pastimes.

TEXT 15

চব্বিশ বৎসর প্রভুর গৃহে অবস্থান ।
তাহাঁ যে করিলা লীলা—'আদি-লীলা' নাম ॥ ১৫ ॥

cabbiśa vatsara prabhura gṛhe avasthāna
tāhāṅ ye karilā līlā——'ādi-līlā' nāma

SYNONYMS

cabbiśa vatsara—for twenty-four years; *prabhura*—of the Lord; *gṛhe*—at home; *avasthāna*—residing; *tāhāṅ*—there; *ye*—whatever; *karilā*—He performed; *līlā*—pastimes; *ādi-līlā nāma*—are called *ādi-līlā*.

TRANSLATION

For twenty-four years, Lord Śrī Caitanya Mahāprabhu remained at home, and whatever pastimes He performed during that time are called the ādi-līlā.

TEXT 16

চব্বিশ বৎসর শেষে যেই মাঘমাস ।
তার শুক্লপক্ষে প্রভু করিলা সন্ন্যাস ॥ ১৬ ॥

cabbiśa vatsara śeṣe yei māgha-māsa
tāra śukla-pakṣe prabhu karilā sannyāsa

SYNONYMS

cabbiśa vatsara—of those twenty-four years; *śeṣe*—at the end; *yei*—which; *māgha-māsa*—the month of Māgha (January-February); *tāra*—of that month; *śukla-pakṣe*—during the fortnight of the waxing moon; *prabhu*—the Lord; *karilā*—accepted; *sannyāsa*—the renounced order of life.

TRANSLATION

At the end of His twenty-fourth year, in the month of Māgha, during the fortnight of the waxing moon, the Lord accepted the renounced order of life, sannyāsa.

TEXT 17

সন্ন্যাস করিয়া চব্বিশ বৎসর অবস্থান ।
তাহাঁ যেই লীলা, তার 'শেষলীলা' নাম ॥ ১৭ ॥

sannyāsa kariyā cabbiśa vatsara avasthāna
tāhāṅ yei līlā, tāra 'śeṣa-līlā' nāma

SYNONYMS

sannyāsa kariyā—after accepting the order of *sannyāsa*; *cabbiśa vatsara*—the twenty-four years; *avasthāna*—remaining in this material world; *tāhāṅ*—in that portion; *yei līlā*—whatever pastimes (were performed); *tāra*—of those pastimes; *śeṣa-līlā*—the pastimes at the end; *nāma*—named.

TRANSLATION

After accepting sannyāsa, Lord Caitanya remained within this material world for another twenty-four years. Within this period, whatever pastimes He enacted are called the śeṣa-līlā, or pastimes occurring at the end.

TEXT 18

শেষলীলার 'মধ্য' 'অন্ত্য',—দুই নাম হয় ।
লীলাভেদে বৈষ্ণব সব নাম-ভেদ কয় ॥ ১৮ ॥

śeṣa-līlāra 'madhya' 'antya',——dui nāma haya
līlā-bhede vaiṣṇava saba nāma-bheda kaya

SYNONYMS

śeṣa-līlāra—of the *śeṣa-līlā,* or pastimes at the end; *madhya*—the middle; *antya*—the final; *dui*—two; *nāma*—names; *haya*—are; *līlā-bhede*—by the difference of pastimes; *vaiṣṇava*—the devotees of the Supreme Lord; *saba*—all; *nāma-bheda*—different names; *kaya*—say.

TRANSLATION

The final pastimes of the Lord, occurring in His last twenty-four years, are called madhya [middle] and antya [final]. All the devotees of the Lord refer to His pastimes according to these divisions.

TEXT 19

তার মধ্যে ছয় বৎসর—গমনাগমন ।
নীলাচল-গৌড়-সেতুবন্ধ-বৃন্দাবন ॥ ১৯ ॥

tāra madhye chaya vatsara——gamanāgamana
nīlācala-gauḍa-setubandha-vṛndāvana

SYNONYMS

tāra madhye—within that period; *chaya vatsara*—for six years; *gamana-āgamana*—going and coming; *nīlācala*—from Jagannātha Purī; *gauḍa*—to Bengal; *setubandha*—and from Cape Comorin; *vṛndāvana*—to Vṛndāvana-dhāma.

TRANSLATION

For six years of the last twenty-four, Śrī Caitanya Mahāprabhu traveled all over India from Jagannātha Purī to Bengal and from Cape Comorin to Vṛndāvana.

TEXT 20

তাহাঁ যেই লীলা, তার 'মধ্যলীলা' নাম ।
তার পাছে লীলা—'অন্ত্যলীলা' অভিধান ॥ ২০ ॥

tāhāṅ yei līlā, tāra 'madhya-līlā' nāma
tāra pāche līlā—'antya-līlā' abhidhāna

SYNONYMS

tāhāṅ—in those places; *yei līlā*—all the pastimes; *tāra*—of those; *madhya-līlā*—the middle pastimes; *nāma*—named; *tāra pāche līlā*—all the pastimes after that period; *antya-līlā*—last pastimes; *abhidhāna*—the nomenclature.

TRANSLATION

All the pastimes performed by the Lord in those places are known as the madhya-līlā, and whatever pastimes were performed after that are called the antya-līlā.

TEXT 21

'আদিলীলা', 'মধ্যলীলা', 'অন্ত্যলীলা' আর ।
এবে 'মধ্যলীলার' কিছু করিয়ে বিস্তার ॥ ২১ ॥

'ādi-līlā', 'madhya-līlā', 'antya-līlā' āra
ebe 'madhya-līlāra' kichu kariye vistāra

SYNONYMS

ādi-līlā madhya-līlā antya-līlā āra—therefore there are three periods, namely the *ādi-līlā, madhya-līlā* and *antya-līlā*; *ebe*—now; *madhya-līlāra*—of the *madhya-līlā*; *kichu*—something; *kariye*—I shall do; *vistāra*—elaboration.

TRANSLATION

The pastimes of the Lord are therefore divided into three periods—the ādi-līlā, madhya-līlā and antya-līlā. Now I shall very elaborately describe the madhya-līlā.

TEXT 22

অষ্টাদশবর্ষ কেবল নীলাচলে স্থিতি ।
আপনি আচরি' জীবে শিখাইলা ভক্তি ॥ ২২ ॥

aṣṭādaśa-varṣa kevala nīlācale sthiti
āpani ācari' jīve śikhāilā bhakti

SYNONYMS

aṣṭādaśa-varṣa—for eighteen years; *kevala*—only; *nīlācale*—in Jagannātha Purī; *sthiti*—staying; *āpani*—personally; *ācari'*—behaving; *jīve*—unto the living entities; *śikhāilā*—instructed; *bhakti*—devotional service.

TRANSLATION

For eighteen continuous years, Lord Śrī Caitanya Mahāprabhu remained at Jagannātha Purī and, through His personal behavior, instructed all living entities in the mode of devotional service.

TEXT 23

তার মধ্যে ছয় বৎসর ভক্তগণ-সঙ্গে ।
প্রেমভক্তি প্রবর্তাইলা নৃত্যগীতরঙ্গে ॥ ২৩ ॥

tāra madhye chaya vatsara bhakta-gaṇa-saṅge
prema-bhakti pravartāilā nṛtya-gīta-raṅge

SYNONYMS

tāra madhye—within that period; *chaya vatsara*—for six years; *bhakta-gaṇa-saṅge*—with all the devotees; *prema-bhakti*—the loving service of the Lord; *pravartāilā*—introduced; *nṛtya-gīta-raṅge*—in the matter of chanting and dancing.

TRANSLATION

Of these eighteen years at Jagannātha Purī, Śrī Caitanya Mahāprabhu spent six years with His many devotees. By chanting and dancing, He introduced the loving service of the Lord.

TEXT 24

নিত্যানন্দ-গোসাঞিরে পাঠাইল গৌড়দেশে ।
তেঁহো গৌড়দেশ ভাসাইল প্রেমরসে ॥ ২৪ ॥

nityānanda-gosāñire pāṭhāila gauḍa-deśe
teṅho gauḍa-deśa bhāsāila prema-rase

SYNONYMS

nityānanda-gosāñire—Nityānanda Gosvāmī; *pāṭhāila*—sent; *gauḍa-deśe*—to Bengal; *teṅho*—He; *gauḍa-deśa*—the tract of land known as Gauḍa-deśa, or Bengal; *bhāsāila*—overflooded; *prema-rase*—with ecstatic love of Kṛṣṇa.

TRANSLATION

Lord Śrī Caitanya Mahāprabhu sent Nityānanda Prabhu from Jagannātha Purī to Bengal, which was known as Gauḍa-deśa, and Lord Nityānanda Prabhu overflooded this country with the transcendental loving service of the Lord.

TEXT 25

সহজেই নিত্যানন্দ—কৃষ্ণপ্রেমোদ্দাম ।
প্রভু-আজ্ঞায় কৈল যাহাঁ তাহাঁ প্রেমদান ॥ ২৫ ॥

sahajei nityānanda——kṛṣṇa-premoddāma
prabhu-ājñāya kaila yāhāṅ tāhāṅ prema-dāna

SYNONYMS

sahajei—by nature; *nityānanda*—Lord Nityānanda Prabhu; *kṛṣṇa-prema-uddāma*—very much inspired in transcendental loving service to Lord Kṛṣṇa; *prabhu-ājñāya*—by the order of the Lord; *kaila*—did; *yāhāṅ tāhāṅ*—anywhere and everywhere; *prema-dāna*—distribution of that love.

TRANSLATION

Śrī Nityānanda Prabhu is by nature very much inspired in rendering transcendental loving service to Lord Kṛṣṇa. Now, being ordered by Śrī Caitanya Mahāprabhu, He distributed this loving service anywhere and everywhere.

TEXT 26

তাঁহার চরণে মোর কোটি নমস্কার ।
চৈতন্যের ভক্তি যেঁহো লওয়াইল সংসার ॥ ২৬ ॥

tāṅhāra caraṇe mora koṭi namaskāra
caitanyera bhakti yeṅho laoyāila saṁsāra

SYNONYMS

tāṅhāra caraṇe—unto His lotus feet; *mora*—my; *koṭi*—unlimited; *namaskāra*—obeisances; *caitanyera*—of Lord Śrī Caitanya Mahāprabhu; *bhakti*—the devotional service; *yeṅho*—one who; *laoyāila*—caused to take; *saṁsāra*—the whole world.

TRANSLATION

I offer innumerable obeisances unto the lotus feet of Śrī Nityānanda Prabhu, who is so kind that He spread the service of Śrī Caitanya Mahāprabhu all over the world.

TEXT 27

চৈতন্য-গোসাঞি যাঁরে বলে 'বড় ভাই' ।
তেঁহো কহে, মোর প্রভু—চৈতন্য-গোসাঞি ॥ ২৭ ॥

caitanya-gosāñi yāṅre bale 'baḍa bhāi'
teṅho kahe, mora prabhu——caitanya-gosāñi

SYNONYMS

caitanya-gosāñi—Lord Śrī Caitanya Mahāprabhu; *yāṅre*—unto whom; *bale*—says; *baḍa bhāi*—elder brother; *teṅho*—He; *kahe*—says; *mora prabhu*—My Lord; *caitanya-gosāñi*—the supreme master, Lord Caitanya Mahāprabhu.

TRANSLATION

Caitanya Mahāprabhu used to address Nityānanda Prabhu as His elder brother, whereas Nityānanda Prabhu addressed Śrī Caitanya Mahāprabhu as His Lord.

TEXT 28

যদ্যপি আপনি হয়ে প্রভু বলরাম ।
তথাপি চৈতন্যের করে দাস-অভিমান ॥ ২৮ ॥

yadyapi āpani haye prabhu balarāma
tathāpi caitanyera kare dāsa-abhimāna

SYNONYMS

yadyapi—although; *āpani*—personally; *haye*—is; *prabhu*—Lord; *balarāma*—Balarāma; *tathāpi*—still; *caitanyera*—of Lord Śrī Caitanya Mahāprabhu; *kare*—accepts; *dāsa-abhimāna*—conception as the eternal servant.

TRANSLATION

Although Nityānanda Prabhu is none other than Balarāma Himself, He nonetheless always thinks of Himself as the eternal servant of Lord Śrī Caitanya Mahāprabhu.

TEXT 29

‘চৈতন্য’ সেব, ‘চৈতন্য’ গাও, লও ‘চৈতন্য’-নাম ।
‘চৈতন্যে’ যে ভক্তি করে, সেই মোর প্রাণ ॥ ২৯ ॥

'caitanya' seva, 'caitanya' gāo, lao 'caitanya'-nāma
'caitanye' ye bhakti kare, sei mora prāṇa

SYNONYMS

caitanya seva—serve Śrī Caitanya Mahāprabhu; *caitanya gāo*—chant about Śrī Caitanya Mahāprabhu; *lao*—always take; *caitanya-nāma*—the name of Lord Caitanya Mahāprabhu; *caitanye*—unto Lord Śrī Caitanya Mahāprabhu; *ye*—anyone who; *bhakti*—devotional service; *kare*—renders; *sei*—that person; *mora*—My; *prāṇa*—life and soul.

TRANSLATION

Nityānanda Prabhu requested everyone to serve Śrī Caitanya Mahāprabhu, chant His glories and utter His name. Nityānanda Prabhu claimed that person to be His life and soul who rendered devotional service unto Śrī Caitanya Mahāprabhu.

TEXT 30

এই মত লোকে চৈতন্য-ভক্তি লওয়াইল ।
দীনহীন, নিন্দক, সবারে নিস্তারিল ॥ ৩০ ॥

ei mata loke caitanya-bhakti laoyāila
dīna-hīna, nindaka, sabāre nistārila

SYNONYMS

ei mata—in this way; *loke*—the people in general; *caitanya*—of Lord Caitanya Mahāprabhu; *bhakti*—the devotional service; *laoyāila*—He caused to accept; *dīna-hīna*—poor fallen souls; *nindaka*—blasphemers; *sabāre*—everyone; *nistārila*—He delivered.

TRANSLATION

In this way, Śrīla Nityānanda Prabhu introduced the cult of Śrī Caitanya Mahāprabhu to everyone without discrimination. Even though the people were fallen souls and blasphemers, they were delivered by this process.

TEXT 31

তবে প্রভু ব্রজে পাঠাইল রূপ-সনাতন।
প্রভু-আজ্ঞায় দুই ভাই আইলা বৃন্দাবন ॥ ৩১ ॥

tabe prabhu vraje pāṭhāila rūpa-sanātana
prabhu-ājñāya dui bhāi āilā vṛndāvana

SYNONYMS

tabe—after this; *prabhu*—Lord Śrī Caitanya Mahāprabhu; *vraje*—to Vṛndāvana-dhāma; *pāṭhāila*—sent; *rūpa-sanātana*—the two brothers Rūpa Gosvāmī and Sanātana Gosvāmī; *prabhu-ājñāya*—upon the order of Śrī Caitanya Mahāprabhu; *dui bhāi*—the two brothers; *āilā*—came; *vṛndāvana*—to Vṛndāvana-dhāma.

TRANSLATION

Lord Śrī Caitanya Mahāprabhu then sent the two brothers Śrīla Rūpa Gosvāmī and Śrīla Sanātana Gosvāmī to Vraja. By His order, they went to Śrī Vṛndāvana-dhāma.

TEXT 32

ভক্তি প্রচারিয়া সর্বতীর্থ প্রকাশিল।
মদনগোপাল-গোবিন্দের সেবা প্রচারিল ॥ ৩২ ॥

bhakti pracāriyā sarva-tīrtha prakāśila
madana-gopāla-govindera sevā pracārila

SYNONYMS

bhakti pracāriyā—broadcasting devotional service; *sarva-tīrtha*—all the places of pilgrimage; *prakāśila*—discovered; *madana-gopāla*—of Śrī Rādhā-Madana-mohana; *govindera*—of Śrī Rādhā-Govindajī; *sevā*—the service; *pracārila*—introduced.

TRANSLATION

After going to Vṛndāvana, the brothers preached devotional service and discovered many places of pilgrimage. They specifically initiated the service of Madana-mohana and Govindajī.

TEXT 33

নানা শাস্ত্র আনি' কৈলা ভক্তিগ্রন্থ সার ।
মূঢ় অধমজনেরে তেঁহো করিলা নিস্তার ॥ ৩৩ ॥

nānā śāstra āni' kailā bhakti-grantha sāra
mūḍha adhama-janere teṅho karilā nistāra

SYNONYMS

nānā śāstra—different types of scriptures; *āni'*—collecting; *kailā*—compiled; *bhakti-grantha*—of books on devotional service; *sāra*—the essence; *mūḍha*—rascals; *adhama-janere*—and fallen souls; *teṅho*—they; *karilā nistāra*—delivered.

TRANSLATION

Both Rūpa Gosvāmī and Sanātana Gosvāmī brought various scriptures to Vṛndāvana and collected the essence of these by compiling many scriptures on devotional service. In this way they delivered all rascals and fallen souls.

PURPORT

Śrīla Śrīnivāsa Ācārya has sung:

nānā-śāstra-vicāraṇaika-nipuṇau sad-dharma-saṁsthāpakau
lokānāṁ hita-kāriṇau tri-bhuvane mānyau śaraṇyākarau
rādhā-kṛṣṇa-padāravinda-bhajanānandena mattālikau
vande rūpa-sanātanau raghu-yugau śrī-jīva gopālakau

The six *gosvāmīs,* under the direction of Śrīla Rūpa Gosvāmī and Śrīla Sanātana Gosvāmī, studied various Vedic literatures and picked up the essence of them, the devotional service of the Lord. This means that all the *gosvāmīs* wrote many scriptures on devotional service with the support of Vedic literature. Devotional service is not a sentimental activity. The essence of Vedic knowledge is devotional service, as confirmed in *Bhagavad-gītā: vedaiś ca sarvair aham eva vedyaḥ* (Bg. 15.15). All the Vedic literature aims at understanding Kṛṣṇa, and how to understand Kṛṣṇa through devotional service has been explained by Śrīla Rūpa and Sanātana Gosvāmīs, with evidence from all Vedic literatures. They have put it so nicely that even a rascal or first-class fool can be delivered by devotional service under the guidance of the *gosvāmīs*.

TEXT 34

প্রভু আজ্ঞায় কৈল সব শাস্ত্রের বিচার ।
ব্রজের নিগূঢ় ভক্তি করিল প্রচার ॥ ৩৪ ॥

prabhu ājñāya kaila saba śāstrera vicāra
vrajera nigūḍha bhakti karila pracāra

SYNONYMS

prabhu ājñāya—upon the order of Lord Śrī Caitanya Mahāprabhu; *kaila*—they did; *saba śāstrera*—of all scriptures; *vicāra*—analytical study; *vrajera*—of Śrī Vṛndāvana-dhāma; *nigūḍha*—most confidential; *bhakti*—devotional service; *karila*—did; *pracāra*—preaching.

TRANSLATION

The gosvāmīs carried out the preaching work of devotional service on the basis of an analytical study of all confidential Vedic literatures. This was in compliance with the order of Śrī Caitanya Mahāprabhu. Thus one can understand the most confidential devotional service of Vṛndāvana.

PURPORT

This proves that bona fide devotional service is based on the conclusions of Vedic literature. It is not based on the type of sentiment exhibited by the *prākṛta-sahajiyās*. The *prākṛta-sahajiyās* do not consult the Vedic literatures, and they are debauchees, woman hunters and smokers of *gañja*. Sometimes they give a theatrical performance and cry for the Lord with tears in their eyes. Of course, all scriptural conclusions are washed off by these tears. The *prākṛta-sahajiyās* do not realize that they are violating the orders of Śrī Caitanya Mahāprabhu, who specifically said that to understand Vṛndāvana and the pastimes of Vṛndāvana, one must have sufficient knowledge of the *śāstras* (Vedic literatures). As stated in *Śrīmad-Bhāgavatam, bhaktyā śruta-gṛhītayā*. This means that devotional service is acquired from Vedic knowledge. *Tac chraddadhānāḥ munayaḥ*. Devotees who are actually serious attain *bhakti*, scientific devotional service, by hearing Vedic literatures (*bhaktyā śruta-gṛhītayā*). It is not that one should create something out of sentimentality, become a *sahajiyā*, and advocate such concocted devotional service. However, Śrīla Bhaktisiddhānta Sarasvatī Ṭhākura considered such *sahajiyās* to be more favorable than the impersonalists, who are hopelessly atheistic. The impersonalists have no idea of the Supreme Personality of Godhead. The position of the *sahajiyās* is far better than that of the Māyāvādī *sannyāsīs*. Although the *sahajiyās* do not think much of Vedic knowledge, they nonetheless have accepted Lord Kṛṣṇa as the Supreme Lord. Unfortunately, they mislead others from authentic devotional service.

TEXT 35

হরিভক্তিবিলাস, আর ভাগবতামৃত ।
দশম-টিপ্পনী, আর দশম-চরিত ॥ ৩৫ ॥

hari-bhakti-vilāsa, āra bhāgavatāmṛta
daśama-ṭippanī, āra daśama-carita

SYNONYMS

hari-bhakti-vilāsa—the scripture named *Hari-bhakti-vilāsa*; *āra*—and; *bhāgavata-amṛta*—the scripture named *Bhāgavatāmṛta*; *daśama-ṭippanī*—comments on the Tenth Canto of *Śrīmad-Bhāgavatam*; *āra*—and; *daśama-carita*—poetry about the Tenth Canto of *Śrīmad-Bhāgavatam*.

TRANSLATION

Some of the books compiled by Śrīla Sanātana Gosvāmī were Hari-bhakti-vilāsa, Bhāgavatāmṛta, Daśama-ṭippanī and Daśama-carita.

PURPORT

In the First Wave of the book known as *Bhakti-ratnākara*, it is said that Sanātana Gosvāmī understood *Śrīmad-Bhāgavatam* by thorough study and explained it in his commentary known as *Vaiṣṇava-toṣaṇī*. All the knowledge that Śrī Sanātana Gosvāmī and Rūpa Gosvāmī directly acquired from Śrī Caitanya Mahāprabhu was broadcast all over the world by their expert service. Sanātana Gosvāmī gave his *Vaiṣṇava-toṣaṇī* commentary to Śrīla Jīva Gosvāmī for editing, and Śrīla Jīva Gosvāmī edited this under the name of *Laghu-toṣaṇī*. Whatever he immediately put down in writing was finished in the year 1476 Śaka. Śrīla Jīva Gosvāmī completed *Laghu-toṣaṇī* in the year Śakābda 1504.

The subject matter of *Hari-bhakti-vilāsa,* by Śrī Sanātana Gosvāmī, was collected by Śrīla Gopāla Bhaṭṭa Gosvāmī and is known as a *vaiṣṇava-smṛti.* This *vaiṣṇava-smṛti-grantha* was finished in twenty chapters, known as *vilāsas.* In the first *vilāsa* there is a description of how a relationship is established between the spiritual master and the disciple, and *mantras* are explained. In the second *vilāsa,* the process of initiation is described. In the third *vilāsa,* the methods of Vaiṣṇava behavior are given, with emphasis on cleanliness, constant remembrance of the Supreme Personality of Godhead, and the chanting of the *mantras* given by the initiating spiritual master. In the fourth *vilāsa* are descriptions of *saṁskāra,* the reformatory method; *tilaka,* the application of twelve *tilakas* on twelve places of the body; *mudrā,* marks on the body; *mālā,* chanting with beads; and *guru-pūjā,* worship of the spiritual master. In the fifth *vilāsa,* one is instructed on how to make a place to sit for meditation, and there are descriptions of breathing exercises, meditation and worship of the *śālagrāma-śilā* representation of Lord Viṣṇu. In the sixth *vilāsa,* the required practices for inviting the transcendental form of the Lord and bathing Him are given. In the seventh *vilāsa,* one is instructed on how to collect flowers used for the worship of Lord Viṣṇu. In the eighth *vilāsa,* there is a description of the Deity and instructions on how to set up incense, light lamps, make offerings, dance, play music, beat drums, garland the Deity, offer prayers and obeisances and counteract offenses. In the ninth *vilāsa,* there are descriptions about collecting *tulasī* leaves, offering oblations to forefathers according to Vaiṣṇava rituals, and offering food. In the tenth *vilāsa* there are descriptions of the devotees of the Lord (Vaiṣṇavas or saintly persons). In the eleventh *vilāsa,* there are elaborate descriptions of Deity worship and the glories of the holy name of the Lord. One is instructed on how to chant the holy name of the Deity, and there are discussions about offenses committed while chanting the holy name, along with methods for getting relief from such offenses. There are also descriptions of the glories of devotional service and the surrendering process. In the twelfth *vilāsa,* Ekādaśī is described. In the thirteenth *vilāsa,* fasting is discussed, as well as observance of the Mahā-dvādaśī ceremony. In the fourteenth *vilāsa,* different duties for different months are outlined. In the fifteenth *vilāsa,* there are instructions on how to observe Ekādaśī fasting without even drinking water. There are also descriptions of branding the body with the symbols of Viṣṇu, and discussions of Cāturmāsya observations during the rainy season, and discussions of Janmāṣṭamī, Pārśvaikādaśī, Śravaṇā-dvādaśī, Rāma-navamī and Vijayā-daśamī. The sixteenth *vilāsa* discusses duties to be observed in the month of Kārttika (October-November), or the Dāmodara month, or Ūrja, when lamps are offered in the Deity room or above the temple. There are also descriptions of the Govardhana-pūjā and Ratha-yātrā. The seventeenth *vilāsa* discusses preparations for Deity worship, *mahā-mantra* chanting and the process of *japa*. In the eighteenth *vilāsa* the different forms of Śrī Viṣṇu are described. The nineteenth *vilāsa* discusses the establishment of the Deity and the rituals observed in bathing the Deity before installation. The twentieth *vilāsa* discusses the construction of temples, referring to those constructed by the great devotees. The details of the *Hari-bhakti-vilāsa-grantha* are given by Śrī Kavirāja Gosvāmī in the *Madhya-līlā* (24.329-345). The descriptions given in those verses by Kṛṣṇadāsa Kavirāja Gosvāmī are actually a description of those portions compiled by Gopāla Bhaṭṭa Gosvāmī. According to Śrīla Bhaktisiddhānta Sarasvatī Ṭhākura, the regulative principles of devotional service compiled by Gopāla Bhaṭṭa Gosvāmī do not strictly follow our Vaiṣṇava principles. Actually, Gopāla Bhaṭṭa Gosvāmī collected only a summary of the elaborate descriptions of Vaiṣṇava regulative principles from *Hari-bhakti-vilāsa*. It is Śrīla Bhaktisiddhānta Sarasvatī Gosvāmī's opinion, however, that to follow the *Hari-bhakti-vilāsa* strictly is to actually follow the Vaiṣṇava rituals in perfect order. He claims that the *smārta-samāja,* which is strictly followed by caste *brāhmaṇas,* has influenced portions that Gopāla Bhaṭṭa Gosvāmī collected from the original *Hari-bhakti-vilāsa*. It is therefore very difficult to find out Vaiṣṇava directions from the book of Gopāla Bhaṭṭa Gosvāmī. It is better to consult the commentary made by Sanātana Gosvāmī himself for *Hari-bhakti-vilāsa* under the name of *Dig-darśinī-ṭīkā*. Some say that the same commentary was compiled by Gopīnātha-pūjā Adhikārī, who was engaged in the service of Śrī Rādhā-ramaṇajī and who happened to be one of the disciples of Gopāla Bhaṭṭa Gosvāmī.

Regarding *Bṛhad-bhāgavatāmṛta,* there are two parts dealing with the discharge of devotional service. The first part is an analytical study of devotional service, in which there is also a description of different planets, including the earth, the heavenly planets, Brahma-loka and Vaikuṇṭha-loka. There are also descriptions of the devotees, including intimate devotees, most intimate devotees and complete devotees. The second part describes the glories of the spiritual world, known as *Goloka-māhātmya-nirūpaṇa,* as well as the process of renunciation of the material world. It also describes real knowledge, devotional service, the spiritual world, love of Godhead, attainment of life's destination, and the bliss of the world. In this way there are seven chapters in each part, fourteen chapters in all.

Daśama-ṭippanī is a commentary on the Tenth Canto of *Śrīmad-Bhāgavatam*. Another name for this commentary is *Bṛhad-vaiṣṇava-toṣaṇī-ṭīkā*. In the *Bhakti-ratnākara,* it is said that *Daśama-ṭippanī* was finished in 1476 Śakābda.

TEXT 36

এই সব গ্রন্থ কৈল গোসাঞি সনাতন ।
রূপগোসাঞি কৈল যত, কে করু গণন ॥ ৩৬ ॥

ei saba grantha kaila gosāñi sanātana
rūpa-gosāñi kaila yata, ke karu gaṇana

SYNONYMS

ei saba—all these; *grantha*—scriptures; *kaila*—compiled; *gosāñi sanātana*—Sanātana Gosvāmī; *rūpa-gosāñi*—Rūpa Gosvāmī; *kaila*—did; *yata*—all; *ke*—who; *karu gaṇana*—can count.

TRANSLATION

We have already given the names of four books compiled by Sanātana Gosvāmī. Similarly, Śrīla Rūpa Gosvāmī has also compiled many books, which no one can even count.

TEXT 37

প্রধান প্রধান কিছু করিয়ে গণন ।
লক্ষ গ্রন্থে কৈল ব্রজবিলাস বর্ণন ॥ ৩৭ ॥

pradhāna pradhāna kichu kariye gaṇana
lakṣa granthe kaila vraja-vilāsa varṇana

SYNONYMS

pradhāna pradhāna—the most important ones; *kichu*—some; *kariye*—I do; *gaṇana*—enumeration; *lakṣa*—hundreds and thousands; *granthe*—in verses; *kaila*—did; *vraja-vilāsa*—of the pastimes of the Lord in Vṛndāvana; *varṇana*—description.

TRANSLATION

I shall therefore enumerate the chief books compiled by Śrīla Rūpa Gosvāmī. He has described the pastimes of Vṛndāvana in thousands of verses.

TEXT 38

রসামৃতসিন্ধু, আর বিদগ্ধমাধব ।
উজ্জ্বলনীলমণি, আর ললিতমাধব ॥ ৩৮ ॥

rasāmṛta-sindhu, āra vidagdha-mādhava
ujjvala-nīlamaṇi, āra lalita-mādhava

SYNONYMS

rasāmṛta-sindhu—of the name *Bhakti-rasāmṛta-sindhu; āra*—and; *vidagdha-mādhava*—of the name *Vidagdha-mādhava; ujjvala-nīla-maṇi*—of the name *Ujjvala-nīlamaṇi; āra*—and; *lalita-mādhava*—of the name *Lalita-mādhava.*

TRANSLATION

The books compiled by Śrī Rūpa Gosvāmī include Bhakti-rasāmṛta-sindhu, Vidagdha-mādhava, Ujjvala-nīlamaṇi and Lalita-mādhava.

TEXTS 39-40

দানকেলিকৌমুদী, আর বহু স্তবাবলী ।
অষ্টাদশ লীলাচ্ছন্দ, আর পদ্যাবলী ॥ ৩৯ ॥
গোবিন্দ-বিরুদাবলী, তাহার লক্ষণ ।
মথুরা-মাহাত্ম্য, আর নাটক-বর্ণন ॥ ৪০ ॥

dāna-keli-kaumudī, āra bahu stavāvalī
aṣṭādaśa līlā-cchanda, āra padyāvalī

govinda-virudāvalī, tāhāra lakṣaṇa
mathurā-māhātmya, āra nāṭaka-varṇana

SYNONYMS

dāna-keli-kaumudī—of the name *Dāna-keli-kaumudī; āra*—and; *bahu stavāvalī*—many prayers; *aṣṭādaśa*—eighteen; *līlā-cchanda*—chronological pastimes; *āra*—and; *padyāvalī*—of the name *Padyāvalī; govinda-virudāvalī*—of the name *Govinda-virudāvalī; tāhāra lakṣaṇa*—the symptoms of the book; *mathurā-māhātmya*—the glories of Mathurā; *āra nāṭaka-varṇana*—and descriptions of drama (*Nāṭaka-candrikā*).

TRANSLATION

Śrīla Rūpa Gosvāmī also compiled Dāna-keli-kaumudī, Stavāvalī, Līlā-cchanda, Padyāvalī, Govinda-virudāvalī, Mathurā-māhātmya and Nāṭaka-varṇana.

TEXT 41

লঘুভাগবতামৃতাদি কে করু গণন।
সর্বত্র করিল ব্রজবিলাস বর্ণন॥ ৪১॥

laghu-bhāgavatāmṛtādi ke karu gaṇana
sarvatra karila vraja-vilāsa varṇana

SYNONYMS

laghu-bhāgavatāmṛta-ādi—another list, containing *Laghu-bhāgavatāmṛta*; *ke*—who; *karu gaṇana*—can count; *sarvatra*—everywhere; *karila*—did; *vraja-vilāsa*—of the pastimes of Vṛndāvana; *varṇana*—description.

TRANSLATION

Who can count the rest of the books (headed by Laghu-bhāgavatāmṛta) written by Śrīla Rūpa Gosvāmī? He has described the pastimes of Vṛndāvana in all of them.

PURPORT

Śrīla Bhaktisiddhānta Sarasvatī has given a description of these books. *Bhakti-rasāmṛta-sindhu* is a great book of instruction on how to develop devotional service to Lord Kṛṣṇa and follow the transcendental process. It was finished in the year 1463 Śakābda. This book is divided into four parts: *pūrva-vibhāga* (eastern division), *dakṣiṇa-vibhāga* (southern division), *paścima-vibhāga* (western division) and *uttara-vibhāga* (northern division). In the *pūrva-vibhāga,* there is a description of the permanent development of devotional service. The general principles of devotional service, the execution of devotional service, ecstasy in devotional service and ultimately the attainment of love of Godhead are described. In this way there are four *laharīs* (waves) in this division of the ocean of the nectar of devotion.

In the *dakṣiṇa-vibhāga* (southern division) there is a general description of the mellow (relationship) called *bhakti-rasa,* which is derived from devotional service. There are also descriptions of the stages known as *vibhāva, anubhāva, sāttvika, vyabhicāri* and *sthāyi-bhāva,* all on this high platform of devotional service. Thus there are five waves in the *dakṣiṇa-vibhāga* division. In the western division (*paścima-vibhāga*) there is a description of the chief transcendental humors derived from devotional service. These are known as *mukhya-bhakti-rasa-nirūpaṇa,* or attainment of the chief humors or feelings in the execution of devotional service. In that part there is a description of devotional service in neutrality, further development in love and affection (called servitude), further development in fraternity, further development in paternity, or paternal love, and finally conjugal love between Kṛṣṇa and His devotees. Thus there are five waves in the western division.

In the northern division (*uttara-vibhāga*) there is a description of the indirect mellows of devotional service—namely, devotional service in laughter, devotional service in wonder, and devotional service in chivalry, pity, anger, dread and ghastliness. There are also mixing of mellows and the transgression of different humors. Thus there are nine waves in this part. This is but a brief outline of *Bhakti-rasāmṛta-sindhu.*

Vidagdha-mādhava is a drama of Lord Kṛṣṇa's pastimes in Vṛndāvana. Śrīla Rūpa Gosvāmī finished this book in the year 1454 Śakābda. The first part of this drama is called *veṇu-nāda-vilāsa,* the second part *manmatha-lekha,* the third part *rādhā-saṅga,* the fourth part *veṇu-haraṇa,* the fifth part *rādhā-prasādana,* the sixth part *śarad-vihāra,* and the seventh and last part *gaurī-vihāra.*

There is also a book called *Ujjvala-nīlamaṇi,* a transcendental account of loving affairs that includes metaphor, analogy and higher *bhakti* sentiments. Devotional service in conjugal love is described briefly in *Bhakti-rasāmṛta-sindhu,* but it is very elaborately discussed in *Ujjvala-nīlamaṇi.* This book describes different types of lovers, their assistants, and those who are very dear to Kṛṣṇa. There is also a description of Śrīmatī Rādhārāṇī and other female lovers, as well as various group leaders. Messengers and the constant associates, as well as others who are very dear to Kṛṣṇa, are all described. The book also relates how love of Kṛṣṇa is awakened and describes the ecstatic situation, the devotional situation, permanent ecstasy, disturbed ecstasy, steady ecstasy, different positions of different dresses, feelings of separation, prior attraction, anger in attraction, varieties of loving affairs, separation from the beloved, meeting with the beloved, and both direct and indirect enjoyment between the lover and the beloved. All this has been very elaborately described.

Similarly, *Lalita-mādhava* is a description of Kṛṣṇa's pastimes in Dvārakā. These pastimes were made into a drama, and the work was finished in the year 1459 Śakābda. The first part deals with festivities in the evening, the second with the killing of the Śaṅkhacūḍa, the third with maddened Śrīmatī Rādhārāṇī, the fourth with Rādhārāṇī's proceeding toward Kṛṣṇa, the fifth with the achievement of Candrāvalī, the sixth with the achievement of Lalitā, the seventh with the meeting in Nava-vṛndāvana, the eighth with the enjoyment in Nava-vṛndāvana, the ninth with looking over pictures, and the tenth with complete satisfaction of the mind. Thus the entire drama is divided into ten parts.

The *Laghu-bhāgavatāmṛta* is divided into two parts. The first is called "The Nectar of Kṛṣṇa" and the second "The Nectar of Devotional Service." The importance of Vedic evidence is stressed in the first part, and this is followed by a description of the original form of the Supreme Personality of Godhead as Śrī Kṛṣṇa and descriptions of His pastimes and expansions in *svāṁśa* (personal forms) and *vibhinnāṁśa*. According to different absorptions, the incarnations are called *āveśa* and *tad-ekātma*. The first incarnation is divided into three *puruṣāvatāras*—namely, Mahā-Viṣṇu, Garbhodakaśāyī Viṣṇu and Kṣīrodakaśāyī Viṣṇu. Then there are the three incarnations of the modes of nature—namely, Brahmā, Viṣṇu and Maheśvara (Śiva). All the paraphernalia used in the service of the Lord is transcendental, beyond the three qualities of this material world. There is also a description of twenty-five *līlā-avatāras*, namely Catuḥsana (the Kumāras), Nārada, Varāha, Matsya, Yajña, Nara-nārāyaṇa Ṛṣi, Kapila, Dattātreya, Hayagrīva, Haṁsa, Pṛśnigarbha, Ṛṣabha, Pṛthu, Nṛsiṁha, Kūrma, Dhanvantari, Mohinī, Vāmana, Paraśurāma, Dāśarathi, Kṛṣṇa-dvaipāyana, Balarāma, Vāsudeva, Buddha and Kalki. There are also fourteen incarnations of Manu: Yajña, Vibhu, Satyasena, Hari, Vaikuṇṭha, Ajita, Vāmana, Sārvabhauma, Ṛṣabha, Viṣvaksena, Dharmasetu, Sudhāmā, Yogeśvara and Bṛhadbhānu. There are also four incarnations for the four *yugas*, and their colors are described as white, red, blackish and black (sometimes yellow, as in the case of Lord Caitanya Mahāprabhu). There are different types of millenniums and incarnations for those millenniums. The categories called *āveśa, prābhava, vaibhava* and *para* constitute different situations for the different incarnations. According to specific pastimes, the names are spiritually empowered. There are also descriptions of the difference between the powerful and the power, and the inconceivable activities of the Supreme Lord.

Śrī Kṛṣṇa is the original Supreme Personality of Godhead, and no one is greater than Him. He is the source of all incarnations. In the *Laghu-bhāgavatāmṛta* there are descriptions of His partial incarnations, a description of the impersonal Brahman effulgence (actually the bodily effulgence of Śrī Kṛṣṇa), the superexcellence of Śrī Kṛṣṇa's pastimes as an ordinary human being with two hands, and so forth. There is nothing to compare with the two-armed form of the Lord. In the spiritual world (*vaikuṇṭha-jagat*) there is no distinction between the owner of the body and the body itself. In the material world the owner of the body is called the soul, and the body is called a material manifestation. In the Vaikuṇṭha world, however, there is no such distinction. Lord Śrī Kṛṣṇa is unborn, and His appearance as an incarnation is perpetual. Kṛṣṇa's pastimes are divided into two parts—manifest and unmanifest. For example, when Kṛṣṇa takes His birth within this material world, His pastimes are considered to be manifest. However, when He disappears, one should not think that He is finished, for His pastimes are going on in an unmanifest form. Varieties of humors, however, are enjoyed by the devotees and Lord Kṛṣṇa during His manifest pastimes. After all, His pastimes in Mathurā, Vṛndāvana and Dvārakā are eternal and are going on perpetually somewhere in some part of the universe.

TEXT 42

তাঁর ভ্রাতুষ্পুত্র নাম—শ্রীজীবগোসাঞি ।
যত ভক্তিগ্রন্থ কৈল, তার অন্ত নাই ॥ ৪২ ॥

tāṅra bhrātuṣputra nāma——śrī-jīva-gosāñi
yata bhakti-grantha kaila, tāra anta nāi

SYNONYMS

tāṅra—his; *bhrātuḥ-putra*—nephew; *nāma*—of the name; *śrī-jīva-gosāñi*—Śrīla Jīva Gosvāmī Prabhupāda; *yata*—all; *bhakti-grantha*—books on devotional service; *kaila*—compiled; *tāra*—that; *anta*—end; *nāi*—there is not.

TRANSLATION

Śrī Rūpa Gosvāmī's nephew, Śrīla Jīva Gosvāmī, has compiled so many books on devotional service that there is no counting them.

TEXT 43

শ্রীভাগবতসন্দর্ভ-নাম গ্রন্থ-বিস্তার ।
ভক্তিসিদ্ধান্তের তাতে দেখাইয়াছেন পার ॥ ৪৩ ॥

śrī-bhāgavata-sandarbha-nāma grantha-vistāra
bhakti-siddhāntera tāte dekhāiyāchena pāra

SYNONYMS

śrī-bhāgavata-sandarbha-nāma—of the name *Bhāgavata-sandarbha*; *grantha*—the book; *vistāra*—very elaborate; *bhakti-siddhāntera*—of the conclusions of devotional service; *tāte*—in that book; *dekhāiyāchena*—he has shown; *pāra*—the limit.

TRANSLATION

In Śrī Bhāgavata-sandarbha, Śrīla Jīva Gosvāmī has written conclusively about the ultimate end of devotional service.

PURPORT

Bhāgavata-sandarbha is also known as *Ṣaṭ-sandarbha.* In the first part, called *Tattva-sandarbha,* it is proved that *Śrīmad-Bhāgavatam* is the most authoritative evidence directly pointing to the Absolute Truth. The second *sandarbha,* called *Bhagavat-sandarbha,* draws a distinction between impersonal Brahman and localized Paramātmā and describes the spiritual world and the domination of the mode of goodness devoid of contamination by the other two material modes. In other words, there is a vivid description of the transcendental position known as *śuddha-sattva.* Material goodness is apt to be contaminated by the other two material qualities—ignorance and passion—but when one is situated in the *śuddha-sattva* position, there is no chance for such contamination. It is a spiritual platform of pure goodness. The potency of the Supreme Lord and the living entity is also described, and there is a description of the inconceivable energies and varieties of energies of the Lord. The potencies are divided into categories—internal, external, personal, marginal and so forth. There are also discussions of the eternality of Deity worship, the omnipotence of the Deity, His all-pervasiveness, His giving shelter to everyone, His subtle and gross potencies, His personal manifestations, His expressions of form, quality and pastimes, His transcendental position and His complete form. It is also stated that everything pertaining to the Absolute has the same potency and that the spiritual world, the associates in the spiritual world and the threefold energies of the Lord in the spiritual world are all transcendental. There are further discussions concerning the difference between the impersonal Brahman and the Personality of Godhead, the fullness of the Personality of Godhead, the objective of all Vedic knowledge, the personal potencies of the Lord, and the Personality of Godhead as the original author of Vedic knowledge.

The third *sandarbha* is called *Paramātma-sandarbha,* and in this book there is a description of Paramātmā (the Supersoul) and an explanation of how the Supersoul exists in millions and millions of living entities. There are discussions of the differences between the qualitative incarnations, and discourses concerning the living entities, *māyā,* the material world, the theory of transformation, the illusory energy, the sameness of this world and the Supersoul, and the truth about this material world. In this connection, the opinions of Śrīdhara Svāmī are given. It is stated that the Supreme Personality of Godhead, although devoid of material qualities, superintends all material activities. There is also a discussion of how the *līlā-avatāra* incarnations respond to the desires of the devotees and how the Supreme Personality of Godhead is characterized by six opulences.

The fourth *sandarbha* is called the *Kṛṣṇa-sandarbha,* and in this book Kṛṣṇa is proved to be the Supreme Personality of Godhead. There are discussions of Kṛṣṇa's pastimes and qualities, His superintendence of the *puruṣa-avatāras,* and so forth. The opinions of Śrīdhara Svāmī are corroborated. In each and every scripture, the supremacy of Kṛṣṇa is stressed. Baladeva, Saṅkarṣaṇa and other expansions of Kṛṣṇa are emanations of Mahā-Saṅkarṣaṇa. All the incarnations and expansions exist simultaneously in the body of Kṛṣṇa, who is described as two-handed. There are also descriptions of the Goloka planet, Vṛndāvana (the eternal place of Kṛṣṇa), the identity of Goloka and Vṛndāvana, the Yādavas and the cowherd boys (both eternal associates of Kṛṣṇa), the adjustment and equality of the manifest and unmanifest pastimes, Śrī Kṛṣṇa's manifestation in Gokula, the queens of Dvārakā as expansions of the internal potency, and, superior to them, the superexcellent *gopīs.* There is also a list of the *gopīs'* names and a discussion of the topmost position of Śrīmatī Rādhārāṇī.

The fifth *sandarbha* is called *Bhakti-sandarbha,* and in this book there is a discussion of how devotional service can be directly executed, and how such service can be adjusted, either directly or indirectly. There is a discussion of the knowledge of all kinds of scripture, the establishment of the Vedic institution of *varṇāśrama*, *bhakti* as superior to fruitive activity, and so forth. It is also stated that without devotional service, even a *brāhmaṇa* is condemned. There are discussions of the process of *karma-tyāga* (the giving of the results of *karma* to the Supreme Personality of Godhead), and the practices of mystic *yoga* and philosophical speculation, which are deprecated as simply hard labor. Worship of the demigods is discouraged, and worship of a Vaiṣṇava is considered exalted. No respect is given to the nondevotees. There are discussions of how one can be liberated even in this life (*jīvan-mukta*), Lord Śiva as a devotee, and how a *bhakta* and his devotional service are eternally existing. It is stated that through *bhakti* one can attain all success, for *bhakti* is transcendental to the material qualities. There is a discussion of how the self is manifest through *bhakti.* There is also a discussion of the self's bliss, as well as how *bhakti,* even imperfectly executed, enables one to attain the lotus feet of the Supreme Personality of Godhead. Unmotivated devotional service is highly praised, and an explanation is given of how each devotee can achieve the platform of unmotivated service by association with other devotees. There is a discussion of the differences between the *mahā-bhāgavata* and the ordinary devotee, the symptoms of philosophical speculation, the symptoms of self-worship, or *ahaṅgrahopāsanā,* the symptoms of devotional service, the symptoms of imaginary perfection, the acceptance of regulative principles, service to the spiritual master, the *mahā-bhāgavata* (liberated devotee) and service to him, service to Vaiṣṇavas in general, the principles of hearing, chanting, remembering and serving the lotus feet of the Lord, offenses in worship, offensive effects, prayers, engaging oneself as an eternal servant of the Lord, making friendships with the Lord and surrendering everything for His pleasure. There is also a discussion of *rāgānugā-bhakti* (spontaneous love of Godhead), of the specific purpose of becoming a devotee of Lord Kṛṣṇa, and a comparative study of other perfectional stages.

The sixth *sandarbha* is called *Prīti-sandarbha,* a thesis on love of Godhead. Here it is stated that through love of Godhead, one becomes perfectly liberated and attains the highest goal of life. A distinction is made between the liberated condition of a personalist and that of an impersonalist, and there is a discussion of liberation during one's lifetime as distinguished from liberation from material bondage. Of all kinds of liberation, liberation in loving service to the Lord is described as the most exalted, and meeting the Supreme Personality of Godhead face to face is shown to be the highest perfection of life. Immediate liberation is contrasted with liberation by a gradual process. Both realization of Brahman and meeting with the Supreme Personality of Godhead are described as liberation within one's lifetime, but meeting with the Supreme Personality of Godhead, both internally and externally, is shown to be superexcellent, above the transcendental realization of the Brahman effulgence. There is a comparative study of liberation as *sālokya, sāmīpya* and *sārūpya. Sāmīpya* is better than *sālokya.* Devotional service is considered to be liberation with greater facilities, and there is a discussion of how to obtain it. There are also discussions of the transcendental state one achieves after attaining the devotional platform, which is the exact position of love of Godhead; the marginal symptoms of transcendental love, and how it is awakened; the distinction between so-called love and transcendental love on the platform of love of Godhead; and different types of humors and mellows enjoyed in relishing the lusty affairs of the *gopīs,* which are different from mundane affairs, which in turn are symbolical representations of pure love for Kṛṣṇa. There are also discussions of *bhakti* mixed with philosophical speculation, the superexcellence of the love of the *gopīs,* the difference between opulent devotional service and loving devotional service, the exalted position of the residents of Gokula, the progressively exalted position of the friends of Kṛṣṇa, the *gopas* and the *gopīs* in parental love with Kṛṣṇa, and finally the superexcellence of the love of the *gopīs* and that of Śrīmatī

Rādhārāṇī. There is also a discussion of how spiritual feelings can be present when one simply imitates them and of how such mellows are far superior to the ordinary mellows of mundane love, and there are descriptions of different ecstasies, the awakening of ecstasy, transcendental qualities, the distinction of *dhīrodātta,* the utmost attractiveness of conjugal love, the ecstatic features, the permanent ecstatic features, the mellows divided in five transcendental features of direct loving service, and indirect loving service, considered in seven divisions. Finally there is a discussion of overlapping of different *rasas,* and there are discussions of *śānta* (neutrality), servitorship, taking shelter, parental love, conjugal love, direct transcendental enjoyment and enjoyment in separation, previous attraction and the glories of Śrīmatī Rādhārāṇī.

TEXT 44

গোপালচম্পূ-নামে গ্রন্থমহাশূর ।
নিত্যলীলা স্থাপন যাহে ব্রজরস-পূর ॥ ৪৪ ॥

gopāla-campū-nāme grantha-mahāśūra
nitya-līlā sthāpana yāhe vraja-rasa-pūra

SYNONYMS

gopāla-campū—*Gopāla-campū; nāme*—by the name; *grantha*—the transcendental literature; *mahā-śūra*—most formidable; *nitya-līlā*—of eternal pastimes; *sthāpana*—establishment; *yāhe*—in which; *vraja-rasa*—the transcendental mellows enjoyed in Vṛndāvana; *pūra*—complete.

TRANSLATION

The most famous and formidable transcendental literature is the book named Gopāla-campū. In this book the eternal pastimes of the Lord are established, and the transcendental mellows enjoyed in Vṛndāvana are completely described.

PURPORT

In his *Anubhāṣya,* Śrīla Bhaktisiddhānta Sarasvatī Ṭhākura gives the following information about *Gopāla-campū. Gopāla-campū* is divided in two parts. The first part is called the eastern wave, and the second part is called the northern wave. In the first part there are thirty-three supplications and in the second part thirty-seven supplications. In the first part, completed in 1510

Śakābda, the following subject matters are discussed: (1) Vṛndāvana and Goloka; (2) the killing of the Pūtanā demon, the *gopīs'* returning home under the instructions of mother Yaśodā, the bathing of Lord Kṛṣṇa and Balarāma, *snigdha-kaṇṭha* and *madhu-kaṇṭha*; (3) the dream of mother Yaśodā; (4) the Janmāṣṭamī ceremony; (5) the meeting between Nanda Mahārāja and Vasudeva, and the killing of the Pūtanā demon; (6) the pastimes of awakening from bed, the deliverance of the demon Śakaṭa, and the name-giving ceremony; (7) the killing of the Tṛṇāvarta demon, Lord Kṛṣṇa's eating dirt, Lord Kṛṣṇa's childish naughtiness, and Lord Kṛṣṇa as a thief; (8) churning of the yogurt, Kṛṣṇa's drinking from the breast of mother Yaśodā, the breaking of the yogurt pot, Kṛṣṇa bound with ropes, the deliverance of the two brothers (Yamalārjuna) and the lamentation of mother Yaśodā; (9) entering Śrī Vṛndāvana; (10) the killing of Vatsāsura, Bakāsura and Vyomāsura; (11) the killing of Aghāsura and the bewilderment of Lord Brahmā; (12) the tending of the cows in the forest; (13) taking care of the cows and chastising the Kāliya serpent; (14) the killing of the Garddabhāsura, and the praise of Kṛṣṇa; (15) the previous attraction of the *gopīs*; (16) the killing of the Pralambāsura and the eating of the forest fire; (17) the *gopīs'* attempt to approach Kṛṣṇa; (18) the lifting of Govardhana Hill; (19) bathing Kṛṣṇa with milk; (20) the return of Nanda Mahārāja from the custody of Varuṇa and the vision of Goloka Vṛndāvana by the *gopīs*; (21) the performance of the rituals in Kātyāyanī-vrata and the worship of the goddess Durgā; (22) the begging of food from the wives of the *brāhmaṇas* performing sacrifices; (23) the meeting of the *gopīs*; (24) enjoying the company of the *gopīs,* the disappearance of Rādhā and Kṛṣṇa from the scene, and the search for Them by the *gopīs*; (25) the reappearance of Kṛṣṇa; (26) the determination of the *gopīs*; (27) pastimes in the waters of the Yamunā; (28) the deliverance of Nanda Mahārāja from the clutches of the serpent; (29) various pastimes in solitary places; (30) the killing of Śaṅkhāsura and the Hori; (31) the killing of Ariṣṭāsura; (32) the killing of the Keśī demon; (33) the appearance of Śrī Nārada Muni and a description of the year in which the book was completed.

In the second part, known as *Uttara-campū,* the following subject matters are discussed: (1) attraction for Vrajabhūmi, (2) the cruel activities of Akrūra, (3) Kṛṣṇa's departure for Mathurā, (4) a description of the city of Mathurā, (5) the killing of Kaṁsa, (6) Nanda Mahārāja's separation from Kṛṣṇa and Balarāma, (7) Nanda Mahārāja's entrance into Vṛndāvana without Kṛṣṇa and Balarāma, (8) the studies of Kṛṣṇa and Balarāma, (9) how the son of the teacher of Kṛṣṇa and Balarāma was returned, (10) Uddhava visits Vṛndāvana, (11) talking with the messenger bumblebee, (12) the return of Uddhava from

Vṛndāvana, (13) the binding of Jarāsandha, (14) the killing of the *yavana* Jarāsandha, (15) the marriage of Balarāma, (16) the marriage of Rukmiṇī, (17) seven marriages, (18) the killing of Narakāsura, the taking of the *pārijāta* flower from heaven and the marriage of 16,000 queens, (19) victory over Bāṇāsura, (20) a description of Balarāma's return to Vraja, (21) the killing of Pauṇḍraka (the imitation Viṣṇu), (22) the killing of Dvivida and thoughts of Hastināpura, (23) departure for Kurukṣetra, (24) how the residents of Vṛndāvana met at Kurukṣetra, (25) consultation with Uddhava, (26) the deliverance of the king, (27) the performance of the Rājasūya sacrifice, (28) the killing of Śālva, (29) considering returning to Vṛndāvana, (30) Kṛṣṇa's revisiting Vṛndāvana, (31) the adjustment of obstructions by Śrīmatī Rādhārāṇī and others, (32) everything completed, (33) the residence of Rādhā and Mādhava, (34) decorating Śrīmatī Rādhārāṇī and Kṛṣṇa, (35) the marriage ceremony of Śrīmatī Rādhārāṇī and Kṛṣṇa, (36) the meeting of Śrīmatī Rādhārāṇī and Kṛṣṇa, and (37) entering Goloka.

TEXT 45

এই মত নানা গ্রন্থ করিয়া প্রকাশ ।
গোষ্ঠী সহিতে কৈলা বৃন্দাবনে বাস ॥ ৪৫ ॥

ei mata nānā grantha kariyā prakāśa
goṣṭhī sahite kailā vṛndāvane vāsa

SYNONYMS

ei mata—in this way; *nānā*—various; *grantha*—books; *kariyā*—making; *prakāśa*—publication; *goṣṭhī*—family members; *sahite*—with; *kailā*—did; *vṛndāvane*—at Vṛndāvana; *vāsa*—residence

TRANSLATION

Thus Śrīla Rūpa Gosvāmī, Sanātana Gosvāmī and their nephew Śrīla Jīva Gosvāmī, as well as practically all of their family members, lived in Vṛndāvana and published important books on devotional service.

TEXT 46

প্রথম বৎসরে অদ্বৈতাদি ভক্তগণ ।
প্রভুরে দেখিতে কৈল, নীলাদ্রি গমন ॥ ৪৬ ॥

prathama vatsare advaitādi bhakta-gaṇa
prabhure dekhite kaila, nīlādri gamana

SYNONYMS

prathama—the first; *vatsare*—in the year; *advaita-ādi*—headed by Advaita Ācārya; *bhakta-gaṇa*—all the devotees; *prabhure*—the Lord; *dekhite*—to see; *kaila*—did; *nīlādri*—to Jagannātha Purī; *gamana*—going.

TRANSLATION

The first year after Śrī Caitanya Mahāprabhu accepted the renounced order of life, all the devotees, headed by Śrī Advaita Prabhu, went to see the Lord at Jagannātha Purī.

TEXT 47

রথযাত্রা দেখি' তাহাঁ রহিলা চারিমাস ।
প্রভুসঙ্গে নৃত্যগীত পরম উল্লাস ॥ ৪৭ ॥

ratha-yātrā dekhi' tāhāṅ rahilā cāri-māsa
prabhu-saṅge nṛtya-gīta parama ullāsa

SYNONYMS

ratha-yātrā—the car festival; *dekhi'*—seeing; *tāhāṅ*—there; *rahilā*—remained; *cāri-māsa*—four months; *prabhu-saṅge*—with the Lord; *nṛtya-gīta*—chanting and dancing; *parama*—greatest; *ullāsa*—pleasure.

TRANSLATION

After attending the Ratha-yātrā ceremony at Jagannātha Purī, all the devotees remained there for four months, greatly enjoying the company of Śrī Caitanya Mahāprabhu by performing kīrtana [chanting and dancing].

TEXT 48

বিদায় সময় প্রভু কহিলা সবারে ।
প্রত্যব্দ আসিবে সবে গুণ্ডিচা দেখিবারে ॥ ৪৮ ॥

vidāya samaya prabhu kahilā sabāre
pratyabda āsibe sabe guṇḍicā dekhibāre

SYNONYMS

vidāya—departing; *samaya*—at the time; *prabhu*—the Lord; *kahilā*—said; *sabāre*—unto everyone; *pratyabda*—every year; *āsibe*—you should come; *sabe*—all; *guṇḍicā*—of the name Guṇḍicā; *dekhibāre*—to see.

TRANSLATION

At the time of departure, the Lord requested all the devotees, "Please come here every year to see the Ratha-yātrā festival of Lord Jagannātha's journey to the Guṇḍicā temple."

PURPORT

There is a temple named Guṇḍicā at Sundarācala. Lord Jagannātha, Baladeva and Subhadrā are pushed in Their three carts from the temple in Purī to the Guṇḍicā temple in Sundarācala. In Orissa, this Ratha-yātrā festival is known as Jagannātha's journey to Guṇḍicā. Whereas others speak of it as the Ratha-yātrā festival, the residents of Orissa refer to it as Guṇḍicā-yātrā.

TEXT 49

প্রভু-অজ্ঞায় ভক্তগণ প্রত্যব্দ আসিয়া।
গুণ্ডিচা দেখিয়া যা'ন প্রভুরে মিলিয়া ॥ ৪৯ ॥

prabhu-ajñāya bhakta-gaṇa pratyabda āsiyā
guṇḍicā dekhiyā yā'na prabhure miliyā

SYNONYMS

prabhu-ajñāya—upon the order of Lord Śrī Caitanya Mahāprabhu; *bhakta-gaṇa*—all the devotees; *pratyabda*—every year; *āsiyā*—coming there; *guṇḍicā*—the festival of Guṇḍicā-yātrā; *dekhiyā*—seeing; *yā'na*—return; *prabhure*—the Lord; *miliyā*—meeting.

TRANSLATION

Following the order of Śrī Caitanya Mahāprabhu, all the devotees used to visit Lord Caitanya Mahāprabhu every year. They would see the Guṇḍicā festival at Jagannātha Purī and then return home after four months.

TEXT 50

বিংশতি বৎসর ঐছে কৈলা গতাগতি।
অন্যোহন্যে দুঁহার দুঁহা বিনা নাহি স্থিতি ॥ ৫০ ॥

viṁśati vatsara aiche kailā gatāgati
anyonye duṅhāra duṅhā vinā nāhi sthiti

SYNONYMS

viṁśati—twenty; *vatsara*—years; *aiche*—thus; *kailā*—did; *gata-āgati*—going and coming; *anyonye*—mutually; *duṅhāra*—of Lord Caitanya and the devotees; *duṅhā*—the two; *vinā*—without; *nāhi*—there is not; *sthiti*—peace.

TRANSLATION

For twenty consecutive years this meeting took place, and the situation became so intense that the Lord and the devotees could not be happy without meeting one another.

TEXT 51

শেষ আর যেই রহে দ্বাদশ বৎসর ।
কৃষ্ণের বিরহলীলা প্রভুর অন্তর ॥ ৫১ ॥

śeṣa āra yei rahe dvādaśa vatsara
kṛṣṇera viraha-līlā prabhura antara

SYNONYMS

śeṣa—at the end; *āra*—the balance; *yei*—whatever; *rahe*—remains; *dvādaśa vatsara*—twelve years; *kṛṣṇera*—of Lord Kṛṣṇa; *viraha-līlā*—the pastimes of separation; *prabhura*—the Lord; *antara*—within.

TRANSLATION

The last twelve years were simply devoted to relishing the pastimes of Kṛṣṇa in separation within the heart of the Lord.

PURPORT

Śrī Kṛṣṇa Caitanya Mahāprabhu enjoyed the position of the *gopīs* in separation from Kṛṣṇa. When Kṛṣṇa left the *gopīs* and went to Mathurā, the *gopīs* cried for Him the rest of their lives, feeling intense separation from Him. This ecstatic feeling of separation was specifically advocated by Lord Caitanya Mahāprabhu through His actual demonstrations.

TEXT 52

**নিরন্তর রাত্রি-দিন বিরহ উন্মাদে।
হাসে, কান্দে, নাচে,গায় পরম বিষাদে ॥ ৫২ ॥**

nirantara rātri-dina viraha unmāde
hāse, kānde, nāce, gāya parama viṣāde

SYNONYMS

nirantara—without cessation; *rātri-dina*—night and day; *viraha*—of separation; *unmāde*—in madness; *hāse*—laughs; *kānde*—cries; *nāce*—dances; *gāya*—chants; *parama*—great; *viṣāde*—in moroseness.

TRANSLATION

In the attitude of separation, Lord Caitanya Mahāprabhu appeared mad both day and night. Sometimes He laughed, and sometimes He cried; sometimes He danced, and sometimes He chanted in great sorrow.

TEXT 53

**যে কালে করেন জগন্নাথ দরশন।
মনে ভাবে, কুরুক্ষেত্রে পাঞাছি মিলন ॥ ৫৩ ॥**

ye kāle karena jagannātha daraśana
mane bhāve, kurukṣetre pāñāchi milana

SYNONYMS

ye kāle—at those times; *karena*—does; *jagannātha*—Lord Jagannātha; *daraśana*—visiting; *mane*—within the mind; *bhāve*—thinks; *kuru-kṣetre*—on the field of Kurukṣetra; *pāñāchi*—I have gotten; *milana*—meeting.

TRANSLATION

At those times, Śrī Caitanya Mahāprabhu would visit Lord Jagannātha. Then His feelings exactly corresponded to those of the gopīs when they saw Kṛṣṇa at Kurukṣetra after long separation. Kṛṣṇa had come to Kurukṣetra with His brother and sister to visit.

PURPORT

When Kṛṣṇa was performing *yajña* (sacrifice) at Kurukṣetra, He invited all the inhabitants of Vṛndāvana to come see Him. Lord Caitanya's heart was always filled with separation from Kṛṣṇa, but as soon as He had the opportunity to visit the Jagannātha temple, He became fully absorbed in the thoughts of the *gopīs* who came to see Kṛṣṇa at Kurukṣetra.

TEXT 54

রথযাত্রায় আগে যবে করেন নর্তন ।
তাহাঁ এই পদ মাত্র করয়ে গায়ন ॥ ৫৪ ॥

ratha-yātrāya āge yabe karena nartana
tāhāṅ ei pada mātra karaye gāyana

SYNONYMS

ratha-yātrāya—in the car festival; *āge*—in front; *yabe*—when; *karena*—does; *nartana*—dancing; *tāhāṅ*—there; *ei*—this; *pada*—stanza; *mātra*—only; *karaye*—does; *gāyana*—singing.

TRANSLATION

When Caitanya Mahāprabhu used to dance before the cart during the festival, He always sang the following two lines.

TEXT 55

"সেইত পরাণ-নাথ পাইনু ।
যাহা লাগি' মদনদহনে ঝুরি গেনু ॥ ৫৫ ॥

seita parāṇa-nātha pāinu
yāhā lāgi' madana-dahane jhuri genu

SYNONYMS

seita—that; *parāṇa-nātha*—Lord of My life; *pāinu*—I have gotten; *yāhā*—whom; *lāgi'*—for; *madana-dahane*—in the fire of lusty desire; *jhuri*—burning; *genu*—I have become.

TRANSLATION

"I have gotten that Lord of My life for whom I was burning in the fire of lusty desires."

PURPORT

In *Śrīmad-Bhāgavatam* (10.29.15) it is stated:

kāmaṁ krodhaṁ bhayaṁ sneham
aikyaṁ sauhṛdam eva ca
nityaṁ harau vidadhato
yānti tanmayatām hi te

The word *kāma* means lusty desire, *bhaya* means fear, and *krodha* means anger. If one somehow or other approaches Kṛṣṇa, his life becomes successful. The *gopīs* approached Kṛṣṇa with lusty desire. Kṛṣṇa was a very beautiful boy, and they wanted to meet and enjoy His company. But this lusty desire is different from that of the material world. It appears like mundane lust, but in actuality it is the highest form of attraction to Kṛṣṇa. Caitanya Mahāprabhu was a *sannyāsī*; He left home and everything else. He could certainly not be induced by any mundane lusty desires. So when He uses the word *madana-dahane* ("in the fire of lusty desire"), He means that out of pure love for Kṛṣṇa He was burning in the fire of separation from Kṛṣṇa. Whenever He met Jagannātha, either in the temple or during the Ratha-yātrā, Caitanya Mahāprabhu used to think, "Now I have gotten the Lord of My life and soul."

TEXT 56

এই ধুয়া-গানে নাচেন দ্বিতীয় প্রহর ।
কৃষ্ণ লঞা ব্রজে যাই—এভাব অন্তর ॥ ৫৬ ॥

ei dhuyā-gāne nācena dvitīya prahara
kṛṣṇa lañā vraje yāi—e-bhāva antara

SYNONYMS

ei dhuyā-gāne—in the repetition of this song; *nācena*—He dances; *dvitīya prahara*—the second period of the day; *kṛṣṇa lañā*—taking Kṛṣṇa; *vraje yāi*—let Me go back to Vṛndāvana; *e-bhāva*—this ecstasy; *antara*—within.

TRANSLATION

Lord Caitanya Mahāprabhu used to sing this song [seita parāṇa-nātha] especially during the latter part of the day, and He would think, "Let Me take Kṛṣṇa and go back to Vṛndāvana." This ecstasy was always filling His heart.

PURPORT

Being always absorbed in the ecstasy of Śrīmatī Rādhārāṇī, Śrī Caitanya Mahāprabhu felt the same separation from Kṛṣṇa that Śrīmatī Rādhārāṇī felt when Kṛṣṇa left Vṛndāvana and went to Mathurā. This ecstatic feeling is very helpful in attaining love of God in separation. Śrī Caitanya Mahāprabhu has taught everyone that one should not be overly anxious to see the Lord, but should rather feel separation from Him in ecstasy. It is actually better to feel separation from Him than to desire to see Him face to face. When the *gopīs* of Vṛndāvana, the residents of Gokula, met Kṛṣṇa at Kurukṣetra during the solar eclipse, they wanted to take Kṛṣṇa back to Vṛndāvana. Śrī Kṛṣṇa Caitanya Mahāprabhu also felt the same ecstasy as soon as He saw Jagannātha in the temple or on the Ratha-yātrā cart. The *gopīs* of Vṛndāvana did not like the opulence of Dvārakā. They wanted to take Kṛṣṇa to the village of Vṛndāvana and enjoy His company in the groves. This desire was also felt by Śrī Caitanya Mahāprabhu, and He danced in ecstasy before the Ratha-yātrā festival when Lord Jagannātha went to Guṇḍicā.

TEXT 57

এই ভাবে নৃত্যমধ্যে পড়ে এক শ্লোক ।
সেই শ্লোকের অর্থ কেহ নাহি বুঝে লোক ॥ ৫৭ ॥

ei bhāve nṛtya-madhye paḍe eka śloka
sei ślokera artha keha nāhi bujhe loka

SYNONYMS

ei bhāve—in this ecstasy; *nṛtya-madhye*—during the dancing; *paḍe*—recites; *eka*—one; *śloka*—verse; *sei ślokera*—of that verse; *artha*—the meaning; *keha*—anyone; *nāhi*—not; *bujhe*—understands; *loka*—person.

TRANSLATION

In that ecstasy, Śrī Caitanya Mahāprabhu recited one verse when dancing in front of Lord Jagannātha. Almost no one could understand the meaning of that verse.

TEXT 58

যঃ কৌমারহরঃ স এব হি বরস্তা এব চৈত্রক্ষপা-
স্তে চোন্মীলিতমালতীসুরভয়ঃ প্রৌঢ়াঃ কদম্বানিলাঃ ।

সা চৈবাস্মি তথাপি তত্র সুরতব্যাপারলীলাবিধৌ
রেবারোধসি বেতসীতরুতলে চেতঃ সমুৎকণ্ঠতে ॥ ৫৮ ॥

yaḥ kaumāra-haraḥ sa eva hi varas tā eva caitra-kṣapās
te conmīlita-mālatī-surabhayaḥ prauḍhāḥ kadambānilāḥ
sā caivāsmi tathāpi tatra surata-vyāpāra-līlā-vidhau
revā-rodhasi vetasī-taru-tale cetaḥ samutkaṇṭhate

SYNONYMS

yaḥ—that same person who; *kaumāra-haraḥ*—the thief of my heart during youth; *saḥ*—he; *eva hi*—certainly; *varaḥ*—lover; *tāḥ*—these; *eva*—certainly; *caitra-kṣapāḥ*—moonlit nights of the month of Caitra; *te*—those; *ca*—and; *unmīlita*—fructified; *mālatī*—of *mālatī* flowers; *surabhayaḥ*—fragrances; *prauḍhāḥ*—full; *kadamba*—with the fragrance of the *kadamba* flower; *anilāḥ*—the breezes; *sā*—that one; *ca*—also; *eva*—certainly; *asmi*—I am; *tathāpi*—still; *tatra*—there; *surata-vyāpāra*—in intimate transactions; *līlā*—of pastimes; *vidhau*—in the manner; *revā*—of the river named Revā; *rodhasi*—on the bank; *vetasī*—of the name Vetasī; *taru-tale*—underneath the tree; *cetaḥ*—my mind; *samutkaṇṭhate*—is very eager to go.

TRANSLATION

"That very personality who stole away my heart during my youth is now again my master. These are the same moonlit nights of the month of Caitra. The same fragrance of mālatī flowers is there, and the same sweet breezes are blowing from the kadamba forest. In our intimate relationship, I am also the same lover, yet still my mind is not happy here. I am eager to go back to that place on the bank of the Revā under the Vetasī tree. That is my desire."

PURPORT

This verse appears in the *Padyāvalī* (382), by Śrīla Rūpa Gosvāmī.

TEXT 59

এই শ্লোকের অর্থ জানে একলে স্বরূপ ।
দৈবে সে বৎসর তাহাঁ গিয়াছেন রূপ ॥ ৫৯ ॥

ei ślokera artha jāne ekale svarūpa
daive se vatsara tāhāṅ giyāchena rūpa

SYNONYMS

ei—this; *ślokera*—of the verse; *artha*—the meaning; *jāne*—knows; *ekale*—alone; *svarūpa*—Svarūpa Dāmodara; *daive*—by chance; *se vatsara*—that year; *tāhāṅ*—there; *giyāchena*—went; *rūpa*—Śrīla Rūpa Gosvāmī.

TRANSLATION

This verse appears to be the hankering between some ordinary boy and girl, but its actual deep meaning was known only to Svarūpa Dāmodara. By chance, one year Rūpa Gosvāmī was also present there.

TEXT 60

প্রভুমুখে শ্লোক শুনি' শ্রীরূপগোসাঞি ।
সেই শ্লোকের অর্থ-শ্লোক করিলা তথাই ॥ ৬০ ॥

prabhu-mukhe śloka śuni' śrī-rūpa-gosāñi
sei ślokera artha-śloka karilā tathāi

SYNONYMS

prabhu-mukhe—in the mouth of Lord Śrī Caitanya Mahāprabhu; *śloka*—the verse; *śuni'*—hearing; *śrī-rūpa-gosāñi*—Śrīla Rūpa Gosvāmī; *sei*—that; *ślokera*—of the first verse; *artha*—giving the meaning; *śloka*—another verse; *karilā*—composed; *tathāi*—immediately.

TRANSLATION

Although the meaning of the verse was known only to Svarūpa Dāmodara, Rūpa Gosvāmī, after hearing it from Śrī Caitanya Mahāprabhu, immediately composed another verse, describing the meaning of the original verse.

TEXT 61

শ্লোক করি' এক তালপত্রেতে লিখিয়া ।
আপন বাসার চালে রাখিল গুঞ্জিয়া ॥ ৬১ ॥

śloka kari' eka tāla-patrete likhiyā
āpana vāsāra cāle rākhila guñjiyā

SYNONYMS

śloka kari'—composing the verse; *eka*—one; *tāla-patrete*—on a palm leaf; *likhiyā*—writing; *āpana*—his own; *vāsāra*—of the residence; *cāle*—on the roof; *rākhila*—kept; *guñjiyā*—pushing.

TRANSLATION

After composing this verse, Rūpa Gosvāmī wrote it on a palm leaf and put it on the roof of the thatched house in which he was living.

TEXT 62

শ্লোক রাখি' গেলা সমুদ্রস্নান করিতে।
হেনকালে আইলা প্রভু তাঁহারে মিলিতে ॥ ৬২ ॥

śloka rākhi' gelā samudra-snāna karite
hena-kāle āilā prabhu tāṅhāre milite

SYNONYMS

śloka rākhi'—keeping the verse in that way; *gelā*—went; *samudra-snāna*—a bath in the sea; *karite*—to take; *hena-kāle*—in the meantime; *āilā*—came; *prabhu*—Lord Śrī Caitanya Mahāprabhu; *tāṅhāre*—him; *milite*—to meet.

TRANSLATION

After composing this verse and putting it on the roof of his house, Śrīla Rūpa Gosvāmī went to bathe in the sea. In the meantime, Lord Caitanya Mahāprabhu went to his hut to meet him.

TEXT 63

হরিদাস ঠাকুর আর রূপ-সনাতন।
জগন্নাথ-মন্দিরে না যা'ন তিন জন ॥ ৬৩ ॥

haridāsa ṭhākura āra rūpa-sanātana
jagannātha-mandire nā yā'na tina jana

SYNONYMS

hari-dāsa ṭhākura—Śrīla Haridāsa Ṭhākura; *āra*—and; *rūpa-sanātana*—Śrīla Rūpa Gosvāmī and Śrīla Sanātana Gosvāmī; *jagannātha-mandire*—in the temple of Lord Jagannātha; *nā*—not; *yā'na*—go; *tina jana*—three persons.

TRANSLATION

To avoid turmoil, three great personalities—Haridāsa Ṭhākura, Śrīla Rūpa Gosvāmī and Śrīla Sanātana Gosvāmī—did not enter the temple of Jagannātha.

PURPORT

It is still the practice at Jagannātha temple not to allow those to enter who do not strictly follow the Vedic culture known as Hinduism. Śrīla Haridāsa Ṭhākura, Śrīla Rūpa Gosvāmī and Śrīla Sanātana Gosvāmī had had previous intimate connections with Mohammedans. Haridāsa Ṭhākura had been born in a Mohammedan family, and Śrīla Rūpa Gosvāmī and Śrīla Sanātana Gosvāmī, having given up their social status in Hindu society, had been appointed ministers in the Mohammedan government. They had even changed their names to Sākara Mallika and Dabira Khāsa. Thus they had supposedly been expelled from *brāhmaṇa* society. Consequently, out of humility, they did not enter the temple of Jagannātha, although the Personality of Godhead, Jagannātha, in His form of Caitanya Mahāprabhu, personally came to see them every day. Similarly, the members of this Kṛṣṇa consciousness society are sometimes refused entrance into some of the temples in India. We should not feel sorry about this as long as we engage in chanting the Hare Kṛṣṇa *mantra*. Kṛṣṇa Himself associates with devotees who are chanting His holy name, and there is no need to be unhappy over not being able to enter a certain temple. Such dogmatic prohibitions were not approved by Lord Caitanya Mahāprabhu. Those who were thought unfit to enter Jagannātha temple were daily visited by Caitanya Mahāprabhu, and this indicates that Caitanya Mahāprabhu did not approve of the prohibitions. To avoid unnecessary turmoil, however, these great personalities would not enter Jagannātha temple.

TEXT 64

মহাপ্রভু জগন্নাথের উপল-ভোগ দেখিয়া ।
নিজগৃহে যা'ন এই তিনেরে মিলিয়া ॥ ৬৪ ॥

mahāprabhu jagannāthera upala-bhoga dekhiyā
nija-gṛhe yā'na ei tinere miliyā

SYNONYMS

mahā-prabhu—Śrī Caitanya Mahāprabhu; *jagannāthera*—of Lord Jagannātha; *upala-bhoga*—offering of food on the stone; *dekhiyā*—after seeing; *nija-gṛhe*—to His own residence; *yā'na*—goes; *ei*—these; *tinere*—three; *miliyā*—meeting.

TRANSLATION

Every day Śrī Caitanya Mahāprabhu used to see the upala-bhoga ceremony at the temple of Jagannātha, and after seeing this, He used to go visit these three great personalities on His way to His own residence.

PURPORT

Upala-bhoga is a particular type of offering performed just behind the Garuḍa-stamba on a stone slab. That stone slab is called the *upala.* All food is offered within the temple room just below the altar of Jagannātha. This *bhoga,* however, was offered on the stone slab within the vision of the public; therefore it is called *upala-bhoga.*

TEXT 65

এই তিন মধ্যে যবে থাকে যেই জন ।
তাঁরে আসি' আপনে মিলে,—প্রভুর নিয়ম ॥ ৬৫ ॥

ei tina madhye yabe thāke yei jana
tāṅre āsi' āpane mile,—prabhura niyama

SYNONYMS

ei tina madhye—of these three; *yabe*—when; *thāke*—remains; *yei jana*—that person who; *tāṅre*—to him; *āsi'*—coming; *āpane mile*—personally meets; *prabhura*—of Śrī Caitanya Mahāprabhu; *niyama*—regular practice.

TRANSLATION

If one of these three was not present, He would meet the others. That was His regular practice.

TEXT 66

দৈবে আসি' প্রভু যবে ঊর্ধ্বেতে চাহিলা ।
চালে গোঁজা তালপত্রে সেই শ্লোক পাইলা ॥ ৬৬ ॥

daive āsi' prabhu yabe ūrdhvete cāhilā
cāle goṅjā tāla-patre sei śloka pāilā

SYNONYMS

daive—accidentally; *āsi'*—coming there; *prabhu*—the Lord; *yabe*—when; *ūrdhvete*—on the roof; *cāhilā*—He looked; *cāle*—in the roof; *goṅjā*—pushed; *tāla-patre*—the palm leaf; *sei*—that; *śloka*—verse; *pāilā*—got.

TRANSLATION

When Śrī Caitanya Mahāprabhu went to the residence of Śrīla Rūpa Gosvāmī, He accidentally saw the palm leaf on the roof, and thus He read the verse composed by him.

TEXT 67

শ্লোক পড়ি' আছে প্রভু আবিষ্ট হইয়া ।
রূপগোসাঞি আসি' পড়ে দণ্ডবৎ হঞা ॥ ৬৭ ॥

śloka paḍi' āche prabhu āviṣṭa ha-iyā
rūpa-gosāñi āsi' paḍe daṇḍavat hañā

SYNONYMS

śloka paḍi'—reading the verse; *āche*—remained; *prabhu*—the Lord; *āviṣṭa*—in an ecstatic mood; *ha-iyā*—being; *rūpa-gosāñi*—Śrīla Rūpa Gosvāmī; *āsi'*—coming; *paḍe*—fell down; *daṇḍavat*—like a rod; *hañā*—becoming.

TRANSLATION

After reading the verse, Śrī Caitanya Mahāprabhu went into an ecstatic mood. While He was in that state, Śrīla Rūpa Gosvāmī came and immediately fell down on the floor like a rod.

PURPORT

The word *daṇḍa* means rod or pole. A rod or pole falls straight; similarly, when one offers obeisances to his superior with all eight *aṅgas* (parts) of the body, he performs what is called *daṇḍavat.* Sometimes we only speak of *daṇḍavats* but actually do not fall down. In any case, *daṇḍavat* means falling down like a rod before one's superior.

TEXT 68

উঠি' মহাপ্রভু তাঁরে চাপড় মারিয়া ।
কহিতে লাগিলা কিছু কোলেতে করিয়া ॥ ৬৮ ॥

uṭhi' mahāprabhu tāṅre cāpaḍa māriyā
kahite lāgilā kichu kolete kariyā

SYNONYMS

uṭhi'—standing up; *mahāprabhu*—Śrī Caitanya Mahāprabhu; *tāṅre*—unto Rūpa Gosvāmī; *cāpaḍa māriyā*—slapping; *kahite*—to say; *lāgilā*—began; *kichu*—something; *kolete*—on the lap; *kariyā*—taking.

TRANSLATION

When Rūpa Gosvāmī fell down like a rod, Śrī Caitanya Mahāprabhu got up and gave him a slap. Then, taking him on His lap, He began to speak to him.

TEXT 69

মোর শ্লোকের অভিপ্রায় না জানে কোন জনে।
মোর মনের কথা তুমি জানিলে কেমনে ? ৬৯ ॥

mora ślokera abhiprāya nā jāne kona jane
mora manera kathā tumi jānile kemane?

SYNONYMS

mora—My; *ślokera*—of the verse; *abhiprāya*—purport; *nā*—does not; *jāne*—know; *kona*—any; *jane*—person; *mora*—My; *manera*—of mind; *kathā*—the intention; *tumi*—you; *jānile*—understood; *kemane*—how.

TRANSLATION

"No one knows the purport of My verse," Caitanya Mahāprabhu said. "How could you understand My intention?"

TEXT 70

এত বলি' তাঁরে বহু প্রসাদ করিয়া।
স্বরূপ-গোসাঞিরে শ্লোক দেখাইল লঞা ॥ ৭০ ॥

eta bali' tāṅre bahu prasāda kariyā
svarūpa-gosāñire śloka dekhāila lañā

SYNONYMS

eta bali'—saying this; *tāṅre*—unto Rūpa Gosvāmī; *bahu*—much; *prasāda*—mercy; *kariyā*—showing; *svarūpa-gosāñire*—unto Svarūpa Gosvāmī; *śloka*—the verse; *dekhāila*—showed; *lañā*—taking.

TRANSLATION

Saying this, Lord Caitanya Mahāprabhu bestowed various benedictions upon Rūpa Gosvāmī, and taking the verse, He later showed it to Svarūpa Gosvāmī.

TEXT 71

স্বরূপে পুছেন প্রভু হইয়া বিস্মিতে।
মোর মনের কথা রূপ জানিল কেমতে ॥ ৭১ ॥

svarūpe puchena prabhu ha-iyā vismite
mora manera kathā rūpa jānila kemate

SYNONYMS

svarūpe—unto Svarūpa Gosvāmī; *puchena*—inquired; *prabhu*—the Lord; *ha-iyā*—becoming; *vismite*—struck with wonder; *mora*—My; *manera*—of the mind; *kathā*—intention; *rūpa*—Rūpa Gosvāmī; *jānila*—understand; *kemate*—how.

TRANSLATION

Having shown the verse to Svarūpa Dāmodara with great wonder, Caitanya Mahāprabhu asked him how Rūpa Gosvāmī could understand the intentions of His mind.

PURPORT

We had the opportunity to receive a similar blessing from Śrīla Bhaktisiddhānta Sarasvatī Gosvāmī when we presented an essay at his birthday ceremony. He was so pleased with that essay that he used to call some of his confidential devotees and show it to them. How could we have understood the intentions of Śrīla Prabhupāda?

TEXT 72

স্বরূপ কহে,—যাতে জানিল তোমার মন।
তাতে জানি,—হয় তোমার কৃপার ভাজন ॥ ৭২ ॥

svarūpa kahe,——yāte jānila tomāra mana
tāte jāni,——haya tomāra kṛpāra bhājana

SYNONYMS

svarūpa kahe—Svarūpa Dāmodara replied; *yāte*—since; *jānila*—he knew; *tomāra*—Your; *mana*—intention; *tāte*—therefore; *jāni*—I can understand; *haya*—he is; *tomāra*—Your; *kṛpāra*—of the mercy; *bhājana*—recipient.

TRANSLATION

Śrīla Svarūpa Dāmodara Gosvāmī replied to Lord Caitanya Mahāprabhu: "If Rūpa Gosvāmī can understand Your mind and intentions, he must have Your Lordship's special benediction."

TEXT 73

প্রভু কহে,—তারে আমি সন্তুষ্ট হঞা।
আলিঙ্গন কৈলু সর্বশক্তি সঞ্চারিয়া ॥ ৭৩ ॥

prabhu kahe,——tāre āmi santuṣṭa hañā
āliṅgana kailu sarva-śakti sañcāriyā

SYNONYMS

prabhu kahe—the Lord said; *tāre*—him; *āmi*—I; *santuṣṭa hañā*—being very much satisfied; *āliṅgana kailu*—embraced; *sarva-śakti*—all potencies; *sañcāriyā*—bestowing.

TRANSLATION

The Lord said: "I was so pleased with Rūpa Gosvāmī that I embraced him and bestowed upon him all necessary potencies for preaching the bhakti cult.

TEXT 74

যোগ্য পাত্র হয় গূঢ়রস-বিবেচনে।
তুমিও কহিও তারে গূঢ়রসাখ্যানে ॥ ৭৪ ॥

yogya pātra haya gūḍha-rasa-vivecane
tumio kahio tāre gūḍha-rasākhyāne

SYNONYMS

yogya—suitable; *pātra*—recipient; *haya*—is; *gūḍha*—confidential; *rasa*—the mellows; *vivecane*—in analyzing; *tumio*—you also; *kahio*—instruct; *tāre*—him; *gūḍha*—confidential; *rasa*—the mellows; *ākhyāne*—in describing.

TRANSLATION

"I accept Śrīla Rūpa Gosvāmī as quite fit to understand the confidential mellows of devotional service, and I recommend that you explain devotional service to him further."

TEXT 75

এসব কহিব আগে বিস্তার করিঞা ।
সংক্ষেপে উদ্দেশ কৈল প্রস্তাব পাইঞা ॥ ৭৫ ॥

e-saba kahiba āge vistāra kariñā
saṅkṣepe uddeśa kaila prastāva pāiñā

SYNONYMS

e-saba—all these; *kahiba*—I shall narrate; *āge*—later; *vistāra*—elaboration; *kariñā*—making; *saṅkṣepe*—in brief; *uddeśa*—reference; *kaila*—did; *prastāva*—opportunity; *pāiñā*—getting.

TRANSLATION

I shall describe all these incidents elaborately later on. Now I have given only a brief reference.

TEXT 76

প্রিয়ঃ সোঽয়ং কৃষ্ণঃ সহচরি কুরুক্ষেত্রমিলিত-
স্তথাহং সা রাধা তদিদমুভয়োঃ সঙ্গমসুখম্ ।
তথাপ্যন্তঃ-খেলন্মধুরমুরলীপঞ্চমজুষে
মনো মে কালিন্দীপুলিনবিপিনায় স্পৃহয়তি ॥ ৭৬ ॥

priyaḥ so 'yaṁ kṛṣṇaḥ sahacari kuru-kṣetra-militas
tathāhaṁ sā rādhā tad idam ubhayoḥ saṅgama-sukham
tathāpy antaḥ-khelan-madhura-muralī-pañcama-juṣe
mano me kālindī-pulina-vipināya spṛhayati

SYNONYMS

priyaḥ—very dear; *saḥ*—He; *ayam*—this; *kṛṣṇaḥ*—Lord Kṛṣṇa; *saha-cari*—O My dear friend; *kuru-kṣetra-militaḥ*—who is met on the field of Kurukṣetra; *tathā*—also; *aham*—I; *sā*—that; *rādhā*—Rādhārāṇī; *tad*—that; *idam*—

this; *ubhayoḥ*—of both of Us; *saṅgama-sukham*—the happiness of meeting; *tathāpi*—still; *antaḥ*—within; *khelan*—playing; *madhura*—sweet; *muralī*—of the flute; *pañcama*—the fifth note; *juṣe*—which delights in; *manaḥ*—the mind; *me*—My; *kālindī*—of the River Yamunā; *pulina*—on the bank; *vipināya*—the trees; *spṛhayati*—desires.

TRANSLATION

[This is a verse spoken by Śrīmatī Rādhārāṇī.] "My dear friend, now I have met My very old and dear friend Kṛṣṇa on this field of Kurukṣetra. I am the same Rādhārāṇī, and now We are meeting together. It is very pleasant, but still I would like to go to the bank of the Yamunā beneath the trees of the forest there. I wish to hear the vibration of His sweet flute playing the fifth note within that forest of Vṛndāvana."

PURPORT

This verse also appears in the *Padyāvalī* (383), by Śrīla Rūpa Gosvāmī.

TEXT 77

এই শ্লোকের সংক্ষেপার্থ শুন, ভক্তগণ ।
জগন্নাথ দেখি' যৈছে প্রভুর ভাবন ॥ ৭৭ ॥

ei ślokera saṅkṣepārtha śuna, bhakta-gaṇa
jagannātha dekhi' yaiche prabhura bhāvana

SYNONYMS

ei—this; *ślokera*—of the verse; *saṅkṣepa-artha*—a brief explanation; *śuna*—hear; *bhakta-gaṇa*—O devotees; *jagannātha*—Lord Jagannātha; *dekhi'*—after seeing; *yaiche*—just as; *prabhura*—of Lord Caitanya; *bhāvana*—the thinking.

TRANSLATION

Now, O devotees, please hear a brief explanation of this verse. Lord Caitanya Mahāprabhu was thinking in this way after having seen the Jagannātha Deity.

TEXT 78

শ্রীরাধিকা কুরুক্ষেত্রে কৃষ্ণের দরশন ।
যদ্যপি পায়েন, তবু ভাবেন ঐছন ॥ ৭৮ ॥

śrī-rādhikā kurukṣetre kṛṣṇera daraśana
yadyapi pāyena, tabu bhāvena aichana

SYNONYMS

śrī-rādhikā—Śrīmatī Rādhārāṇī; *kuru-kṣetre*—in the field of Kurukṣetra; *kṛṣṇera*—of Lord Kṛṣṇa; *daraśana*—meeting; *yadyapi*—although; *pāyena*—She gets; *tabu*—still; *bhāvena*—thinks; *aichana*—in this way.

TRANSLATION

The subject of His thoughts was Śrīmatī Rādhārāṇī, who met Kṛṣṇa in the field of Kurukṣetra. Although She met Kṛṣṇa there, She was nonetheless thinking of Him in the following way.

TEXT 79

রাজবেশ, হাতী, ঘোড়া, মনুষ্য গহন।
কাহাঁ গোপ-বেশ, কাহাঁ নির্জন বৃন্দাবন ॥ ৭৯ ॥

rāja-veśa, hātī, ghoḍā, manuṣya gahana
kāhāṅ gopa-veśa, kāhāṅ nirjana vṛndāvana

SYNONYMS

rāja-veśa—royal dress; *hātī*—elephants; *ghoḍā*—horses; *manuṣya*—men; *gahana*—crowds; *kāhāṅ*—where; *gopa-veśa*—the dress of a cowherd boy; *kāhāṅ*—where; *nirjana*—solitary; *vṛndāvana*—of the name Vṛndāvana.

TRANSLATION

She thought of Him in the calm and quiet atmosphere of Vṛndāvana, dressed as a cowherd boy. But at Kurukṣetra He was in a royal dress and was accompanied by elephants, horses and crowds of men. Thus the atmosphere was not congenial for Their meeting.

TEXT 80

সেই ভাব, সেই কৃষ্ণ, সেই বৃন্দাবন।
যবে পাই, তবে হয় বাঞ্ছিত পূরণ ॥ ৮০ ॥

sei bhāva, sei kṛṣṇa, sei vṛndāvana
yabe pāi, tabe haya vāñchita pūraṇa

SYNONYMS

sei bhāva—that circumstance; *sei kṛṣṇa*—that Kṛṣṇa; *sei vṛndāvana*—that Vṛndāvana; *yabe pāi*—if I get; *tabe*—then; *haya*—is; *vāñchita*—desired object; *pūraṇa*—fulfilled.

TRANSLATION

Thus meeting with Kṛṣṇa and thinking of the Vṛndāvana atmosphere, Rādhārāṇī longed for Kṛṣṇa to take Her to Vṛndāvana again to fulfill Her desire in that calm atmosphere.

TEXT 81

আহুশ্চ তে নলিননাভ পদারবিন্দং
যোগেশ্বরৈর্হৃদি বিচিন্ত্যমগাধবোধৈঃ ।
সংসারকূপপতিতোত্তরণাবলম্বং
গেহং জুষামপি মনস্যুদিয়াৎ সদা নঃ ॥ ৮১ ॥

āhuś ca te nalina-nābha padāravindaṁ
yogeśvarair hṛdi vicintyam agādha-bodhaiḥ
saṁsāra-kūpa-patitottaraṇāvalambaṁ
gehaṁ juṣām api manasy udiyāt sadā naḥ

SYNONYMS

āhuḥ—the *gopīs* said; *ca*—and; *te*—Your; *nalina-nābha*—O Lord, whose navel is just like a lotus flower; *pada-aravindam*—lotus feet; *yoga-īśvaraiḥ*—by the great mystic *yogīs*; *hṛdi*—within the heart; *vicintyam*—to be meditated upon; *agādha-bodhaiḥ*—who were highly learned philosophers; *saṁsāra-kūpa*—the dark well of material existence; *patita*—of those fallen; *uttaraṇa*—of deliverers; *avalambam*—the only shelter; *geham*—family affairs; *juṣām*—of those engaged; *api*—although; *manasi*—in the minds; *udiyāt*—let be awakened; *sadā*—always; *naḥ*—our.

TRANSLATION

The gopīs spoke thus: "Dear Lord, whose navel is just like a lotus flower, Your lotus feet are the only shelter for those who have fallen into the deep well of material existence. Your feet are worshiped and meditated upon by great mystic yogīs and highly learned philosophers. We

wish that these lotus feet may also be awakened within our hearts, although we are only ordinary persons engaged in household affairs."

PURPORT

This is a verse from the *Śrīmad-Bhāgavatam* (10.82.49).

TEXT 82

তোমার চরণ মোর ব্রজপুরঘরে ।
উদয় করয়ে যদি, তবে বাঞ্ছা পূরে ॥ ৮২ ॥

tomāra caraṇa mora vraja-pura-ghare
udaya karaye yadi, tabe vāñchā pūre

SYNONYMS

tomāra—Your; *caraṇa*—lotus feet; *mora*—my; *vraja-pura-ghare*—at the home in Vṛndāvana; *udaya*—awaken; *karaye*—I do; *yadi*—if; *tabe*—then; *vāñchā*—desires; *pūre*—are fulfilled.

TRANSLATION

The gopīs thought: "Dear Lord, if Your lotus feet again come to our home in Vṛndāvana, our desires will be fulfilled."

PURPORT

In his *Anubhāṣya,* Śrīla Bhaktisiddhānta Sarasvatī Ṭhākura comments: "The *gopīs* are purely engaged in the service of the Lord without motive. They are not captivated by the opulence of Kṛṣṇa, nor by the understanding that He is the Supreme Personality of Godhead." Naturally the *gopīs* were inclined to love Kṛṣṇa, for He was an attractive young boy of Vṛndāvana village. Being village girls, they were not very much attracted to the field of Kurukṣetra, where Kṛṣṇa was present with elephants, horses and royal dress. Indeed, they did not very much appreciate Kṛṣṇa in that atmosphere. Kṛṣṇa was not attracted by the opulence or personal beauty of the *gopīs* but by their pure devotional service. Similarly, the *gopīs* were attracted to Kṛṣṇa as a cowherd boy, not in sophisticated guise. Lord Kṛṣṇa is inconceivably powerful. To understand Him, great *yogīs* and saintly persons give up all material engagements and meditate upon Him. Similarly, those who are overly attracted to material enjoyment, to enhancement of material opulence, to family maintenance or to liberation from the entanglements of this material world take shelter of the Supreme Personality of Godhead. But such activities and motivations are unknown to the *gopīs;* they are not at all expert in executing such auspicious activities. Already transcendentally enlightened, they simply engage their purified senses in the service of the Lord in the remote village of Vṛndāvana. The *gopīs* are not interested in dry speculation, in the arts, in music, or other conditions of material life. They are bereft of all understanding of material enjoyment and renunciation. Their only desire is to see Kṛṣṇa return and enjoy spiritual, transcendental pastimes with them. The *gopīs* want Him simply to stay in Vṛndāvana so that they can render service unto Him, for His pleasure. There is not even a tinge of personal sense gratification.

TEXT 83

ভাগবতের শ্লোক-গূঢ়ার্থ বিশদ করিঞা ।
রূপ-গোসাঞি শ্লোক কৈল লোক বুঝাইঞা ॥ ৮৩ ॥

bhāgavatera śloka-gūḍhārtha viśada kariñā
rūpa-gosāñi śloka kaila loka bujhāiñā

SYNONYMS

bhāgavatera—of *Śrīmad-Bhāgavatam;* *śloka*—the verse; *gūḍha-artha*—confidential meaning; *viśada*—elaborate description; *kariñā*—doing; *rūpa-gosāñi*—Śrīla Rūpa Gosvāmī; *śloka*—the verse; *kaila*—compiled; *loka*—the people in general; *bujhāiñā*—making understand.

TRANSLATION

In one verse, Śrīla Rūpa Gosvāmī has explained the confidential meaning of the verse of Śrīmad-Bhāgavatam for the understanding of the general populace.

TEXT 84

যা তে লীলারসপরিমলোদ্গারিবন্যাপরীতা
ধন্যা ক্ষৌণী বিলসতি বৃতা মাথুরী মাধুরীভিঃ ।
তত্রাস্মাভিশ্চটুলপশুপীভাবমুগ্ধান্তরাভিঃ
সম্বীতস্ত্বং কলয় বদনোল্লাসি-বেণুর্বিহারম্ ॥ ৮৪ ॥

yā te līlā-rasa-parimalodgāri-vanyāparītā
dhanyā kṣauṇī vilasati vṛtā māthurī mādhurībhiḥ

tatrāsmābhiś caṭula-paśupī-bhāva-mugdhāntarābhiḥ
saṁvītas tvaṁ kalaya vadanollāsi-veṇur vihāram

SYNONYMS

yā—that; *te*—Your; *līlā-rasa*—of the mellows tasted in the pastimes; *parimala*—the fragrance; *udgāri*—spreading; *vanya-āparītā*—filled with forests; *dhanyā*—glorious; *kṣauṇī*—the land; *vilasati*—enjoys; *vṛtā*—surrounded; *māthurī*—the Mathurā district; *mādhurībhiḥ*—by the beauties; *tatra*—there; *asmābhiḥ*—by us; *caṭula*—flickering; *paśupī-bhāva*—with ecstatic enjoyment as *gopīs*; *mugdha-antarābhiḥ*—by those whose hearts are enchanted; *saṁvītaḥ*—surrounded; *tvam*—You; *kalaya*—kindly perform; *vadana*—on the mouth; *ullāsi*—playing; *veṇuḥ*—with the flute; *vihāram*—playful pastimes.

TRANSLATION

The gopīs continued: "Dear Kṛṣṇa, the fragrance of the mellows of Your pastimes is spread throughout the forests of the glorious land of Vṛndāvana, which is surrounded by the sweetness of the district of Mathurā. In the congenial atmosphere of that wonderful land, You may enjoy Your pastimes, with Your flute dancing on Your lips, and surrounded by us, the gopīs, whose hearts are always enchanted by unpredictable ecstatic emotions."

PURPORT

This is a verse from the *Lalita-mādhava* (10.38), by Śrīla Rūpa Gosvāmī.

TEXT 85

এইমত মহাপ্রভু দেখি' জগন্নাথে ।
সুভদ্রা-সহিত দেখে, বংশী নাহি হাতে ॥ ৮৫ ॥

ei-mata mahāprabhu dekhi' jagannāthe
subhadrā-sahita dekhe, vaṁśī nāhi hāte

SYNONYMS

ei-mata—in this way; *mahā-prabhu*—Śrī Caitanya Mahāprabhu; *dekhi'*—after seeing; *jagannāthe*—Lord Jagannātha; *su-bhadrā*—Subhadrā; *sahita*—with; *dekhe*—He sees; *vaṁśī*—the flute; *nāhi*—not; *hāte*—in the hand.

TRANSLATION

In this way, when Śrī Caitanya Mahāprabhu saw Jagannātha, He saw that the Lord was with His sister Subhadrā and was not holding a flute in His hand.

TEXT 86

ত্রিভঙ্গ-সুন্দর ব্রজে ব্রজেন্দ্রনন্দন ।
কাহাঁ পাব, এই বাঞ্ছা বাড়ে অনুক্ষণ ॥ ৮৬ ॥

tri-bhaṅga-sundara vraje vrajendra-nandana
kāhāṅ pāba, ei vāñchā bāḍe anukṣaṇa

SYNONYMS

tri-bhaṅga—bent in three places; *sundara*—beautiful; *vraje*—in Vṛndāvana; *vrajendra-nandana*—the son of Nanda Mahārāja; *kāhāṅ*—where; *pāba*—shall I get; *ei*—this; *vāñchā*—desire; *bāḍe*—increases; *anukṣaṇa*—incessantly.

TRANSLATION

Absorbed in the ecstasy of the gopīs, Lord Caitanya Mahāprabhu wished to see Lord Jagannātha in His original form as Kṛṣṇa, the son of Nanda Mahārāja, standing in Vṛndāvana and appearing very beautiful, His body curved in three places. His desire to see that form was always increasing.

TEXT 87

রাধিকা-উন্মাদ যৈছে উদ্ধব-দর্শনে ।
উদ্‌ঘূর্ণা-প্রলাপ তৈছে প্রভুর রাত্রি-দিনে ॥ ৮৭ ॥

rādhikā-unmāda yaiche uddhava-darśane
udghūrṇā-pralāpa taiche prabhura rātri-dine

SYNONYMS

rādhikā-unmāda—the madness of Śrīmatī Rādhārāṇī; *yaiche*—just like; *uddhava-darśane*—in seeing Uddhava; *udghūrṇā-pralāpa*—talking inconsistently in madness; *taiche*—similarly; *prabhura*—of Lord Caitanya; *rātri-dine*—night and day.

TRANSLATION

Just as Śrīmatī Rādhārāṇī talked inconsistently with a bumblebee in the presence of Uddhava, Śrī Caitanya Mahāprabhu in His ecstasy talked crazily and inconsistently day and night.

PURPORT

This *unmāda* (madness) is not ordinary madness. When Śrī Caitanya Mahāprabhu talked inconsistently, almost like a crazy fellow, He was in the transcendental ecstasy of love. In the highest transcendental ecstasy there is a feeling of being enchanted in the presence of the enchanter. When the enchanter and the enchanted become separated, *mohana,* or bewilderment, occurs. When so bewildered due to separation, one becomes stunned, and at that time all the bodily symptoms of transcendental ecstasy are manifested. When they are manifest, one appears inconceivably crazy. This is called transcendental madness. In this state, there is imaginative discourse, and one experiences emotions like those of a madman. The madness of Śrīmatī Rādhārāṇī was explained to Kṛṣṇa by Uddhava, who said, "My dear Kṛṣṇa, because of extreme feelings of separation from You, Śrīmatī Rādhārāṇī is sometimes making Her bed in the groves of the forest, sometimes rebuking a bluish cloud, and sometimes wandering about in the dense darkness of the forest. Thus She has become like a crazy woman."

TEXT 88

দ্বাদশ বৎসর শেষ ঐছে গোঙাইল ।
এই মত শেষলীলা ত্রিবিধানে কৈল ॥ ৮৮ ॥

dvādaśa vatsara śeṣa aiche goṅāila
ei mata śeṣa-līlā tri-vidhāne kaila

SYNONYMS

dvādaśa—twelve; *vatsara*—years; *śeṣa*—final; *aiche*—in that way; *goṅāila*—passed away; *ei mata*—in this way; *śeṣa-līlā*—the last pastimes; *tri-vidhāne*—in three ways; *kaila*—executed.

TRANSLATION

The last twelve years of Śrī Caitanya Mahāprabhu were passed in this transcendental craziness. Thus He executed His last pastimes in three ways.

TEXT 89

সন্ন্যাস করি' চব্বিশ বৎসর কৈলা যে যে কর্ম।
অনন্ত, অপার—তার কে জানিবে মর্ম ॥ ৮৯ ॥

sannyāsa kari' cabbiśa vatsara kailā ye ye karma
ananta, apāra——tāra ke jānibe marma

SYNONYMS

sannyāsa kari'—after accepting the renounced order; *cabbiśa vatsara*—twenty-four years; *kailā*—did; *ye ye*—whatever; *karma*—activities; *ananta*—unlimited; *apāra*—insurmountable; *tāra*—of that; *ke*—who; *jānibe*—will know; *marma*—the purport.

TRANSLATION

For the twenty-four years after Śrī Caitanya Mahāprabhu accepted the renounced order, whatever pastimes He executed were unlimited and unfathomable. Who can understand the purport of such pastimes?

TEXT 90

উদ্দেশ করিতে করি দিগ্-দরশন।
মুখ্য মুখ্য লীলার করি সূত্র গণন ॥ ৯০ ॥

uddeśa karite kari dig-daraśana
mukhya mukhya līlāra kari sūtra gaṇana

SYNONYMS

uddeśa—indication; *karite*—to make; *kari*—I do; *dig-daraśana*—a general survey; *mukhya mukhya*—the chief; *līlāra*—of the pastimes; *kari*—I do; *sūtra*—synopsis; *gaṇana*—enumeration.

TRANSLATION

Just to indicate those pastimes, I am presenting a general survey of the chief pastimes in the form of a synopsis.

TEXT 91

প্রথম সূত্র প্রভুর সন্ন্যাসকরণ।
সন্ন্যাস করি' চলিলা প্রভু শ্রীবৃন্দাবন ॥ ৯১ ॥

prathama sūtra prabhura sannyāsa-karaṇa
sannyāsa kari' calilā prabhu śrī-vṛndāvana

SYNONYMS

prathama—first; *sūtra*—synopsis; *prabhura*—of the Lord; *sannyāsa-karaṇa*—accepting the *sannyāsa* order; *sannyāsa kari'*—after accepting the renounced order; *calilā*—went; *prabhu*—the Lord; *śrī-vṛndāvana*—toward Vṛndāvana.

TRANSLATION

This is the first synopsis: After accepting the sannyāsa order, Caitanya Mahāprabhu proceeded toward Vṛndāvana.

PURPORT

Clearly these statements are a real account of Śrī Caitanya Mahāprabhu's acceptance of the renounced order of life. His acceptance of this renounced order is not at all comparable to the acceptance of *sannyāsa* by Māyāvādīs. After accepting *sannyāsa,* Caitanya Mahāprabhu's aim was to reach Vṛndāvana. He was unlike the Māyāvādī *sannyāsīs,* who desire to merge into the existence of the Absolute. For a Vaiṣṇava, acceptance of *sannyāsa* means getting relief from all material activities and completely devoting oneself to the transcendental loving service of the Lord. This is confirmed by Śrīla Rūpa Gosvāmī (B.r.s. 1.2.255): *anāsaktasya viṣayān yathārham upayuñjataḥ/ nirbandhaḥ kṛṣṇa-sambandhe yuktaṁ vairāgyam ucyate.* For a Vaiṣṇava, the renounced order means completely giving up attachment for material things and engaging nonstop in the transcendental loving service of the Lord. The Māyāvādī *sannyāsīs,* however, do not know how to engage everything in the service of the Lord. Because they have no devotional training , they think material objects to be untouchable. *Brahma-satyaṁ jagan-mithyā.* The Māyāvādīs think that the world is false, but the Vaiṣṇava *sannyāsīs* do not think like this. Vaiṣṇavas say, "Why should the world be false? It is reality, and it is meant for the service of the Supreme Personality of Godhead." For a Vaiṣṇava *sannyāsī,* renunciation means not accepting anything for personal sense enjoyment. Devotional service means engaging everything for the satisfaction of the Supreme Personality of Godhead.

TEXT 92

প্রেমেতে বিহ্বল বাহ্য নাহিক স্মরণ ।
রাঢ়দেশে তিন দিন করিলা ভ্রমণ ॥ ৯২ ॥

premete vihvala bāhya nāhika smaraṇa
rāḍha-deśe tina dina karilā bhramaṇa

SYNONYMS

premete—in ecstatic love of Kṛṣṇa; *vihvala*—overwhelmed; *bāhya*—external; *nāhika*—there is not; *smaraṇa*—remembrance; *rāḍha-deśe*—in the Rāḍha countries; *tina dina*—three days; *karilā*—did; *bhramaṇa*—traveling.

TRANSLATION

When proceeding toward Vṛndāvana, Śrī Caitanya Mahāprabhu was overwhelmed with ecstatic love for Kṛṣṇa, and He lost all remembrance of the external world. In this way He traveled continuously for three days in Rāḍha-deśa, the country where the Ganges River does not flow.

TEXT 93

নিত্যানন্দ প্রভু মহাপ্রভু ভুলাইয়া ।
গঙ্গাতীরে লঞা আইলা 'যমুনা' বলিয়া ॥ ৯৩ ॥

nityānanda prabhu mahāprabhu bhulāiyā
gaṅgā-tīre lañā āilā 'yamunā' baliyā

SYNONYMS

nityānanda prabhu—Lord Nityānanda Prabhu; *mahā-prabhu*—Śrī Caitanya Mahāprabhu; *bhulāiyā*—bewildering; *gaṅgā-tīre*—on the bank of the Ganges; *lañā*—taking; *āilā*—brought; *yamunā*—the River Yamunā; *baliyā*—informing.

TRANSLATION

First of all, Lord Nityānanda bewildered Śrī Caitanya Mahāprabhu by bringing Him along the banks of the Ganges, saying that it was the River Yamunā.

TEXT 94

শান্তিপুরে আচার্যের গৃহে আগমন ।
প্রথম ভিক্ষা কৈল তাহাঁ, রাত্রে সংকীর্তন ॥ ৯৪ ॥

śāntipure ācāryera gṛhe āgamana
prathama bhikṣā kaila tāhāṅ, rātre saṅkīrtana

SYNONYMS

śāntipure—in the city of Śāntipura; *ācāryera*—of Advaita Ācārya; *gṛhe*—to the home; *āgamana*—coming; *prathama*—first; *bhikṣā*—accepting alms; *kaila*—did; *tāhāṅ*—there; *rātre*—at night; *saṅkīrtana*—performance of congregational chanting.

TRANSLATION

After three days, Lord Caitanya Mahāprabhu came to the house of Advaita Ācārya at Śāntipura and accepted alms there. This was His first acceptance of alms. At night He performed congregational chanting there.

PURPORT

It appears that in His transcendental ecstasy, Śrī Caitanya Mahāprabhu forgot to eat for three continuous days. He was then misled by Nityānanda Prabhu, who said that the River Ganges was the Yamunā. Because the Lord was in the ecstasy of going to Vṛndāvana, He was engladdened to see the Yamunā, although in actuality the river was the Ganges. In this way the Lord was brought to the house of Advaita Prabhu at Śāntipura after three days, and He accepted food there. As long as the Lord remained there, He saw His mother, Śacīdevī, and every night executed congregational chanting with all the devotees.

TEXT 95

মাতা ভক্তগণের তাহাঁ করিল মিলন।
সর্ব সমাধান করি' কৈল নীলাদ্রিগমন ॥ ৯৫ ॥

mātā bhakta-gaṇera tāhāṅ karila milana
sarva samādhāna kari' kaila nīlādri-gamana

SYNONYMS

mātā—the mother; *bhakta-gaṇera*—of the devotees; *tāhāṅ*—in that place; *karila*—did; *milana*—meeting; *sarva*—all; *samādhāna*—adjustments; *kari'*—executing; *kaila*—did; *nīlādri-gamana*—going to Jagannātha Purī.

TRANSLATION

At the house of Advaita Prabhu, He met His mother as well as all the devotees from Māyāpura. He adjusted everything and then went to Jagannātha Purī.

PURPORT

Śrī Caitanya Mahāprabhu knew very well that His acceptance of *sannyāsa* was a thunderbolt for His mother. He therefore called for His mother and the devotees from Māyāpura, and by the arrangement of Śrī Advaita Ācārya, He met them for the last time after His acceptance of *sannyāsa*. His mother was overwhelmed with grief when she saw that He was clean-shaven. There was no longer any beautiful hair on His head. Mother Śacī was pacified by all the devotees, and Lord Caitanya Mahāprabhu asked her to cook for Him because He was very hungry, not having taken anything for three days. His mother immediately agreed, and, forgetting everything else, she cooked for Śrī Caitanya Mahāprabhu during all the days she was at the house of Śrī Advaita Prabhu. Then, after a few days, Śrī Caitanya Mahāprabhu requested His mother's permission to go to Jagannātha Purī. At His mother's request, He made Jagannātha Purī His headquarters after His acceptance of *sannyāsa*. Thus everything was adjusted, and with His mother's permission Śrī Caitanya Mahāprabhu proceeded toward Jagannātha Purī.

TEXT 96

পথে নানা লীলারস, দেব-দরশন।
মাধবপুরীর কথা, গোপাল-স্থাপন ॥ ৯৬ ॥

pathe nānā līlā-rasa, deva-daraśana
mādhava-purīra kathā, gopāla-sthāpana

SYNONYMS

pathe—on the way; *nānā*—various; *līlā-rasa*—transcendental pastimes; *deva-daraśana*—visiting the temples; *mādhava-purīra*—of Mādhavendra Purī; *kathā*—incidents; *gopāla*—of Gopāla; *sthāpana*—the installation.

TRANSLATION

On the way toward Jagannātha Purī, Caitanya Mahāprabhu performed many other pastimes. He visited various temples and heard the story about Mādhavendra Purī and the installation of Gopāla.

PURPORT

This Mādhava Purī is Mādhavendra Purī. Another Mādhava Purī is Mādhavācārya, who was the spiritual master of a devotee in the line of Gadādhara Paṇḍita and who wrote a book known as *Śrī Maṅgala-bhāṣya.*

Mādhavācārya, however, is different from Mādhavendra Purī, who is mentioned in this verse.

TEXT 97

ক্ষীর-চুরি-কথা, সাক্ষি-গোপাল-বিবরণ ।
নিত্যানন্দ কৈল প্রভুর দণ্ড-ভঞ্জন ॥ ৯৭ ॥

kṣīra-curi-kathā, sākṣi-gopāla-vivaraṇa
nityānanda kaila prabhura daṇḍa-bhañjana

SYNONYMS

kṣīra-curi-kathā—the narration of the stealing of the condensed milk; *sākṣi-gopāla-vivaraṇa*—the description of witness Gopāla; *nityānanda*—Nityānanda Prabhu; *kaila*—did; *prabhura*—of the Lord; *daṇḍa-bhañjana*—breaking the *sannyāsa* rod.

TRANSLATION

From Nityānanda Prabhu, Lord Caitanya Mahāprabhu heard the story of Kṣīra-curī Gopinātha and of the witness Gopāla. Then Nityānanda Prabhu broke the sannyāsa rod belonging to Lord Caitanya Mahāprabhu.

PURPORT

This Kṣīra-curī Gopinātha is situated about five miles away from the Bāleśvara station on the Northeastern Railway, formerly known as the Bengal-Māyāpura Railway. This station is situated a few miles away from the famous Kargapura Junction station. Sometimes the charge of the temple was given to Śyāmasundara Adhikārī from Gopīvallabhapura, which lies on the border of the district of Medinīpura. Śyāmasundara Adhikārī was a descendant of Rasikānanda Murāri, the chief disciple of Śyāmānanda Gosvāmī.

A few miles before the Jagannātha Purī station is a small station called Sākṣi-gopāla. Near this station is a village named Satyavādī, where the temple of Sākṣi-gopāla is situated.

TEXT 98

ক্রুদ্ধ হঞা একা গেলা জগন্নাথ দেখিতে ।
দেখিয়া মূর্চ্ছিত হঞা পড়িলা ভূমিতে ॥ ৯৮ ॥

kruddha hañā ekā gelā jagannātha dekhite
dekhiyā mūrcchita hañā paḍilā bhūmite

SYNONYMS

kruddha—angry; *hañā*—becoming; *ekā*—alone; *gelā*—went; *jagannātha*—Lord Jagannātha; *dekhite*—to see; *dekhiyā*—after seeing Jagannātha; *mūrcchita*—senseless; *hañā*—becoming; *paḍilā*—fell down; *bhūmite*—on the ground.

TRANSLATION

After His sannyāsa rod was broken by Nityānanda Prabhu, Caitanya Mahāprabhu apparently became very angry and left His company to travel alone to the Jagannātha temple. When Caitanya Mahāprabhu entered the Jagannātha temple and saw Lord Jagannātha, He immediately lost His senses and fell down on the ground.

TEXT 99

সার্বভৌম লঞা গেলা আপন-ভবন ।
তৃতীয় প্রহরে প্রভুর হইল চেতন ॥ ৯৯ ॥

sārvabhauma lañā gelā āpana-bhavana
tṛtīya prahare prabhura ha-ila cetana

SYNONYMS

sārvabhauma—Sārvabhauma Bhaṭṭācārya; *lañā*—taking; *gelā*—went; *āpana-bhavana*—to his own house; *tṛtīya prahare*—in the afternoon; *prabhura*—of Lord Caitanya Mahāprabhu; *ha-ila*—there was; *cetana*—consciousness.

TRANSLATION

After Lord Caitanya Mahāprabhu saw Lord Jagannātha in the temple and fell down unconscious, Sārvabhauma Bhaṭṭācārya took Him to his home. The Lord remained unconscious until the afternoon, when He finally regained His consciousness.

TEXT 100

নিত্যানন্দ, জগদানন্দ, দামোদর, মুকুন্দ ।
পাছে আসি' মিলি' সবে পাইল আনন্দ ॥ ১০০ ॥

nityānanda, jagadānanda, dāmodara, mukunda
pāche āsi' mili' sabe pāila ānanda

SYNONYMS

nityānanda—of the name Nityānanda; *jagadānanda*—of the name Jagadānanda; *dāmodara*—of the name Dāmodara; *mukunda*—of the name Mukunda; *pāche āsi'*—coming; *mili'*—meeting; *sabe*—all; *pāila*—got; *ānanda*—pleasure.

TRANSLATION

The Lord had left Nityānanda's company and had gone alone to the Jagannātha temple, but later Nityānanda, Jagadānanda, Dāmodara and Mukunda came to see Him, and after seeing Him they were very pleased.

TEXT 101

তবে সার্বভৌমে প্রভু প্রসাদ করিল ।
আপন-ঈশ্বরমূর্তি তাঁরে দেখাইল ॥ ১০১ ॥

tabe sārvabhaume prabhu prasāda karila
āpana-īśvara-mūrti tāṅre dekhāila

SYNONYMS

tabe—at that time; *sārvabhaume*—unto Sārvabhauma Bhaṭṭācārya; *prabhu*—Lord Śrī Caitanya Mahāprabhu; *prasāda karila*—bestowed mercy; *āpana*—His own; *īśvara-mūrti*—original form as the Lord; *tāṅre*—unto him; *dekhāila*—showed.

TRANSLATION

After this incident, Lord Caitanya Mahāprabhu bestowed His mercy upon Sārvabhauma Bhaṭṭācārya by showing him His original form as the Lord.

TEXT 102

তবে ত' করিলা প্রভু দক্ষিণ গমন ।
কূর্মক্ষেত্রে কৈল বাসুদেব বিমোচন ॥ ১০২ ॥

tabe ta' karilā prabhu dakṣiṇa gamana
kūrma-kṣetre kaila vāsudeva vimocana

SYNONYMS

tabe ta'—thereafter; *karilā*—did; *prabhu*—Lord Caitanya Mahāprabhu; *dakṣiṇa*—to southern India; *gamana*—traveling; *kūrma-kṣetre*—at the pilgrimage site known as Kūrma-kṣetra; *kaila*—did; *vāsudeva*—of the name Vāsudeva; *vimocana*—deliverance.

TRANSLATION

After bestowing mercy upon Sārvabhauma Bhaṭṭācārya, the Lord started for southern India. When He came to Kūrma-kṣetra, He delivered a person named Vāsudeva.

TEXT 103

জিয়ড়-নৃসিংহে কৈল নৃসিংহ-স্তবন ।
পথে-পথে গ্রামে-গ্রামে নামপ্রবর্তন ॥ ১০৩ ॥

jiyaḍa-nṛsiṁhe kaila nṛsiṁha-stavana
pathe-pathe grāme-grāme nāma-pravartana

SYNONYMS

jiyaḍa-nṛsiṁhe—the place of pilgrimage known as Jiyaḍa-nṛsiṁha; *kaila*—did; *nṛsiṁha*—to Nṛsiṁha; *stavana*—praying; *pathe-pathe*—on the way; *grāme-grāme*—every village; *nāma-pravartana*—introduction of the holy name of the Lord.

TRANSLATION

After visiting Kūrma-kṣetra, the Lord visited the south Indian temple of Jiyaḍa-nṛsiṁha and offered His prayers to Lord Nṛsiṁhadeva. On His way, He introduced the chanting of the Hare Kṛṣṇa mahā-mantra in every village.

TEXT 104

গোদাবরীতীর-বনে বৃন্দাবন-ভ্রম ।
রামানন্দ রায় সহ তাহাঞি মিলন ॥ ১০৪ ॥

godāvarī-tīra-vane vṛndāvana-bhrama
rāmānanda rāya saha tāhāñi milana

SYNONYMS

godāvarī-tīra—on the bank of the River Godāvarī; *vane*—in the forest; *vṛndāvana-bhrama*—mistook as Vṛndāvana; *rāmānanda rāya*—of the name Rāmānanda Rāya; *saha*—with; *tāhāñi*—there; *milana*—meeting.

TRANSLATION

Once the Lord mistook the forest on the bank of the River Godāvarī to be Vṛndāvana. In that place He happened to meet Rāmānanda Rāya.

TEXT 105

ত্রিমল্ল-ত্রিপদী-স্থান কৈল দরশন ।
সর্বত্র করিল কৃষ্ণনাম প্রচারণ ॥ ১০৫ ॥

trimalla-tripadī-sthāna kaila daraśana
sarvatra karila kṛṣṇa-nāma pracāraṇa

SYNONYMS

trimalla—a place named Trimalla; *tripadī*—or Tirupati; *sthāna*—the place; *kaila*—did; *daraśana*—visit; *sarvatra*—everywhere; *karila*—did; *kṛṣṇa-nāma*—the holy name of Lord Kṛṣṇa; *pracāraṇa*—preaching.

TRANSLATION

He visited the place known as Trimalla, or Tirupati, and there He extensively preached the chanting of the Lord's holy name.

PURPORT

This holy place is situated in the district of Tāñjor, south India. The temple of Tripadī is situated in the valley of Vyeṅkaṭācala and contains a Deity of Lord Rāmacandra. On top of Vyeṅkaṭācala is the famous temple of Bālājī.

TEXT 106

তবে ত' পাষণ্ডিগণে করিল দলন ।
অহোবল-নৃসিংহাদি কৈল দরশন ॥ ১০৬ ॥

tabe ta' pāṣaṇḍi-gaṇe karila dalana
ahovala-nṛsiṁhādi kaila daraśana

SYNONYMS

tabe ta'—thereafter; *pāṣaṇḍi-gaṇe*—unto the atheists; *karila*—did; *dalana*—subduing; *ahovala-nṛsiṁha-ādi*—Nṛsiṁhadeva, named Ahovala or at Ahovala; *kaila*—did; *daraśana*—visit.

TRANSLATION

After visiting the temple of Trimalla or Tripadī, Śrī Caitanya Mahāprabhu had to subdue some atheists. He then visited the temple of Ahovala-nṛsiṁha.

PURPORT

This Ahovala temple is situated in Dakṣiṇātya in the district of Karṇula within the subdivision of Sārbela. Throughout the whole district this very famous temple is much appreciated by the people. There are nine other temples also, and all of them together are called the Nava-nṛsiṁha temples. There is much wonderful architecture and artistic engraving work in these temples. However, as stated in the local gazette, the *Karṇula Manual,* the work is not complete.

TEXT 107

শ্রীরঙ্গক্ষেত্র আইলা কাবেরীর তীর ।
শ্রীরঙ্গ দেখিয়া প্রেমে হইলা অস্থির ॥ ১০৭ ॥

śrī-raṅga-kṣetra āilā kāverīra tīra
śrī-raṅga dekhiyā preme ha-ilā asthira

SYNONYMS

śrī-raṅga-kṣetra—to the place where the temple of Raṅganātha is situated; *āilā*—came; *kāverīra*—of the River Kāverī; *tīra*—the bank; *śrī-raṅga dekhiyā*—after seeing this temple; *preme*—in love of Godhead; *ha-ilā*—became; *asthira*—agitated.

TRANSLATION

When Śrī Caitanya Mahāprabhu came to the land of Śrī Raṅga-kṣetra on the bank of the Kāverī, He visited the temple of Śrī Raṅganātha and was there overwhelmed in the ecstasy of love of Godhead.

TEXT 108

ত্রিমল্ল ভট্টের ঘরে কৈল প্রভু বাস ।
তাহাঞি রহিলা প্রভু বর্ষা চারি মাস ॥ ১০৮ ॥

trimalla bhaṭṭera ghare kaila prabhu vāsa
tāhāñi rahilā prabhu varṣā cāri māsa

SYNONYMS

trimalla bhaṭṭera—of Trimalla Bhaṭṭa; *ghare*—at the house; *kaila*—did; *prabhu*—the Lord; *vāsa*—residence; *tāhāñi*—there; *rahilā*—lived; *prabhu*—the Lord; *varṣā*—the rainy season; *cāri*—four; *māsa*—months.

TRANSLATION

Śrī Caitanya Mahāprabhu lived at the house of Trimalla Bhaṭṭa for the four months of the rainy season.

TEXT 109

শ্রীবৈষ্ণব ত্রিমল্লভট্ট—পরম পণ্ডিত ।
গোসাঞির পাণ্ডিত্য-প্রেমে হইলা বিস্মিত ॥ ১০৯

śrī-vaiṣṇava trimalla-bhaṭṭa——parama paṇḍita
gosāñira pāṇḍitya-preme ha-ilā vismita

SYNONYMS

śrī-vaiṣṇava trimalla-bhaṭṭa—Trimalla Bhaṭṭa was a Śrī Vaiṣṇava; *parama*—highly; *paṇḍita*—learned scholar; *gosāñira*—of Lord Caitanya Mahāprabhu; *pāṇḍitya*—scholarship; *preme*—as well as in the love of Godhead; *ha-ilā*—was; *vismita*—astonished.

TRANSLATION

Śrī Trimalla Bhaṭṭa was both a member of the Śrī Vaiṣṇava community and a learned scholar; therefore when he saw Caitanya Mahāprabhu, who was both a great scholar and a great devotee of the Lord, he was very much astonished.

TEXT 110

চাতুর্মাস্য তাঁহা প্রভু শ্রীবৈষ্ণবের সনে ।
গোঙাইল নৃত্য-গীত-কৃষ্ণসংকীর্তনে ॥ ১১০ ॥

cāturmāsya tāṅhā prabhu śrī-vaiṣṇavera sane
goṅāila nṛtya-gīta-kṛṣṇa-saṅkīrtane

SYNONYMS

cāturmāsya—observance of the four months of the rainy season; *tāṇhā*—there; *prabhu*—the Lord; *śrī-vaiṣṇavera sane*—with the Śrī Vaiṣṇavas; *goṅāila*—passed; *nṛtya*—dancing; *gīta*—singing; *kṛṣṇa-saṅkīrtane*—in chanting the holy name of Lord Kṛṣṇa.

TRANSLATION

Lord Śrī Caitanya Mahāprabhu passed the Cāturmāsya months with the Śrī Vaiṣṇavas, dancing, singing and chanting the holy name of the Lord.

TEXT 111

চাতুর্মাস্য-অন্তে পুনঃ দক্ষিণ গমন ।
পরমানন্দপুরী সহ তাহাঁঞি মিলন ॥ ১১১ ॥

cāturmāsya-ante punaḥ dakṣiṇa gamana
paramānanda-purī saha tāhāñi milana

SYNONYMS

cāturmāsya-ante—at the end of the Cāturmāsya; *punaḥ*—again; *dakṣiṇa gamana*—traveling in southern India; *paramānanda-purī*—of the name Paramānanda Purī; *saha*—with; *tāhāñi*—there; *milana*—meeting.

TRANSLATION

After the end of the Cāturmāsya, Lord Caitanya Mahāprabhu continued traveling throughout southern India. At that time He met Paramānanda Purī.

TEXT 112

তবে ভট্টথারি হৈতে কৃষ্ণদাসের উদ্ধার ।
রামজপী বিপ্রমুখে কৃষ্ণনাম প্রচার ॥ ১১২ ॥

tabe bhaṭṭathāri haite kṛṣṇa-dāsera uddhāra
rāma-japī vipra-mukhe kṛṣṇa-nāma pracāra

SYNONYMS

tabe—after this; *bhaṭṭa-thāri*—a Bhaṭṭathāri; *haite*—from; *kṛṣṇa-dāsera*—of Kṛṣṇadāsa; *uddhāra*—the deliverance; *rāma-japī*—chanters of the name of

Lord Rāma; *vipra-mukhe*—unto *brāhmaṇas; kṛṣṇa-nāma*—the name of Lord Kṛṣṇa; *pracāra*—preaching.

TRANSLATION

After this, Kṛṣṇadāsa, the servant of Lord Caitanya Mahāprabhu, was delivered from the clutches of a Bhaṭṭathāri. Caitanya Mahāprabhu then preached that Lord Kṛṣṇa's name should also be chanted by brāhmaṇas who were accustomed to chanting Lord Rāma's name.

PURPORT

In the Mālābāra district, a section of the *brāhmaṇas* are known as *nambudri-brāhmaṇas,* and the Bhaṭṭathāris are their priests. Bhaṭṭathāris know many tantric black arts, such as the art of killing a person, of bringing him under submission, and of destroying or devastating him. They are very expert in these black arts, and one such Bhaṭṭathāri bewildered the personal servant of Śrī Caitanya Mahāprabhu while the servant accompanied the Lord in His travels through south India. Somehow or other Śrī Caitanya Mahāprabhu delivered this Kṛṣṇadāsa from the clutches of the Bhaṭṭathāri. Śrī Caitanya Mahāprabhu is well known as Patita-pāvana, the savior of all fallen souls, and He proved this in His behavior toward His personal servant, Kṛṣṇadāsa, whom He saved. Sometimes the word Bhaṭṭathāri is misspelled in Bengal as Bhaṭṭamāri.

TEXT 113

শ্রীরঙ্গপুরী সহ তাহাঞি মিলন ।
রামদাস বিপ্রের কৈল দুঃখবিমোচন ॥ ১১৩ ॥

śrī-raṅga-purī saha tāhāñi milana
rāma-dāsa viprera kaila duḥkha-vimocana

SYNONYMS

śrī-raṅga-purī—of the name Śrī Raṅga-purī; *saha*—with; *tāhāñi*—there; *milana*—meeting; *rāma-dāsa*—of the name Rāmadāsa; *viprera*—of the *brāhmaṇa; kaila*—did; *duḥkha-vimocana*—deliverance from all sufferings.

TRANSLATION

Śrī Caitanya Mahāprabhu then met Śrī Raṅgapurī and mitigated all the sufferings of a brāhmaṇa named Rāmadāsa.

TEXT 114

তত্ত্ববাদী সহ কৈল তত্ত্বের বিচার ।
আপনাকে হীনবুদ্ধি হৈল তাঁ-সবার ॥ ১১৪ ॥

tattva-vādī saha kaila tattvera vicāra
āpanāke hīna-buddhi haila tāṅ-sabāra

SYNONYMS

tattva-vādī—a section of the Madhvācārya-sampradāya; *saha*—with; *kaila*—did; *tattvera*—of the Absolute Truth; *vicāra*—discussion; *āpanāke*—themselves; *hīna-buddhi*—consideration as inferior in quality; *haila*—was; *tāṅ-sabāra*—of all the opposing parties.

TRANSLATION

Caitanya Mahāprabhu also had a discussion with the Tattvavādī community, and the Tattvavādīs felt themselves to be inferior Vaiṣṇavas.

PURPORT

The Tattvavādī sect belongs to Madhvācārya's Vaiṣṇava community, but its behavior differs from the strict Madhvācārya Vaiṣṇava principles. There is one monastery named Uttararāḍī, and its commander is named Raghuvarya-tīrtha-madhvācārya.

TEXT 115

অনন্ত, পুরুষোত্তম, শ্রীজনার্দন ।
পদ্মনাভ, বাসুদেব কৈল দরশন ॥ ১১৫ ॥

ananta, puruṣottama, śrī-janārdana
padmanābha, vāsudeva kaila daraśana

SYNONYMS

ananta—Anantadeva; *puruṣottama*—of the name Puruṣottama; *śrī-janārdana*—of the name Śrī Janārdana; *padma-nābha*—of the name Padmanābha; *vāsudeva*—of the name Vāsudeva; *kaila*—did; *daraśana*—visit.

TRANSLATION

Śrī Caitanya Mahāprabhu then visited the Viṣṇu temples of Anantadeva, Puruṣottama, Śrī Janārdana, Padmanābha and Vāsudeva.

PURPORT

A temple of Ananta Padmanābha Viṣṇu is situated in the Trivāndrama district. This temple is very famous in those quarters. Another Viṣṇu temple, named Śrī Janārdana, is situated about twenty-six miles north of the Trivāndrama district near a railway station called Varkālā.

TEXT 116

তবে প্রভু কৈল সপ্ততাল বিমোচন ।
সেতুবন্ধে স্নান, রামেশ্বর দরশন ॥ ১১৬ ॥

tabe prabhu kaila saptatāla vimocana
setu-bandhe snāna, rāmeśvara daraśana

SYNONYMS

tabe—thereafter; *prabhu*—the Lord; *kaila*—did; *sapta-tāla-vimocana*—deliverance of the Saptatāla tree; *setu-bandhe*—at Cape Comorin; *snāna*—bathing; *rāmeśvara*—temple of Rāmeśvara; *daraśana*—visit.

TRANSLATION

After that, Lord Caitanya Mahāprabhu delivered the celebrated Saptatāla tree, took His bath at Setubandha Rāmeśvara and visited the temple of Lord Śiva known as Rāmeśvara.

PURPORT

It is said that the Saptatāla tree is a very old, massive palm tree. There was once a fight between Bali and his brother Sugrīva, and Lord Rāmacandra took the side of Sugrīva and killed Bali, keeping Himself behind this celebrated tree. When Lord Caitanya Mahāprabhu toured south India, He embraced this tree, which was delivered and directly promoted to Vaikuṇṭha.

TEXT 117

তাহাঞি করিল কূর্মপুরাণ শ্রবণ ।
মায়াসীতা নিলেক রাবণ, তাহাতে লিখন ॥ ১১৭ ॥

tāhāñi karila kūrma-purāṇa śravaṇa
māyā-sītā nileka rāvaṇa, tāhāte likhana

SYNONYMS

tāhāñi—there; *karila*—did; *kūrma-purāṇa*—of the *Kūrma Purāṇa*; *śravaṇa*—hearing; *māyā-sītā*—a false Sītā; *nileka*—kidnapped; *rāvaṇa*—by Rāvaṇa; *tāhāte*—in that book; *likhana*—it is stated.

TRANSLATION

At Rāmeśvara, Śrī Caitanya Mahāprabhu had a chance to read the Kūrma Purāṇa, in which He discovered that the form of Sītā kidnapped by Rāvaṇa was not that of the real Sītā but a mere shadow representation.

PURPORT

The *Kūrma Purāṇa* states that this shadowy Sītā was placed into a fire as a test of chastity. It was Māyā-sītā who entered the fire and the real Sītā who came out of the fire.

TEXT 118

শুনিয়া প্রভুর আনন্দিত হৈল মন ।
রামদাস বিপ্রের কথা হইল স্মরণ ॥ ১১৮ ॥

śuniyā prabhura ānandita haila mana
rāma-dāsa viprera kathā ha-ila smaraṇa

SYNONYMS

śuniyā—hearing this; *prabhura*—of Lord Caitanya Mahāprabhu; *ānandita*—very happy; *haila*—became; *mana*—the mind; *rāma-dāsa*—of the name Rāmadāsa; *viprera*—with the *brāhmaṇa; kathā*—of the conversation; *ha-ila*—was; *smaraṇa*—remembrance.

TRANSLATION

Śrī Caitanya Mahāprabhu was very glad to read about the false Sītā, and He remembered His meeting with Rāmadāsa Vipra, who was very sorry that mother Sītā had been kidnapped by Rāvaṇa.

TEXT 119

সেই পুরাতন পত্র আগ্রহ করি' নিল ।
রামদাসে দেখাইয়া দুঃখ খণ্ডাইল ॥ ১১৯ ॥

sei purātana patra āgraha kari' nila
rāmadāse dekhāiyā duḥkha khaṇḍāila

SYNONYMS

sei—that; *purātana*—old; *patra*—page; *āgraha*—with great enthusiasm; *kari'*—doing; *nila*—took; *rāma-dāse*—to the *brāhmaṇa* Rāmadāsa; *dekhāiyā*—showing; *duḥkha*—unhappiness; *khaṇḍāila*—mitigated.

TRANSLATION

Indeed, Lord Caitanya Mahāprabhu eagerly tore this page from the Kūrma Purāṇa, although the book was very old, and He later showed it to Rāmadāsa Vipra, whose unhappiness was mitigated.

TEXT 120

ব্রহ্মসংহিতা, কর্ণামৃত, দুই পুঁথি পাঞা ।
দুই পুস্তক লঞা আইলা উত্তম জানিঞা ॥ ১২০ ॥

brahma-saṁhitā, karṇāmṛta, dui puṅthi pāñā
dui pustaka lañā āilā uttama jāniñā

SYNONYMS

brahma-saṁhitā—the book named *Brahma-saṁhitā; karṇāmṛta*—the book named *Kṛṣṇa-karṇāmṛta; dui*—two; *puṅthi*—scriptures; *pāñā*—obtaining; *dui*—two; *pustaka*—books; *lañā*—carrying; *āilā*—came back; *uttama*—very good; *jāniñā*—knowing.

TRANSLATION

Śrī Caitanya Mahāprabhu also found two other books—namely, Brahma-saṁhitā and Kṛṣṇa-karṇāmṛta. Knowing these books to be excellent, He took them to present to His devotees.

PURPORT

In the olden days, there were no presses, and all the important scriptures were hand-written and kept in large temples. Caitanya Mahāprabhu found *Brahma-saṁhitā* and *Kṛṣṇa-karṇāmṛta* in hand-written texts, and knowing them to be very authoritative, He took them with Him to present to His devotees. Of course, He obtained the permission of the temple commander. Now both *Brahma-saṁhitā* and *Kṛṣṇa-karṇāmṛta* are available in print with commentaries by Śrīla Bhaktisiddhānta Sarasvatī Ṭhākura.

TEXT 121

পুনরপি নীলাচলে গমন করিল।
ভক্তগণে মেলিয়া স্নানযাত্রা দেখিল ॥ ১২১ ॥

punarapi nīlācale gamana karila
bhakta-gaṇe meliyā snāna-yātrā dekhila

SYNONYMS

punarapi—again; *nīlācale*—to Jagannātha Purī; *gamana*—going back; *karila*—did; *bhakta-gaṇe*—all the devotees; *meliyā*—meeting; *snāna-yātrā*—the bathing ceremony of Lord Jagannātha; *dekhila*—saw.

TRANSLATION

After collecting these books, Śrī Caitanya Mahāprabhu returned to Jagannātha Purī. At that time, the bathing ceremony of Jagannātha was taking place, and He saw it.

TEXT 122

অনবসরে জগন্নাথের না পাঞা দরশন।
বিরহে আলালনাথ করিলা গমন ॥ ১২২ ॥

anavasare jagannāthera nā pāñā daraśana
virahe ālālanātha karilā gamana

SYNONYMS

anavasare—during the absence; *jagannāthera*—of Lord Jagannātha; *nā*—not; *pāñā*—getting; *daraśana*—visit; *virahe*—in separation; *ālālanātha*—of the place named Ālālanātha; *karilā*—did; *gamana*—going.

TRANSLATION

When Jagannātha was absent from the temple, Caitanya Mahāprabhu, who could not see Him, felt separation and left Jagannātha Purī to go to a place known as Ālālanātha.

PURPORT

Ālālanātha is also known as Brahmagiri. This place is about fourteen miles from Jagannātha Purī and is also on the beach. There is a temple of Jagannātha there. At the present moment a police station and post office are situated there because so many people come to see the temple.

The word *anavasara* is used when Śrī Jagannāthajī cannot be seen in the temple. After the bathing ceremony (*snāna-yātrā*), Lord Jagannātha is supposed to become sick. He is therefore removed to His private apartment, where no one can see Him. Actually, during this period renovations are made on the body of the Jagannātha Deity. This is called *nava-yauvana*. During the Ratha-yātrā ceremony, Lord Jagannātha once again comes before the public. Thus for fifteen days after the bathing ceremony, Lord Jagannātha is not visible to any visitors.

TEXT 123

ভক্তসনে দিন কত তাহাঞি রহিলা।
গৌড়ের ভক্ত আইসে, সমাচার পাইলা ॥ ১২৩ ॥

bhakta-sane dina kata tāhāñi rahilā
gauḍera bhakta āise, samācāra pāilā

SYNONYMS

bhakta-sane—with the devotees; *dina kata*—some days; *tāhāñi*—there at Ālālanātha; *rahilā*—remained; *gauḍera*—of Bengal; *bhakta*—devotees; *āise*—come; *samācāra*—news; *pāilā*—He got.

TRANSLATION

Śrī Caitanya Mahāprabhu remained for some days at Ālālanātha. In the meantime, Caitanya Mahāprabhu received news that all the devotees from Bengal were coming to Jagannātha Purī.

TEXT 124

নিত্যানন্দ-সার্বভৌম আগ্রহ করিঞা।
নীলাচলে আইলা মহাপ্রভুকে লইঞা ॥ ১২৪ ॥

nityānanda-sārvabhauma āgraha kariñā
nīlācale āilā mahāprabhuke la-iñā

SYNONYMS

nityānanda—Lord Nityānanda Prabhu; *sārvabhauma*—Sārvabhauma Bhaṭṭācārya; *āgraha kariñā*—showing great eagerness; *nīlācale*—to Jagannātha

Purī; *āilā*—returned; *mahāprabhuke*—Śrī Caitanya Mahāprabhu; *la-iñā*—taking.

TRANSLATION

When the devotees from Bengal arrived at Jagannātha Purī, both Nityānanda Prabhu and Sārvabhauma Bhaṭṭācārya greatly endeavored to take Śrī Caitanya Mahāprabhu back to Jagannātha Purī.

TEXT 125

বিরহে বিহ্বল প্রভু না জানে রাত্রি-দিনে ।
হেনকালে আইলা গৌড়ের ভক্তগণে ॥ ১২৫ ॥

virahe vihvala prabhu nā jāne rātri-dine
hena-kāle āilā gauḍera bhakta-gaṇe

SYNONYMS

virahe—in separation; *vihvala*—overwhelmed; *prabhu*—Lord Śrī Caitanya Mahāprabhu; *nā*—not; *jāne*—knows; *rātri-dine*—day and night; *hena-kāle*—at this time; *āilā*—arrived; *gauḍera*—of Bengal; *bhakta-gaṇe*—all the devotees.

TRANSLATION

When Lord Caitanya Mahāprabhu finally left Ālālanātha to return to Jagannātha Purī, He was overwhelmed both day and night due to separation from Jagannātha. His lamentation knew no bounds. During this time, all the devotees from different parts of Bengal, and especially from Navadvīpa, arrived in Jagannātha Purī.

TEXT 126

সবে মিলি' যুক্তি করি' কীর্তন আরম্ভিল ।
কীর্তন-আবেশে প্রভুর মন স্থির হৈল ॥ ১২৬ ॥

sabe mili' yukti kari' kīrtana ārambhila
kīrtana-āveśe prabhura mana sthira haila

SYNONYMS

sabe mili'—meeting all together; *yukti kari'*—after due consideration; *kīrtana*—congregational chanting of the holy name; *ārambhila*—began;

kīrtana-āveśe—in the ecstasy of *kīrtana; prabhura*—of Lord Caitanya Mahāprabhu; *mana*—the mind; *sthira*—pacified; *haila*—became.

TRANSLATION

After due consideration, all the devotees began chanting the holy name congregationally. Lord Caitanya's mind was thus pacified by the ecstasy of the chanting.

PURPORT

Being absolute, Lord Jagannātha is identical in person, form, picture, *kīrtana* and all other circumstances. Therefore when Caitanya Mahāprabhu heard the chanting of the holy name of the Lord, He was pacified. Previously, He had been feeling very morose due to separation from Jagannātha. The conclusion is that whenever a *kīrtana* of pure devotees takes place, the Lord is immediately present. By chanting the holy names of the Lord, we associate with the Lord personally.

TEXT 127

পূর্বে যবে প্রভু রামানন্দেরে মিলিলা ।
নীলাচলে আসিবারে তাঁরে আজ্ঞা দিলা ॥ ১২৭ ॥

pūrve yabe prabhu rāmānandere mililā
nīlācale āsibāre tāṅre ājñā dilā

SYNONYMS

pūrve—before this; *yabe*—while; *prabhu*—Lord Śrī Caitanya Mahāprabhu; *rāmānandere*—Śrī Rāmānanda Rāya; *mililā*—met; *nīlācale*—to Jagannātha Purī; *āsibāre*—to come; *tāṅre*—him; *ājñā dilā*—ordered.

TRANSLATION

Previously, when Śrī Caitanya Mahāprabhu had been touring South India, He had met Rāmānanda Rāya on the banks of the Godāvarī. At that time it had been decided that Rāmānanda Rāya would resign from his post as governor and return to Jagannātha Purī to live with Śrī Caitanya Mahāprabhu.

TEXT 128

রাজ-আজ্ঞা লঞা তেঁহো আইলা কত দিনে ।
রাত্রি-দিনে কৃষ্ণকথা রামানন্দসনে ॥ ১২৮ ॥

rāja-ājñā lañā teṅho āilā kata dine
rātri-dine kṛṣṇa-kathā rāmānanda-sane

SYNONYMS

rāja-ājñā—the permission of the King, Pratāparudra; *lañā*—getting; *teṅho*—Rāmānanda Rāya; *āilā*—returned; *kata dine*—in some days; *rātri-dine*—day and night; *kṛṣṇa-kathā*—talks of Lord Kṛṣṇa and His pastimes; *rāmānanda-sane*—in the company of Rāmānanda Rāya.

TRANSLATION

Upon the order of Śrī Caitanya Mahāprabhu, Śrī Rāmānanda Rāya took leave of the King and returned to Jagannātha Purī. After he arrived, Śrī Caitanya Mahāprabhu very much enjoyed talking with him both day and night about Lord Kṛṣṇa and His pastimes.

TEXT 129

কাশীমিশ্রে কৃপা, প্রদ্যুম্ন মিশ্রাদি-মিলন।
পরমানন্দপুরী-গোবিন্দ-কাশীশ্বরাগমন ॥ ১২৯ ॥

kāśī-miśre kṛpā, pradyumna miśrādi-milana
paramānanda-purī-govinda-kāśīśvarāgamana

SYNONYMS

kāśī-miśre kṛpā—His mercy to Kāśī Miśra; *pradyumna miśra-ādi-milana*—meeting with Pradyumna Miśra; *paramānanda-purī*—of the name Paramānanda Purī; *govinda*—of the name Govinda; *kāśīśvara*—of the name Kāśīśvara; *āgamana*—coming.

TRANSLATION

After Rāmānanda Rāya's arrival, Śrī Caitanya Mahāprabhu bestowed His mercy upon Kāśī Miśra and met Pradyumna Miśra. At that time three personalities—Paramānanda Purī, Govinda and Kāśīśvara—came to see Lord Caitanya at Jagannātha Purī.

TEXT 130

দামোদরস্বরূপ-মিলনে পরম আনন্দ।
শিখিমাহিতি-মিলন, রায় ভবানন্দ ॥ ১৩০ ॥

dāmodara-svarūpa-milane parama ānanda
śikhi-māhiti-milana, rāya bhavānanda

SYNONYMS

dāmodara-svarūpa—Svarūpa Dāmodara; *milane*—in meeting; *parama*—great; *ānanda*—pleasure; *śikhi-māhiti*—of the name Śikhi Māhiti; *milana*—meeting; *rāya bhavānanda*—Bhavānanda, the father of Rāmānanda Rāya.

TRANSLATION

Eventually there was a meeting with Svarūpa Dāmodara Gosvāmī, and the Lord became very greatly pleased. Then there was a meeting with Śikhi Māhiti and with Bhavānanda Rāya, the father of Rāmānanda Rāya.

TEXT 131

গৌড় হইতে সর্ব বৈষ্ণবের আগমন ।
কুলীনগ্রামবাসি-সঙ্গে প্রথম মিলন ॥ ১৩১ ॥

gauḍa ha-ite sarva vaiṣṇavera āgamana
kulīna-grāma-vāsi-saṅge prathama milana

SYNONYMS

gauḍa ha-ite—from Bengal; *sarva*—all; *vaiṣṇavera*—of the Vaiṣṇavas; *āgamana*—appearance; *kulīna-grāma-vāsi*—the residents of Kulīna-grāma; *saṅge*—with them; *prathama*—first; *milana*—meeting.

TRANSLATION

All the devotees from Bengal gradually began arriving at Jagannātha Purī. At this time, the residents of Kulīna-grāma also came to see Śrī Caitanya Mahāprabhu for the first time.

TEXT 132

নরহরি দাস আদি যত খণ্ডবাসী ।
শিবানন্দসেন-সঙ্গে মিলিলা সবে আসি' ॥ ১৩২ ॥

narahari dāsa ādi yata khaṇḍa-vāsī
śivānanda-sena-saṅge mililā sabe āsi'

SYNONYMS

narahari dāsa—of the name Narahari dāsa; *ādi*—heading the list; *yata*—all; *khaṇḍa-vāsī*—devotees of the place known as Khaṇḍa; *śivānanda-sena*—of the name Śivānanda Sena; *saṅge*—with; *mililā*—He met; *sabe*—all; *āsi'*—coming there.

TRANSLATION

Eventually Narahari dāsa and other inhabitants of Khaṇḍa, along with Śivānanda Sena, all arrived, and Śrī Caitanya Mahāprabhu met them.

TEXT 133

স্নানযাত্রা দেখি' প্রভু সঙ্গে ভক্তগণ ।
সবা লঞা কৈলা প্রভু গুণ্ডিচা মার্জন ॥ ১৩৩ ॥

snāna-yātrā dekhi' prabhu saṅge bhakta-gaṇa
sabā lañā kailā prabhu guṇḍicā mārjana

SYNONYMS

snāna-yātrā—the bathing ceremony; *dekhi'*—seeing; *prabhu*—Lord Caitanya Mahāprabhu; *saṅge*—with Him; *bhakta-gaṇa*—the devotees; *sabā*—all; *lañā*—taking; *kailā*—did; *prabhu*—Lord Caitanya Mahāprabhu; *guṇḍicā mārjana*—washing and cleaning the Guṇḍicā temple.

TRANSLATION

After seeing the bathing ceremony of Lord Jagannātha, Śrī Caitanya Mahāprabhu washed and cleaned Śrī Guṇḍicā temple with the assistance of many devotees.

TEXT 134

সবা-সঙ্গে রথযাত্রা কৈল দরশন ।
রথ-অগ্রে নৃত্য করি' উদ্যানে গমন ॥ ১৩৪ ॥

sabā-saṅge ratha-yātrā kaila daraśana
ratha-agre nṛtya kari' udyāne gamana

SYNONYMS

sabā-saṅge—with all of them; *ratha-yātrā*—the car festival; *kaila*—did; *daraśana*—seeing; *ratha-agre*—in front of the car; *nṛtya*—dancing; *kari'*—doing; *udyāne*—in the garden; *gamana*—going.

TRANSLATION

After this, Lord Caitanya Mahāprabhu and all the devotees saw the Ratha-yātrā, the car festival ceremony. Caitanya Mahāprabhu Himself danced in front of the car, and after dancing He entered a garden.

TEXT 135

প্রতাপরুদ্রেরে কৃপা কৈল সেই স্থানে।
গৌড়ীয়াভক্তে আজ্ঞা দিল বিদায়ের দিনে ॥ ১৩৫ ॥

pratāparudrere kṛpā kaila sei sthāne
gauḍīyā-bhakte ājñā dila vidāyera dine

SYNONYMS

pratāparudrere—unto King Pratāparudra; *kṛpā*—mercy; *kaila*—did; *sei sthāne*—in that garden; *gauḍīyā-bhakte*—to all the devotees of Bengal; *ājñā*—the order; *dila*—gave; *vidāyera*—of departure; *dine*—on the day.

TRANSLATION

In that garden, Lord Caitanya Mahāprabhu bestowed His mercy upon King Pratāparudra. Afterwards, when the Bengali devotees were about to return home, the Lord gave separate orders to almost every one of them.

TEXT 136

প্রত্যব্দ আসিবে রথযাত্রা-দরশনে।
এই ছলে চাহে ভক্তগণের মিলনে ॥ ১৩৬ ॥

pratyabda āsibe ratha-yātrā-daraśane
ei chale cāhe bhakta-gaṇera milane

SYNONYMS

prati-abda—every year; *āsibe*—you should all come; *ratha-yātrā*—the car festival; *daraśane*—to see; *ei chale*—under this plea; *cāhe*—desires; *bhakta-gaṇera*—of all the devotees; *milane*—the meeting.

TRANSLATION

Śrī Caitanya Mahāprabhu desired to meet all the devotees of Bengal every year. Therefore He ordered them to come to see the Ratha-yātrā festival every year.

TEXT 137

সার্বভৌম-ঘরে প্রভুর ভিক্ষা-পরিপাটী।
ষাঠীর মাতা কহে, যাতে রাণ্ডী হউক্ ষাঠী ॥ ১৩৭ ॥

sārvabhauma-ghare prabhura bhikṣā-paripāṭī
ṣāṭhīra mātā kahe, yāte rāṇḍī hauk ṣāṭhī

SYNONYMS

sārvabhauma-ghare—at the house of Sārvabhauma Bhaṭṭācārya; *prabhura*—of the Lord; *bhikṣā*—eating; *paripāṭī*—sumptuously; *ṣāṭhīra mātā*—the mother of Ṣāṭhī, who was the daughter of Sārvabhauma Bhaṭṭācārya; *kahe*—says; *yāte*—by which; *rāṇḍī*—widow; *hauk*—let her become; *ṣāṭhī*—Ṣāṭhī, the daughter.

TRANSLATION

Śrī Caitanya Mahāprabhu was invited to dine at the house of Sārvabhauma Bhaṭṭācārya. While He was eating sumptuously, the son-in-law of Sārvabhauma Bhaṭṭācārya [the husband of his daughter Ṣāṭhī] criticized Him. Because of this, Ṣāṭhī's mother cursed him by praying that Ṣāṭhī would become a widow. In other words, she cursed her son-in-law to die.

TEXT 138

বর্ষান্তরে অদ্বৈতাদি ভক্তের আগমন।
প্রভুরে দেখিতে সবে করিলা গমন ॥ ১৩৮ ॥

varṣāntare advaitādi bhaktera āgamana
prabhure dekhite sabe karilā gamana

SYNONYMS

varṣa-antare—at the end of the year; *advaita-ādi*—headed by Advaita Ācārya; *bhaktera*—of all the devotees; *āgamana*—coming to Jagannātha Purī; *prabhure*—the Lord; *dekhite*—to see; *sabe*—all of them; *karilā*—did; *gamana*—going to Jagannātha Purī.

TRANSLATION

At the end of the year, all the devotees from Bengal, headed by Advaita Ācārya, again came to see the Lord. Indeed, there was a great rush of devotees to Jagannātha Purī.

TEXT 139

আনন্দে সবারে নিয়া দেন বাসস্থান ।
শিবানন্দ সেন করে সবার পালন ॥ ১৩৯ ॥

ānande sabāre niyā dena vāsa-sthāna
śivānanda sena kare sabāra pālana

SYNONYMS

ānande—in great pleasure; *sabāre*—all the devotees; *niyā*—taking; *dena*—gives; *vāsa-sthāna*—residential quarters; *śivānanda sena*—of the name Śivānanda Sena; *kare*—does; *sabāra*—of all; *pālana*—maintenance.

TRANSLATION

When all the devotees from Bengal arrived, Śrī Caitanya Mahāprabhu allotted them residential quarters, and Śivānanda Sena was put in charge of their maintenance.

TEXT 140

শিবানন্দের সঙ্গে আইলা কুক্কুর ভাগ্যবান্ ।
প্রভুর চরণ দেখি' কৈল অন্তর্ধান ॥ ১৪০ ॥

śivānandera saṅge āilā kukkura bhāgyavān
prabhura caraṇa dekhi' kaila antardhāna

SYNONYMS

śivānandera saṅge—with Śivānanda Sena; *āilā*—came; *kukkura*—a dog; *bhāgyavān*—fortunate; *prabhura*—of the Lord; *caraṇa*—the lotus feet; *dekhi'*—seeing; *kaila*—did; *antardhāna*—disappearing.

TRANSLATION

A dog accompanied Śivānanda Sena and the devotees, and that dog was so fortunate that after seeing the lotus feet of Lord Caitanya Mahāprabhu, it was liberated and went back home, back to Godhead.

TEXT 141

পথে সার্বভৌম সহ সবার মিলন ।
সার্বভৌম ভট্টাচার্যের কাশীতে গমন ॥ ১৪১ ॥

pathe sārvabhauma saha sabāra milana
sārvabhauma bhaṭṭācāryera kāśīte gamana

SYNONYMS

pathe—on the way; *sārvabhauma*—Sārvabhauma Bhaṭṭācārya; *saha*—with; *sabāra*—of everyone; *milana*—meeting; *sārvabhauma bhaṭṭācāryera*—of the devotee named Sārvabhauma Bhaṭṭācārya; *kāśīte*—to Vārāṇasī; *gamana*—going.

TRANSLATION

Everyone met Sārvabhauma Bhaṭṭācārya on his way to Vārāṇasī.

TEXT 142

প্রভুরে মিলিলা সর্ব বৈষ্ণব আসিয়া ।
জলক্রীড়া কৈল প্রভু সবারে লইয়া ॥ ১৪২ ॥

prabhure mililā sarva vaiṣṇava āsiyā
jala-krīḍā kaila prabhu sabāre la-iyā

SYNONYMS

prabhure—Lord Caitanya Mahāprabhu; *mililā*—met; *sarva*—all; *vaiṣṇava*—devotees; *āsiyā*—arriving at Jagannātha Purī; *jala-krīḍā*—sporting in the water; *kaila*—performed; *prabhu*—the Lord; *sabāre*—all the devotees; *la-iyā*—taking.

TRANSLATION

After arriving at Jagannātha Purī, all the Vaiṣṇavas met with Śrī Caitanya Mahāprabhu. Later, Śrī Caitanya Mahāprabhu sported in the water, taking all the devotees with Him.

TEXT 143

সবা লঞা কৈল গুণ্ডিচা-গৃহ-সংমার্জন ।
রথযাত্রা-দরশনে প্রভুর নর্তন ॥ ১৪৩ ॥

sabā lañā kaila guṇḍicā-gṛha-sammārjana
ratha-yātrā-daraśane prabhura nartana

SYNONYMS

sabā lañā—taking all of them; *kaila*—performed; *guṇḍicā-gṛha-sammār-jana*—washing of the Guṇḍicā temple; *ratha-yātrā*—the car festival; *daraśane*—in seeing; *prabhura*—of the Lord; *nartana*—dancing.

TRANSLATION

First the Lord washed the temple of Guṇḍicā very thoroughly. Then everyone saw the Ratha-yātrā festival and the Lord's dancing before the car.

TEXT 144

উপবনে কৈল প্রভু বিবিধ বিলাস ।
প্রভুর অভিষেক কৈল বিপ্র কৃষ্ণদাস ॥ ১৪৪ ॥

upavane kaila prabhu vividha vilāsa
prabhura abhiṣeka kaila vipra kṛṣṇadāsa

SYNONYMS

upavane—in the forest by the road; *kaila*—performed; *prabhu*—Lord Caitanya Mahāprabhu; *vividha*—varieties of; *vilāsa*—pastimes; *prabhura*—of Lord Caitanya Mahāprabhu; *abhiṣeka*—bathing; *kaila*—did; *vipra*—the *brāhmaṇa; kṛṣṇa-dāsa*—of the name Kṛṣṇadāsa.

TRANSLATION

In the forest along the road from the Jagannātha temple to Guṇḍicā, Lord Caitanya Mahāprabhu performed various pastimes. A brāhmaṇa named Kṛṣṇadāsa performed the bathing ceremony of Lord Śrī Caitanya Mahāprabhu.

TEXT 145

গুণ্ডিচাতে নৃত্য-অন্তে কৈল জলকেলি ।
হেরা-পঞ্চমীতে দেখিল লক্ষ্মীদেবীর কেলী ॥ ১৪৫ ॥

guṇḍicāte nṛtya-ante kaila jala-keli
herā-pañcamīte dekhila lakṣmī-devīra kelī

SYNONYMS

guṇḍicāte—in the neighborhood of Guṇḍicā temple; *nṛtya-ante*—after dancing; *kaila*—performed; *jala-keli*—sporting in the water; *herā-pañcamīte*—on the day of Herā-pañcamī; *dekhila*—saw; *lakṣmī-devīra*—of the goddess of fortune; *kelī*—activities.

TRANSLATION

After dancing in the Guṇḍicā temple, the Lord sported in the water with His devotees, and on Herā-pañcamī day they all saw the activities of the goddess of fortune, Lakṣmīdevī.

TEXT 146

কৃষ্ণজন্ম-যাত্রাতে প্রভু গোপবেশ হৈলা ।
দধিভার বহি' তবে লগুড় ফিরাইলা ॥ ১৪৬ ॥

kṛṣṇa-janma-yātrāte prabhu gopa-veśa hailā
dadhi-bhāra vahi' tabe laguḍa phirāilā

SYNONYMS

kṛṣṇa-janma-yātrāte—on the birthday ceremony of Lord Kṛṣṇa; *prabhu*—Lord Caitanya Mahāprabhu; *gopa-veśa*—dressed like a cowherd boy; *hailā*—was; *dadhi-bhāra*—a balance for pots of yogurt; *vahi'*—carrying; *tabe*—at that time; *laguḍa*—a log; *phirāilā*—encircled.

TRANSLATION

On Janmāṣṭamī, Lord Kṛṣṇa's birthday, Śrī Caitanya Mahāprabhu dressed Himself as a cowherd boy and, carrying a balance with pots of yogurt, encircled a log.

TEXT 147

গৌড়ের ভক্তগণে তবে করিল বিদায় ।
সঙ্গের ভক্ত লঞা করে কীর্তন সদায় ॥ ১৪৭ ॥

gauḍera bhakta-gaṇe tabe karila vidāya
saṅgera bhakta lañā kare kīrtana sadāya

SYNONYMS

gauḍera—of Gauḍa-deśa (Bengal); *bhakta-gaṇe*—to the devotees; *tabe*—then; *karila*—gave; *vidāya*—farewell; *saṅgera*—of constant companionship; *bhakta*—devotees; *lañā*—taking; *kare*—performs; *kīrtana*—congregational chanting; *sadāya*—always.

TRANSLATION

After this, Śrī Caitanya Mahāprabhu bade farewell to all the devotees from Gauḍa-deśa [Bengal] and continued chanting with His intimate devotees who constantly remained with Him.

TEXT 148

বৃন্দাবন যাইতে কৈল গৌড়েরে গমন ।
প্রতাপরুদ্র কৈল পথে বিবিধ সেবন ॥ ১৪৮ ॥

vṛndāvana yāite kaila gauḍere gamana
pratāparudra kaila pathe vividha sevana

SYNONYMS

vṛndāvana yāite—to go to Vṛndāvana; *kaila*—did; *gauḍere*—to Bengal; *gamana*—going; *pratāparudra*—King Pratāparudra; *kaila*—performed; *pathe*—on the road; *vividha*—various; *sevana*—services.

TRANSLATION

To visit Vṛndāvana, the Lord went to Gauḍa-deśa [Bengal]. On the way, King Pratāparudra performed a variety of service to please the Lord.

TEXT 149

পুরীগোসাঞি-সঙ্গে বস্ত্রপ্রদান-প্রসঙ্গ ।
রামানন্দ রায় আইলা ভদ্রক পর্যন্ত ॥ ১৪৯ ॥

purī-gosāñi-saṅge vastra-pradāna-prasaṅga
rāmānanda rāya āilā bhadraka paryanta

SYNONYMS

purī-gosāñi-saṅge—with Purī Gosvāmī; *vastra-pradāna-prasaṅga*—incidents of exchanging cloth; *rāmānanda rāya*—of the name Rāmānanda Rāya; *āilā*—came; *bhadraka*—a place of the name Bhadraka; *paryanta*—as far as.

TRANSLATION

On the way to Vṛndāvana via Bengal, there was an incident wherein some cloth was exchanged with Purī Gosāñi. Śrī Rāmānanda Rāya accompanied the Lord as far as the city of Bhadraka.

TEXT 150

আসি' বিদ্যাবাচস্পতির গৃহেতে রহিলা ।
প্রভুরে দেখিতে লোকসংঘট্ট হইলা ॥ ১৫০ ॥

āsi' vidyā-vācaspatira gṛhete rahilā
prabhure dekhite loka-saṅghaṭṭa ha-ilā

SYNONYMS

āsi'—coming to Bengal; *vidyā-vācaspatira*—of Vidyā-vācaspati; *gṛhete*—at the home; *rahilā*—remained; *prabhure*—unto Lord Caitanya Mahāprabhu; *dekhite*—to see; *loka-saṅghaṭṭa*—crowds of men; *ha-ilā*—there were.

TRANSLATION

When Śrī Caitanya Mahāprabhu reached Vidyānagara, Bengal, on the way to Vṛndāvana, He stopped at the house of Vidyā-vācaspati, who was the brother of Sārvabhauma Bhaṭṭācārya. When Lord Caitanya Mahāprabhu suddenly arrived at his house, great crowds of people gathered.

TEXT 151

পঞ্চদিন দেখে লোক নাহিক বিশ্রাম ।
লোকভয়ে রাত্রে প্রভু আইলা কুলিয়া-গ্রাম ॥১৫১॥

pañca-dina dekhe loka nāhika viśrāma
loka-bhaye rātre prabhu āilā kuliyā-grāma

SYNONYMS

pañca-dina—continuously for five days; *dekhe*—see; *loka*—people; *nāhika*—there is not; *viśrāma*—rest; *loka-bhaye*—on account of fearing the crowds of men; *rātre*—at night; *prabhu*—the Lord; *āilā*—went; *kuliyā-grāma*—to the place known as Kuliyā.

TRANSLATION

For five consecutive days all the people gathered to see the Lord, and still there was no rest. Out of fear of the crowd, Lord Caitanya Mahāprabhu left at night and went to the town of Kuliyā [present-day Navadvīpa].

PURPORT

If one considers the statements of the *Caitanya-bhāgavata* along with the description by Locana dāsa Ṭhākura, it is clear that present-day Navadvīpa was formerly known as Kuliyā-grāma. While at Kuliyā-grāma, Śrī Caitanya Mahāprabhu bestowed His favor upon Devānanda Paṇḍita and delivered Gopāla Cāpala and many others who had previously committed offenses at His lotus feet. At that time, to go from Vidyānagara to Kuliyā-grāma one had to cross a branch of the Ganges. All of those old places still exist. Cināḍāṅgā was formerly situated in Kuliyā-grāma, which is now known as Kolera Gañja.

TEXT 152

কুলিয়া-গ্রামেতে প্রভুর শুনিয়া আগমন ।
কোটি কোটি লোক আসি' কৈল দরশন ॥ ১৫২ ॥

kuliyā-grāmete prabhura śuniyā āgamana
koṭi koṭi loka āsi' kaila daraśana

SYNONYMS

kuliyā-grāmete—in that place known as Kuliyā-grāma; *prabhura*—of the Lord; *śuniyā*—hearing; *āgamana*—about the arrival; *koṭi koṭi*—hundreds of thousands; *loka*—of people; *āsi'*—coming; *kaila*—took; *daraśana*—audience.

TRANSLATION

Hearing of the Lord's arrival in Kuliyā-grāma, many hundreds and thousands of people came to see Him.

TEXT 153

কুলিয়া-গ্রামে কৈল দেবানন্দেরে প্রসাদ ।
গোপাল-বিপ্রেরে ক্ষমাইল শ্রীবাসাপরাধ ॥ ১৫৩ ॥

kuliyā-grāme kaila devānandere prasāda
gopāla-viprere kṣamāila śrīvāsāparādha

SYNONYMS

kuliyā-grāme—in that village known as Kuliyā-grāma; *kaila*—showed; *devānandere prasāda*—mercy to Devānanda Paṇḍita; *gopāla-viprere*—and to the *brāhmaṇa* known as Gopāla Cāpala; *kṣamāila*—excused; *śrīvāsa-aparādha*—the offense to the lotus feet of Śrīvasa Ṭhākura.

TRANSLATION

The specific acts performed by Śrī Caitanya Mahāprabhu at this time were His showing favor upon Devānanda Paṇḍita and excusing the brāhmaṇa known as Gopāla Cāpala from the offense he had committed at the lotus feet of Śrīvāsa Ṭhākura.

TEXT 154

পাষণ্ডী নিন্দক আসি' পড়িলা চরণে ।
অপরাধ ক্ষমি' তারে দিল কৃষ্ণপ্রেমে ॥ ১৫৪ ॥

pāṣaṇḍī nindaka āsi' paḍilā caraṇe
aparādha kṣami' tāre dila kṛṣṇa-preme

SYNONYMS

pāṣaṇḍī—atheists; *nindaka*—blasphemers; *āsi'*—coming there; *paḍilā*—fell down; *caraṇe*—at the lotus feet of the Lord; *aparādha kṣami'*—excusing them of their offenses; *tāre*—unto them; *dila*—gave; *kṛṣṇa-preme*—love of Kṛṣṇa.

TRANSLATION

Many atheists and blasphemers came and fell at the lotus feet of the Lord, and the Lord in return excused them and gave them love of Kṛṣṇa.

TEXT 155

বৃন্দাবন যাবেন প্রভু শুনি' নৃসিংহানন্দ ।
পথ সাজাইল মনে পাইয়া আনন্দ ॥ ১৫৫ ॥

vṛndāvana yābena prabhu śuni' nṛsiṁhānanda
patha sājāila mane pāiyā ānanda

SYNONYMS

vṛndāvana—to Vṛndāvana; *yābena*—will go; *prabhu*—the Lord; *śuni'*—hearing; *nṛsiṁhānanda*—of the name Nṛsiṁhānanda; *patha*—the way; *sā-jāila*—decorated; *mane*—within the mind; *pāiyā*—getting; *ānanda*—pleasure.

TRANSLATION

When Śrī Nṛsiṁhānanda Brahmacārī heard that Lord Caitanya Mahāprabhu would go to Vṛndāvana, he became very pleased and mentally began decorating the way there.

TEXT 156

কুলিয়া নগর হৈতে পথ রত্নে বান্ধাইল ।
নিবৃন্ত পুষ্পশয্যা উপরে পাতিল ॥ ১৫৬ ॥

kuliyā nagara haite patha ratne bāndhāila
nivṛnta puṣpa-śayyā upare pātila

SYNONYMS

kuliyā nagara—the city of Kuliyā; *haite*—from; *patha*—way; *ratne*—with jewels; *bāndhāila*—constructed; *nivṛnta*—stemless; *puṣpa-śayyā*—flower bed; *upare*—on top; *pātila*—laid down.

TRANSLATION

First Nṛsiṁhānanda Brahmacārī contemplated a broad road starting from the city of Kuliyā. He bedecked the road with jewels, upon which he then laid a bed of stemless flowers.

TEXT 157

পথে দুই দিকে পুষ্পবকুলের শ্রেণী ।
মধ্যে মধ্যে দুইপাশে দিব্য পুষ্করিণী ॥ ১৫৭ ॥

pathe dui dike puṣpa-bakulera śreṇī
madhye madhye dui-pāśe divya puṣkariṇī

SYNONYMS

pathe—on the road; *dui dike*—on both sides; *puṣpa-bakulera*—of bakula flower trees; *śreṇī*—rows; *madhye madhye*—in the middle; *dui-pāśe*—on both sides; *divya*—transcendental; *puṣkariṇī*—lakes.

TRANSLATION

He mentally decorated both sides of the road with bakula flower trees, and at intervals on both sides he placed lakes of a transcendental nature.

TEXT 158

রত্নবাঁধা ঘাট, তাহে প্রফুল্ল কমল ।
নানা পক্ষি-কোলাহল, সুধা-সম জল ॥ ১৫৮ ॥

ratna-bāṅdhā ghāṭa, tāhe praphulla kamala
nānā pakṣi-kolāhala, sudhā-sama jala

SYNONYMS

ratna-bāṅdhā—constructed with jewels; *ghāṭa*—bathing places; *tāhe*—there; *praphulla*—fully blossoming; *kamala*—lotus flowers; *nānā*—various; *pakṣi*—of birds; *kolāhala*—vibrations; *sudhā*—nectar; *sama*—like; *jala*—water.

TRANSLATION

These lakes had bathing places constructed with jewels, and they were filled with blossoming lotus flowers. There were various birds chirping, and the water was exactly like nectar.

TEXT 159

শীতল সমীর বহে নানা গন্ধ লঞা ।
'কানাইর নাটশালা' পর্যন্ত লইল বান্ধিঞা ॥ ১৫৯ ॥

śītala samīra vahe nānā gandha lañā
'kānāira nāṭaśālā' paryanta la-ila bāndhiñā

SYNONYMS

śītala—very cool; *samīra*—breezes; *vahe*—blowing; *nānā*—various; *gandha*—fragrances; *lañā*—carrying; *kānāira nāṭa-śālā* —the place named Kānāi Nāṭaśālā; *paryanta*—as far as; *la-ila*—carried; *bāndhiñā*—constructing.

TRANSLATION

The entire road was surcharged with many cool breezes, which carried the fragrances from various flowers. He carried the construction of this road as far as Kānāi Nāṭaśālā.

PURPORT

Kānāi Nāṭaśālā is about 202 miles from Calcutta on the Loop line of the Eastern Railway. The railway station is named Tālajhāḍi, and after one gets off at that station, he has to go about two miles to find Kānāi Nāṭaśālā.

TEXT 160

আগে মন নাহি চলে, না পারে বান্ধিতে।
পথবান্ধা না যায়, নৃসিংহ হৈলা বিস্মিতে ॥ ১৬০ ॥

āge mana nāhi cale, nā pāre bāndhite
patha-bāndhā nā yāya, nṛsiṁha hailā vismite

SYNONYMS

āge—beyond this; *mana*—the mind; *nāhi*—does not; *cale*—go; *nā*—is not; *pāre*—able; *bāndhite*—to construct the road; *patha-bāndhā*—construction of the road; *nā yāya*—is not possible; *nṛsiṁha*—Nṛsiṁhānanda Brahmacārī; *hailā*—became; *vismite*—astonished.

TRANSLATION

Within the mind of Nṛsiṁhānanda Brahmacārī, the road could not be constructed beyond Kānāi Nāṭaśālā. He could not understand why the road's construction could not be completed, and thus he was astonished.

TEXT 161

নিশ্চয় করিয়া কহি, শুন, ভক্তগণ।
এবার না যাবেন প্রভু শ্রীবৃন্দাবন ॥ ১৬১ ॥

niścaya kariyā kahi, śuna, bhakta-gaṇa
ebāra nā yābena prabhu śrī-vṛndāvana

SYNONYMS

niścaya—assurance; *kariyā*—making; *kahi*—I say; *śuna*—please hear; *bhakta-gaṇa*—my dear devotees; *ebāra*—this time; *nā*—not; *yābena*—will go; *prabhu*—Lord Caitanya Mahāprabhu; *śrī-vṛndāvana*—to Vṛndāvana.

TRANSLATION

With great assurance he then told the devotees that Lord Caitanya would not go to Vṛndāvana at that time.

PURPORT

Śrīla Nṛsiṁhānanda Brahmacārī was a great devotee of Lord Caitanya Mahāprabhu; therefore when he heard that from Kuliyā Śrī Caitanya Mahāprabhu was going to Vṛndāvana, although he had no material wealth he began to construct within his mind a very attractive path or road for Caitanya Mahāprabhu to traverse. Some of the description of this path is given above. But even mentally he could not construct the road beyond Kānāi Nāṭaśālā. Therefore he concluded that Caitanya Mahāprabhu would not go to Vṛndāvana at that time.

For a pure devotee, it is the same whether he materially constructs a path or constructs one within his mind. This is because the Supreme Personality of Godhead, Janārdana, is *bhāva-grāhī,* or appreciative of the sentiment. For Him a path made with actual jewels and a path made of mental jewels are the same. Though subtle, mind is also matter, so any path—indeed, anything for the service of the Lord, whether in gross matter or in subtle matter—is accepted equally by the Supreme Personality of Godhead. The Lord accepts the attitude of His devotee and sees how much he is prepared to serve Him. The devotee is at liberty to serve the Lord either in gross matter or in subtle matter. The important point is that the service be in relation with the Supreme Personality of Godhead. This is confirmed in *Bhagavad-gītā* (9.26):

patraṁ puṣpaṁ phalaṁ toyaṁ
yo me bhaktyā prayacchati
tad ahaṁ bhakty-upahṛtam
aśnāmi prayatātmanaḥ

"If one offers Me with love and devotion a leaf, a flower, fruit or water, I will accept it." The real ingredient is *bhakti* (devotion). Pure devotion is uncontaminated by the modes of material nature. *Ahaituky apratihatā:* unconditional devotional service cannot be checked by any material condition. This means that one does not have to be very rich to serve the Supreme Personality of Godhead. Even the poorest man can equally serve the Supreme Personality of Godhead if he has pure devotion. If there is no ulterior motive, devotional service cannot be checked by any material condition.

TEXT 162

'কানাঞির নাটশালা' হৈতে আসিব ফিরিঞা ।
জানিবে পশ্চাৎ, কহিলু নিশ্চয় করিঞা ॥ ১৬২ ॥

'kānāñira nāṭaśālā' haite āsiba phiriñā
jānibe paścāt, kahilu niścaya kariñā

SYNONYMS

kānāñira nāṭa-śālā—the place of the name Kānāi Nāṭaśālā; *haite*—from; *āsiba*—will come; *phiriñā*—returning; *jānibe*—you will know; *paścāt*—later; *kahilu*—I say; *niścaya*—assurance; *kariñā*—making.

TRANSLATION

Nṛsiṁhānanda Brahmacārī said: "The Lord will go to Kānāi Nāṭaśālā and then will return. All of you will come to know of this later, but I now say this with great assurance."

TEXT 163

গোসাঞি কুলিয়া হৈতে চলিলা বৃন্দাবন ।
সঙ্গে সহস্রেক লোক যত ভক্তগণ ॥ ১৬৩ ॥

gosāñi kuliyā haite calilā vṛndāvana
saṅge sahastreka loka yata bhakta-gaṇa

SYNONYMS

gosāñi—Lord Caitanya Mahāprabhu; *kuliyā haite*—from Kuliyā; *calilā*—proceeded; *vṛndāvana*—toward Vṛndāvana; *saṅge*—with Him; *sahastreka*—thousands; *loka*—of people; *yata*—all; *bhakta-gaṇa*—the devotees.

TRANSLATION

When Lord Caitanya Mahāprabhu began to proceed from Kuliyā toward Vṛndāvana, thousands of men were with Him, and all of them were devotees.

TEXT 164

যাহাঁ যায় প্রভু, তাহাঁ কোটিসংখ্য লোক ।
দেখিতে আইসে, দেখি' খণ্ডে দুঃখ-শোক ॥ ১৬৪ ॥

yāhāṅ yāya prabhu, tāhāṅ koṭi-saṅkhya loka
dekhite āise, dekhi' khaṇḍe duḥkha-śoka

SYNONYMS

yāhāṅ—wherever; *yāya*—goes; *prabhu*—the Lord; *tāhāṅ*—everywhere; *koṭi-saṅkhya loka*—an unlimited number of people; *dekhite āise*—come to see Him; *dekhi'*—after seeing; *khaṇḍe*—removes; *duḥkha*—unhappiness; *śoka*—lamentation.

TRANSLATION

Wherever the Lord visited, crowds of innumerable people came to see Him. When they saw Him, all their unhappiness and lamentation disappeared.

TEXT 165

যাহাঁ যাহাঁ প্রভুর চরণ পড়য়ে চলিতে ।
সে মৃত্তিকা লয় লোক, গর্ত হয় পথে ॥ ১৬৫ ॥

yāhāṅ yāhāṅ prabhura caraṇa paḍaye calite
se mṛttikā laya loka, garta haya pathe

SYNONYMS

yāhāṅ yāhāṅ—wherever; *prabhura*—of the Lord; *caraṇa*—lotus feet; *paḍaye*—touch; *calite*—while walking; *se*—that; *mṛttikā*—dirt; *laya*—take; *loka*—the people; *garta*—a hole; *haya*—there becomes; *pathe*—on the road.

TRANSLATION

Wherever the Lord touched the ground with His lotus feet, people immediately came and gathered the dirt. Indeed, they gathered so much that many holes were created in the road.

TEXT 166

ঐছে চলি, আইলা প্রভু 'রামকেলি' গ্রাম।
গৌড়ের নিকট গ্রাম অতি অনুপাম ॥ ১৬৬ ॥

aiche cali, āilā prabhu 'rāmakeli' grāma
gauḍera nikaṭa grāma ati anupāma

SYNONYMS

aiche—in that way; *cali*—walking; *āilā*—came; *prabhu*—Lord Śrī Caitanya Mahāprabhu; *rāma-keli grāma*—to the village of the name Rāmakeli; *gauḍera*—Bengal; *nikaṭa*—near; *grāma*—the village; *ati*—very; *anupāma*—exquisite.

TRANSLATION

Lord Caitanya Mahāprabhu eventually arrived at a village named Rāmakeli. This village is situated on the border of Bengal and is very exquisite.

PURPORT

Rāmakeli-grāma is situated on the banks of the Ganges on the border of Bengal. Śrīla Rūpa and Sanātana Gosvāmīs had their residences in this village.

TEXT 167

তাহাঁ নৃত্য করে প্রভু প্রেমে অচেতন।
কোটি কোটি লোক আইসে দেখিতে চরণ ॥ ১৬৭ ॥

tāhāṅ nṛtya kare prabhu preme acetana
koṭi koṭi loka āise dekhite caraṇa

SYNONYMS

tāhāṅ—there; *nṛtya*—dancing; *kare*—performed; *prabhu*—Lord Caitanya Mahāprabhu; *preme*—in love of Godhead; *acetana*—unconscious; *koṭi koṭi*—innumerable *loka*—people; *āise*—came; *dekhite*—to see; *caraṇa*—His lotus feet.

TRANSLATION

While performing saṅkīrtana in Rāmakeli-grāma, the Lord danced and sometimes lost consciousness due to love of God. While He was at

Rāmakeli-grāma, an unlimited number of people came to see His lotus feet.

TEXT 168

গৌড়েশ্বর যবন-রাজা প্রভাব শুনিঞা ।
কহিতে লাগিল কিছু বিস্মিত হঞা ॥ ১৬৮ ॥

gauḍeśvara yavana-rājā prabhāva śuniñā
kahite lāgila kichu vismita hañā

SYNONYMS

gauḍa-īśvara—king of Bengal; *yavana-rājā*—Mohammedan king; *prabhāva*—influence; *śuniñā*—hearing; *kahite*—to say; *lāgila*—began; *kichu*—something; *vismita*—astonished; *hañā*—becoming.

TRANSLATION

When the Mohammedan King of Bengal heard of Caitanya Mahāprabhu's influence in attracting innumerable people, he became very astonished and began to speak as follows.

PURPORT

At that time the Mohammedan king of Bengal was Nawab Husen Sāhā Bādasāha.

TEXT 169

বিনা দানে এত লোক যাঁর পাছে হয় ।
সেই ত' গোসাঞা, ইহা জানিহ নিশ্চয় ॥ ১৬৯ ॥

vinā dāne eta loka yāṅra pāche haya
sei ta' gosāñā, ihā jāniha niścaya

SYNONYMS

vinā—without; *dāne*—charity; *eta*—so many; *loka*—persons; *yāṅra*—whom; *pāche*—after; *haya*—become; *sei ta'*—He certainly; *gosāñā*—a prophet; *ihā*—this; *jāniha*—know; *niścaya*—surely.

TRANSLATION

"Such a person, who is followed by so many people without giving them charity, must be a prophet. I can surely understand this fact."

TEXT 170

কাজী, যবন ইহার না করিহ হিংসন।
আপন-ইচ্ছায় বুলুন, যাহাঁ উঁহার মন ॥ ১৭০ ॥

kājī, yavana ihāra nā kariha hiṁsana
āpana-icchāya buluna, yāhāṅ uṅhāra mana

SYNONYMS

kājī—magistrate; *yavana*—Mohammedan; *ihāra*—of Him; *nā*—do not; *kariha*—make; *hiṁsana*—jealousy; *āpana-icchāya*—at His own will; *buluna*—let Him go; *yāhāṅ*—wherever; *uṅhāra*—of Him; *mana*—mind.

TRANSLATION

The Mohammedan King ordered the magistrate: "Do not disturb this Hindu prophet out of jealousy. Let Him do His own will wherever He likes."

PURPORT

Even a Mohammedan king could understand Śrī Caitanya Mahāprabhu's transcendental position as a prophet; therefore He ordered the local magistrate not to disturb Him but to let Him do whatever He liked.

TEXT 171

কেশব-ছত্রীরে রাজা বার্তা পুছিল।
প্রভুর মহিমা ছত্রী উড়াইয়া দিল ॥ ১৭১ ॥

keśava-chatrīre rājā vārtā puchila
prabhura mahimā chatrī uḍāiyā dila

SYNONYMS

keśava-chatrīre—from the person named Keśava Chatrī; *rājā*—King; *vārtā*—news; *puchila*—inquired; *prabhura*—of the Lord; *mahimā*—glories; *chatrī*—Keśava Chatrī; *uḍāiyā*—attaching no importance; *dila*—gave.

TRANSLATION

When the Mohammedan King asked his assistant, Keśava Chatrī, for news of the influence of Śrī Caitanya Mahāprabhu, Keśava Chatrī, al-

though knowing everything about Caitanya Mahāprabhu, tried to avoid the conversation by not giving any importance to Caitanya Mahāprabhu's activities.

PURPORT

Keśava Chatrī became a diplomat when questioned about Śrī Caitanya Mahāprabhu. Although he knew everything about Him, he was afraid that the Mohammedan King might become His enemy. He gave no importance to the Lord's activities, so that the Mohammedan King would take Him to be an ordinary man and would not give Him any trouble.

TEXT 172

ভিখারী সন্ন্যাসী করে তীর্থ পর্যটন ।
তাঁরে দেখিবারে আইসে দুই চারি জন ॥ ১৭২ ॥

bhikhārī sannyāsī kare tīrtha paryaṭana
tāṅre dekhibāre āise dui cāri jana

SYNONYMS

bhikhārī—beggar; *sannyāsī*—mendicant; *kare*—does; *tīrtha*—of holy places; *paryaṭana*—touring; *tāṅre*—Him; *dekhibāre*—to see; *āise*—come; *dui cāri jana*—only a few people.

TRANSLATION

Keśava Chatrī informed the Mohammedan King that Caitanya Mahāprabhu was a mendicant touring different places of pilgrimage and that, as such, only a few people came to see Him.

TEXT 173

যবনে তোমার ঠাঞি করয়ে লাগানি ।
তাঁর হিংসায় লাভ নাহি, হয় আর হানি ॥ ১৭৩ ॥

yavane tomāra ṭhāñi karaye lāgāni
tāṅra hiṁsāya lābha nāhi, haya āra hāni

SYNONYMS

yavane—your Mohammedan servant; *tomāra*—your; *ṭhāñi*—place; *karaye*—does; *lāgāni*—instigation; *tāṅra*—of Him; *hiṁsāya*—to become jealous; *lābha nāhi*—there is no profit; *haya*—there is; *āra*—rather; *hāni*—loss.

TRANSLATION

Keśava Chatrī said: "Out of jealousy your Mohammedan servant plots against Him. I think that you should not be very interested in Him, for there is no profit in it. Rather, there is simply loss."

TEXT 174

রাজারে প্রবোধি' কেশব ব্রাহ্মণ পাঠাঞা ।
চলিবার তরে প্রভুরে পাঠাইল কহিঞা ॥ ১৭৪ ॥

rājāre prabodhi' keśava brāhmaṇa pāṭhāñā
calibāra tare prabhure pāṭhāila kahiñā

SYNONYMS

rājāre—unto the King; *prabodhi'*—pacifying; *keśava*—of the name Keśava Chatrī; *brāhmaṇa*—one *brāhmaṇa; pāṭhāñā*—sending there; *calibāra tare*—for the sake of leaving; *prabhura*—unto the Lord; *pāṭhāila*—sent; *kahiñā*—telling.

TRANSLATION

After pacifying the King in this way, Keśava Chatrī sent a brāhmaṇa messenger to Lord Caitanya Mahāprabhu, requesting Him to leave without delay.

TEXT 175

দবির খাসেরে রাজা পুছিল নিভৃতে ।
গোসাঞির মহিমা তেঁহো লাগিল কহিতে ॥ ১৭৫ ॥

dabira khāsere rājā puchila nibhṛte
gosāñira mahimā teṅho lāgila kahite

SYNONYMS

dabira khāsere—of the name Dabira Khāsa (then the name of Śrīla Rūpa Gosvāmī); *rājā*—the King; *puchila*—inquired; *nibhṛte*—in privacy; *gosāñira*—of Lord Caitanya Mahāprabhu; *mahimā*—glories; *teṅho*—he; *lāgila*—began; *kahite*—to speak.

TRANSLATION

In private, the King inquired from Dabira Khāsa [Śrīla Rūpa Gosvāmī], who began to speak about the glories of the Lord.

TEXT 176

যে তোমারে রাজ্য দিল, যে তোমার গোসাঞা ।
তোমার দেশে তোমার ভাগ্যে জন্মিলা আসিঞা ॥

ye tomāre rājya dila, ye tomāra gosāñā
tomāra deśe tomāra bhāgye janmilā āsiñā

SYNONYMS

ye—that one who; *tomāre*—unto you; *rājya*—kingdom; *dila*—gave; *ye*—the one who; *tomāra*—your; *gosāñā*—prophet; *tomāra deśe*—in your country; *tomāra bhāgye*—on account of your good fortune; *janmilā*—took birth; *āsiñā*—coming.

TRANSLATION

Śrīla Rūpa Gosvāmī said: "The Supreme Personality of Godhead, who gave you this kingdom and whom you accept as a prophet, has taken birth in your country due to your good fortune.

TEXT 177

তোমার মঙ্গল বাঞ্ছে, কার্যসিদ্ধি হয় ।
ইহার আশীর্বাদে তোমার সর্বত্রই জয় ॥ ১৭৭ ॥

tomāra maṅgala vāñche, kārya-siddhi haya
ihāra āśīrvāde tomāra sarvatra-i jaya

SYNONYMS

tomāra—your; *maṅgala*—good fortune; *vāñche*—He desires; *kārya*—of business; *siddhi*—the perfection; *haya*—is; *ihāra*—of Him; *āśīrvāde*—by the blessings; *tomāra*—your; *sarvatra-i*—everywhere; *jaya*—victory.

TRANSLATION

"This prophet always desires your good fortune. By His grace, all your business is successful. By His blessings, you will attain victory everywhere.

TEXT 178

মোরে কেন পুছ, তুমি পুছ আপন-মন ।
তুমি নরাধিপ হও বিষ্ণু-অংশ সম ॥ ১৭৮ ॥

more kena pucha, tumi pucha āpana-mana
tumi narādhipa hao viṣṇu-aṁśa sama

SYNONYMS

more—unto me; *kena*—why; *pucha*—you inquire; *tumi*—you; *pucha*—inquire; *āpana-mana*—your own mind; *tumi*—you; *nara-adhipa*—King of the people; *hao*—you are; *viṣṇu-aṁśa sama*—representative of the Supreme Personality of Godhead.

TRANSLATION

"Why are you questioning me? Better that you question your own mind. Because you are the King of the people, you are the representative of the Supreme Personality of Godhead. Therefore you can understand this better than I."

TEXT 179

তোমার চিত্তে চৈতন্যেরে কৈছে হয় জ্ঞান ।
তোমার চিত্তে যেই লয়, সেই ত' প্রমাণ ॥ ১৭৯ ॥

tomāra citte caitanyere kaiche haya jñāna
tomāra citte yei laya, sei ta' pramāṇa

SYNONYMS

tomāra citte—in your mind; *caitanyere*—of Lord Caitanya Mahāprabhu; *kaiche*—how; *haya*—there is; *jñāna*—knowledge; *tomāra*—your; *citte*—mind; *yei*—whatever; *laya*—takes; *sei ta' pramāṇa*—that is evidence.

TRANSLATION

Thus Śrīla Rūpa Gosvāmī informed the King about his mind as a way of knowing Śrī Caitanya Mahāprabhu. He assured the King that whatever occurred in his mind could be considered evidence.

TEXT 180

রাজা কহে, শুন, মোর মনে যেই লয়।
সাক্ষাৎ ঈশ্বর ইহঁ নাহিক সংশয়॥ ১৮০ ॥

rājā kahe, śuna, mora mane yei laya
sākṣāt īśvara ihaṅ nāhika saṁśaya

SYNONYMS

rājā kahe—the King replied; *śuna*—hear; *mora*—my; *mane*—mind; *yei*—what; *laya*—takes; *sākṣāt*—personally; *īśvara*—the Supreme Personality; *ihaṅ*—He; *nāhika*—there is not; *saṁśaya*—doubt.

TRANSLATION

The King replied: "I consider Śrī Caitanya Mahāprabhu to be the Supreme Personality of Godhead. There is no doubt about it."

TEXT 181

এত কহি' রাজা গেলা নিজ অভ্যন্তরে।
তবে দবির খাস আইলা আপনার ঘরে ॥ ১৮১ ॥

eta kahi' rājā gelā nija abhyantare
tabe dabira khāsa āilā āpanāra ghare

SYNONYMS

eta kahi'—saying this; *rājā*—the King; *gelā*—went; *nija*—own; *abhyantare*—to the private house; *tabe*—at that time; *dabira khāsa*—Śrīla Rūpa Gosvāmī; *āilā*—returned; *āpanāra*—his own; *ghare*—to the residence.

TRANSLATION

After having this conversation with Rūpa Gosvāmī, the King entered his private house. Rūpa Gosvāmī, then known as Dabira Khāsa, also returned to his residence.

PURPORT

A monarch is certainly a representative of the Supreme Personality of Godhead. As stated in *Bhagavad-gītā, sarva-loka-maheśvaram:* the Supreme Personality of Godhead is the proprietor of all planetary systems. In each and every planet there must be some king, governmental head or executive. Such a person is supposed to be the representative of Lord Viṣṇu. On behalf of the Supreme Personality of Godhead, he must see to the interest of all the people. Therefore Lord Viṣṇu, as Paramātmā, gives the king all intelligence to execute governmental affairs. Śrīla Rūpa Gosvāmī therefore asked the King what was in his mind concerning Śrī Caitanya Mahāprabhu and indicated that whatever the King thought about Him was correct.

TEXT 182

ঘরে আসি' দুই ভাই যুকতি করিঞা।
প্রভু দেখিবারে চলে বেশ লুকাঞা ॥ ১৮২ ॥

ghare āsi' dui bhāi yukati kariñā
prabhu dekhibāre cale veśa lukāñā

SYNONYMS

ghare āsi'—after returning home; *dui bhāi*—two brothers; *yukati*—arguments; *kariñā*—making; *prabhu*—Lord Caitanya Mahāprabhu; *dekhibāre*—to see; *cale*—go; *veśa*—dress; *lukāñā*—hiding.

TRANSLATION

After returning to his residence, Dabira Khāsa and his brother decided after much consideration to go see the Lord incognito.

TEXT 183

অর্ধরাত্রে দুই ভাই আইলা প্রভু-স্থানে।
প্রথমে মিলিলা নিত্যানন্দ-হরিদাস সনে ॥ ১৮৩ ॥

ardha-rātre dui bhāi āilā prabhu-sthāne
prathame mililā nityānanda-haridāsa sane

SYNONYMS

ardha-rātre—in the dead of night; *dui bhāi*—the two brothers; *āilā*—came; *prabhu-sthāne*—to the place of Lord Caitanya; *prathame*—first; *mililā*—met; *nityānanda-haridāsa*—Lord Nityānanda and Haridāsa Ṭhākura; *sane*—with.

TRANSLATION

Thus in the dead of night the two brothers, Dabira Khāsa and Sākara Mallika, went to see Śrī Caitanya Mahāprabhu incognito. First they met Nityānanda Prabhu and Haridāsa Ṭhākura.

TEXT 184

তাঁরা দুইজন জানাইলা প্রভুর গোচরে ।
রূপ, সাকরমল্লিক আইলা তোমা' দেখিবারে ॥১৮৪॥

tāṅrā dui-jana jānāilā prabhura gocare
rūpa, sākara-mallika āilā tomā' dekhibāre

SYNONYMS

tāṅrā—they; *dui-jana*—two persons; *jānāilā*—informed; *prabhura*—of Lord Caitanya Mahāprabhu; *gocare*—in the presence; *rūpa*—Rūpa Gosvāmī; *sākara-mallika*—and Sanātana Gosvāmī; *āilā*—have come; *tomā'*—You; *dekhibāre*—to see.

TRANSLATION

Śrī Nityānanda Prabhu and Haridāsa Ṭhākura told Lord Caitanya Mahāprabhu that two personalities—Śrī Rūpa and Sanātana—had come to see Him.

PURPORT

Sākara Mallika was the name of Sanātana Gosvāmī, and Dabira Khāsa was the name of Rūpa Gosvāmī. They were recognized by these names in the service of the Mohammedan King; therefore these are Mohammedan names. As officials, the brothers adopted all kinds of Mohammedan customs.

TEXT 185

দুই গুচ্ছ তৃণ দুঁহে দশনে ধরিঞা ।
গলে বস্ত্র বান্ধি' পড়ে দণ্ডবৎ হঞা ॥ ১৮৫ ॥

dui guccha tṛṇa duṅhe daśane dhariñā
gale vastra bāndhi' paḍe daṇḍavat hañā

SYNONYMS

dui—two; *guccha*—bunches; *tṛṇa*—of straw; *duṅhe*—both of them; *daśane*—in the teeth; *dhariñā*—catching; *gale*—on the neck; *vastra*—cloth; *bāndhi'*—binding; *paḍe*—fall; *daṇḍavat*—like rods; *hañā*—becoming.

TRANSLATION

In great humility, both brothers took bunches of straw between their teeth, and, each binding a cloth around his neck, they fell down like rods before the Lord.

TEXT 186

দৈন্য রোদন করে, আনন্দে বিহ্বল ।
প্রভু কহে,—উঠ, উঠ, হইল মঙ্গল ॥ ১৮৬ ॥

dainya rodana kare, ānande vihvala
prabhu kahe,——uṭha, uṭha, ha-ila maṅgala

SYNONYMS

dainya—humility; *rodana*—crying; *kare*—perform; *ānande*—in ecstasy; *vihvala*—overwhelmed; *prabhu kahe*—the Lord said; *uṭha uṭha*—stand up, stand up; *ha-ila maṅgala*—all auspiciousness unto you.

TRANSLATION

Upon seeing Lord Caitanya Mahāprabhu, the two brothers were overwhelmed with joy, and out of humility they began to cry. Lord Caitanya Mahāprabhu asked them to get up and assured them of all good fortune.

TEXT 187

উঠি' দুই ভাই তবে দন্তে তৃণ ধরি' ।
দৈন্য করি' স্তুতি করে করযোড় করি ॥ ১৮৭ ॥

uṭhi' dui bhāi tabe dante tṛṇa dhari'
dainya kari' stuti kare karayoḍa kari

SYNONYMS

uṭhi'—standing up; *dui*—two; *bhāi*—brothers; *tabe*—then; *dante*—in the teeth; *tṛṇa*—straw; *dhari'*—holding; *dainya kari'*—in all humbleness; *stuti kare*—offer prayer; *kara-yoḍa*—folded hands; *kari'*—making.

TRANSLATION

The two brothers got up, and again taking straw between their teeth, they humbly offered their prayers with folded hands.

TEXT 188

জয় জয় শ্রীকৃষ্ণচৈতন্য দয়াময় ।
পতিতপাবন জয়, জয় মহাশয় ॥ ১৮৮ ॥

jaya jaya śrī-kṛṣṇa-caitanya dayā-maya
patita-pāvana jaya, jaya mahāśaya

SYNONYMS

jaya jaya—all glories; *śrī-kṛṣṇa-caitanya*—unto Lord Śrī Caitanya Mahāprabhu; *dayā-maya*—the most merciful; *patita-pāvana*—the savior of the fallen souls; *jaya*—glories; *jaya*—glories; *mahāśaya*—to the great personality.

TRANSLATION

"All glories to Śrī Kṛṣṇa Caitanya Mahāprabhu, the most merciful savior of the fallen souls! All glories to the Supreme Personality!

TEXT 189

নীচ-জাতি, নীচ-সঙ্গী, করি নীচ কাজ ।
তোমার অগ্রেতে প্রভু কহিতে বাসি লাজ ॥ ১৮৯ ॥

nīca-jāti, nīca-saṅgī, kari nīca kāja
tomāra agrete prabhu kahite vāsi lāja

SYNONYMS

nīca-jāti—classified among the fallen; *nīca-saṅgī*—associated with fallen souls; *kari*—we perform; *nīca*—abominable; *kāja*—work; *tomāra*—of You; *agrete*—in front; *prabhu*—O Lord; *kahite*—to say; *vāsi*—we feel; *lāja*—ashamed.

TRANSLATION

"Sir, we belong to the lowest class of men, and our associates and employment are also of the lowest type. Therefore we cannot introduce ourselves to You. We feel very much ashamed, standing here before You.

PURPORT

Although the two brothers, Rūpa and Sanātana (at that time Dabira Khāsa and Sākara Mallika), presented themselves as being born in a low family, they nonetheless belonged to a most respectable *brāhmaṇa* family that was originally from Karṇāta. Thus they actually belonged to the *brāhmaṇa* caste. Unfortunately, because of being associated with the Mohammedan governmental service, their customs and behavior resembled those of the Mohammedans. Therefore they presented themselves as *nīca-jāti.* The word *jāti* means birth. According to *śāstra,* there are three kinds of birth. The first birth is from the womb of the mother, the second birth is the acceptance of the reformatory method, and the third birth is acceptance by the spiritual master (initiation). One becomes abominable by adopting an abominable profession or by associating with people who are naturally abominable. Rūpa and Sanātana, as Dabira Khāsa and Sākara Mallika, associated with Mohammedans, who were naturally opposed to brahminical culture and cow protection. In *Śrīmad-Bhāgavatam* (Seventh Canto) it is stated that every person belongs to a certain classification. A person is identifiable by the special symptoms mentioned in the *śāstras*. By one's symptoms, one is known to belong to a certain caste. Both Dabira Khāsa and Sākara Mallika belonged to the *brāhmaṇa* caste, but because they were employed by Mohammedans, their original habits degenerated into those of the Mohammedan community. Since the symptoms of brahminical culture were almost nil, they identified themselves with the lowest caste. In the *Bhakti-ratnākara* it is clearly stated that because Sākara Mallika and Dabira Khāsa associated with lower-class men, they introduced themselves as belonging to the lower classes. Actually, however, they had been born in respectable *brāhmaṇa* families.

TEXT 190

মত্তুল্যো নাস্তি পাপাত্মা নাপরাধী চ কশ্চন ।
পরিহারেঽপি লজ্জা মে কিং ব্রুবে পুরুষোত্তম ॥১৯০॥

mat-tulyo nāsti pāpātmā
nāparādhī ca kaścana
parihāre 'pi lajjā me
kiṁ bruve puruṣottama

SYNONYMS

mat—me; *tulyaḥ*—like; *na asti*—there is not; *pāpa-ātmā*—sinful man; *na aparādhī*—nor an offender; *ca*—also; *kaścana*—anyone; *parihāre*—in begging pardon; *api lajjā*—ashamed; *me*—of me; *kim*—what; *bruve*—I shall say; *puruṣottama*—O Supreme Personality of Godhead.

TRANSLATION

"Dear Lord, let us inform you that no one is more sinful than us, nor is there any offender like us. Even if we wanted to mention our sinful activities, we would immediately become ashamed. And what to speak of giving them up!"

PURPORT

This verse is from the *Bhakti-rasāmṛta-sindhu* (1.2.154) by Śrīla Rūpa Gosvāmī.

TEXT 191

পতিত-পাবন-হেতু তোমার অবতার ।
আমা-বই জগতে, পতিত নাহি আর ॥ ১৯১ ॥

patita-pāvana-hetu tomāra avatāra
āmmā-va-i jagate, patita nāhi āra

SYNONYMS

patita-pāvana—deliverance of the fallen; *hetu*—for the matter of; *tomāra*—Your; *avatāra*—incarnation; *āmā-va-i*—than us; *jagate*—in this world; *patita*—fallen; *nāhi*—there is not; *āra*—more.

TRANSLATION

Both brothers submitted: "Dear Lord, You have incarnated to deliver the fallen souls. You should consider that in this world there is none so fallen as us.

TEXT 192

জগাই-মাধাই দুই করিলে উদ্ধার ।
তাহাঁ উদ্ধারিতে শ্রম নহিল তোমার ॥ ১৯২ ॥

jagāi-mādhāi dui karile uddhāra
tāhāṅ uddhārite śrama nahila tomāra

SYNONYMS

jagāi-mādhāi—the two brothers Jagāi and Mādhāi; *dui*—two; *karile*—You did; *uddhāra*—deliverance; *tāhāṅ*—there; *uddhārite*—to deliver; *śrama*—exertion; *nahila*—there was not; *tomāra*—of You.

TRANSLATION

"You have delivered the two brothers Jagāi and Mādhāi, but to deliver them You did not have to exert Yourself very much.

TEXT 193

ব্রাহ্মণজাতি তারা, নবদ্বীপে ঘর ।
নীচ-সেবা নাহি করে, নহে নীচের কূর্পর ॥ ১৯৩ ॥

brāhmaṇa-jāti tārā, nava-dvīpe ghara
nīca-sevā nāhi kare, nahe nīcera kūrpara

SYNONYMS

brāhmaṇa-jāti—born in a *brāhmaṇa* family; *tārā*—they; *nava-dvīpe*—the holy place of Navadvīpa-dhāma; *ghara*—their house; *nīca-sevā*—service to degraded persons; *nāhi*—not; *kare*—do; *nahe*—not; *nīcera*—of low persons; *kūrpara*—an instrument.

TRANSLATION

"The brothers Jagāi and Mādhāi belonged to the brāhmaṇa caste, and their residence was in the holy place of Navadvīpa. They never served low-class persons, nor were they instruments to abominable activities.

TEXT 194

সবে এক দোষ তার, হয় পাপাচার ।
পাপরাশি দহে নামাভাসেই তোমার ॥ ১৯৪ ॥

sabe eka doṣa tāra, haya pāpācāra
pāpa-rāśi dahe nāmābhāsei tomāra

SYNONYMS

sabe—in all; *eka*—one only; *doṣa*—fault; *tāra*—of them; *haya*—they are; *pāpa-ācāra*—attached to sinful activities; *pāpa-rāśi*—volumes of sinful activities; *dahe*—become burned; *nāma-ābhāsei*—simply by the dim reflection of chanting the holy name; *tomāra*—of Your Lordship.

TRANSLATION

"Jagāi and Mādhāi had but one fault—they were addicted to sinful activity. However, volumes of sinful activity can be burned to ashes simply by a dim reflection of the chanting of Your holy name.

PURPORT

Śrīla Rūpa Gosvāmī and Sanātana Gosvāmī presented themselves as being lower than the two brothers Jagāi and Mādhāi, who were delivered by Śrī Caitanya Mahāprabhu. When Rūpa and Sanātana compared themselves to Jagāi and Mādhāi, they found themselves inferior because the Lord had no trouble in delivering two drunken brothers. This was so because, despite the fact that they were addicted to sinful activity, in other ways their life was brilliant. They belonged to the *brāhmaṇa* caste of Navadvīpa, and such *brāhmaṇas* were pious by nature. Although they had been addicted to some sinful activities due to bad association, those unwanted things could vanish simply because of the chanting of the holy name of the Lord. Another point for Jagāi and Mādhāi was that, as members of a *brāhmaṇa* family, they did not accept service under anyone. The *śāstras* strictly forbid a *brāhmaṇa* to accept service under anyone. The idea is that by accepting a master, one accepts the occupation of a dog. In other words, a dog cannot thrive without having a master, and for the sake of pleasing the master, dogs offend many people. They bark at innocent people just to please the master. Similarly, when one is a servant, he has to perform abominable activities according to the orders of the master. Therefore, when Dabira Khāsa and Sākara Mallika compared their position to that of Jagāi and Mādhāi, they found Jagāi and Mādhāi's position far better. Jagāi and Mādhāi never accepted the service of a low-class person; nor were they forced to execute abominable activities under the order of a low-class master. Jagāi and Mādhāi chanted the name of Śrī Caitanya Mahāprabhu by way of blasphemy, but because they simply chanted His name, they immediately became free from the reactions of sinful activities. Thus later they were saved.

TEXT 195

তোমার নাম লঞা তোমার করিল নিন্দন ।
সেই নাম হইল তার মুক্তির কারণ ॥ ১৯৫ ॥

tomāra nāma lañā tomāra karila nindana
sei nāma ha-ila tāra muktira kāraṇa

SYNONYMS

tomāra—Your; *nāma*—holy name; *lañā*—taking; *tomāra*—of You; *karila*—did; *nindana*—blaspheming; *sei*—that; *nāma*—holy name; *ha-ila*—became; *tāra*—of them; *muktira*—of deliverance; *kāraṇa*—the cause.

TRANSLATION

"Jagāi and Mādhāi uttered Your holy name by way of blaspheming You. Fortunately, that holy name became the cause of their deliverance.

TEXT 196

জগাই-মাধাই হৈতে কোটী কোটী গুণ ।
অধম পতিত পাপী আমি দুই জন ॥ ১৯৬ ॥

jagāi-mādhāi haite koṭī koṭī guṇa
adhama patita pāpī āmi dui jana

SYNONYMS

jagāi-mādhāi—of the name Jagāi and Mādhāi; *haite*—than; *koṭī koṭī*—millions and millions; *guṇa*—of times; *adhama*—degraded; *patita*—fallen; *pāpī*—sinful; *āmi*—we; *dui*—two; *jana*—persons.

TRANSLATION

"We two are millions and millions of times inferior to Jagāi and Mādhāi. We are more degraded, fallen and sinful than they.

TEXT 197

ম্লেচ্ছজাতি, ম্লেচ্ছসেবী, করি ম্লেচ্ছকর্ম ।
গো-ব্রাহ্মণ-দ্রোহি-সঙ্গে আমার সঙ্গম ॥ ১৯৭ ॥

mleccha-jāti, mleccha-sevī, kari mleccha-karma
go-brāhmaṇa-drohi-saṅge āmāra saṅgama

SYNONYMS

mleccha-jāti—belonging to the meat-eater caste; *mleccha-sevī*—servants of the meat-eaters; *kari*—we execute; *mleccha-karma*—the work of meat-eaters; *go*—cows; *brāhmaṇa*—*brāhmaṇas; drohi*—those inimical to; *saṅge*—with; *āmāra*—our; *saṅgama*—association.

TRANSLATION

"Actually we belong to the caste of meat-eaters because we are servants of meat-eaters. Indeed, our activities are exactly like those of the meat-eaters. Because we always associate with such people, we are inimical toward the cows and brāhmaṇas."

PURPORT

There are two kinds of meat-eaters—one who is born in a family of meat-eaters and one who has learned to associate with meat-eaters. From Śrīla Rūpa and Sanātana Gosvāmīs (formerly Dabira Khāsa and Sākara Mallika) we can learn how one attains the character of a meat-eater simply by associating with meat-eaters. At the present moment in India the presidential offices are occupied by many so-called *brāhmaṇas,* but the state maintains slaughterhouses for killing cows and makes propaganda against Vedic civilization. The first principle of Vedic civilization is the avoidance of meat-eating and intoxication. Presently in India, intoxication and meat-eating are encouraged, and the so-called learned *brāhmaṇas* presiding over this state of affairs have certainly become degraded according to the standard given herein by Śrīla Rūpa Gosvāmī and Sanātana Gosvāmī. These so-called *brāhmaṇas* give sanction to slaughterhouses for the sake of a fat salary, and they do not protest these abominable activities. By deprecating the principles of Vedic civilization and supporting cow killing, they are immediately degraded to the platform of *mlecchas* and *yavanas.* A *mleccha* is a meat-eater, and a *yavana* is one who has deviated from Vedic culture. Unfortunately, such *mlecchas* and *yavanas* are in executive power. How, then, can there be peace and prosperity in the state? The king or the president must be the representative of the Supreme Personality of Godhead. When Mahārāja Yudhiṣṭhira accepted the rule of Bhārata-varṣa (formerly this entire planet, including all the seas and land), he took sanction from authorities like Bhīṣmadeva and Lord Kṛṣṇa. He thus ruled the entire world according to religious principles. At the present moment, however, heads of state do not care for religious principles. If irreligious people vote on an issue, even though it be against the principles of the *śāstras,* the bills will be passed. The president and heads of state become sinful by agreeing to such abominable activities. Sanātana and Rūpa Gosvāmīs pleaded guilty to such activities; they therefore classified themselves among the *mlecchas,* although born in a *brāhmaṇa* family.

TEXT 198

মোর কর্ম, মোর হাতে-গলায় বান্ধিয়া ।
কু-বিষয়-বিষ্ঠা-গর্তে দিয়াছে ফেলাইয়া ॥ ১৯৮ ॥

mora karma, mora hāte-galāya bāndhiyā
ku-viṣaya-viṣṭhā-garte diyāche phelāiyā

SYNONYMS

mora—our; *karma*—activities; *mora*—our; *hāte*—on the hand; *galāya*—on the neck; *bāndhiyā*—binding; *ku-viṣaya*—of abominable objects of sense gratification; *viṣṭhā*—of the stool; *garte*—in the ditch; *diyāche phelāiyā*—have been thrown.

TRANSLATION

The two brothers, Sākara Mallika and Dabira Khāsa, very humbly submitted that due to their abominable activities, they were now bound by the neck and hands and had been thrown into a ditch filled with abominable stool-like objects of material sense enjoyment.

PURPORT

Śrīla Bhaktisiddhānta Sarasvatī Ṭhākura has explained *ku-viṣaya garta* as follows: "Because of the activities of the senses, we become subjected to many sense gratificatory processes and are thus entangled by the laws of material nature." This entanglement is called *viṣaya.* When the sense gratificatory processes are executed by pious activity, they are called *su-viṣaya.* The word *su* means "good," and *viṣaya* means "sense objects." When the sense gratificatory activities are performed under sinful conditions, they are called *ku-viṣaya,* bad sense enjoyment. In either case, either *ku-viṣaya* or *su-viṣaya,* these are material activities. As such, they are compared to stool. In other words, such things are to be avoided. To become free from *su-viṣaya* and *ku-viṣaya,* one must engage himself in the transcendental loving service of Kṛṣṇa, the Supreme Personality of Godhead. The activities of devotional service are free from the contamination of material qualities. Therefore, to be free from the reactions of *su-viṣaya* and *ku-viṣaya,* one must take to Kṛṣṇa consciousness. In that way, one will save himself from contamination. In this connection, Śrīla Narottama dāsa Ṭhākura has sung:

karma-kāṇḍa, jñāna-kāṇḍa, kevala viṣera bhāṇḍa
amṛta baliyā yeba khāya
nānā yoni sadā phire, kadarya bhakṣaṇa kare
tāra janma adhaḥ-pāte yāya

Su-viṣaya and *ku-viṣaya* both fall under the category of *karma-kāṇḍa.* There is another *kāṇḍa* (platform of activity) called *jñāna-kāṇḍa,* or philosophical speculation about the effects of *ku-viṣaya* and *su-viṣaya* with the intention to find out the means of deliverance from material entanglement. On the platform of *jñāna-kaṇḍa,* one may give up the objects of *ku-viṣaya* and *su-viṣaya.* But that is not the perfection of life. Perfection is transcendental to both *jñāna-kāṇḍa* and *karma-kāṇḍa;* it is on the platform of devotional service. If we do not take to devotional service in Kṛṣṇa consciousness, we have to remain within this material world and endure the repetition of birth and death due to the effects of *jñāna-kāṇḍa* and *karma-kāṇḍa.* Therefore Narottama dāsa Ṭhākura says:

nānā yoni sadā phire, kadarya bhakṣaṇa kare
tāra janma adhaḥ-pāte yāya

"One travels throughout various species of life and eats all kinds of nonsense. Thus he spoils his existence." A man in material existence and attached to *ku-viṣaya* or *su-viṣaya* is in the same position as that of a worm in stool. After all, whether it be moist or dry, stool is stool. Similarly, material activities may be either pious or impious, but because they are all material, they are compared to stool. Worms cannot get out of stool by their own endeavor; similarly, those who are overly attached to material existence cannot get out of materialism and suddenly become Kṛṣṇa conscious. Attachment is there. As explained by Prahlāda Mahārāja in *Śrīmad-Bhāgavatam* (7.5.30):

matir na kṛṣṇe parataḥ svato vā
mitho 'bhipadyeta gṛha-vratānām
adānta-gobhir viśatāṁ tamisraṁ
punaḥ punaś carvita-carvaṇānām

"Those who have made up their minds to remain in this material world and enjoy sense gratification cannot become Kṛṣṇa conscious. Because of their attachment to material activity, they cannot attain liberation, neither by the instructions of superior persons nor by their own endeavor, nor by passing resolutions in big conferences. Because their senses are uncontrolled, they gradually descend to the darkest regions of material existence to repeat the same process of birth and death in desirable or undesirable species of life."

TEXT 199

আমা উদ্ধারিতে বলী নাহি ত্রিভুবনে ।
পতিতপাবন তুমি—সবে তোমা বিনে ॥ ১৯৯ ॥

āmā uddhārite balī nāhi tri-bhuvane
patita-pāvana tumi——sabe tomā vine

SYNONYMS

āmā—us; *uddhārite*—to deliver; *balī*—powerful; *nāhi*—there is not; *tri-bhuvane*—within the three worlds; *patita-pāvana*—deliverer of the fallen; *tumi*—You; *sabe*—only; *tomā*—You; *vine*—except.

TRANSLATION

"No one within the three worlds is sufficiently powerful to deliver us. You are the only savior of the fallen souls; therefore there is no one but You.

TEXT 200

আমা উদ্ধারিয়া যদি দেখাও নিজ-বল ।
'পতিতপাবন' নাম তবে সে সফল ॥ ২০০ ॥

āmā uddhāriyā yadi dekhāo nija-bala
'patita-pāvana' nāma tabe se saphala

SYNONYMS

āmā—us; *uddhāriyā*—by delivering; *yadi*—if; *dekhāo*—You show; *nija-bala*—Your own strength; *patita-pāvana*—savior of the fallen; *nāma*—this name; *tabe*—then; *se*—that; *sa-phala*—successful.

TRANSLATION

"If You simply deliver us by Your transcendental strength, then certainly Your name will be known as the savior of the fallen souls.

TEXT 201

সত্য এক বাত কহোঁ, শুন, দয়াময়।
মো-বিনু দয়ার পাত্র জগতে না হয়॥ ২০১॥

satya eka bāta kahoṅ, śuna, dayā-maya
mo-vinu dayāra pātra jagate nā haya

SYNONYMS

satya—truthful; *eka*—one; *bāta*—word; *kahoṅ*—we say; *śuna*—please hear; *dayā-maya*—O all-merciful Lord; *mo-vinu*—except for us; *dayāra*—of mercy; *pātra*—objects; *jagate*—in the world; *nā*—not; *haya*—there is.

TRANSLATION

"Let us speak one word that is very true. Plainly hear us, O merciful one. There is no other object of mercy within the three worlds but us.

TEXT 202

মোরে দয়া করি' কর স্বদয়া সফল।
অখিল ব্রহ্মাণ্ড দেখুক তোমার দয়া-বল॥ ২০২॥

more dayā kari' kara sva-dayā saphala
akhila brahmāṇḍa dekhuka tomāra dayā-bala

SYNONYMS

more—to us; *dayā*—mercy; *kari'*—showing; *kara*—make; *sva-dayā*—Your own mercy; *sa-phala*—successful; *akhila*—throughout; *brahmāṇḍa*—the universe; *dekhuka*—let it be seen; *tomāra*—Your; *dayā-bala*—power of mercy.

TRANSLATION

"We are the most fallen; therefore by showing us Your mercy, Your mercy is most successful. Let the power of Your mercy be exhibited throughout the entire universe!

TEXT 203

ন মৃষা পরমার্থমেব মে, শৃণু বিজ্ঞাপনমেকমগ্রতঃ ।
যদি মে ন দয়িষ্যসে তদা, দয়নীয়স্তব নাথ দুর্লভঃ ॥২০৩॥

na mṛṣā paramārtham eva me,
śṛṇu vijñāpanam ekam agrataḥ
yadi me na dayiṣyase tadā,
dayanīyas tava nātha durlabhaḥ

SYNONYMS

na—not; *mṛṣā*—untruth; *parama-artham*—full of meaning; *eva*—certainly; *me*—my; *śṛṇu*—kindly hear; *vijñāpanam*—submission; *ekam*—one; *agrataḥ*—first; *yadi*—if; *me*—unto me; *na dayiṣyase*—You will not show mercy; *tadā*—then; *dayanīyaḥ*—candidate for mercy; *tava*—Your; *nātha*—O Lord; *durlabhaḥ*—difficult to find.

TRANSLATION

" 'Let us submit one piece of information before You, dear Lord. It is not at all false, but is full of meaning. It is this: If You are not merciful upon us, then it will be very, very difficult to find more suitable candidates for Your mercy.'

PURPORT

This verse is from the *Stotra-ratna* (47) by Śrī Yāmunācārya.

TEXT 204

আপনে অযোগ্য দেখি' মনে পাঙ ক্ষোভ ।
তথাপি তোমার গুণে উপজয় লোভ ॥ ২০৪ ॥

āpane ayogya dekhi' mane pāṅ kṣobha
tathāpi tomāra guṇe upajaya lobha

SYNONYMS

āpane—ourselves; *ayogya*—most unfit; *dekhi'*—seeing; *mane*—within the mind; *pāṅ*—get; *kṣobha*—lamentation; *tathāpi*—still; *tomāra*—Your; *guṇe*—in transcendental qualities; *upajaya*—there is; *lobha*—attraction.

TRANSLATION

"We are very depressed at being unfit candidates for Your mercy. Yet since we have heard of Your transcendental qualities, we are very much attracted to You.

TEXT 205

বামন যৈছে চাঁদ ধরিতে চাহে করে ।
তৈছে এই বাঞ্ছা মোর উঠয়ে অন্তরে ॥ ২০৫ ॥

vāmana yaiche cāṅda dharite cāhe kare
taiche ei vāñchā mora uṭhaye antare

SYNONYMS

vāmana—a dwarf; *yaiche*—as; *cāṅda*—the moon; *dharite*—to capture; *cāhe*—wants; *kare*—does; *taiche*—similarly; *ei*—this; *vāñchā*—desire; *mora*—our; *uṭhaye*—awakens; *antare*—within the mind.

TRANSLATION

"Indeed, we are like a dwarf who wants to capture the moon. Although we are completely unfit, a desire to receive Your mercy is awakening within our minds.

TEXT 206

ভবন্তমেবানুচরন্নিরন্তরঃ
প্রশান্তনিঃশেষমনোরথান্তরঃ ।
কদাহমৈকান্তিকনিত্যকিঙ্করঃ
প্রহর্ষয়িষ্যামি সনাথজীবিতম্ ॥ ২০৬ ॥

bhavantam evānucaran nirantaraḥ
praśānta-niḥśeṣa-mano-rathāntaraḥ
kadāham aikāntika-nitya-kiṅkaraḥ
praharṣayiṣyāmi sanātha-jīvitam

SYNONYMS

bhavantam—You; *eva*—certainly; *anucaran*—serving; *nirantaraḥ*—always; *praśānta*—pacified; *niḥśeṣa*—all; *manaḥ-ratha*—desires; *antaraḥ*—other;

kadā—when; *aham*—I; *aikāntika*—exclusive; *nitya*—eternal; *kiṅkaraḥ*—servant; *praharṣayiṣyāmi*—I shall become joyful; *sa-nātha*—with a fitting master; *jīvitam*—living.

TRANSLATION

" 'By serving You constantly, one is freed from all material desires and is completely pacified. When shall I engage as Your permanent eternal servant and always feel joyful to have such a fitting master?' "

PURPORT

In His teachings to Sanātana Gosvāmī, Śrī Caitanya Mahāprabhu has declared every living entity to be an eternal servitor of the Supreme Personality of Godhead. This is the constitutional position of all living entities. Just as a dog or servant is very satisfied to get a competent, perfect master, or as a child is completely satisfied to possess a competent father, so the living entity is satisifed by completely engaging in the service of the Supreme Lord. He thereby knows that he has a competent master to save him from all kinds of danger. Unless the living entity comes to the guaranteed protection of the Supreme Lord, He is full of anxiety. This life of anxiety is called material existence. To be completely satisfied and devoid of anxiety, one must come to the position of eternally rendering service to the Supreme Lord. This verse is also from the *Stotra-ratna* (43) by Śrī Yāmunācārya.

TEXT 207

শুনি' মহাপ্রভু কহে,—শুন, দবির-খাস ।
তুমি দুই ভাই—মোর পুরাতন দাস ॥ ২০৭ ॥

śuni' mahāprabhu kahe,——śuna, dabira-khāsa
tumi dui bhāi——mora purātana dāsa

SYNONYMS

śuni'—hearing this; *mahā-prabhu*—Lord Caitanya Mahāprabhu; *kahe*—says; *śuna*—please hear; *dabira khāsa*—Dabira Khāsa; *tumi*—you; *dui bhāi*—two brothers; *mora*—My; *purātana*—old; *dāsa*—servants.

TRANSLATION

After hearing the prayer of Dabira Khāsa and Sākara Mallika, Śrī Caitanya Mahāprabhu said: "My dear Dabira Khāsa, you two brothers are My old servants.

TEXT 208

আজি হৈতে দুঁহার নাম 'রূপ' 'সনাতন'।
দৈন্য ছাড়, তোমার দৈন্যে ফাটে মোর মন ॥ ২০৮ ॥

āji haite duṅhāra nāma 'rūpa' 'sanātana'
dainya chāḍa, tomāra dainye phāṭe mora mana

SYNONYMS

āji haite—from this day; *duṅhāra*—of both of you; *nāma*—these names; *rūpa*—Śrī Rūpa; *sanātana*—Śrī Sanātana; *dainya chāḍa*—give up your humility; *tomāra*—your; *dainye*—humility; *phāṭe*—breaks; *mora*—My; *mana*—heart.

TRANSLATION

"My dear Sākara Mallika, from this day your names will be changed to Śrīla Rūpa and Śrīla Sanātana. Now please abandon your humility, for My heart is breaking to see you so humble.

PURPORT

Actually this is Śrī Caitanya Mahāprabhu's initiation of Dabira Khāsa and Sākara Mallika. They approached the Lord with all humility, and the Lord accepted them as old servants, as eternal servants, and He changed their names. It is to be understood from this that it is essential for a disciple to change his name after initiation.

śaṅkha-cakrādy-ūrdhva-puṇḍra-
dhāraṇādy-ātma-lakṣaṇam
tan nāma-karaṇaṁ caiva
vaiṣṇavatvam ihocyate

"After initiation, the disciple's name must be changed to indicate that he is a servant of Lord Viṣṇu. The disciple should also immediately begin marking his body with *tilaka* (*ūrdhva-puṇḍra*), especially his forehead. These are spiritual marks, symptoms of a perfect Vaiṣṇava." This is a verse from the *Padma Purāṇa, Uttara-khaṇḍa.* A member of the *sahajiyā-sampradāya* does not change his name; therefore he cannot be accepted as a Gauḍīya Vaiṣṇava. If a person does not change his name after initiation, it is to be understood that he will continue in his bodily conception of life.

TEXT 209

দৈন্যপত্রী লিখি' মোরে পাঠালে বার বার ।
সেই পত্রীদ্বারা জানি তোমার ব্যবহার ॥ ২০৯ ॥

dainya-patrī likhi' more pāṭhāle bāra bāra
sei patrī-dvārā jāni tomāra vyavahāra

SYNONYMS

dainya-patrī—humble letters; *likhi'*—writing; *more*—unto Me; *pāṭhāle*—you sent; *bāra bāra*—again and again; *sei*—those; *patrī-dvārā*—by the letters; *jāni*—I can understand; *tomāra*—your; *vyavahāra*—behavior.

TRANSLATION

"You have written several letters showing your humility. I can understand your behavior from those letters.

TEXT 210

তোমার হৃদয় আমি জানি পত্রীদ্বারে ।
তোমা শিখাইতে শ্লোক পাঠাইল তোমারে ॥ ২১০ ॥

tomāra hṛdaya āmi jāni patrī-dvāre
tomā śikhāite śloka pāṭhāila tomāre

SYNONYMS

tomāra—your; *hṛdaya*—hearts; *āmi*—I; *jāni*—understand; *patrī-dvāre*—by those letters; *tomā*—you; *śikhāite*—to instruct; *śloka*—a verse; *pāṭhāila*—I sent; *tomāre*—unto you.

TRANSLATION

"By your letters, I could understand your heart. Therefore, in order to teach you, I sent you one verse, which reads as follows.

TEXT 211

পরব্যসনিনী নারী ব্যগ্রাপি গৃহকর্মসু ।
তদেবাস্বাদয়ত্যন্তর্নবসঙ্গরসায়নম্ ॥ ২১১ ॥

para-vyasaninī nārī
vyagrāpi gṛha-karmasu
tad evāsvādayaty antar
nava-saṅga-rasāyanam

SYNONYMS

para-vyasaninī—attached to another man; *nārī*—a woman; *vyagrā api*—although zealous; *gṛha-karmasu*—in household affairs; *tat eva*—that only; *āsvādayati*—tastes; *antaḥ*—within herself; *nava-saṅga*—of new association; *rasa-ayanam*—mellow.

TRANSLATION

" 'If a woman is attached to a man other than her husband, she will appear very busy in carrying out her household affairs, but within her heart she is always relishing feelings of association with her paramour.'

TEXT 212

গৌড়-নিকট আসিতে নাহি মোর প্রয়োজন ।
তোমা-দুঁহা দেখিতে মোর ইহাঁ আগমন ॥ ২১২ ॥

gauḍa-nikaṭa āsite nāhi mora prayojana
tomā-duṅhā dekhite mora ihāṅ āgamana

SYNONYMS

gauḍa-nikaṭa—to Bengal; *āsite*—to come; *nāhi*—there was none; *mora*—My; *prayojana*—necessity; *tomā*—you; *duṅhā*—two; *dekhite*—to see; *mora*—My; *ihāṅ*—here; *āgamana*—coming.

TRANSLATION

"I really had no business in coming to Bengal, but I have come just to see you two brothers.

TEXT 213

এই মোর মনের কথা কেহ নাহি জানে ।
সবে বলে, কেনে আইলা রামকেলি-গ্রামে ॥ ২১৩ ॥

ei mora manera kathā keha nāhi jāne
sabe bale, kene āilā rāma-keli-grāme

SYNONYMS

ei—this; *mora*—My; *manera*—of the mind; *kathā*—intention; *keha*—anyone; *nāhi*—not; *jāne*—knows; *sabe*—everyone; *bale*—says; *kene*—why; *āilā*—You came; *rāma-keli-grāme*—to this village named Rāmakeli.

TRANSLATION

"Everyone is asking why I have come to this village of Rāmakeli. No one knows My intentions.

TEXT 214

ভাল হৈল, দুই ভাই আইলা মোর স্থানে।
ঘরে যাহ, ভয় কিছু না করিহ মনে॥ ২১৪॥

bhāla haila, dui bhāi āilā mora sthāne
ghare yāha, bhaya kichu nā kariha mane

SYNONYMS

bhāla haila—it was very good; *dui bhāi*—you two brothers; *āilā*—came; *mora*—My; *sthāne*—to the place; *ghare*—home; *yāha*—go; *bhaya*—fear; *kichu*—any; *nā*—do not; *kariha*—have; *mane*—within the mind.

TRANSLATION

"It is very good that you two brothers have come to see Me. Now you can go home. Do not fear anything.

TEXT 215

জন্মে জন্মে তুমি দুই—কিঙ্কর আমার।
অচিরাতে কৃষ্ণ তোমায় করিবে উদ্ধার॥ ২১৫॥

janme janme tumi dui——kiṅkara āmāra
acirāte kṛṣṇa tomāya karibe uddhāra

SYNONYMS

janme janme—birth after birth; *tumi*—you; *dui*—two; *kiṅkara*—servants; *āmāra*—My; *acirāte*—very soon; *kṛṣṇa*—Lord Kṛṣṇa; *tomāya*—of both of you; *karibe*—will do; *uddhāra*—deliverance.

TRANSLATION

"Birth after birth you have been My eternal servants. I am sure that Kṛṣṇa will deliver you very soon."

TEXT 216

এত বলি দুঁহার শিরে ধরিল দুই হাতে ।
দুই ভাই প্রভু-পদ নিল নিজ মাথে ॥ ২১৬ ॥

eta bali duṅhāra śire dharila dui hāte
dui bhāi prabhu-pada nila nija māthe

SYNONYMS

eta bali—saying this; *duṅhāra śire*—on the heads of both of them; *dharila*—placed; *dui*—two; *hāte*—hands; *dui bhāi*—the two brothers; *prabhu-pada*—the lotus feet of the Lord; *nila*—took; *nija māthe*—on their own heads.

TRANSLATION

The Lord then placed His two hands on the heads of both of them, and in return they immediately placed the lotus feet of the Lord on their heads.

TEXT 217

দোঁহা আলিঙ্গিয়া প্রভু বলিল ভক্তগণে ।
সবে কৃপা করি' উদ্ধারহ দুই জনে ॥ ২১৭ ॥

doṅhā āliṅgiyā prabhu balila bhakta-gaṇe
sabe kṛpā kari' uddhāraha dui jane

SYNONYMS

doṅhā—both of them; *āliṅgiyā*—embracing; *prabhu*—the Lord; *balila*—said; *bhakta-gaṇe*—unto the devotees; *sabe*—all of you; *kṛpā*—mercy; *kari'*—showing; *uddhāraha*—deliver; *dui*—the two; *jane*—persons.

TRANSLATION

After this, the Lord embraced both of them and requested all of the devotees present to be merciful upon them and deliver them.

TEXT 218

দুই জনে প্রভুর কৃপা দেখি' ভক্তগণে ।
'হরি' 'হরি' বলে সবে আনন্দিত-মনে ॥ ২১৮ ॥

dui jane prabhura kṛpā dekhi' bhakta-gaṇe
'hari' 'hari' bale sabe ānandita-mane

SYNONYMS

dui jane—unto the two persons; *prabhura*—of the Lord; *kṛpā*—the mercy; *dekhi'*—seeing; *bhakta-gaṇe*—all the devotees; *hari hari*—the holy name of the Lord; *bale*—chant; *sabe*—all; *ānandita*—cheerful; *mane*—in the mind.

TRANSLATION

When all of the devotees saw the mercy of the Lord upon the two brothers, they were very gladdened, and they began to chant the holy name of the Lord, "Hari! Hari!"

PURPORT

Śrīla Narottama dāsa Ṭhākura says, *chāḍiyā vaiṣṇava sevā nistāra peche kebā:* unless one serves a Vaiṣṇava, he cannot be delivered. The spiritual master initiates the disciple to deliver him, and if the disciple executes the order of the spiritual master and does not offend other Vaiṣṇavas, his path is clear. Consequently Śrī Caitanya Mahāprabhu requested all the Vaiṣṇavas present to show mercy toward the two brothers, Rūpa and Sanātana, who had just been initiated by the Lord. When a Vaiṣṇava sees that another Vaiṣṇava is a recipient of the Lord's mercy, he becomes very happy. Vaiṣṇavas are not envious. If a Vaiṣṇava, by the mercy of the Lord, is empowered by Him to distribute the Lord's holy name all over the world, other Vaiṣṇavas become very joyful—that is, if they are truly Vaiṣṇavas. One who is envious of the success of a Vaiṣṇava is certainly not a Vaiṣṇava himself, but an ordinary mundane man. Envy and jealousy are manifested by mundane people, not by Vaiṣṇavas. Why should a Vaiṣṇava be envious of another Vaiṣṇava who is successful in spreading the holy name of the Lord? An actual Vaiṣṇava is very pleased to accept another Vaiṣṇava who is bestowing the Lord's mercy. A mundane person in the dress of a Vaiṣṇava should not be respected but rejected. This is enjoined in the *śāstras* (*upekṣā*). The word *upekṣā* means neglect. One should neglect an envious person. A preacher's duty is to love the Supreme Personality of Godhead, make friendships with Vaiṣṇavas, show mercy to the innocent and reject or neglect those who are envious or jealous. There are many jealous people in the dress of Vaiṣṇavas in this Kṛṣṇa consciousness movement, and they should be completely neglected. There is no need to serve a jealous person who is in the dress of a Vaiṣṇava. When Narottama dāsa Ṭhākura says *chāḍiyā vaiṣṇava sevā nistāra peche kebā,* he is indicating an actual Vaiṣṇava, not an envious or jealous person in the dress of a Vaiṣṇava.

TEXT 219

নিত্যানন্দ, হরিদাস, শ্রীবাস, গদাধর ।
মুকুন্দ, জগদানন্দ, মুরারি, বক্রেশ্বর ॥ ২১৯ ॥

nityānanda, haridāsa, śrīvāsa, gadādhara
mukunda, jagadānanda, murāri, vakreśvara

SYNONYMS

nityānanda—Lord Nityānanda; *hari-dāsa*—Haridāsa Ṭhākura; *śrīvāsa*—Śrīvāsa Ṭhākura; *gadādhara*—Gadādhara Paṇḍita; *mukunda*—Mukunda; *jagadānanda*—Jagadānanda; *murāri*—Murāri; *vakreśvara*—Vakreśvara.

TRANSLATION

All the Vaiṣṇava associates of the Lord were present, including Nityānanda, Haridāsa Ṭhākura, Śrīvāsa Ṭhākura, Gadādhara Paṇḍita, Mukunda, Jagadānanda, Murāri and Vakreśvara.

TEXT 220

সবার চরণে ধরি, পড়ে দুই ভাই ।
সবে বলে,—ধন্য তুমি, পাইলে গোসাঞি ॥ ২২০ ॥

sabāra caraṇe dhari, paḍe dui bhāi
sabe bale,——dhanya tumi, pāile gosāñi

SYNONYMS

sabāra—of all of them; *caraṇe*—the lotus feet; *dhari*—touching; *paḍe*—fall down; *dui bhāi*—the two brothers; *sabe bale*—all the Vaiṣṇavas say; *dhanya tumi*—you are so fortunate; *pāile gosāñi*—you have gotten the shelter of the lotus feet of Lord Caitanya Mahāprabhu.

TRANSLATION

In accordance with the instructions of Śrī Caitanya Mahāprabhu, the two brothers, Rūpa and Sanātana, immediately touched the lotus feet of these Vaiṣṇavas, who all became very happy and congratulated the two brothers for having received the mercy of the Lord.

PURPORT

This behavior is indicative of real Vaiṣṇavas. When they saw that Rūpa and Sanātana were fortunate enough to receive the mercy of the Lord, they were so pleased that they all congratulated the two brothers. A jealous person in the dress of a Vaiṣṇava is not at all happy to see the success of another Vaiṣṇava in receiving the Lord's mercy. Unfortunately in this age of Kali there are many mundane persons in the dress of Vaiṣṇavas, and Śrīla Bhaktivinoda Ṭhākura has described them as disciples of Kali. He says, *kali-celā.* He indicates that there is another Vaiṣṇava, a pseudo-Vaiṣṇava with *tilaka* on his nose and *kunti* beads around his neck. Such a pseudo-Vaiṣṇava associates with money and women and is jealous of successful Vaiṣṇavas. Although passing for a Vaiṣṇava, his only business is earning money in the dress of a Vaiṣṇava. Bhaktivinoda Ṭhākura therefore says that such a pseudo-Vaiṣṇava is not a Vaiṣṇava at all but a disciple of Kali-yuga. A disciple of Kali cannot become an *ācārya* by the decision of some high court. Mundane votes have no jurisdiction to elect a Vaiṣṇava *ācārya.* A Vaiṣṇava *ācārya* is self-effulgent, and there is no need for any court judgment. A false *ācārya* may try to override a Vaiṣṇava by a high-court decision, but Bhaktivinoda Ṭhākura says that he is nothing but a disciple of Kali-yuga.

TEXT 221

সবা-পাশ আজ্ঞা মাগি' চলন-সময় ।
প্রভু-পদে কহে কিছু করিয়া বিনয় ॥ ২২১ ॥

sabā-pāśa ājñā māgi' calana-samaya
prabhu-pade kahe kichu kariyā vinaya

SYNONYMS

sabā—all of them; *pāśa*—from; *ājñā*—order; *māgi'*—taking; *calana-samaya*—at the time of departure; *prabhu-pade*—at the lotus feet of the Lord; *kahe*—say; *kichu*—something; *kariyā*—doing; *vinaya*—submission.

TRANSLATION

After begging the permission of all the Vaiṣṇavas present, the two brothers, at the time of their departure, humbly submitted something at the lotus feet of the Lord.

TEXT 222

ইহাঁ হৈতে চল, প্রভু, ইহাঁ নাহি কায ।
যদ্যপি তোমারে ভক্তি করে গৌড়রাজ ॥ ২২২ ॥

ihāṅ haite cala, prabhu, ihāṅ nāhi kāya
yadyapi tomāre bhakti kare gauḍa-rāja

SYNONYMS

ihāṅ haite—from this place; *cala*—please depart; *prabhu*—dear Lord; *ihāṅ*—in this place; *nāhi kāya*—there is no other business; *yadyapi*—although; *tomāre*—unto You; *bhakti*—respect; *kare*—shows; *gauḍa-rāja*—the King of Bengal.

TRANSLATION

They said: "Dear Lord, although the King of Bengal, Nawab Husena Sāhā, is very respectful toward You, You have no other business here. Kindly depart from this place.

TEXT 223

তথাপি যবন জাতি, না করি প্রতীতি ।
তীর্থযাত্রায় এত সংঘট্ট ভাল নহে রীতি ॥ ২২৩ ॥

tathāpi yavana jāti, nā kari pratīti
tīrtha-yātrāya eta saṅghaṭṭa bhāla nahe rīti

SYNONYMS

tathāpi—still; *yavana jāti*—by caste a Mohammedan; *nā*—does not; *kari*—do; *pratīti*—confidence; *tīrtha-yātrāya*—in going for a pilgrimage; *eta*—so; *saṅghaṭṭa*—crowd; *bhāla*—good; *nahe*—not; *rīti*—etiquette.

TRANSLATION

"Although the King is respectful toward You, he still belongs to the yavana class and should not be believed. We think that there is no need

for such a great crowd to accompany You on Your pilgrimage to Vṛndāvana.

TEXT 224

যার সঙ্গে চলে এই লোক লক্ষকোটি ।
বৃন্দাবন-যাত্রার এ নহে পরিপাটী ॥ ২২৪ ॥

yāra saṅge cale ei loka lakṣa-koṭi
vṛndāvana-yātrāra e nahe paripāṭī

SYNONYMS

yāra—of whom; *saṅge*—in the company; *cale*—follow; *ei*—these; *loka*—people; *lakṣa-koṭi*—hundreds and thousands; *vṛndāvana-yātrāra*—of going to Vṛndāvana; *e*—this; *nahe*—not; *paripāṭī*—method.

TRANSLATION

"Dear Lord, You are going to Vṛndāvana with hundreds and thousands of people following You, and this is not a fitting way to go on a pilgrimage."

PURPORT

Sometimes, for business purposes, large crowds of men are taken to different places of pilgrimage, and money is collected from them. That is a very lucrative business, but Rūpa and Sanātana Gosvāmīs, expressing their opinion in the presence of Lord Caitanya Mahāprabhu, disapproved of such crowded pilgrimages. Actually when Lord Caitanya visited Vṛndāvana, He visited it alone and accepted a servant only at His devotees' request. He never visited Vṛndāvana with crowds of people for a commercial purpose.

TEXT 225

যদ্যপি বস্তুতঃ প্রভুর কিছু নাহি ভয় ।
তথাপি লৌকিকলীলা, লোক-চেষ্টাময় ॥ ২২৫ ॥

yadyapi vastutaḥ prabhura kichu nāhi bhaya
tathāpi laukika-līlā, loka-ceṣṭā-maya

SYNONYMS

yadyapi—although; *vastutaḥ*—in fact; *prabhura*—of the Lord; *kichu*—any; *nāhi*—there is not; *bhaya*—fear; *tathāpi*—still; *laukika-līlā*—general pastimes; *loka-ceṣṭā-maya*—consisting of popular behavior.

TRANSLATION

Although Śrī Caitanya Mahāprabhu was Śrī Kṛṣṇa Himself, the Supreme Lord, and was therefore not at all fearful, He still acted like a human being to teach neophytes how to act.

TEXT 226

এত বলি' চরণ বন্দি' গেলা দুইজন ।
প্রভুর সেই গ্রাম হৈতে চলিতে হৈল মন ॥ ২২৬ ॥

eta bali' caraṇa vandi' gelā dui-jana
prabhura sei grāma haite calite haila mana

SYNONYMS

eta bali'—saying this; *caraṇa vandi'*—offering prayers to the lotus feet of Lord Caitanya; *gelā*—went back; *dui-jana*—the two brothers; *prabhura*—of Śrī Caitanya Mahāprabhu; *sei*—that; *grāma*—village; *haite*—from; *calite*—to go; *haila*—there was; *mana*—the mind.

TRANSLATION

Having spoken thus, the two brothers offered prayers to the lotus feet of the Lord and returned to their homes. Lord Caitanya Mahāprabhu then desired to leave that village.

TEXT 227

প্রাতে চলি' আইলা প্রভু 'কানাইর নাটশালা' ।
দেখিল সকল তাহাঁ কৃষ্ণচরিত্র-লীলা ॥ ২২৭ ॥

prāte cali' āilā prabhu 'kānāira nāṭaśālā'
dekhila sakala tāhāṅ kṛṣṇa-caritra-līlā

SYNONYMS

prāte—in the morning; *cali'*—departing; *āilā*—came; *prabhu*—the Lord; *kānāira nāṭaśālā*—to the place of the name Kānāi Nāṭaśālā; *dekhila*—saw; *sakala*—all; *tāhāṅ*—there; *kṛṣṇa-caritra-līlā*—the pastimes of Kṛṣṇa.

TRANSLATION

In the morning, the Lord left and went to a place known as Kānāi Nāṭaśālā. While there, He saw many pastimes of Lord Kṛṣṇa.

PURPORT

In those days in Bengal there were many places known as Kānāi Nāṭaśālā, where pictures of the pastimes of Lord Kṛṣṇa were kept. People used to go there to see them. This is called *kṛṣṇa-caritra-līlā.* In Bengal there are still many places called *hari-sabhā,* which indicates a place where local people gather to chant the Hare Kṛṣṇa *mahā-mantra* and discuss the pastimes of Lord Kṛṣṇa. The word *kānāi* means "Lord Kṛṣṇa's," and *nāṭaśālā* indicates a place where pastimes are demonstrated. So those places which at the present moment are called *hari-sabhā* may previously have been known as Kānāi Nāṭaśālā.

TEXT 228

সেই রাত্রে প্রভু তাহাঁ চিন্তে মনে মন ।
সঙ্গে সংঘট্ট ভাল নহে, কৈল সনাতন ॥ ২২৮ ॥

sei rātre prabhu tāhāṅ cinte mane mana
saṅge saṅghaṭṭa bhāla nahe, kaila sanātana

SYNONYMS

sei rātre—that night; *prabhu*—the Lord; *tāhāṅ*—there; *cinte*—thinks; *mane*—within His mind; *mana*—the mind; *saṅge*—with Him; *saṅghaṭṭa*—crowds of men; *bhāla nahe*—is not good; *kaila sanātana*—Sanātana has so spoken.

TRANSLATION

That night the Lord considered Sanātana Gosvāmī's proposal that He should not go to Vṛndāvana followed by so many people.

TEXT 229

মথুরা যাইব আমি এত লোক সঙ্গে ।
কিছু সুখ না পাইব, হবে রসভঙ্গে ॥ ২২৯ ॥

mathurā yāiba āmi eta loka saṅge
kichu sukha nā pāiba, habe rasa-bhaṅge

SYNONYMS

mathurā—the holy place of the name Mathurā; *yāiba*—shall go; *āmi*—I; *eta*—so many; *loka*—people; *saṅge*—with; *kichu*—any; *sukha*—happiness;

nā—not; *pāiba*—I shall get; *habe*—there will be; *rasa-bhaṅge*—a disturbance in the atmosphere.

TRANSLATION

The Lord thought: "If I go to Mathurā with such crowds behind Me, it would not be a very happy situation, for the atmosphere would be disturbed."

PURPORT

Śrī Caitanya Mahāprabhu confirms that visiting a holy place like Vṛndāvana with so many people is simply disturbing. He would not find the happiness He desired by visiting such holy places in that way.

TEXT 230

একাকী যাইব, কিম্বা সঙ্গে এক জন।
তবে সে শোভয়ে বৃন্দাবনেরে গমন ॥ ২৩০ ॥

ekākī yāiba, kimvā saṅge eka jana
tabe se śobhaye vṛndāvanere gamana

SYNONYMS

ekākī—alone; *yāiba*—I shall go; *kimvā*—or; *saṅge*—with; *eka*—one; *jana*—person; *tabe*—then only; *se*—that; *śobhaye*—becomes beautiful; *vṛndāvanere*—to Vṛndāvana; *gamana*—going.

TRANSLATION

The Lord concluded that He would go alone to Vṛndāvana or, at most, would take only one person as His companion. In that way, going to Vṛndāvana would be very pleasant.

TEXT 231

এত চিন্তি প্রাতঃকালে গঙ্গাস্নান করি'।
'নীলাচলে যাব' বলি' চলিলা গৌরহরি ॥ ২৩১ ॥

eta cinti prātaḥ-kāle gaṅgā-snāna kari'
'nīlācale yāba' bali' calilā gaurahari

SYNONYMS

eta cinti—thus thinking; *prātaḥ-kāle*—in the morning; *gaṅgā-snāna*—bathing in the Ganges; *kari'*—performing; *nīlācale yāba*—I shall go to Nīlācala (Jagannātha Purī); *bali'*—saying; *calilā*—started; *gaurahari*—Śrī Caitanya Mahāprabhu.

TRANSLATION

Thinking like this, the Lord took His morning bath in the Ganges and started for Nīlācala, saying "I shall go there."

TEXT 232

এই মত চলি' চলি' আইলা শান্তিপুরে ।
দিন পাঁচ-সাত রহিলা আচার্যের ঘরে ॥ ২৩২ ॥

ei mata cali' cali' āilā śāntipure
dina pāṅca-sāta rahilā ācāryera ghare

SYNONYMS

ei mata—in this way; *cali' cali'*—walking; *āilā*—came; *śāntipure*—to Śāntipura; *dina pāṅca-sāta*—five or seven days; *rahilā*—remained; *ācāryera ghare*—at the house of Advaita Ācārya.

TRANSLATION

Walking and walking, Śrī Caitanya Mahāprabhu arrived at Śāntipura and remained at the house of Advaita Ācārya for five to seven days.

TEXT 233

শচীদেবী আনি' তাঁরে কৈল নমস্কার ।
সাত দিন তাঁর ঠাঞি ভিক্ষা-ব্যবহার ॥ ২৩৩ ॥

śacī-devī āni' tāṅre kaila namaskāra
sāta dina tāṅra ṭhāñi bhikṣā-vyavahāra

SYNONYMS

śacī-devī—mother Śacīdevī; *āni'*—calling her; *tāṅre*—unto Lord Caitanya Mahāprabhu; *kaila*—did; *namaskāra*—obeisances; *sāta dina*—seven days; *tāṅra ṭhāñi*—from Śacīdevī; *bhikṣā-vyavahāra*—accepting meals.

TRANSLATION

Taking this opportunity, Śrī Advaita Ācārya Prabhu sent for mother Śacīdevī, and she remained at His house for seven days to prepare the meals for Śrī Caitanya Mahāprabhu.

TEXT 234

তাঁর আজ্ঞা লঞা পুনঃ করিলা গমনে।
বিনয় করিয়া বিদায় দিল ভক্তগণে ॥ ২৩৪ ॥

tāṅra ājñā lañā punaḥ karilā gamane
vinaya kariyā vidāya dila bhakta-gaṇe

SYNONYMS

tāṅra ājñā lañā—taking the permission of mother Śacīdevī; *punaḥ*—again; *karilā*—did; *gamane*—starting; *vinaya kariyā*—by submitting pleasing words; *vidāya*—farewell; *dila*—gave; *bhakta-gaṇe*—to all the devotees.

TRANSLATION

Taking permission from His mother, Lord Caitanya Mahāprabhu started for Jagannātha Purī. When the devotees followed Him, He humbly begged them to remain and bade them all farewell.

TEXT 235

জনা দুই সঙ্গে আমি যাব নীলাচলে।
আমারে মিলিবা আসি' রথযাত্রা-কালে ॥ ২৩৫ ॥

janā dui saṅge āmi yāba nīlācale
āmāre milibā āsi' ratha-yātrā-kāle

SYNONYMS

janā—persons; *dui*—two; *saṅge*—with; *āmi*—I; *yāba*—shall go; *nīlācale*—to Jagannātha Purī; *āmāre*—Me; *milibā*—will meet; *āsi'*—coming there; *ratha-yātrā-kāle*—during the time of the car festival.

TRANSLATION

Śrī Caitanya Mahāprabhu, although requesting all the devotees to go back, allowed two people to follow Him. He requested all the devotees to come to Jagannātha Purī and meet Him during the car festival.

TEXT 236

বলভদ্র ভট্টাচার্য, আর পণ্ডিত দামোদর।
দুইজন-সঙ্গে প্রভু আইলা নীলাচল ॥ ২৩৬ ॥

balabhadra bhaṭṭācārya, āra paṇḍita dāmodara
dui-jana-saṅge prabhu āilā nīlācala

SYNONYMS

bala-bhadra bhaṭṭācārya—of the name Balabhadra Bhaṭṭācārya; *āra*—and; *paṇḍita dāmodara*—Dāmodara Paṇḍita; *dui-jana*—two persons; *saṅge*—with; *prabhu*—the Lord; *āilā*—went back; *nīlācala*—to Jagannātha Purī.

TRANSLATION

Two persons named Balabhadra Bhaṭṭācārya and Dāmodara Paṇḍita accompanied Śrī Caitanya Mahāprabhu to Jagannātha Purī [Nīlācala].

TEXT 237

দিন কত তাহাঁ রহি' চলিলা বৃন্দাবন।
লুকাঞা চলিলা রাত্রে, না জানে কোন জন ॥ ২৩৭ ॥

dina kata tāhāṅ rahi' calilā vṛndāvana
lukāñā calilā rātre, nā jāne kona jana

SYNONYMS

dina kata—a few days; *tāhāṅ*—at Jagannātha Purī; *rahi'*—remaining; *calilā*—started; *vṛndāvana*—for Vṛndāvana; *lukāñā*—keeping secret; *calilā*—started; *rātre*—at night; *nā jāne*—did not know; *kona*—some; *jana*—person.

TRANSLATION

After remaining at Jagannātha Purī for a few days, the Lord secretly started for Vṛndāvana at night. He did this without anyone's knowledge.

TEXT 238

বলভদ্র ভট্টাচার্য রহে মাত্র সঙ্গে।
ঝারিখণ্ড-পথে কাশী আইলা মহারঙ্গে ॥ ২৩৮ ॥

balabhadra bhaṭṭācārya rahe mātra saṅge
jhārikhaṇḍa-pathe kāśī āilā mahā-raṅge

SYNONYMS

bala-bhadra bhaṭṭācārya—of the name Balabhadra Bhaṭṭācārya; *rahe*—remains; *mātra*—only; *saṅge*—with Him; *jhāri-khaṇḍa-pathe*—on the way through Jhārikhaṇḍa (Madhya Pradesh); *kāśī*—in Benares; *āilā*—arrived; *mahā-raṅge*—with great delight.

TRANSLATION

When Śrī Caitanya Mahāprabhu left Jagannātha Purī for Vṛndāvana, only Balabhadra Bhaṭṭācārya was with Him. Thus He traveled on the path through Jhārikhaṇḍa and arrived in Benares with great delight.

TEXT 239

দিন চার কাশীতে রহি' গেলা বৃন্দাবন ।
মথুরা দেখিয়া দেখে দ্বাদশ কানন ॥ ২৩৯ ॥

dina cāra kāśīte rahi' gelā vṛndāvana
mathurā dekhiyā dekhe dvādaśa kānana

SYNONYMS

dina cāra—only four days; *kāśīte*—at Benares; *rahi'*—remaining; *gelā*—started for; *vṛndāvana*—the holy place Vṛndāvana; *mathurā*—the holy place Mathurā; *dekhiyā*—after seeing; *dekhe*—visits; *dvādaśa*—twelve; *kānana*—forests.

TRANSLATION

Śrī Caitanya Mahāprabhu stayed at Benares only four days and then left for Vṛndāvana. After seeing the town of Mathurā, He visited the twelve forests.

PURPORT

Those who visit the Vṛndāvana area today also generally visit twelve places, known as the twelve forests. They start at Mathurā, where there is Kāmya-vana. From there they go to Tāla-vana, Tamāla-vana, Madhu-vana, Kusuma-vana, Bhāṇḍīra-vana, Bilva-vana, Bhadra-vana, Khadira-vana, Loha-vana, Kumuda-vana and Gokula-mahāvana.

TEXT 240

লীলাস্থল দেখি' প্রেমে হইলা অস্থির ।
বলভদ্র কৈল তাঁরে মথুরার বাহির ॥ ২৪০ ॥

līlā-sthala dekhi' preme ha-ilā asthira
balabhadra kaila tāṅre mathurāra bāhira

SYNONYMS

līlā-sthala—all the holy places of Lord Kṛṣṇa's pastimes; *dekhi'*—visiting; *preme*—in great ecstasy; *ha-ilā*—became; *asthira*—agitated; *bala-bhadra*—of the name Balabhadra; *kaila*—assisted; *tāṅre*—Lord Caitanya Mahāprabhu; *mathurāra*—of the town of Mathurā; *bāhira*—outside.

TRANSLATION

When Śrī Caitanya Mahāprabhu visited all twelve places of Śrī Kṛṣṇa's pastimes, He became very agitated because of ecstasy. Balabhadra Bhaṭṭācārya somehow or other got Him out of Mathurā.

TEXT 241

গঙ্গাতীর-পথে লঞা প্রয়াগে আইলা ।
শ্রীরূপ আসি' প্রভুকে তথাই মিলিলা ॥ ২৪১ ॥

gaṅgā-tīra-pathe lañā prayāge āilā
śrī-rūpa āsi' prabhuke tathāi mililā

SYNONYMS

gaṅgā-tīra-pathe—the path on the bank of the Ganges; *lañā*—taking; *prayāge*—in Allahabad; *āilā*—arrived; *śrī-rūpa*—of the name Śrī Rūpa; *āsi'*—coming there; *prabhuke*—Lord Śrī Caitanya Mahāprabhu; *tathāi*—there; *mililā*—met.

TRANSLATION

After leaving Mathurā, the Lord began to walk along a path on the bank of the Ganges, and finally He reached the holy place named Prayāga [Allahabad]. It was there that Śrīla Rūpa Gosvāmī came and met the Lord.

TEXT 242

দণ্ডবৎ করি' রূপ ভূমিতে পড়িলা ।
পরম আনন্দে প্রভু আলিঙ্গন দিলা ॥ ২৪২ ॥

daṇḍavat kari' rūpa bhūmite paḍilā
parama ānande prabhu āliṅgana dilā

SYNONYMS

daṇḍavat kari'—offering obeisances; *rūpa*—Śrīla Rūpa Gosvāmī; *bhūmite*—on the ground; *paḍilā*—fell; *parama*—great; *ānande*—in delight; *prabhu*—the Lord; *āliṅgana*—embracing; *dilā*—gave.

TRANSLATION

At Prayāga, Rūpa Gosvāmī fell down on the ground to offer obeisances to the Lord, and the Lord embraced him with great delight.

TEXT 243

শ্রীরূপে শিক্ষা করাই' পাঠাইলা বৃন্দাবন ।
আপনে করিলা বারাণসী আগমন ॥ ২৪৩ ॥

śrī-rūpe śikṣā karāi' pāṭhāilā vṛndāvana
āpane karilā vārāṇasī āgamana

SYNONYMS

śrī-rūpe śikṣā karāi'—teaching Śrīla Rūpa Gosvāmī; *pāṭhāilā*—sent; *vṛndāvana*—toward Vṛndāvana; *āpane*—Himself; *karilā*—did; *vārāṇasī*—to Benares; *āgamana*—coming.

TRANSLATION

After instructing Śrīla Rūpa Gosvāmī at Prayāga at the Daśāśvamedha-ghāṭa, Caitanya Mahāprabhu ordered him to go to Vṛndāvana. The Lord then returned to Vārāṇasī.

TEXT 244

কাশীতে প্রভুকে আসি' মিলিলা সনাতন ।
দুই মাস রহি' তাঁরে করাইলা শিক্ষণ ॥ ২৪৪ ॥

kāśīte prabhuke āsi' mililā sanātana
dui māsa rahi' tāṅre karāilā śikṣaṇa

SYNONYMS

kāśīte—at Vārāṇasī; *prabhuke*—the Lord; *āsi'*—arriving; *mililā*—met; *sanātana*—of the name Sanātana Gosvāmī; *dui*—two; *māsa*—months; *rahi'*—remaining; *tāṅre*—unto him; *karāilā*—did; *śikṣaṇa*—instruction.

TRANSLATION

When Lord Caitanya Mahāprabhu arrived at Vārāṇasī, Sanātana Gosvāmī met Him there. The Lord remained there for two months and instructed Sanātana Gosvāmī perfectly.

TEXT 245

মথুরা পাঠাইলা তাঁরে দিয়া ভক্তিবল ।
সন্ন্যাসীরে কৃপা করি' গেলা নীলাচল ॥ ২৪৫ ॥

mathurā pāṭhāilā tāṅre diyā bhakti-bala
sannyāsīre kṛpā kari' gelā nīlācala

SYNONYMS

mathurā—to Mathurā; *pāṭhāilā*—sent; *tāṅre*—him; *diyā*—giving; *bhakti-bala*—the strength of devotion; *sannyāsīre*—unto the Māyāvādī *sannyāsīs; kṛpā*—mercy; *kari'*—giving; *gelā*—went back; *nīlācala*—to Jagannātha Purī.

TRANSLATION

After fully instructing Sanātana Gosvāmī, Śrī Caitanya Mahāprabhu sent him to Mathurā with empowered devotional service. In Benares He also bestowed His mercy upon the Māyāvādī sannyāsīs. He then returned to Nīlācala [Jagannātha Purī].

TEXT 246

ছয় বৎসর ঐছে প্রভু করিলা বিলাস ।
কভু ইতি-উতি, কভু ক্ষেত্রবাস ॥ ২৪৬ ॥

chaya vatsara aiche prabhu karilā vilāsa
kabhu iti-uti, kabhu kṣetra-vāsa

SYNONYMS

chaya vatsara—six years; *aiche*—in that way; *prabhu*—the Lord; *karilā*—did; *vilāsa*—pastimes; *kabhu*—sometimes; *iti-uti*—here and there; *kabhu*—sometimes; *kṣetra-vāsa*—residing at Jagannātha Purī.

TRANSLATION

The Lord traveled all over India for six years. He was sometimes here and sometimes there performing His transcendental pastimes, and sometimes He remained at Jagannātha Purī.

TEXT 247

আনন্দে ভক্ত-সঙ্গে সদা কীর্তন-বিলাস ।
জগন্নাথ-দরশন, প্রেমের বিলাস ॥ ২৪৭ ॥

ānande bhakta-saṅge sadā kīrtana-vilāsa
jagannātha-daraśana, premera vilāsa

SYNONYMS

ānande—in great delight; *bhakta-saṅge*—with devotees; *sadā*—always; *kīrtana*—of chanting; *vilāsa*—enjoyment; *jagannātha*—Lord Jagannātha; *daraśana*—visiting; *premera*—of ecstasy; *vilāsa*—pastimes.

TRANSLATION

While at Jagannātha Purī, the Lord passed His time in great joy by performing saṅkīrtana and visiting the temple of Jagannātha in great ecstasy.

TEXT 248

মধ্যলীলার কৈলুঁ এই সূত্র-বিবরণ ।
অন্ত্যলীলার সূত্র এবে শুন, ভক্তগণ ॥ ২৪৮ ॥

madhya-līlāra kailuṅ ei sūtra-vivaraṇa
antya-līlāra sūtra ebe śuna, bhakta-gaṇa

SYNONYMS

madhya-līlāra—of the *madhya-līlā,* the middle portion of His pastimes; *kailuṅ*—I made; *ei*—this; *sūtra*—synopsis; *vivaraṇa*—description; *antya-*

līlāra—of the pastimes at the end, known as *antya-līlā; sūtra*—synopsis; *ebe*—now; *śuna*—hear; *bhakta-gaṇa*—all devotees.

TRANSLATION

Thus I have given a synopsis of the madhya-līlā, the middle pastimes of the Lord. Now, O devotees, kindly hear the synopsis of the final pastimes of the Lord, known as antya-līlā.

TEXT 249

বৃন্দাবন হৈতে যদি নীলাচলে আইলা ।
আঠার বর্ষ তাহাঁ বাস, কাহাঁ নাহি গেলা ॥ ২৪৯ ॥

vṛndāvana haite yadi nīlācale āilā
āṭhāra varṣa tāhāṅ vāsa, kāhāṅ nāhi gelā

SYNONYMS

vṛndāvana haite—from Vṛndāvana; *yadi*—though; *nīlācale*—to Jagannātha Purī; *āilā*—came back; *āṭhāra*—eighteen; *varṣa*—years; *tāhāṅ*—at Jagannātha Purī; *vāsa*—residence; *kāhāṅ*—anywhere; *nāhi*—not; *gelā*—went.

TRANSLATION

When the Lord returned to Jagannātha Purī from Vṛndāvana, He remained there and did not go anywhere else for eighteen years.

TEXT 250

প্রতিবর্ষ আইসেন তাহাঁ গৌড়ের ভক্তগণ ।
চারি মাস রহে প্রভুর সঙ্গে সম্মিলন ॥ ২৫০ ॥

prativarṣa āisena tāhāṅ gauḍera bhakta-gaṇa
cāri māsa rahe prabhura saṅge sanmilana

SYNONYMS

prativarṣa—each year; *āisena*—visit; *tāhāṅ*—there; *gauḍera*—of Bengal; *bhakta-gaṇa*—all the devotees; *cāri*—four; *māsa*—months; *rahe*—remain; *prabhura*—Lord Caitanya Mahāprabhu; *saṅge*—with; *sanmilana*—meeting.

TRANSLATION

During those eighteen years, all the devotees of Bengal used to visit Him at Jagannātha Purī every year. They would remain there for four continuous months and enjoy the company of the Lord.

TEXT 251

নিরন্তর নৃত্যগীত কীর্তন-বিলাস।
আচণ্ডালে প্রেমভক্তি করিলা প্রকাশ ॥ ২৫১ ॥

nirantara nṛtya-gīta kīrtana-vilāsa
ācaṇḍāle prema-bhakti karilā prakāśa

SYNONYMS

nirantara—without stopping; *nṛtya-gīta*—chanting and dancing; *kīrtana*—of *saṅkīrtana; vilāsa*—enjoyment; *ācaṇḍāle*—to everyone, even to the lowest person; *prema-bhakti*—love of Godhead; *karilā*—did; *prakāśa*—manifestation.

TRANSLATION

At Jagannātha Purī, Śrī Caitanya Mahāprabhu performed chanting and dancing unceasingly. Thus He enjoyed the pastime of saṅkīrtana. He manifested His causeless mercy, pure love of God, to everyone, including the lowest man.

TEXT 252

পণ্ডিত-গোসাঞি কৈল নীলাচলে বাস।
বক্রেশ্বর, দামোদর, শঙ্কর, হরিদাস ॥ ২৫২ ॥

paṇḍita-gosāñi kaila nīlācale vāsa
vakreśvara, dāmodara, śaṅkara, haridāsa

SYNONYMS

paṇḍita-gosāñi—Gadādhara Paṇḍita; *kaila*—did; *nīlācale*—at Jagannātha Purī; *vāsa*—living; *vakreśvara*—of the name Vakreśvara; *dāmodara*—Dāmodara Paṇḍita; *śaṅkara*—of the name Śaṅkara; *hari-dāsa*—Haridāsa Ṭhākura.

TRANSLATION

Residing with the Lord at Jagannātha Purī were Paṇḍita Gosāñi and other devotees, such as Vakreśvara, Dāmodara, Śaṅkara and Haridāsa Ṭhākura.

TEXT 253

জগদানন্দ, ভগবান্, গোবিন্দ, কাশীশ্বর ।
পরমানন্দপুরী, আর স্বরূপ-দামোদর ॥ ২৫৩ ॥

jagadānanda, bhagavān, govinda, kāsīśvara
paramānanda-purī, āra svarūpa-dāmodara

SYNONYMS

jagadānanda—of the name Jagadānanda; *bhagavān*—of the name Bhagavān; *govinda*—of the name Govinda; *kāsīśvara*—of the name Kāsīśvara; *paramānanda-purī*—of the name Paramānanda Purī; *āra svarūpa-dāmodara*—and Svarūpa Dāmodara, His secretary.

TRANSLATION

Jagadānanda, Bhagavān, Govinda, Kāśīśvara, Paramānanda Purī and Svarūpa Dāmodara were other devotees who also lived with the Lord.

TEXT 254

ক্ষেত্রবাসী রামানন্দ রায় প্রভৃতি ।
প্রভুসঙ্গে এই সব কৈল নিত্যস্থিতি ॥ ২৫৪ ॥

kṣetra-vāsī rāmānanda rāya prabhṛti
prabhu-saṅge ei saba kaila nitya-sthiti

SYNONYMS

kṣetra-vāsī—residents of Jagannātha Purī; *rāmānanda rāya*—of the name Rāmānanda Rāya; *prabhṛti*—and others; *prabhu-saṅge*—with the Lord; *ei saba*—all of them; *kaila*—did; *nitya-sthiti*—permanently living.

TRANSLATION

Śrīla Rāmānanda Rāya and other devotees who were residents of Jagannātha Purī also remained permanently with the Lord.

TEXTS 255-256

অদ্বৈত, নিত্যানন্দ, মুকুন্দ, শ্রীবাস ।
বিদ্যানিধি, বাসুদেব, মুরারি,—যত দাস ॥ ২৫৫ ॥
প্রতিবর্ষে আইসে সঙ্গে রহে চারিমাস ।
তাঁ-সবা লঞা প্রভুর বিবিধ বিলাস ॥ ২৫৬ ॥

advaita, nityānanda, mukunda, śrīvāsa
vidyānidhi, vāsudeva, murāri,——yata dāsa

prativarṣe āise saṅge rahe cāri-māsa
tāṅ-sabā lañā prabhura vividha vilāsa

SYNONYMS

advaita—of the name Advaita; *nityānanda*—of the name Nityānanda; *mukunda*—of the name Mukunda; *śrīvāsa*—of the name Śrīvāsa; *vidyā-nidhi*—of the name Vidyānidhi; *vāsu-deva*—of the name Vāsudeva; *murāri*—of the name Murāri; *yata dāsa*—all servitors of the Lord; *prativarṣe*—each year; *āise*—go there; *saṅge*—in association; *rahe*—remain; *cāri-māsa*—four months; *tāṅ-sabā*—all of them; *lañā*—taking; *prabhura*—of the Lord; *vividha*—various; *vilāsa*—pastimes.

TRANSLATION

Other devotees of the Lord—headed by Advaita Ācārya, Nityānanda Prabhu, Mukunda, Śrīvāsa, Vidyānidhi, Vāsudeva and Murāri—used to visit Jagannātha Purī and remain with the Lord for four continuous months. The Lord enjoyed various pastimes in their company.

TEXT 257

হরিদাসের সিদ্ধিপ্রাপ্তি,—অদ্ভুত সে সব ।
আপনি মহাপ্রভু যাঁর কৈল মহোৎসব ॥ ২৫৭ ॥

haridāsera siddhi-prāpti,——adbhuta se saba
āpani mahāprabhu yāṅra kaila mahotsava

SYNONYMS

hari-dāsera—of Ṭhākura Haridāsa; *siddhi-prāpti*—passing away; *adbhuta*—wonderful; *se*—those; *saba*—all incidents; *āpani*—personally;

mahā-prabhu—Śrī Caitanya Mahāprabhu; *yāṅra*—whose; *kaila*—performed; *mahā-utsava*—festival.

TRANSLATION

At Jagannātha Purī, Haridāsa Ṭhākura passed away. The incident was very wonderful because the Lord Himself performed the festival of Ṭhākura Haridāsa's departure.

TEXT 258

তবে রূপ-গোসাঞির পুনরাগমন ।
তাঁহার হৃদয়ে কৈল প্রভু শক্তি-সঞ্চারণ ॥ ২৫৮ ॥

tabe rūpa-gosāñira punar-āgamana
tāṅhāra hṛdaye kaila prabhu śakti-sañcāraṇa

SYNONYMS

tabe—thereafter; *rūpa-gosāñira*—of Śrīla Rūpa Gosvāmī; *punaḥ-āgamana*—again coming there; *tāṅhāra*—of him; *hṛdaye*—in the heart; *kaila*—did; *prabhu*—the Lord; *śakti-sañcāraṇa*—invoking of transcendental power.

TRANSLATION

At Jagannātha Purī Śrīla Rūpa Gosvāmī met the Lord again, and the Lord invested his heart with all transcendental power.

TEXT 259

তবে ছোট হরিদাসে প্রভু কৈল দণ্ড ।
দামোদর-পণ্ডিত কৈল প্রভুকে বাক্য-দণ্ড ॥ ২৫৯ ॥

tabe choṭa haridāse prabhu kaila daṇḍa
dāmodara-paṇḍita kaila prabhuke vākya-daṇḍa

SYNONYMS

tabe—thereafter; *choṭa hari-dāse*—unto Junior Haridāsa; *prabhu*—the Lord; *kaila*—did; *daṇḍa*—punishment; *dāmodara-paṇḍita*—of the name Dāmodara Paṇḍita; *kaila*—did; *prabhuke*—unto the Lord; *vākya-daṇḍa*—chastisement as a warning.

TRANSLATION

After this, the Lord punished the Junior Haridāsa, and Dāmodara Paṇḍita gave some warning to the Lord.

PURPORT

Actually Dāmodara Paṇḍita was the eternal servant of the Lord. He could not punish the Lord at any time, nor had he any desire to, but He did give some warning to the Lord so that others would not blaspheme Him. Of course, He should have known that the Lord is the Supreme Personality of Godhead and is free to act in any way. There is no need to warn Him, and such an action is not very much appreciated by advanced devotees.

TEXT 260

তবে সনাতন-গোসাঞিির পুনরাগমন ।
জ্যৈষ্ঠমাসে প্রভু তাঁরে কৈল পরীক্ষণ ॥ ২৬০ ॥

tabe sanātana-gosāñira punar-āgamana
jyaiṣṭha-māse prabhu tāṅre kaila parīkṣaṇa

SYNONYMS

tabe—thereafter; *sanātana-gosāñira*—of Sanātana Gosvāmī; *punaḥ-āgamana*—again coming; *jyaiṣṭha-māse*—in the month of Jyaiṣṭha (May-June); *prabhu*—the Lord; *tāṅre*—him; *kaila*—did; *parīkṣaṇa*—examination.

TRANSLATION

Thereafter Sanātana Gosvāmī met the Lord again, and the Lord tested him in scorching heat during the month of Jyaiṣṭha.

TEXT 261

তুষ্ট হঞা প্রভু তাঁরে পাঠাইলা বৃন্দাবন ।
অদ্বৈতের হস্তে প্রভুর অদ্ভুত ভোজন ॥ ২৬১ ॥

tuṣṭa hañā prabhu tāṅre pāṭhāilā vṛndāvana
advaitera haste prabhura adbhuta bhojana

SYNONYMS

tuṣṭa hañā—being very much pleased; *prabhu*—the Lord; *tāṅre*—him; *pāṭhāilā*—sent back; *vṛndāvana*—to Vṛndāvana; *advaitera*—of Advaita

Ācārya; *haste*—in the hands; *prabhura*—of the Lord; *adbhuta*—wonderful; *bhojana*—feasting.

TRANSLATION

Being pleased, the Lord sent Sanātana Gosvāmī back to Vṛndāvana. After that, He was fed wonderfully by the hands of Śrī Advaita Ācārya.

TEXT 262

নিত্যানন্দ-সঙ্গে যুক্তি করিয়া নিভৃতে ।
তাঁরে পাঠাইলা গৌড়ে প্রেম প্রচারিতে ॥ ২৬২ ॥

nityāṇanda-saṅge yukti kariyā nibhṛte
tāṅre pāṭhāilā gauḍe prema pracārite

SYNONYMS

nityānanda-saṅge—with Nityānanda Prabhu; *yukti*—discussion; *kariyā*—making; *nibhṛte*—in privacy; *tāṅre*—Him; *pāṭhāilā*—sent; *gauḍe*—to Bengal; *prema*—love of Godhead; *pracārite*—to preach.

TRANSLATION

After sending Sanātana Gosvāmī back to Vṛndāvana, the Lord privately consulted with Śrī Nityānanda Prabhu. He then sent Him to Bengal to preach love of Godhead.

TEXT 263

তবে ত' বল্লভ ভট্ট প্রভুরে মিলিলা ।
কৃষ্ণনামের অর্থ প্রভু তাঁহারে কহিলা ॥ ২৬৩ ॥

tabe ta' vallabha bhaṭṭa prabhure mililā
kṛṣṇa-nāmera artha prabhu tāṅhāre kahilā

SYNONYMS

tabe ta'—thereafter; *vallabha bhaṭṭa*—of the name Vallabha Bhaṭṭa; *prabhure*—Lord Śrī Caitanya Mahāprabhu; *mililā*—met; *kṛṣṇa-nāmera*—of the holy name of Kṛṣṇa; *artha*—import; *prabhu*—the Lord; *tāṅhāre*—unto him; *kahilā*—explained.

TRANSLATION

Soon afterward, Vallabha Bhaṭṭa met the Lord at Jagannātha Purī, and the Lord explained to him the import of the holy name of Kṛṣṇa.

PURPORT

This Vallabha Bhaṭṭa is the head of the Vaiṣṇava *sampradāya* known as the Vallabhācārya-sampradāya in western India. There is a long story about Vallabha Ācārya narrated in the *Caitanya-caritāmṛta,* specifically in the Seventh Chapter of *Antya-līlā* and the Nineteenth Chapter of *Madhya-līlā.* Lord Caitanya Mahāprabhu visited the house of Vallabha Ācārya on the other side of Prayāga in a place known as Ādāila-grāma. Later, Vallabha Bhaṭṭa saw Caitanya Mahāprabhu at Jagannātha Purī to explain his commentary on *Śrīmad-Bhāgavatam.* He was very proud of his writings, but Śrī Caitanya Mahāprabhu corrected him, telling him that a Vaiṣṇava should be humble and follow in the footsteps of his predecessors. The Lord told him that his pride in being superior to Śrīdhara Svāmī was not at all befitting a Vaiṣṇava.

TEXT 264

প্রদ্যুম্ন মিশ্রেরে প্রভু রামানন্দ-স্থানে ।
কৃষ্ণকথা শুনাইল কহি' তাঁর গুণে ॥ ২৬৪ ॥

pradyumna miśrere prabhu rāmānanda-sthāne
kṛṣṇa-kathā śunāila kahi' tāṅra guṇe

SYNONYMS

pradyumna miśrere—of the name Pradyumna Miśra; *prabhu*—Lord Caitanya Mahāprabhu; *rāmānanda-sthāne*—at the place of Rāmānanda Rāya; *kṛṣṇa-kathā*—topics of Lord Śrī Kṛṣṇa; *śunāila*—caused to hear; *kahi'*—explaining; *tāṅra*—of Rāmānanda Rāya; *guṇe*—the transcendental qualities.

TRANSLATION

After explaining the transcendental qualities of Rāmānanda Rāya, the Lord sent Pradyumna Miśra to the residence of Rāmānanda Rāya, and Pradyumna Miśra learned kṛṣṇa-kathā from him.

TEXT 265

গোপীনাথ পট্টনায়ক—রামানন্দ-ভ্রাতা ।
রাজা মারিতেছিল, প্রভু হৈল ত্রাতা ॥ ২৬৫ ॥

gopīnātha paṭṭanāyaka——rāmānanda-bhrātā
rājā māritechila, prabhu haila trātā

SYNONYMS

gopīnātha paṭṭa-nāyaka—of the name Gopīnātha Paṭṭanāyaka; *rāmānanda-bhrātā*—the brother of Śrī Rāmānanda Rāya; *rājā*—the King; *māritechila*—condemned to death; *prabhu*—Lord Caitanya Mahāprabhu; *haila*—became; *trātā*—the deliverer.

TRANSLATION

After this, Lord Caitanya Mahāprabhu saved Gopīnātha Paṭṭanāyaka, the younger brother of Rāmānanda Rāya, from being condemned to death by the King.

TEXT 266

রামচন্দ্রপুরী-ভয়ে ভিক্ষা ঘাটাইলা ।
বৈষ্ণবের দুঃখ দেখি' অর্দ্ধেক রাখিলা ॥ ২৬৬ ॥

rāmacandra-purī-bhaye bhikṣā ghāṭāilā
vaiṣṇavera duḥkha dekhi' ardheka rākhilā

SYNONYMS

rāmacandra-purī-bhaye—by the fear of Rāmacandra Purī; *bhikṣā*—the proportion of eating; *ghāṭāilā*—decreased; *vaiṣṇavera*—of all the Vaiṣṇavas; *duḥkha*—unhappiness; *dekhi'*—understanding; *ardheka*—half of the portion; *rākhilā*—kept.

TRANSLATION

Rāmacandra Purī criticized Lord Caitanya Mahāprabhu's eating; therefore the Lord reduced His eating to a minimum. However, when all the Vaiṣṇavas became very sorry, the Lord increased His portion to half as much as usual.

TEXT 267

ব্রহ্মাণ্ড-ভিতরে হয় চৌদ্দ ভুবন ।
চৌদ্দভুবনে বৈসে যত জীবগণ ॥ ২৬৭ ॥

brahmāṇḍa-bhitare haya caudda bhuvana
caudda-bhuvane baise yata jīva-gaṇa

SYNONYMS

brahmāṇḍa-bhitare—within the universe; *haya*—there are; *caudda bhuvana*—fourteen planetary systems; *caudda-bhuvane*—in those fourteen planetary systems; *baise*—reside; *yata*—as many as there are; *jīva-gaṇa*—living entities.

TRANSLATION

There are fourteen planetary systems within the universe, and all living entities reside in those planetary systems.

TEXT 268

মনুষ্যের বেশ ধরি' যাত্রিকের ছলে ।
প্রভুর দর্শন করে আসি' নীলাচলে ॥ ২৬৮ ॥

manuṣyera veśa dhari' yātrikera chale
prabhura darśana kare āsi' nīlācale

SYNONYMS

manuṣyera—of human beings; *veśa dhari'*—dressing themselves; *yātrikera chale*— as if pilgrims; *prabhura*—of Lord Caitanya Mahāprabhu; *darśana kare*—visit; *āsi'*—coming; *nīlācale*—to Jagannātha Purī.

TRANSLATION

Dressing like human beings on pilgrimage, they all used to come to Jagannātha Purī to visit Śrī Caitanya Mahāprabhu.

TEXT 269

একদিন শ্রীবাসাদি যত ভক্তগণ ।
মহাপ্রভুর গুণ গাঞা করেন কীর্তন ॥ ২৬৯ ॥

eka-dina śrīvāsādi yata bhakta-gaṇa
mahāprabhura guṇa gāñā karena kīrtana

SYNONYMS

eka-dina—one day; *śrīvāsa-ādi*—Śrīvāsa Ṭhākura and others; *yata*—all; *bhakta-gaṇa*—devotees; *mahāprabhura*—of Lord Caitanya Mahāprabhu; *guṇa*— qualities; *gāñā*—describing; *karena*—perform; *kīrtana*—chanting.

TRANSLATION

One day all the devotees, headed by Śrīvāsa Ṭhākura, were chanting the transcendental qualities of Śrī Caitanya Mahāprabhu.

TEXT 270

শুনি' ভক্তগণে কহে সক্রোধ বচনে ।
কৃষ্ণ-নাম-গুণ ছাড়ি, কি কর কীর্তনে ॥ ২৭০ ॥

śuni' bhakta-gaṇe kahe sa-krodha vacane
kṛṣṇa-nāma-guṇa chāḍi, ki kara kīrtane

SYNONYMS

śuni'—hearing this; *bhakta-gaṇe*—to all the devotees; *kahe*—the Lord says; *sa-krodha vacane*—talking in an angry mood; *kṛṣṇa-nāma-guṇa chāḍi*—leaving aside the transcendental qualities and the name of the Lord; *ki kara kīrtane*—what kind of chanting are you performing.

TRANSLATION

Not liking the chanting of His transcendental qualities, Śrī Caitanya Mahāprabhu chastised them as if He were angry. "What kind of chanting is this?" He asked. "Are you leaving aside the chanting of the holy name of the Lord?"

TEXT 271

ঔদ্ধত্য করিতে হৈল সবাকার মন ।
স্বতন্ত্র হইয়া সবে নাশা'বে ভুবন ॥ ২৭১ ॥

auddhatya karite haila sabākāra mana
svatantra ha-iyā sabe nāśā 'be bhuvana

SYNONYMS

auddhatya—impudence; *karite*—to do; *haila*—was; *sabākāra*—of all of you; *mana*—the mind; *svatantra*—independent; *ha-iyā*—becoming; *sabe*—all of you; *nāśā 'be*—will spoil; *bhuvana*—the whole world.

TRANSLATION

Thus Śrī Caitanya Mahāprabhu chastised all the devotees, telling them not to show impudence and spoil the entire world by becoming independent.

PURPORT

Śrī Caitanya Mahāprabhu warned all His followers not to become independent or impudent. Unfortunately, after the disappearance of Lord Caitanya Mahāprabhu, many *apa-sampradāyas* (so-called followers) invented many ways not approved by the *ācāryas*. Bhaktivinoda Ṭhākura has described them as: the *āula, bāula, karttābhajā, neḍā, daraveśa, sāni sahajiyā, sakhībhekī, smārta, jāta-gosāñi, ativāḍī, cūḍādhārī* and *gaurāṅga-nāgarī.*

The *āula-sampradāya, bāula-sampradāya* and others invented their own ways of understanding Lord Caitanya's philosophy without following in the footsteps of the *ācāryas.* Śrī Caitanya Mahāprabhu Himself indicates herein that all such attempts would simply spoil the spirit of His cult.

TEXT 272

দশদিকে কোটী কোটী লোক হেন কালে।
'জয় কৃষ্ণচৈতন্য' বলি' করে কোলাহলে ॥ ২৭২ ॥

daśa-dike koṭī koṭī loka hena kāle
'jaya kṛṣṇa-caitanya' bali' kare kolāhale

SYNONYMS

daśa-dike—in the ten directions; *koṭī koṭī*—many thousands of men; *loka*—people; *hena kāle*—at this time; *jaya kṛṣṇa-caitanya*—all glories to Lord Caitanya Mahāprabhu; *bali'*—loudly crying; *kare*—make; *kolāhale*—a tumultuous sound.

TRANSLATION

When Śrī Caitanya Mahāprabhu was apparently in an angry mood and chastising His devotees, many thousands of people outside loudly cried in a tumultuous voice: "All glories to Śrī Caitanya Mahāprabhu!"

TEXT 273

জয় জয় মহাপ্রভু—ব্রজেন্দ্রকুমার।
জগৎ তারিতে প্রভু, তোমার অবতার ॥ ২৭৩ ॥

jaya jaya mahāprabhu——vrajendra-kumāra
jagat tārite prabhu, tomāra avatāra

SYNONYMS

jaya jaya mahāprabhu—all glories to Lord Caitanya Mahāprabhu; *vrajendra-kumāra*—originally Lord Kṛṣṇa, the son of Mahārāja Nanda; *jagat*—the whole world; *tārite*—to deliver; *prabhu*—the Lord; *tomāra*—Your; *avatāra*—incarnation.

TRANSLATION

All the people began to call very loudly: "All glories to Śrī Caitanya Mahāprabhu, who is the son of Mahārāja Nanda! Now You have appeared to deliver the whole world!

TEXT 274

বহুদূর হৈতে আইনু হঞা বড় আর্ত ।
দরশন দিয়া প্রভু করহ কৃতার্থ ॥ ২৭৪ ॥

bahu-dūra haite āinu hañā baḍa ārta
daraśana diyā prabhu karaha kṛtārtha

SYNONYMS

bahu-dūra—a long distance; *haite*—from; *āinu*—we have come; *hañā*—becoming; *baḍa*—very much; *ārta*—aggrieved; *daraśana*—audience; *diyā*—giving; *prabhu*—O Lord; *karaha*—kindly show; *kṛta-artha*—favor.

TRANSLATION

"O Lord, we are very unhappy. We have come a long distance to see You. Please be merciful and show us Your favor."

TEXT 275

শুনিয়া লোকের দৈন্য দ্রবিলা হৃদয় ।
বাহিরে আসি' দরশন দিলা দয়াময় ॥ ২৭৫ ॥

śuniyā lokera dainya dravilā hṛdaya
bāhire āsi' daraśana dilā dayā-maya

SYNONYMS

śuniyā—hearing; *lokera*—of the people; *dainya*—humility; *dravilā*—became softened; *hṛdaya*—the heart; *bāhire*—outside; *āsi'*—coming; *daraśana*—audience; *dilā*—gave; *dayā-maya*—the merciful.

TRANSLATION

When the Lord heard the humble petition made by the people, his heart softened. Being very merciful, He immediately came out and gave audience to all of them.

TEXT 276

বাহু তুলি' বলে প্রভু বল' 'হরি' 'হরি' ।
উঠিল—শ্রীহরিধ্বনি চতুর্দিক্ ভরি' ॥ ২৭৬ ॥

bāhu tuli' bale prabhu bala' 'hari' 'hari'
uṭhila——śrī-hari-dhvani catur-dik bhari'

SYNONYMS

bāhu tuli'—raising the arms; *bale*—says; *prabhu*—the Lord; *bala'*—speak; *hari hari*—the holy name of the Lord, Hari; *uṭhila*—arose; *śrī-hari-dhvani*—vibration of the sound Hari; *catuḥ-dik*—the four directions; *bhari'*—filling.

TRANSLATION

Raising His arms, the Lord asked everyone to chant loudly the vibration of the holy name of Lord Hari. There immediately arose a great stir, and the vibration of "Hari!" filled all directions.

TEXT 277

প্রভু দেখি' প্রেমে লোক আনন্দিত মন ।
প্রভুকে ঈশ্বর বলি' করয়ে স্তবন ॥ ২৭৭ ॥

prabhu dekhi' preme loka ānandita mana
prabhuke īśvara bali' karaye stavana

SYNONYMS

prabhu dekhi'—seeing the Lord; *preme*—in ecstasy; *loka*—all people; *ānandita*—joyous; *mana*—the mind; *prabhuke*—the Lord; *īśvara*—as the Supreme Lord; *bali'*—accepting; *karaye*—did; *stavana*—prayer.

TRANSLATION

Seeing the Lord, everyone became joyful out of love. Everyone accepted the Lord as the Supreme, and thus they offered their prayers.

TEXT 278

স্তব শুনি' প্রভুকে কহেন শ্রীনিবাস।
ঘরে গুপ্ত হও, কেনে বাহিরে প্রকাশ ॥ ২৭৮ ॥

stava śuni' prabhuke kahena śrīnivāsa
ghare gupta hao, kene bāhire prakāśa

SYNONYMS

stava—prayers; *śuni'*—hearing; *prabhuke*—unto the Lord; *kahena*—says; *śrīnivāsa*—Śrīnivāsa Ācārya; *ghare*—at home; *gupta*—covered; *hao*—You are; *kene*—why; *bāhire*—outside; *prakāśa*—manifested.

TRANSLATION

While the people were offering their prayers unto the Lord, Śrīnivāsa Ācārya sarcastically said to the Lord: "At home, You wanted to be covered. Why have You exposed Yourself outside?"

TEXT 279

কে শিখাল এই লোকে, কহে কোন্ বাত।
ইহা-সবার মুখ ঢাক দিয়া নিজ হাত ॥ ২৭৯ ॥

ke śikhāla ei loke, kahe kon vāta
ihā-sabāra mukha ḍhāka diyā nija hāta

SYNONYMS

ke—who; *śikhāla*—taught; *ei*—these; *loke*—people; *kahe*—they say; *kon*—what; *vāta*—topics; *ihā*—of them; *sabāra*—of all; *mukha*—the mouths; *ḍhāka*—just cover; *diyā*—with; *nija*—Your own; *hāta*—hand.

TRANSLATION

Śrīnivāsa Ācārya continued: "Who has taught these people? What are they saying? Now You can cover their mouths with Your own hand.

TEXT 280

সূর্য যৈছে উদয় করি' চাহে লুকাইতে ।
বুঝিতে না পারি তৈছে তোমার চরিতে ॥ ২৮০ ॥

sūrya yaiche udaya kari' cāhe lukāite
bujhite nā pāri taiche tomāra carite

SYNONYMS

sūrya—the sun; *yaiche*—just like; *udaya*—appearance; *kari'*—making; *cāhe*—wants; *lukāite*—to hide; *bujhite*—to understand; *nā*—not; *pāri*—able; *taiche*—similarly; *tomāra*—Your; *carite*—in the character.

TRANSLATION

"It is as if the sun, after rising, wanted to hide itself. We cannot understand such characteristics in Your behavior."

TEXT 281

প্রভু কহেন,—শ্রীনিবাস, ছাড় বিড়ম্বনা ।
সবে মেলি' কর মোর কতেক লাঞ্ছনা ॥ ২৮১ ॥

prabhu kahena,—śrīnivāsa, chāḍa viḍambanā
sabe meli' kara mora kateka lāñcanā

SYNONYMS

prabhu—the Lord; *kahena*—says; *śrīnivāsa*—My dear Śrīnivāsa; *chāḍa*—give up; *viḍambanā*—all these jokes; *sabe*—all of you; *meli'*—together; *kara*—do; *mora*—of Me; *kateka*—so much; *lāñcanā*—humiliation.

TRANSLATION

The Lord replied: "My dear Śrīnivāsa, please stop joking. You have all combined together to humiliate Me in this way."

TEXT 282

এত বলি' লোকে করি' শুভদৃষ্টি দান ।
অভ্যন্তরে গেলা, লোকের পূর্ণ হৈল কাম ॥ ২৮২ ॥

eta bali' loke kari' śubha-dṛṣṭi dāna
abhyantare gelā, lokera pūrṇa haila kāma

SYNONYMS

eta bali'—thus saying; *loke*—unto the people; *kari'*—doing; *śubha-dṛṣṭi*—auspicious glance; *dāna*—charity; *abhyantare*—within the room; *gelā*—went; *lokera*—of all the people; *pūrṇa*—fulfilled; *haila*—was; *kāma*—the desire.

TRANSLATION

Thus speaking, the Lord entered His room after glancing auspiciously upon the people out of charity. In this way the desires of the people were completely fulfilled.

TEXT 283

রঘুনাথ-দাস নিত্যানন্দ-পাশে গেলা ।
চিড়া-দধি-মহোৎসব তাহাঁই করিলা ॥ ২৮৩ ॥

raghunātha-dāsa nityānanda-pāśe gelā
ciḍā-dadhi-mahotsava tāhāṅi karilā

SYNONYMS

raghunātha-dāsa—of the name Raghunātha dāsa; *nityānanda*—Lord Nityānanda; *pāśe*—near; *gelā*—went; *ciḍā*—chipped rice; *dadhi*—curd; *mahotsava*—festival; *tāhāṅi*—there; *karilā*—performed.

TRANSLATION

At this time, Raghunātha dāsa approached Śrī Nityānanda Prabhu and, according to His order, prepared a feast and distributed prasāda composed of chipped rice and curd.

PURPORT

There is a special preparation in Bengal wherein chipped rice is mixed with curd and sometimes with *sandeśa* and mango. It is a very palatable food offered to the Deity and then distributed to the public. Raghunātha dāsa Gosvāmī, who was a householder at this time, met Nityānanda Prabhu. According to His advice, he executed this festival of *dadhi-ciḍā-prasāda*.

TEXT 284

তাঁর আজ্ঞা লঞা গেলা প্রভুর চরণে ।
প্রভু তাঁরে সমর্পিলা স্বরূপের স্থানে ॥ ২৮৪ ॥

tāṅra ājñā lañā gelā prabhura caraṇe
prabhu tāṅre samarpilā svarūpera sthāne

SYNONYMS

tāṅra—His; *ājñā*—order; *lañā*—taking; *gelā*—approached; *prabhura*—of Caitanya Mahāprabhu; *caraṇe*—the lotus feet; *prabhu*—the Lord; *tāṅre*—him; *samarpilā*—handed over; *svarūpera*—of Svarūpa Dāmodara; *sthāne*—to the place.

TRANSLATION

Later, Śrīla Raghunātha dāsa Gosvāmī left home and took shelter of Śrī Caitanya Mahāprabhu at Jagannātha Purī. At that time, the Lord received him and placed him under the care of Svarūpa Dāmodara for spiritual enlightenment.

PURPORT

In this regard, Śrīla Raghunātha dāsa Gosvāmī writes in *Vilāpa-kusumāñjali* (5):

yo māṁ dustara-geha-nirjala-mahā-kūpād apāra-klamāt
sadyaḥ sāndra-dayāmbudhiḥ prakṛtitaḥ svairī-kṛpāraj-jubhiḥ
uddhṛty-ātma-saroja-nindi-caraṇa-prāntaṁ prapādya svayaṁ
śrī-dāmodara-sāc cakāra tam ahaṁ caitanya-candraṁ bhaje

"Let me offer my respectful obeisances unto the lotus feet of Śrī Caitanya Mahāprabhu, who, by His unreserved mercy, kindly saved me from household life, which is exactly like a blind well without water, and placed me in the ocean of transcendental joy under the care of Svarūpa Dāmodara Gosvāmī."

TEXT 285

ব্রহ্মানন্দ-ভারতীর ঘুচাইল চর্মাম্বর ।
এই মত লীলা কৈল ছয় বৎসর ॥ ২৮৫ ॥

brahmānanda-bhāratīra ghucāila carmāmbara
ei mata līlā kaila chaya vatsara

SYNONYMS

brahmānanda-bhāratīra—of Brahmānanda Bhāratī; *ghucāila*—vanquished; *carma-ambara*—dress of skin; *ei mata*—in this way; *līlā*—pastimes; *kaila*—performed; *chaya vatsara*—six years.

TRANSLATION

Later, Śrī Caitanya Mahāprabhu stopped Brahmānanda Bhāratī's habit of wearing deerskin. The Lord thus enjoyed His pastimes continuously for six years, experiencing varieties of transcendental bliss.

TEXT 286

এই ত' কহিল মধ্যলীলার সূত্রগণ ।
শেষ দ্বাদশ বৎসরের শুন বিবরণ ॥ ২৮৬ ॥

ei ta' kahila madhya-līlāra sūtra-gaṇa
śeṣa dvādaśa vatsarera śuna vivaraṇa

SYNONYMS

ei ta'—thus; *kahila*—explained; *madhya-līlāra*—of the middle pastimes; *sūtra-gaṇa*—the codes; *śeṣa*—last; *dvādaśa*—twelve; *vatsarera*—of the years; *śuna*—hear; *vivaraṇa*—the description.

TRANSLATION

I have thus given the codes of the madhya-līlā. Now please hear the pastimes the Lord performed during the last twelve years.

PURPORT

Thus Śrīla Kavirāja Gosvāmī, strictly following in the footsteps of Śrī Vyāsadeva, gives a synopsis of the *līlās* of *Caitanya-caritāmṛta*. He has given such a description at the end of each canto. In the *Ādi-līlā* he outlined the pastimes of the Lord in the five stages of boyhood, leaving the details of the description to Śrīla Vṛndāvana dāsa Ṭhākura. Now in this chapter the pastimes that took place at the end of the Lord's life are summarized. These are described in the *Madhya-līlā* and *Antya-līlā*. The rest of the pastimes have been described in codes in the Second Chapter of *Madhya-līlā*. In this way the author has gradually described both the *Madhya-līlā* and *Antya-līlā*.

TEXT 287

শ্রীরূপ-রঘুনাথ-পদে যার আশ।
চৈতন্যচরিতামৃত কহে কৃষ্ণদাস ॥ ২৮৭ ॥

śrī-rūpa-raghunātha-pade yāra āśa
caitanya-caritāmṛta kahe kṛṣṇadāsa

SYNONYMS

śrī-rūpa—Śrīla Rūpa Gosvāmī; *raghunātha*—Śrīla Raghunātha dāsa Gosvāmī; *pade*—at the lotus feet; *yāra*—whose; *āśa*—expectation; *caitanya-caritāmṛta*—the book named *Caitanya-caritāmṛta; kahe*—describes; *kṛṣṇa-dāsa*—Śrīla Kṛṣṇadāsa Kavirāja Gosvāmī.

TRANSLATION

Praying at the lotus feet of Śrī Rūpa and Śrī Raghunātha, always desiring their mercy, I, Kṛṣṇadāsa, narrate Śrī-Caitanya-caritāmṛta, following in their footsteps.

Thus end the Bhaktivedanta purports of the Śrī Caitanya-caritāmṛta, Madhya-līlā, *Chapter One, summarizing the later pastimes of Lord Śrī Caitanya Mahāprabhu.*

CHAPTER 2

The Ecstatic Manifestations of Lord Śrī Caitanya Mahāprabhu

In the Second Chapter of *Madhya-līlā,* the author describes the pastimes the Lord performed during the last twelve years of His life. Thus he has also described some of the pastimes of *Antya-līlā.* Why he has done so is very difficult for an ordinary person to understand. The author expects that reading the pastimes of the Lord will gradually help a person awaken his dormant love of Kṛṣṇa. Actually this *Caitanya-caritāmṛta* was compiled by the author during very old age. Therefore the codes of *Antya-līlā* are also described in the Second Chapter. Śrīla Kavirāja Gosvāmī has confirmed that the opinion of Svarūpa Dāmodara is authoritative in the matter of devotional service. Over and above this are the notes of Svarūpa Dāmodara, memorized by Raghunātha dāsa Gosvāmī, who also helped in the compilation of *Caitanya-caritāmṛta.* After the disappearance of Svarūpa Dāmodara Gosvāmī, Raghunātha dāsa Gosvāmī went to see Vṛndāvana. At that time the author, Śrīla Kavirāja Gosvāmī, met Raghunātha dāsa Gosvāmī, by whose mercy he also could memorize all the notes. In this way the author was able to complete this transcendental literature, *Śrī Caitanya-caritāmṛta.*

TEXT 1

বিচ্ছেদেঽস্মিন্ প্রভোরন্ত্যলীলা-সূত্রানুবর্ণনে ।
গৌরস্য কৃষ্ণবিচ্ছেদপ্রলাপাদ্যনুবর্ণ্যতে ॥ ১ ॥

vicchede 'smin prabhor antya-
līlā-sūtrānuvarṇane
gaurasya kṛṣṇa-viccheda-
pralāpādy anuvarṇyate

SYNONYMS

vicchede—in the chapter; *asmin*—this; *prabhoḥ*—of the Lord; *antya-līlā*—of the last division of His pastimes; *sūtra*—of the codes; *anuvarṇane*—in the matter of description; *gaurasya*—of Lord Śrī Caitanya Mahāprabhu; *kṛṣṇa-vic-cheda*—of separation from Kṛṣṇa; *pralāpa*—craziness; *ādi*—other subject matters; *anuvarṇyate*—is being described.

TRANSLATION

While relating in synopsis form the last division of the pastimes of Lord Caitanya Mahāprabhu, in this chapter I shall describe the Lord's transcendental ecstasy, which appears like madness due to His separation from Kṛṣṇa.

PURPORT

In this Second Chapter, the activities of Lord Caitanya that took place after the Lord accepted *sannyāsa* are generally described. Śrī Caitanya Mahāprabhu is specifically mentioned here as being *gaura,* or of fair complexion. Kṛṣṇa is generally known to be blackish, but when He is absorbed in the thought of the *gopīs,* who are all of fair complexion, Kṛṣṇa Himself also becomes fair. Śrī Caitanya Mahāprabhu in particular felt separation from Kṛṣṇa very deeply, exactly like a lover who is dejected in separation from the beloved. Such feelings, which were expressed by Śrī Caitanya Mahāprabhu for nearly twelve years at the end of His pastimes, are described in brief in this Second Chapter of *Madhya-līlā.*

TEXT 2

জয় জয় শ্রীচৈতন্য জয় নিত্যানন্দ ।
জয়াদ্বৈতচন্দ্র জয় গৌরভক্তবৃন্দ ॥ ২ ॥

jaya jaya śrī-caitanya jaya nityānanda
jayādvaitacandra jaya gaura-bhakta-vṛnda

SYNONYMS

jaya jaya śrī-caitanya—all glories to Śrī Caitanya Mahāprabhu; *jaya nityā-nanda*—all glories to Lord Nityānanda; *jaya advaita-candra*—all glories to Advaita Prabhu; *jaya gaura-bhakta-vṛnda*—all glories to the devotees of the Lord.

TRANSLATION

All glories to Śrī Caitanya Mahāprabhu! All glories to Lord Nityānanda! All glories to Advaitacandra! All glories to all the devotees of the Lord!

TEXT 3

শেষ যে রহিল প্রভুর দ্বাদশ বৎসর ।
কৃষ্ণের বিয়োগ-স্ফূর্তি হয় নিরন্তর ॥ ৩ ॥

śeṣa ye rahila prabhura dvādaśa vatsara
kṛṣṇera viyoga-sphūrti haya nirantara

SYNONYMS

śeṣa—at the end; *ye*—those; *rahila*—remained; *prabhura*—of Lord Śrī Caitanya Mahāprabhu; *dvādaśa vatsara*—twelve years; *kṛṣṇera*—of Lord Kṛṣṇa; *viyoga*—of separation; *sphūrti*—manifestation; *haya*—is; *nirantara*—always.

TRANSLATION

During His last twelve years, Śrī Caitanya Mahāprabhu always manifested all the symptoms of ecstasy in separation from Kṛṣṇa.

TEXT 4

শ্রীরাধিকার চেষ্টা যেন উদ্ধব-দর্শনে ।
এইমত দশা প্রভুর হয় রাত্রি-দিনে ॥ ৪ ॥

śrī-rādhikāra ceṣṭā yena uddhava-darśane
ei-mata daśā prabhura haya rātri-dine

SYNONYMS

śrī-rādhikāra—of Śrīmatī Rādhārāṇī; *ceṣṭā*—the activities; *yena*—just like; *uddhava-darśane*—in seeing Uddhava at Vṛndāvana; *ei-mata*—in this way; *daśā*—the condition; *prabhura*—of the Lord; *haya*—is; *rātri-dine*—day and night.

TRANSLATION

Śrī Caitanya Mahāprabhu's state of mind, day and night, was practically identical to Rādhārāṇī's state of mind when Uddhava came to Vṛndāvana to see the gopīs.

TEXT 5

নিরন্তর হয় প্রভুর বিরহ-উন্মাদ ।
ভ্রমময় চেষ্টা সদা, প্রলাপময় বাদ ॥ ৫ ॥

nirantara haya prabhura viraha-unmāda
bhrama-maya ceṣṭā sadā, pralāpa-maya vāda

SYNONYMS

nirantara—constantly; *haya*—is; *prabhura*—of the Lord; *viraha*—of separation; *unmāda*—the madness; *bhrama-maya*—forgetful; *ceṣṭā*—activities; *sadā*—always; *pralāpa-maya*—full of delirium; *vāda*—philosophy.

TRANSLATION

The Lord constantly exhibited a state of mind reflecting the madness of separation. All His activities were based on forgetfulness, and His talks were always based on madness.

TEXT 6

রোমকূপে রক্তোদ্গম, দন্ত সব হালে ।
ক্ষণে অঙ্গ ক্ষীণ হয়, ক্ষণে অঙ্গ ফুলে ॥ ৬ ॥

roma-kūpe raktodgama, danta saba hāle
kṣaṇe aṅga kṣīṇa haya, kṣaṇe aṅga phule

SYNONYMS

roma-kūpe—the pores of the body; *rakta-udgama*—exuding blood; *danta*—teeth; *saba*—all; *hāle*—loosen; *kṣaṇe*—in one moment; *aṅga*—the whole body; *kṣīṇa*—slender; *haya*—becomes; *kṣaṇe*—in another moment; *aṅga*—the body; *phule*—fattens.

TRANSLATION

Blood flowed from all the pores of His body, and all His teeth were loosened. At one moment His whole body became slender, and at another moment His whole body became fat.

TEXT 7

গম্ভীরা-ভিতরে রাত্রে নাহি নিদ্রা-লব ।
ভিত্তে মুখ-শির ঘষে, ক্ষত হয় সব ॥ ৭ ॥

gambhīrā-bhitare rātre nāhi nidrā-lava
bhitte mukha-śira ghaṣe, kṣata haya saba

SYNONYMS

gambhīrā-bhitare—inside the inner room; *rātre*—at night; *nāhi*—there is not; *nidrā-lava*—a fraction of sleep; *bhitte*—on the ground; *mukha*—mouth; *śira*—head; *ghaṣe*—grind; *kṣata*—injuries; *haya*—there are; *saba*—all.

TRANSLATION

The small room beyond the corridor is called the Gambhīrā. Śrī Caitanya Mahāprabhu used to stay in that room, but He did not sleep for a moment. All night He used to grind His mouth and head on the ground, and His face sustained injuries all over.

TEXT 8

তিন দ্বারে কপাট, প্রভু যায়েন বাহিরে ।
কভু সিংহদ্বারে পড়ে, কভু সিন্ধুনীরে ॥ ৮ ॥

tina dvāre kapāṭa, prabhu yāyena bāhire
kabhu siṁha-dvāre paḍe, kabhu sindhu-nīre

SYNONYMS

tina dvāre—the three doors; *kapāṭa*—completely closed; *prabhu*—the Lord; *yāyena*—goes; *bāhire*—outside; *kabhu*—sometimes; *siṁha-dvāre*—at the gate of the temple of Jagannātha, known as Siṁha-dvāra; *paḍe*—falls flat; *kabhu*—sometimes; *sindhu-nīre*—in the water of the sea.

TRANSLATION

Although the three doors of the house were always closed, the Lord would nonetheless go out and sometimes would be found at Jagannātha Temple before the gate known as Siṁha-dvāra. And sometimes the Lord would fall flat into the sea.

TEXT 9

চটক পর্বত দেখি' 'গোবর্ধন' ভ্রমে ।
ধাঞা চলে আর্তনাদ করিয়া ক্রন্দনে ॥ ৯ ॥

caṭaka parvata dekhi' 'govardhana' bhrame
dhāñā cale ārta-nāda kariyā krandane

SYNONYMS

caṭaka parvata—the sandhills; *dekhi'*—seeing; *govardhana*—Govardhana Hill in Vṛndāvana; *bhrame*—mistakes; *dhāñā*—running; *cale*—goes; *ārta-nāda*—wail; *kariyā*—making; *krandane*—cries.

TRANSLATION

Śrī Caitanya Mahāprabhu would also run very fast across the sandhills, mistaking them to be Govardhana. As He ran, He would wail and cry loudly.

PURPORT

Because of the winds of the sea, sometimes the sand would form dunes. Such sand dunes are called *caṭaka parvata.* Instead of seeing these sand dunes simply as hills of sand, the Lord would take them to be Govardhana Hill. Sometimes He would run toward these dunes at high speed, crying very loudly, expressing the state of mind exhibited by Rādhārāṇī. Thus Caitanya Mahāprabhu was absorbed in thoughts of Kṛṣṇa and His pastimes. His state of mind brought Him the atmosphere of Vṛndāvana and Govardhana Hill, and thus He enjoyed the transcendental bliss of separation and meeting.

TEXT 10

উপবনোদ্যান দেখি' বৃন্দাবন-জ্ঞান।
তাহাঁ যাই' নাচে, গায়, ক্ষণে মূর্চ্ছা যা'ন ॥ ১০ ॥

upavanodyāna dekhi' vṛndāvana-jñāna
tāhāṅ yāi' nāce, gāya, kṣaṇe mūrcchā yā'na

SYNONYMS

upavana-udyāna—small parks; *dekhi'*—seeing; *vṛndāvana-jñāna*—took them to be the forests of Vṛndāvana; *tāhāṅ*—there; *yāi'*—going; *nāce*—dances; *gāya*—sings; *kṣaṇe*—in a moment; *mūrcchā*—unconsciousness; *yā'na*—goes.

TRANSLATION

Sometimes Caitanya Mahāprabhu mistook the small parks of the city for Vṛndāvana. Sometimes He would go there, dance and chant and sometimes fall unconscious in spiritual ecstasy.

TEXT 11

কাহাঁ নাহি শুনি যেই ভাবের বিকার।
সেই ভাব হয় প্রভুর শরীরে প্রচার ॥ ১১ ॥

kāhāṅ nāhi śuni yei bhāvera vikāra
sei bhāva haya prabhura śarīre pracāra

SYNONYMS

kāhāṅ—anywhere; *nāhi*—not; *śuni*—we hear; *yei*—that; *bhāvera*—of ecstasy; *vikāra*—transformation; *sei*—that; *bhāva*—ecstasy; *haya*—is; *prabhura*—of the Lord; *śarīre*—in the body; *pracāra*—manifest.

TRANSLATION

The extraordinary transformations of the body due to transcendental feelings would never have been possible for anyone but the Lord, in whose body all transformations were manifest.

PURPORT

The ecstatic transformations of the body as described in such exalted literatures as *Bhakti-rasāmṛta-sindhu* are practically not seen in this material world. However, these symptoms were perfectly present in the body of Śrī Caitanya Mahāprabhu. These symptoms are indicative of *mahābhāva,* or the highest ecstasy. Sometimes *sahajiyās* artificially imitate these symptoms, but experienced devotees reject them immediately. The author admits herein that these symptoms are not to be found anywhere but in the body of Śrī Caitanya Mahāprabhu.

TEXT 12

হস্তপদের সন্ধি সব বিতস্তি-প্রমাণে।
সন্ধি ছাড়ি' ভিন্ন হয়ে, চর্ম রহে স্থানে ॥ ১২ ॥

hasta-padera sandhi saba vitasti-pramāṇe
sandhi chāḍi' bhinna haye, carma rahe sthāne

SYNONYMS

hasta-padera—of the hands and legs; *sandhi*—joints; *saba*—all; *vitasti*—about eight inches; *pramāṇe*—in length; *sandhi*—joints; *chāḍi'*—dislocated;

bhinna—separated; *haye*—become; *carma*—skin; *rahe*—remains; *sthāne*—in the place.

TRANSLATION

The joints of His hands and legs would sometimes become separated by eight inches, and they remained connected only by the skin.

TEXT 13

হস্ত, পদ, শির, সব শরীর-ভিতরে ।
প্রবিষ্ট হয়—কূর্মরূপ দেখিয়ে প্রভুরে ॥ ১৩ ॥

hasta, pada, śira, saba śarīra-bhitare
praviṣṭa haya——kūrma-rūpa dekhiye prabhure

SYNONYMS

hasta—the hands; *pada*—the legs; *śira*—head; *saba*—all; *śarīra*—the body; *bhitare*—within; *praviṣṭa*—entered; *haya*—is; *kūrma-rūpa*—like a tortoise; *dekhiye*—one sees; *prabhure*—the Lord.

TRANSLATION

Sometimes Śrī Caitanya Mahāprabhu's hands, legs and head would all enter within His body, just like the withdrawn limbs of a tortoise.

TEXT 14

এই মত অদ্ভুত-ভাব শরীরে প্রকাশ ।
মনেতে শূন্যতা, বাক্যে হাহা-হুতাশ ॥ ১৪ ॥

ei mata adbhuta-bhāva śarīre prakāśa
manete śūnyatā, vākye hā-hā-hutāśa

SYNONYMS

ei mata—in this way; *adbhuta*—wonderful; *bhāva*—ecstasy; *śarīre*—in the body; *prakāśa*—manifestation; *manete*—in the mind; *śūnyatā*—vacancy; *vākye*—in speaking; *hā-hā*—despondency; *hutāśa*—disappointment.

TRANSLATION

In this way Śrī Caitanya Mahāprabhu used to manifest wonderful ecstatic symptoms. His mind appeared vacant, and there were only hopelessness and disappointment in His words.

TEXT 15

কাহাঁ মোর প্রাণনাথ মুরলীবদন ।
কাহাঁ করোঁ কাহাঁ পাঙ ব্রজেন্দ্রনন্দন ॥ ১৫ ॥

kāhāṅ mora prāṇa-nātha muralī-vadana
kāhāṅ karoṅ kāhāṅ pāṅ vrajendra-nandana

SYNONYMS

kāhāṅ—where; *mora*—My; *prāṇa-nātha*—Lord of the life; *muralī-vadana*—playing the flute; *kāhāṅ*—what; *karoṅ*—shall I do; *kāhāṅ*—where; *pāṅ*—I shall get; *vrajendra-nandana*—the son of Mahārāja Nanda.

TRANSLATION

Śrī Caitanya Mahāprabhu used to express His mind in this way: "Where is the Lord of My life, who is playing His flute? What shall I do now? Where should I go to find the son of Mahārāja Nanda?

TEXT 16

কাহারে কহিব, কেবা জানে মোর দুঃখ ।
ব্রজেন্দ্রনন্দন বিনু ফাটে মোর বুক ॥ ১৬ ॥

kāhāre kahiba, kebā jāne mora duḥkha
vrajendra-nandana vinu phāṭe mora buka

SYNONYMS

kāhāre—unto whom; *kahiba*—I shall speak; *kebā*—who; *jāne*—knows; *mora*—My; *duḥkha*—disappointment; *vrajendra-nandana*—Kṛṣṇa, the son of Nanda Mahārāja; *vinu*—without; *phāṭe*—breaks; *mora*—My; *buka*—heart.

TRANSLATION

"To whom should I speak? Who can understand My disappointment? Without the son of Nanda Mahārāja, My heart is broken."

TEXT 17

এইমত বিলাপ করে বিহ্বল অন্তর ।
রায়ের নাটক-শ্লোক পড়ে নিরন্তর ॥ ১৭ ॥

ei-mata vilāpa kare vihvala antara
rāyera nāṭaka-śloka paḍe nirantara

SYNONYMS

ei-mata—in this way; *vilāpa*—lamentation; *kare*—does; *vihvala*—bewildered; *antara*—within; *rāyera*—of Śrī Rāmānanda Rāya; *nāṭaka*—drama; *śloka*—verses; *paḍe*—reads; *nirantara*—constantly.

TRANSLATION

In this way Śrī Caitanya Mahāprabhu always expressed bewilderment and lamented in separation from Kṛṣṇa. At such times He used to read the ślokas from Rāmānanda Rāya's drama known as Jagannātha-vallabha-nāṭaka.

TEXT 18

প্রেমচ্ছেদরুজোঽবগচ্ছতি হরির্নায়ং ন চ প্রেম বা
স্থানাস্থানমবৈতি নাপি মদনো জানাতি নো দুর্বলাঃ।
অন্যো বেদ ন চান্যদুঃখমখিলং নো জীবনং বাশ্রবং
দ্বিত্রাণ্যেব দিনানি যৌবনমিদং হাহা বিধে কা গতিঃ ॥১৮

prema-ccheda-rujo 'vagacchati harir nāyaṁ na ca prema vā
sthānāsthānam avaiti nāpi madano jānāti no durbalāḥ
anyo veda na cānya-duḥkham akhilaṁ no jīvanaṁ vāśravaṁ
dvi-trāṇy eva dināni yauvanam idaṁ hā-hā vidhe kā gatiḥ

SYNONYMS

prema-cheda-rujaḥ—the sufferings of a broken loving relationship; *avagacchati*—knows; *hariḥ*—the Supreme Lord; *na*—not; *ayam*—this; *na ca*—nor; *prema*—love; *vā*—nor; *sthāna*—the proper place; *asthānam*—an unsuitable place; *avaiti*—knows; *na*—not; *api*—also; *madanaḥ*—Cupid; *jānāti*—knows; *naḥ*—us; *durbalāḥ*—very weak; *anyaḥ*—another; *veda*—knows; *na*—not; *ca*—also; *anya-duḥkham*—the difficulties of others; *akhilam*—all; *naḥ*—our; *jīvanam*—life; *vā*—or; *āśravam*—simply full of miseries; *dvi*—two; *trāṇi*—three; *eva*—certainly; *dināni*—days; *yauvanam*—youth; *idam*—this; *hā-hā*—alas; *vidhe*—O creator; *kā*—what; *gatiḥ*—our destination.

TRANSLATION

[Śrīmatī Rādhārāṇī used to lament:] " 'Our Kṛṣṇa does not realize what we have suffered from injuries inflicted in the course of loving affairs. We

are actually misused by love because love does not know where to strike and where not to strike. Even Cupid does not know of our very weakened condition. What should I tell anyone? No one can understand another's difficulties. Our life is actually not under our control, for youth will remain for two or three days and soon be finished. In this condition, O creator, what will be our destination?'

PURPORT

This verse is from the *Jagannātha-vallabha-nāṭaka* (3.9) of Rāmānanda Rāya.

TEXT 19

উপজিল প্রেমাঙ্কুর, ভাঙ্গিল যে দুঃখ-পূর,
কৃষ্ণ তাহা নাহি করে পান ।
বাহিরে নাগররাজ, ভিতরে শঠের কাজ,
পরনারী বধে সাবধান ॥ ১৯ ॥

upajila premāṅkura, bhāṅgila ye duḥkha-pūra,
kṛṣṇa tāhā nāhi kare pāna
bāhire nāgara-rāja, bhitare śaṭhera kāja,
para-nārī vadhe sāvadhāna

SYNONYMS

upajila—grew up; *prema-aṅkura*—fructification of love of God; *bhāṅgila*—was broken; *ye*—that; *duḥkha-pūra*—full of miseries; *kṛṣṇa*—Lord Kṛṣṇa; *tāhā*—that; *nāhi*—not; *kare*—does; *pāna*—drinking; *bāhire*—externally; *nāgara-rāja*—the most attractive person; *bhitare*—within; *śaṭhera*—of a cheater; *kāja*—activities; *para-nārī*—others' wives; *vadhe*—kills; *sāvadhāna*—very careful.

TRANSLATION

[Śrīmatī Rādhārāṇī spoke thus, in distress due to separation from Kṛṣṇa.] "Oh, what shall I say of My distress? After I met Kṛṣṇa My loving propensities sprouted, but upon separating from Him, I sustained a great shock, which is now continuing like the sufferings of a disease. The only physician for this disease is Kṛṣṇa Himself, but He is not taking care of this sprouting plant of devotional service. What can I say about the behavior of Kṛṣṇa? Outwardly He is a very attractive young lover, but at heart He is a great cheat, very expert in killing others' wives."

TEXT 20

সখি হে, না বুঝিয়ে বিধির বিধান।
সুখ লাগি' কৈলুঁ প্রীত, হৈল দুঃখ বিপরীত,
এবে যায়, না রহে পরাণ॥ ২০ ॥ ধ্রু ॥

sakhi he, nā bujhiye vidhira vidhāna
sukha lāgi' kailuṅ prīta, haila duḥkha viparīta,
ebe yāya, nā rahe parāṇa

SYNONYMS

sakhi he—(My dear) friend; *nā bujhiye*—I do not understand; *vidhira*—of the Creator; *vidhāna*—the regulation; *sukha lāgi'*—for happiness; *kailuṅ*—I did; *prīta*—love; *haila*—it became; *duḥkha*—unhappiness; *viparīta*—the opposite; *ebe*—now; *yāya*—going; *nā*—does not; *rahe*—remain; *parāṇa*—life.

TRANSLATION

[Śrīmatī Rādhārāṇī continued lamenting about the consequences of loving Kṛṣṇa.] "My dear friend, I do not understand the regulative principles given by the Creator. I loved Kṛṣṇa for happiness, but the result was just the opposite. I am now in an ocean of distress. It must be that now I am going to die, for My vital force no longer remains. This is My state of mind.

TEXT 21

কুটিল প্রেমা অগেয়ান, নাহি জানে স্থানাস্থান,
ভাল-মন্দ নারে বিচারিতে।
ক্রূর শঠের গুণডোরে, হাতে-গলে বান্ধি' মোরে,
রাখিয়াছে, নারি' উকাশিতে॥ ২১ ॥

kuṭila premā ageyāna, nāhi jāne sthānāsthāna,
bhāla-manda nāre vicārite
krūra śaṭhera guṇa-ḍore, hāte-gale bāndhi' more,
rākhiyāche, nāri' ukāśite

SYNONYMS

kuṭila—crooked; *premā*—love of Kṛṣṇa; *ageyāna*—ignorant; *nāhi*—does not; *jāne*—know; *sthāna-asthāna*—a suitable place or unsuitable place;

bhāla-manda—what is good or what is bad; *nāre*—not able; *vicārite*—to consider; *krūra*—very cruel; *śaṭhera*—of the cheater; *guṇa-ḍore*—by the ropes of the good qualities; *hāte*—on the hands; *gale*—on the neck; *bāndhi'*—binding; *more*—Me; *rākhiyāche*—has kept; *nāri'*—being unable; *ukāśite*—to get relief.

TRANSLATION

"By nature loving affairs are very crooked. They are not entered with sufficient knowledge, nor do they consider whether a place is suitable or not, nor do they look forward to the results. By the ropes of His good qualities, Kṛṣṇa, who is so unkind, has bound My neck and hands, and I am unable to get relief.

TEXT 22

যে মদন তনুহীন, পরদ্রোহে পরবীণ,
পাঁচ বাণ সন্ধে অনুক্ষণ ।
অবলার শরীরে, বিন্ধি' কৈল জরজরে,
দুঃখ দেয়, না লয় জীবন ॥ ২২ ॥

ye madana tanu-hīna, para-drohe paravīṇa,
pāñca bāṇa sandhe anukṣaṇa
abalāra śarīre, vindhi' kaila jarajare,
duḥkha deya, nā laya jīvana

SYNONYMS

ye madana—that Cupid; *tanu-hīna*—without a body; *para-drohe*—in putting others in difficulty; *paravīṇa*—very expert; *pāñca*—five; *bāṇa*—arrows; *sandhe*—fixes; *anukṣaṇa*—constantly; *abalāra*—of an innocent woman; *śarīre*—in the body; *vindhi'*—piercing; *kaila*—made; *jarajare*—almost invalid; *duḥkha deya*—gives tribulation; *nā*—does not; *laya*—take; *jīvana*—the life.

TRANSLATION

"In My loving affairs, there is a person named Madana. His qualities are thus: Personally He possesses no gross body, yet He is very expert in giving pains to others. He has five arrows, and fixing them on His bow, He shoots them into the bodies of innocent women. Thus these women become invalids. It would be better if He took My life without hesitation, but He does not do so. He simply gives Me pain.

TEXT 23

অন্যের যে দুঃখ মনে, অন্যে তাহা নাহি জানে,
সত্য এই শাস্ত্রের বিচারে ।
অন্য জন কাহাঁ লিখি, না জানয়ে প্রাণসখী,
যাতে কহে ধৈর্য ধরিবারে ॥ ২৩ ॥

anyera ye duḥkha mane, anye tāhā nāhi jāne,
satya ei śāstrera vicāre
anya jana kāhāṅ likhi, nā jānaye prāṇa-sakhī,
yāte kahe dhairya dharibāre

SYNONYMS

anyera—of others; *ye*—that; *duḥkha*—unhappiness; *mane*—in the minds; *anye*—others; *tāhā*—that; *nāhi*—do not; *jāne*—know; *satya*—truth; *ei*—this; *śāstrera*—of scripture; *vicāre*—in the judgment; *anya jana*—other persons; *kāhāṅ*—what; *likhi*—I shall write; *nā jānaye*—do not know; *prāṇa-sakhī*—My dear friends; *yāte*—by which; *kahe*—speak; *dhairya dharibāre*—to take patience.

TRANSLATION

"In the scriptures it is said that one person can never know the unhappiness in the mind of another. Therefore what can I say of My dear friends, Lalitā and the others? Nor can they understand the unhappiness within Me. They simply try to console Me repeatedly, saying, 'Dear friend, be patient.'

TEXT 24

'কৃষ্ণ—কৃপা-পারাবার, কভু করিবেন অঙ্গীকার',
সখি, তোর এ ব্যর্থ বচন ।
জীবের জীবন চঞ্চল, যেন পদ্মপত্রের জল,
তত দিন জীবে কোন্ জন ॥ ২৪ ॥

'kṛṣṇa——kṛpā-pārāvāra, kabhu karibena aṅgīkāra,'
sakhi, tora e vyartha vacana
jīvera jīvana cañcala, yena padma-patrera jala,
tata dina jīve kon jana

SYNONYMS

kṛṣṇa—Lord Kṛṣṇa; *kṛpā-pārāvāra*—an ocean of mercy; *kabhu*—sometimes; *karibena*—will make; *aṅgīkāra*—acceptance; *sakhi*—My dear friend; *tora*—your; *e*—these; *vyartha*—untruthful; *vacana*—complimentary words; *jīvera*—of the living entity; *jīvana*—life; *cañcala*—flickering; *yena*—like; *padma-patrera*—of the leaf of the lotus flower; *jala*—the water; *tata*—so many; *dina*—days; *jīve*—lives; *kon*—what; *jana*—person.

TRANSLATION

"I say, 'My dear friends, you are asking Me to be patient, saying that Kṛṣṇa is an ocean of mercy and that some time in the future He will accept Me. However, I must say that this will not console Me. A living entity's life is very flickering. It is like water on the leaf of a lotus flower. Who will live long enough to expect Kṛṣṇa's mercy?

TEXT 25

শত বৎসর পর্যন্ত, জীবের জীবন অন্ত,
এই বাক্য কহ না বিচারি' ।
নারীর যৌবন-ধন, যারে কৃষ্ণ করে মন,
সে যৌবন—দিন দুই-চারি ॥ ২৫ ॥

śata vatsara paryanta, jīvera jīvana anta,
ei vākya kaha nā vicāri'
nārīra yauvana-dhana, yāre kṛṣṇa kare mana,
se yauvana——dina dui-cāri

SYNONYMS

śata vatsara paryanta—up to one hundred years; *jīvera*—of the living entity; *jīvana*—of the life; *anta*—the end; *ei vākya*—this word; *kaha*—you speak; *nā*—without; *vicāri'*—making consideration; *nārīra*—of a woman; *yauvana-dhana*—the wealth of youthfulness; *yāre*—in which; *kṛṣṇa*—Lord Kṛṣṇa; *kare*—does; *mana*—intention; *se yauvana*—that youthfulness; *dina*—days; *dui-cāri*—two or four.

TRANSLATION

" 'A human being does not live more than a hundred years. You should also consider that the youthfulness of a woman, which is the only attraction for Kṛṣṇa, remains for only a few days.

TEXT 26

অগ্নি যৈছে নিজ-ধাম, দেখাইয়া অভিরাম,
পতঙ্গীরে আকর্ষিয়া মারে ।
কৃষ্ণ ঐছে নিজ-গুণ, দেখাইয়া হরে মন,
পাছে দুঃখ-সমুদ্রেতে ডারে ॥ ২৬ ॥

agni yaiche nija-dhāma, dekhāiyā abhirāma,
pataṅgīre ākarṣiyā māre
kṛṣṇa aiche nija-guṇa, dekhāiyā hare mana,
pāche duḥkha-samudrete ḍāre

SYNONYMS

agni—fire; *yaiche*—like; *nija-dhāma*—his own place; *dekhāiyā*—showing; *abhirāma*—attractive; *pataṅgīre*—the flies; *ākarṣiyā*—attracting; *māre*—kills; *kṛṣṇa*—Lord Kṛṣṇa; *aiche*—in that way; *nija-guṇa*—His transcendental qualities; *dekhāiyā*—showing; *hare mana*—attracts our mind; *pāche*—in the end; *duḥkha-samudrete*—in an ocean of unhappiness; *ḍāre*—drowns.

TRANSLATION

" 'If you say that Kṛṣṇa is an ocean of transcendental qualities and therefore must be merciful some day, I can only say that He is like fire, which attracts flies by its dazzling brightness and kills them. Such are the qualities of Kṛṣṇa. By showing us His transcendental qualities, He attracts our minds, and then later, by separating from us, He drowns us in an ocean of unhappiness.' "

TEXT 27

এতেক বিলাপ করি', বিষাদে শ্রীগৌরহরি,
উঘাড়িয়া দুঃখের কপাট ।
ভাবের তরঙ্গ-বলে, নানারূপে মন চলে,
আর এক শ্লোক কৈল পাঠ ॥ ২৭ ॥

eteka vilāpa kari', viṣāde śrī-gaura-hari,
ughāḍiyā duḥkhera kapāṭa
bhāvera taraṅga-bale, nānā-rūpe mana cale,
āra eka śloka kaila pāṭha

SYNONYMS

eteka—in this way; *vilāpa*—lamentation; *kari'*—doing; *viṣāde*—in moroseness; *śrī-gaura-hari*—Lord Śrī Caitanya Mahāprabhu; *ughāḍiyā*—opening; *duḥkhera*—of unhappiness; *kapāṭa*—doors; *bhāvera*—of ecstasy; *taraṅga-bale*—by the force of the waves; *nānā-rūpe*—in various ways; *mana*—His mind; *cale*—wanders; *āra eka*—another one; *śloka*—verse; *kaila*—did; *pāṭha*—read.

TRANSLATION

In this way, Lord Śrī Caitanya Mahāprabhu lamented in a great ocean of sadness, and thus He opened the doors of His unhappiness. Forced by the waves of ecstasy, His mind wandered over transcendental mellows, and in this way He would read another verse [as follows].

TEXT 28

শ্রীকৃষ্ণরূপাদিনিষেবণং বিনা
ব্যর্থানি মেঽহান্যখিলেন্দ্রিয়াণ্যলম্ ।
পাষাণশুষ্কেন্ধনভারকাণ্যহো
বিভর্মি বা তানি কথং হতত্রপঃ ॥ ২৮ ॥

śrī-kṛṣṇa-rūpādi-niṣevaṇaṁ vinā
vyarthāni me 'hāny akhilendriyāṇy alam
pāṣāṇa-śuṣkendhana-bhārakāṇy aho
vibharmi vā tāni kathaṁ hata-trapaḥ

SYNONYMS

śrī-kṛṣṇa-rūpa-ādi—of the transcendental form and pastimes of Lord Śrī Kṛṣṇa; *niṣevaṇam*—the service; *vinā*—without; *vyarthāni*—meaningless; *me*—My; *ahāni*—days; *akhila*—all; *indriyāṇi*—senses; *alam*—entirely; *pāṣāṇa*—dead stones; *śuṣka*—dry; *indhana*—wood; *bhārakāṇi*—burdens; *aho*—alas; *vibharmi*—I bear; *vā*—or; *tāni*—all of them; *katham*—how; *hata-trapaḥ*—without shame.

TRANSLATION

" 'My dear friends, unless I serve the transcendental form, qualities and pastimes of Śrī Kṛṣṇa, all My days and all My senses will become entirely useless. Now I am uselessly bearing the burden of My senses, which are

like stone blocks and dried wood. I do not know how long I will be able to continue without shame.'

TEXT 29

বংশীগানামৃত-ধাম, লাবণ্যামৃত-জন্মস্থান,
যে না দেখে সে চাঁদ বদন ।
সে নয়নে কিবা কাজ, পড়ুক তার মুণ্ডে বাজ,
সে নয়ন রহে কি কারণ ॥ ২৯ ॥

vaṁśī-gānāmṛta-dhāma, lāvaṇyāmṛta-janma-sthāna,
ye nā dekhe se cāṅda vadana
se nayane kibā kāja, paḍuka tāra muṇḍe vāja,
se nayana rahe ki kāraṇa

SYNONYMS

vaṁśī-gāna-amṛta-dhāma—the abode of the nectar derived from the songs of the flute; *lāvaṇya-amṛta-janma-sthāna*—the birthplace of the nectar of beauty; *ye*—anyone who; *nā*—not; *dekhe*—sees; *se*—that; *cāṅda*—moonlike; *vadana*—face; *se*—those; *nayane*—eyes; *kibā kāja*—what is the use; *paḍuka*—let there be; *tāra*—his; *muṇḍe*—on the head; *vāja*—thunderbolt; *se*—those; *nayana*—eyes; *rahe*—keeps; *ki*—what; *kāraṇa*—reason.

TRANSLATION

"Of what use are eyes if one does not see the face of Kṛṣṇa, which resembles the moon and is the birthplace of all beauty and the reservoir of the nectarean songs of His flute? Oh, let a thunderbolt strike his head! Why does he keep such eyes?

PURPORT

The moonlike face of Kṛṣṇa is the reservoir of nectarean songs and abode of His flute. It is also the root of all bodily beauty. If the eyes of the *gopīs* are not engaged in seeing the beautiful face of Kṛṣṇa, it is better that they be struck by a thunderbolt. For the *gopīs,* to see anything but Kṛṣṇa is uninteresting and, indeed, detestful. The *gopīs* are never pleased to see anything but Kṛṣṇa. The only solace for their eyes is the beautiful moonlike face of Kṛṣṇa, the worshipful object of all senses. When they cannot see the beautiful face of Kṛṣṇa, they actually see everything as vacant, and they desire to be struck by a thunderbolt. They do not find any reason to maintain their eyes when they are bereft of the beauty of Kṛṣṇa.

TEXT 30

সখি হে, শুন, মোর হত বিধিবল ।
মোর বপু-চিত্ত-মন, সকল ইন্দ্রিয়গণ,
কৃষ্ণ বিনু সকল বিফল ॥ ৩০ ॥ ধ্রু ॥

sakhi he, śuna, mora hata vidhi-bala
mora vapu-citta-mana, sakala indriya-gaṇa,
kṛṣṇa vinu sakala viphala

SYNONYMS

sakhi he—O My dear friend; *śuna*—please hear; *mora*—My; *hata*—lost; *vidhi-bala*—the strength of providence; *mora*—My; *vapu*—body; *citta*—consciousness; *mana*—mind; *sakala*—all; *indriya-gaṇa*—senses; *kṛṣṇa*—Lord Kṛṣṇa; *vinu*—without; *sakala*—everything; *viphala*—futile.

TRANSLATION

"My dear friends, please hear Me. I have lost all providential strength. Without Kṛṣṇa, My body, consciousness and mind, as well as all My senses, are useless.

TEXT 31

কৃষ্ণের মধুর বাণী, অমৃতের তরঙ্গিণী,
তার প্রবেশ নাহি যে শ্রবণে ।
কাণাকড়ি-ছিদ্র সম, জানিহ সে শ্রবণ,
তার জন্ম হৈল অকারণে ॥ ৩১ ॥

kṛṣṇera madhura vāṇī, amṛtera taraṅgiṇī,
tāra praveśa nāhi ye śravaṇe
kāṇākaḍi-chidra sama, jāniha se śravaṇa,
tāra janma haila akāraṇe

SYNONYMS

kṛṣṇera—of Lord Kṛṣṇa; *madhura*—sweet; *vāṇī*—words; *amṛtera*—of nectar; *taraṅgiṇī*—waves; *tāra*—of those; *praveśa*—entrance; *nāhi*—there is not; *ye*—which; *śravaṇe*—in the ear; *kāṇākaḍi*—of a damaged conchshell; *chidra*—the hole; *sama*—like; *jāniha*—please know; *se*—that; *śravaṇa*—ear; *tāra*—his; *janma*—birth; *haila*—was; *akāraṇe*—without purpose.

TRANSLATION

"Topics about Kṛṣṇa are like waves of nectar. If such nectar does not enter one's ear, the ear is no better than the hole of a damaged conchshell. Such an ear is created for no purpose.

PURPORT

In this connection, Śrīla Bhaktisiddhānta Sarasvatī Ṭhākura quotes the following verses from *Śrīmad-Bhāgavatam* (2.3.17-24):

āyur harati vai puṁsām
udyann astaṁ ca yann asau
tasyarte yat-kṣaṇo nīta
uttama-śloka-vārtayā

taravaḥ kiṁ na jīvanti
bhastrāḥ kiṁ na śvasanty uta
na khādanti na mehanti
kiṁ grāme paśavo 'pare

śva-viḍ-varāhoṣṭra-kharaiḥ
saṁstutaḥ puruṣaḥ paśuḥ
na yat-karṇa-pathopeto
jātu nāma gadāgrajaḥ

bile batorukrama-vikramān ye
na śṛṇvataḥ karṇa-puṭe narasya
jihvāsatī dārdurikeva sūta
na copagāyaty urugāya-gāthāḥ

bhāraḥ paraṁ paṭṭa-kirīṭa-juṣṭam
apy uttamāṅgaṁ na namen mukundam
śāvau karau no kurute saparyāṁ
harer lasat-kāñcana-kaṅkaṇau vā

barhāyite te nayane narāṇāṁ
liṅgāni viṣṇor na nirīkṣato ye
pādau nṛṇāṁ tau druma-janma-bhājau
kṣetrāṇi nānuvrajato harer yau

jīvañ-chavo bhāgavatāṅghri-reṇuṁ
na jātu martyo 'bhilabheta yas tu
śrī-viṣṇu-padyā manu-jas tulasyāḥ
śvasañ-chavo yas tu na veda gandham

tad aśma-sāraṁ hṛdayaṁ batedaṁ
yad gṛhyamāṇair hari-nāma-dheyaiḥ
na vikriyetātha yadā vikāro
netre jalaṁ gātra-ruheṣu harṣaḥ

"Both by rising and setting, the sun decreases the duration of life of everyone, except one who utilizes the time by discussing topics of the all-good Personality of Godhead. Do the trees not live? Do the bellows of the blacksmith not breathe? All around us, do the beasts not eat and discharge semen? Men who are like dogs, hogs, camels and asses praise those men who never listen to the transcendental pastimes of Lord Śrī Kṛṣṇa, the deliverer from evils. One who has not listened to the messages about the prowess and marvelous acts of the Personality of Godhead and has not sung or chanted loudly the worthy songs about the Lord should be considered to possess ears like the holes of snakes and a tongue like that of a frog. The upper portion of the body, though crowned with a silk turban, is only a heavy burden if not bowed down before the Personality of Godhead, who can award *mukti* [freedom]. And the hands, though decorated with glittering bangles, are like those of a dead man if not engaged in the service of the Personality of Godhead Hari. The eyes which do not look at the symbolic representations of the Personality of Godhead Viṣṇu [His forms, name, quality, etc.] are like those printed on the plumes of a peacock, and the legs which do not move to the holy places [where the Lord is remembered] are considered to be like tree trunks. The person who has not at any time received upon his head the dust from the feet of a pure devotee of the Lord is certainly a dead body. And the person who has never experienced the flavor of the *tulasī* leaves from the lotus feet of the Lord is also a dead body, although breathing. Certainly that heart is steel-framed which, in spite of one's chanting the holy name of the Lord with concentration, does not change when ecstasy takes place, tears fill the eyes and the hairs stand on end."

TEXT 32

কৃষ্ণের অধরামৃত, কৃষ্ণ-গুণ-চরিত,
সুধাসার-স্বাদ-বিনিন্দন।
তার স্বাদ যে না জানে, জন্মিয়া না মৈল কেনে,
সে রসনা ভেক জিহ্বা সম ॥ ৩২ ॥

kṛṣṇera adharāmṛta, kṛṣṇa-guṇa-carita,
sudhā-sāra-svāda-vinindana
tāra svāda ye nā jāne, janmiyā nā maila kene,
se rasanā bheka jihvā sama

SYNONYMS

kṛṣṇera—of Lord Kṛṣṇa; *adhara-amṛta*—the nectar of the lips; *kṛṣṇa*—of Lord Kṛṣṇa; *guṇa*—the qualities; *carita*—the activities; *sudhā-sāra*—of the essence of all nectar; *svāda*—the taste; *vinindana*—surpassing; *tāra*—of that; *svāda*—the taste; *ye*—anyone who; *nā jāne*—does not know; *janmiyā*—taking birth; *nā maila*—did not die; *kene*—why; *se*—that; *rasanā*—tongue; *bheka*—of the frog; *jihvā*—the tongue; *sama*—like.

TRANSLATION

"The nectar from the lips of Lord Kṛṣṇa and His transcendental qualities and characteristics surpass the taste of the essence of all nectar, and there is no fault in tasting such nectar. If one does not taste it, he should die immediately after birth, and his tongue is to be considered no better than the tongue of a frog.

TEXT 33

মৃগমদ নীলোৎপল, মিলনে যে পরিমল,
যেই হরে তার গর্ব-মান।
হেন কৃষ্ণ-অঙ্গ-গন্ধ, যার নাহি সে সম্বন্ধ,
সেই নাসা ভস্ত্রার সমান ॥ ৩৩ ॥

mṛga-mada nīlotpala, milane ye parimala,
yei hare tāra garva-māna
hena kṛṣṇa-aṅga-gandha, yāra nāhi se sambandha,
sei nāsā bhastrāra samāna

SYNONYMS

mṛga-mada—the fragrance of musk; *nīla-utpala*—and the bluish lotus flower; *milane*—in mixing; *ye*—that; *parimala*—fragrance; *yei*—which; *hare*—vanquishes; *tāra*—of them; *garva*—pride; *māna*—and prestige; *hena*—such; *kṛṣṇa*—of Lord Kṛṣṇa; *aṅga*—of the body; *gandha*—the aroma; *yāra*—whose; *nāhi*—not; *se*—that; *sambandha*—relationship; *sei*—such; *nāsā*—nose; *bhastrāra*—to the bellows; *samāna*—equal.

TRANSLATION

"One's nostrils are no better than the bellows of a blacksmith if he has not smelled the fragrance of Kṛṣṇa's body, which is like the aroma of musk combined with that of the bluish lotus flower. Indeed, such combinations are actually defeated by the aroma of Kṛṣṇa's body.

TEXT 34

কৃষ্ণ-কর-পদতল, কোটিচন্দ্র-সুশীতল,
তার স্পর্শ যেন স্পর্শমণি ।
তার স্পর্শ নাহি যার, সে যাউক্ ছারখার,
সেই বপু লৌহ-সম জানি ॥ ৩৪ ॥

kṛṣṇa-kara-pada-tala, koṭi-candra-suśītala,
tāra sparśa yena sparśa-maṇi
tāra sparśa nāhi yāra, se yāuk chārakhāra,
sei vapu lauha-sama jāni

SYNONYMS

kṛṣṇa—of Lord Kṛṣṇa; *kara*—the palms; *pada-tala*—the soles of His feet; *koṭi-candra*—like the light of millions of moons; *su-śītala*—cool and pleasing; *tāra*—of them; *sparśa*—the touch; *yena*—like; *sparśa-maṇi*—touchstone; *tāra*—his; *sparśa*—touch; *nāhi*—not; *yāra*—of whom; *se*—that person; *yāuk*—let him go; *chārakhāra*—to ruin; *sei vapu*—that body; *lauha-sama*—like iron; *jāni*—I know.

TRANSLATION

"The palms of Kṛṣṇa's hands and the soles of His feet are so cool and pleasant that they can be compared only to the light of millions of moons. One who has touched such hands and feet has indeed tasted the effects of touchstone. If one has not touched them, his life is spoiled, and his body is like iron."

TEXT 35

করি' এত বিলপন, প্রভু শচীনন্দন,
উঘাড়িয়া হৃদয়ের শোক ।
দৈন্য-নির্বেদ-বিষাদে, হৃদয়ের অবসাদে,
পুনরপি পড়ে এক শ্লোক ॥ ৩৫ ॥

kari' eta vilapana, prabhu śacī-nandana,
ughāḍiyā hṛdayera śoka
dainya-nirveda-viṣāde, hṛdayera avasāde,
punarapi paḍe eka śloka

SYNONYMS

kari'—doing; *eta*—such; *vilapana*—lamenting; *prabhu*—the Lord; *śacī-nandana*—the son of mother Śacī; *ughāḍiyā*—opening; *hṛdayera*—of the heart; *śoka*—the lamentation; *dainya*—humility; *nirveda*—disappointment; *viṣāde*—in moroseness; *hṛdayera*—of the heart; *avasāde*—in despondency; *punarapi*—again and again; *paḍe*—reads; *eka*—one; *śloka*—verse.

TRANSLATION

Lamenting in this way, Śrī Caitanya Mahāprabhu opened the doors of grief within His heart. Morose, humble and disappointed, He read a verse again and again with a despondent heart.

PURPORT

In *Bhakti-rasāmṛta-sindhu,* the word *dainya* (humility) is explained as follows: "When unhappiness, fearfulness and the sense of having offended combine, one feels condemned. This sense of condemnation is described as *dīnatā,* humility. When one is subjected to such humility, he feels bodily inactive, he apologizes, and his consciousness is disturbed. His mind is also restless, and many other symptoms are visible." The word *nirveda* is also explained in *Bhakti-rasāmṛta-sindhu.* "One may feel unhappiness and separation, as well as jealousy and lamentation due to not discharging one's duties. The despondency that results is called *nirveda.* When one is captured by this despondency, thoughts, tears, loss of bodily luster, humility and heavy breathing result." *Viṣāda* is also explained in *Bhakti-rasāmṛta-sindhu*: "When one fails to achieve the desired goal of life and repents for all his offenses, there is a state of regret called *viṣāda*." The symptoms of *viṣāda* are also explained. "One hankers to revive his original condition and inquires how to do so. There are also deep thought, heavy breathing, crying and lamentation as well as a changing of the bodily color and drying up of the tongue."

In *Bhakti-rasāmṛta-sindhu* thirty-three such destructive symptoms are mentioned. They are expressed in words, in the eyebrows and in the eyes. These symptoms are called *vyabhicārī bhāva,* destructive ecstasy. If they continue, they are sometimes called *sañcārī,* or continued ecstasy.

TEXT 36

যদা যাতো দৈবান্মধুরিপুরসৌ লোচনপথং
তদাস্মাকং চেতো মদনহতকেনাহৃতমভূৎ ।
পুনর্যস্মিন্নেষ ক্ষণমপি দৃশোরেতি পদবীং
বিধাস্যামস্তস্মিন্নখিলঘটিকা রত্নখচিতাঃ ॥ ৩৬ ॥

yadā yāto daivān madhu-ripur asau locana-pathaṁ
tadāsmākaṁ ceto madana-hatakenāhṛtam abhūt
punar yasminn eṣa kṣaṇam api dṛśor eti padavīṁ
vidhāsyāmas tasminn akhila-ghaṭikā ratna-khacitāḥ

SYNONYMS

yadā—when; *yātaḥ*—entered upon; *daivāt*—by chance; *madhu-ripuḥ*—the enemy of the demon Madhu; *asau*—He; *locana-patham*—the path of the eyes; *tadā*—at that time; *asmākam*—our; *cetaḥ*—consciousness; *madana-hatakena*—by wretched Cupid; *āhṛtam*—stolen; *abhūt*—has become; *punaḥ*—again; *yasmin*—when; *eṣaḥ*—Kṛṣṇa; *kṣaṇam api*—even for a moment; *dṛśoḥ*—of the two eyes; *eti*—goes to; *padavīm*--the path; *vidhāsyāmaḥ*—we shall make; *tasmin*—at that time; *akhila*—all; *ghaṭikāḥ*—indications of time; *ratna-khacitāḥ*—bedecked with jewels.

TRANSLATION

" 'If, by chance, the transcendental form of Kṛṣṇa comes before My path of vision, My heart, injured from being beaten, will be stolen away

by Cupid, happiness personified. Because I could not see the beautiful form of Kṛṣṇa to My heart's content, when I again see His form I shall decorate the phases of time with many jewels.'

PURPORT

This verse is spoken by Śrīmatī Rādhārāṇī in the *Jagannātha-vallabha-nāṭaka* (3.11) of Rāmānanda Rāya.

TEXT 37

যে কালে বা স্বপনে, দেখিনু বংশীবদনে,
সেই কালে আইলা দুই বৈরি ।
'আনন্দ' আর 'মদন', হরি' নিল মোর মন,
দেখিতে না পাইনু নেত্র ভরি' ॥ ৩৭ ॥

ye kāle vā svapane, dekhinu vaṁśī-vadane,
sei kāle āilā dui vairi
'ānanda' āra 'madana', hari' nila mora mana,
dekhite nā pāinu netra bhari'

SYNONYMS

ye kāle—at the time; *vā svapane*—or in dreams; *dekhinu*—I saw; *vaṁśī-vadane*—Lord Kṛṣṇa's face with His flute; *sei kāle*—at that time; *āilā*—appeared; *dui*—two; *vairi*—enemies; *ānanda*—pleasure; *āra*—and; *madana*—Cupid; *hari'*—stealing; *nila*—took; *mora*—My; *mana*—mind; *dekhite*—to see; *nā*—not; *pāinu*—I was able; *netra*—eyes; *bhari'*—fulfilling.

TRANSLATION

"Whenever I had the chance to see Lord Kṛṣṇa's face and His flute, even in a dream, two enemies would appear before Me. They were pleasure and Cupid, and since they took away My mind, I was not able to see the face of Kṛṣṇa to the full satisfaction of My eyes.

TEXT 38

পুনঃ যদি কোন ক্ষণ, কয়ায় কৃষ্ণ দরশন,
তবে সেই ঘটী-ক্ষণ-পল ।

দিয়া মাল্যচন্দন, নানা রত্ন-আভরণ,
অলঙ্কৃত করিমু সকল ॥ ৩৮ ॥

punaḥ yadi kona kṣaṇa, kayāya kṛṣṇa daraśana,
tabe sei ghaṭī-kṣaṇa-pala
diyā mālya-candana, nānā ratna-ābharaṇa,
alaṅkṛta karimu sakala

SYNONYMS

punaḥ—again; *yadi*—if; *kona*—some; *kṣaṇa*—moment; *kayāya*—helps; *kṛṣṇa*—Lord Kṛṣṇa; *daraśana*—seeing; *tabe*—then; *sei*—that; *ghaṭī-kṣaṇa-pala*—seconds, moments and hours; *diyā*—offering; *mālya-candana*—garlands and sandalwood pulp; *nānā*—various; *ratna*—jewels; *ābharaṇa*—ornaments; *alaṅkṛta*—decorated; *karimu*—I shall make; *sakala*—all.

TRANSLATION

"If by chance such a moment comes when I can once again see Kṛṣṇa, then I shall worship those seconds, moments and hours with flower garlands and pulp of sandalwood and decorate them with all kinds of jewels and ornaments."

TEXT 39

ক্ষণে বাহ্য হৈল মন, আগে দেখে দুই জন,
তাঁরে পুছে,—আমি না চৈতন্য ?
স্বপ্নপ্রায় কি দেখিনু, কিবা আমি প্রলাপিনু,
তোমরা কিছু শুনিয়াছ দৈন্য ? ৩৯ ॥

kṣaṇe bāhya haila mana, āge dekhe dui jana,
tāṅre puche,—āmi nā caitanya?
svapna-prāya ki dekhinu, kibā āmi pralāpinu,
tomarā kichu śuniyācha dainya?

SYNONYMS

kṣaṇe—in an instant; *bāhya*—outside; *haila*—became; *mana*—the mind; *āge*—in front; *dekhe*—sees; *dui jana*—two persons; *tāṅre*—unto them; *puche*—inquires; *āmi*—I; *nā*—not; *caitanya*—conscious; *svapna-prāya*—

almost dreaming; *ki*—what; *dekhinu*—I have seen; *kibā*—what; *āmi*—I; *pralāpinu*—spoke in craziness; *tomarā*—you; *kichu*—something; *śuniyācha*—have heard; *dainya*—humility.

TRANSLATION

In an instant, Śrī Caitanya Mahāprabhu regained external consciousness and saw two persons before Him. Questioning them, He asked, "Am I conscious? What dreams have I been seeing? What craziness have I spoken? Have you heard some expressions of humility?"

PURPORT

When Śrī Caitanya Mahāprabhu thus spoke in ecstasy, He saw two persons before Him. One was His secretary, Svarūpa Dāmodara, and the other was Rāya Rāmānanda. Coming to His external consciousness, He saw them both present, and although He was still talking in the ecstasy of Śrīmatī Rādhārāṇī, He immediately began to question whether He was the same Śrī Caitanya Mahāprabhu.

TEXT 40

শুন মোর প্রাণের বান্ধব ।
নাহি কৃষ্ণ-প্রেমধন, দরিদ্র মোর জীবন,
দেহেন্দ্রিয় বৃথা মোর সব ॥ ৪০ ॥

śuna mora prāṇera bāndhava
nāhi kṛṣṇa-prema-dhana, daridra mora jīvana,
dehendriya vṛthā mora saba

SYNONYMS

śuna—kindly hear; *mora*—My; *prāṇera*—of life; *bāndhava*—friends; *nāhi*—there is none; *kṛṣṇa-prema-dhana*—wealth of love of Kṛṣṇa; *daridra*—poverty-stricken; *mora*—My; *jīvana*—life; *deha-indriya*—all the limbs and senses of My body; *vṛthā*—fruitless; *mora*—My; *saba*—all.

TRANSLATION

Śrī Caitanya Mahāprabhu continued: "My dear friends, you are all My life and soul; therefore I tell you that I possess no wealth of love for Kṛṣṇa. Consequently My life is poverty-stricken. My limbs and senses are useless."

TEXT 41

পুনঃ কহে,—হায় হায়, শুন, স্বরূপ-রামরায়,
এই মোর হৃদয়-নিশ্চয়।
শুনি, করহ বিচার, হয়, নয়—কহ সার,
এত বলি' শ্লোক উচ্চারয় ॥ ৪১ ॥

punaḥ kahe,——hāya hāya, śuna, svarūpa-rāmarāya,
ei mora hṛdaya-niścaya
śuni, karaha vicāra, haya, naya——kaha sāra,
eta bali' śloka uccāraya

SYNONYMS

punaḥ—again; *kahe*—says; *hāya hāya*—alas; *śuna*—kindly hear; *svarūpa-rāma-rāya*—My dear Svarūpa Dāmodara and Rāmānanda Rāya; *ei*—this; *mora*—My; *hṛdaya-niścaya*—the certainty in My heart; *śuni*—hearing; *karaha*—just make; *vicāra*—judgment; *haya, naya*—correct or not; *kaha sāra*—tell Me the essence; *eta bali'*—saying this; *śloka*—another verse; *uccāraya*—recites.

TRANSLATION

Again He addressed both Svarūpa Dāmodara and Rāya Rāmānanda, speaking despondently: "Alas! My friends, you can now know the certainty within My heart, and after knowing My heart you should judge whether I am correct or not. You can speak of this properly." Śrī Caitanya Mahāprabhu then began to chant another verse.

TEXT 42

কইঅবরহিঅং পেম্মং ণ হি হোই মাণুসে লোএ।
জই হোই কস্স বিরহে হোন্তম্মি কো জীঅই ॥ ৪২ ॥

kai-ava-rahi-aṁ pemmaṁ ṇa hi hoi māṇuse loe
ja-i hoi kassa virahe hontammi ko jīa-i

SYNONYMS

kai-ava-rahi-am—without any cheating propensity, without any motive concerning the four principles of material existence (namely religiosity, economic development, sense gratification and liberation); *pemmam*—love of Godhead; *ṇa*—never; *hi*—certainly; *hoi*—becomes; *māṇuse*—in human society; *loe*—in this world; *ja-i*—if; *hoi*—there is; *kassa*—whose; *virahe*—in separation; *hontammi*—is; *ko*—who; *jīa-i*—lives.

TRANSLATION

" 'Love of Godhead, devoid of cheating propensities, is not possible within this material world. If there is such a love, there cannot be separation, for if there is separation, how can one live?'

PURPORT

This is a verse in a common language called *prākṛta,* and the exact Sanskrit transformation is *kaitava-rahitaṁ prema na hi bhavati mānuṣe loke/ yadi bhavati kasya viraho virahe saty api ko jīvati.*

TEXT 43

অকৈতব কৃষ্ণপ্রেম, যেন জাম্বুনদ-হেম,
সেই প্রেমা নৃলোকে না হয়।
যদি হয় তার যোগ, না হয় তবে বিয়োগ,
বিয়োগ হৈলে কেহ না জীয়য় ॥ ৪৩ ॥

akaitava kṛṣṇa-prema, yena jāmbū-nada-hema,
sei premā nṛloke nā haya
yadi haya tāra yoga, nā haya tabe viyoga,
viyoga haile keha nā jīyaya

SYNONYMS

akaitava kṛṣṇa-prema—unalloyed love of Kṛṣṇa; *yena*—like; *jāmbū-nada-hema*—gold from the Jāmbū River; *sei premā*—that love of Godhead; *nṛ-loke*—in the material world; *nā haya*—is not possible; *yadi*—if; *haya*—there is; *tāra*—with it; *yoga*—connection; *nā*—not; *haya*—is; *tabe*—then; *viyoga*—separation; *viyoga*—separation; *haile*—if there is; *keha*—someone; *nā jīyaya*—cannot live.

TRANSLATION

"Pure love for Kṛṣṇa, just like gold from the Jāmbū River, does not exist in human society. If it existed, there could not be separation. If separation were there, one could not live."

TEXT 44

এত কহি' শচীসুত, শ্লোক পড়ে অদ্ভুত,
শুনে দুঁহে এক-মন হঞা।
আপন-হৃদয়-কাজ, কহিতে বাসিয়ে লাজ,
তবু কহি লাজবীজ খাঞা ॥ ৪৪ ॥

eta kahi' śacī-suta, śloka paḍe adbhuta,
śune duṅhe eka-mana hañā
āpana-hṛdaya-kāja, kahite vāsiye lāja,
tabu kahi lāja-bīja khāñā

SYNONYMS

eta kahi'—thus saying; *śacī-suta*—the son of Śrīmatī Śacīmātā; *śloka*—verse; *paḍe*—recites; *adbhuta*—wonderful; *śune*—hear; *duṅhe*—the two persons; *eka-mana hañā*—with rapt attention; *āpana-hṛdaya-kāja*—the activities of one's own heart; *kahite*—to speak; *vāsiye*—I feel; *lāja*—shameful; *tabu*—still; *kahi*—I speak; *lāja-bīja*—the seed of bashfulness; *khāñā*—finishing.

TRANSLATION

Thus speaking, the son of Śrīmatī Śacīmātā recited another wonderful verse, and Rāmānanda Rāya and Svarūpa Dāmodara heard this verse with rapt attention. Śrī Caitanya Mahāprabhu said, "I feel shameful to disclose the activities of My heart. Nonetheless, I shall be done with all formalities and speak from the heart. Please hear."

TEXT 45

ন প্রেমগন্ধোঽস্তি দরাপি মে হরৌ
ক্রন্দামি সৌভাগ্যভরং প্রকাশিতুম্।
বংশীবিলাস্যাননলোকনং বিনা
বিভর্মি যৎ প্রাণপতঙ্গকান্ বৃথা ॥ ৪৫ ॥

na prema-gandho 'sti darāpi me harau
krandāmi saubhāgya-bharaṁ prakāśitum
vaṁśī-vilāsy-ānana-lokanaṁ vinā
vibharmi yat prāṇa-pataṅgakān vṛthā

SYNONYMS

na—never; *prema-gandhaḥ*—a scent of love of Godhead; *asti*—there is; *darā api*—even in a slight proportion; *me*—My; *harau*—in the Supreme Personality of Godhead; *krandāmi*—I cry; *saubhāgya-bharam*—the volume of My fortune; *prakāśitum*—to exhibit; *vaṁśī-vilāsi*—of the great flute player; *ānana*—at the face; *lokanam*—looking; *vinā*—without; *vibharmi*—I carry; *yat*—because; *prāṇa-pataṅgakān*—My insect-like life; *vṛthā*—with no purpose.

TRANSLATION

Śrī Caitanya Mahāprabhu continued: "My dear friends, I have not the slightest tinge of love of Godhead within My heart. When you see Me crying in separation, I am just falsely exhibiting a demonstration of My great fortune. Indeed, not seeing the beautiful face of Kṛṣṇa playing His flute, I continue to live My life like an insect, without purpose.

TEXT 46

দূরে শুদ্ধপ্রেমগন্ধ, কপট প্রেমের বন্ধ,
সেহ মোর নাহি কৃষ্ণ-পায় ।
তবে যে করি ক্রন্দন, স্বসৌভাগ্য প্রখ্যাপন,
করি, ইহা জানিহ নিশ্চয় ॥ ৪৬ ॥

dūre śuddha-prema-gandha, kapaṭa premera bandha,
seha mora nāhi kṛṣṇa-pāya
tabe ye kari krandana, sva-saubhāgya prakhyāpana,
kari, ihā jāniha niścaya

SYNONYMS

dūre—far away; *śuddha-prema-gandha*—a scent of pure devotional love; *kapaṭa*—false; *premera*—of love of Godhead; *bandha*—binding; *seha*—that; *mora*—My; *nāhi*—there is not; *kṛṣṇa-pāya*—at the lotus feet of Kṛṣṇa; *tabe*—but; *ye*—that; *kari*—I do; *krandana*—crying; *sva-saubhāgya*—My own fortune; *prakhyāpana*—demonstration; *kari*—I do; *ihā*—this; *jāniha*—know; *niścaya*—certainly.

TRANSLATION

"Actually, My love for Kṛṣṇa is far, far away. Whatever I do is actually false. When you see Me cry, I am simply exhibiting My great fortune. Please try to understand this beyond a doubt.

TEXT 47

যাতে বংশীধ্বনি-সুখ, না দেখি' সে চাঁদ মুখ,
যদ্যপি নাহিক 'আলম্বন'।
নিজ-দেহে করি প্রীতি, কেবল কামের রীতি,
প্রাণ-কীটের করিয়ে ধারণ ॥ ৪৭ ॥

yāte vaṁśī-dhvani-sukha, nā dekhi' se cāṅda mukha,
yadyapi nāhika 'ālambana'
nija-dehe kari prīti, kevala kāmera rīti,
prāṇa-kīṭera kariye dhāraṇa

SYNONYMS

yāte—in which; *vaṁśī-dhvani-sukha*—the happiness of hearing the playing of the flute; *nā dekhi'*—not seeing; *se*—that; *cāṅda mukha*—moonlike face; *yadyapi*—although; *nāhika*—there is not; *'ālambana'*—the meeting of the lover and beloved; *nija*—own; *dehe*—in the body; *kari*—I do; *prīti*—affection; *kevala*—only; *kāmera*—of lust; *rīti*—the way; *prāṇa*—of life; *kīṭera*—of the fly; *kariye*—I do; *dhāraṇa*—continuing.

TRANSLATION

"Even though I do not see the moonlike face of Kṛṣṇa playing on His flute and although there is no possibility of My meeting Him, still I take care of My own body. That is the way of lust. In this way, I maintain My fly-like life.

PURPORT

In this connection, Śrīla Bhaktisiddhānta Sarasvatī Ṭhākura says that the lovable Supreme Lord is the supreme shelter. The Lord is the supreme subject, and the devotees are the object. The coming together of a subject and object is called *ālambana*. The object hears, and the subject plays the flute. That the object cannot see the moonlike face of Kṛṣṇa and has no eagerness to see Him is the sign of being without *ālambana*. Externally imagining such a thing simply satisfies one's lusty desires, and thus one lives without purpose.

TEXT 48

কৃষ্ণপ্রেমা সুনির্মল, যেন শুদ্ধগঙ্গাজল,
সেই প্রেমা—অমৃতের সিন্ধু।

নির্মল সে অনুরাগে, না লুকায় অন্য দাগে,
শুক্লবস্ত্রে যৈছে মসীবিন্দু ॥ ৪৮ ॥

kṛṣṇa-premā sunirmala, yena śuddha-gaṅgā-jala,
sei premā——amṛtera sindhu
nirmala se anurāge, nā lukāya anya dāge,
śukla-vastre yaiche masī-bindu

SYNONYMS

kṛṣṇa-premā—love of Kṛṣṇa; *su-nirmala*—without material contamination; *yena*—exactly like; *śuddha-gaṅgā-jala*—the pure water of the Ganges; *sei premā*—that love; *amṛtera sindhu*—the ocean of nectar; *nirmala*—pure; *se*—that; *anurāge*—attraction; *nā lukāya*—does not conceal; *anya*—other; *dāge*—spot; *śukla-vastre*—on white cloth; *yaiche*—as; *masī-bindu*—a spot of ink.

TRANSLATION

"Love for Lord Kṛṣṇa is very pure, just like the waters of the Ganges. That love is an ocean of nectar. That pure attachment to Kṛṣṇa does not conceal any spot, which would appear just like a spot of ink on a white cloth.

PURPORT

Unalloyed love of Kṛṣṇa is just like a big sheet of white cloth. Absence of attachment is compared to a black spot on that white cloth. Just as the black spot is prominent, so the absence of love of Godhead is prominent on the platform of pure love of Godhead.

TEXT 49

শুদ্ধপ্রেম-সুখসিন্ধু, পাই তার এক বিন্দু,
সেই বিন্দু জগৎ ডুবায় ।
কহিবার যোগ্য নয়, তথাপি বাউলে কয়,
কহিলে বা কেবা পাতিয়ায় ॥ ৪৯ ॥

śuddha-prema-sukha-sindhu, pāi tāra eka bindu,
sei bindu jagat ḍubāya
kahibāra yogya naya, tathāpi bāule kaya,
kahile vā kebā pātiyāya

SYNONYMS

śuddha-prema—unalloyed love; *sukha-sindhu*—the ocean of happiness; *pāi*—if I get; *tāra*—of that; *eka*—one; *bindu*—drop; *sei bindu*—that drop; *jagat*—the whole world; *ḍubāya*—drowns; *kahibāra*—to speak; *yogya naya*—is not fit; *tathāpi*—still; *bāule*—a madman; *kaya*—speaks; *kahile*—if spoken; *vā*—or; *kebā pātiyāya*—who believes.

TRANSLATION

"Unalloyed love of Kṛṣṇa is like the ocean of happiness. If someone gets one drop of it, the whole world can drown in that drop. It is not befitting to express such love of Godhead, yet a madman must speak. However, even though he speaks, no one believes him."

TEXT 50

এই মত দিনে দিনে, স্বরূপ-রামানন্দ-সনে,
নিজ-ভাব করেন বিদিত।
বাহ্যে বিষজ্বালা হয়, ভিতরে আনন্দময়,
কৃষ্ণপ্রেমার অদ্ভুত চরিত ॥ ৫০ ॥

ei mata dine dine, svarūpa-rāmānanda-sane,
nija-bhāva karena vidita
bāhye viṣa-jvālā haya, bhitare ānanda-maya,
kṛṣṇa-premāra adbhuta carita

SYNONYMS

ei mata—in this way; *dine dine*—day after day; *svarūpa*—Svarūpa Dāmodara; *rāmānanda*—Rāmānanda Rāya; *sane*—with; *nija*—own; *bhāva*—ecstasy; *karena*—makes; *vidita*—known; *bāhye*—externally; *viṣa-jvālā haya*—there is suffering from poisonous effects; *bhitare*—within; *ānanda-maya*—transcendental ecstasy; *kṛṣṇa-premāra*—of love of Kṛṣṇa; *adbhuta*—wonderful; *carita*—characteristic.

TRANSLATION

In this way, Lord Caitanya used to revel in ecstasy day after day and exhibit these ecstasies before Svarūpa and Rāmānanda Rāya. Externally there appeared severe tribulation, as if He were suffering from poisonous effects, but internally He was experiencing bliss. This is characteristic of transcendental love of Kṛṣṇa.

TEXT 51

এই প্রেমা-আস্বাদন, তপ্ত-ইক্ষু-চর্বণ,
মুখ জ্বলে, না যায় ত্যজন ।
সেই প্রেমা যাঁর মনে, তার বিক্রম সেই জানে,
বিষামৃতে একত্র মিলন ॥ ৫১ ॥

ei premā-āsvādana, tapta-ikṣu-carvaṇa,
mukha jvale, nā yāya tyajana
sei premā yāṅra mane, tāra vikrama sei jāne,
viṣāmṛte ekatra milana

SYNONYMS

ei—this; *premā*—love of Kṛṣṇa; *āsvādana*—tasting; *tapta*—hot; *ikṣu-carvaṇa*—chewing sugarcane; *mukha jvale*—the mouth burns; *nā yāya tyajana*—still not possible to give up; *sei*—that; *premā*—love of Godhead; *yāṅra mane*—in someone's mind; *tāra*—of that; *vikrama*—the power; *sei jāne*—he knows; *viṣa-amṛte*—poison and nectar; *ekatra*—in oneness; *milana*—meeting.

TRANSLATION

If one tastes such love of Godhead, he can compare it to hot sugarcane. When one chews hot sugarcane, his mouth burns, yet he cannot give it up. Similarly, if one has but a little love of Godhead, he can perceive its powerful effects. It can only be compared to poison and nectar mixed together.

TEXT 52

পীড়াভির্নবকালকূট-কটুতাগর্বস্য নির্বাসনো
নিস্যন্দেন মুদাং সুধা-মধুরিমাহঙ্কারসঙ্কোচনঃ ।
প্রেমা সুন্দরি নন্দনন্দনপরো জাগর্তি যস্যান্তরে
জ্ঞায়ন্তে স্ফুটমস্য বক্রমধুরাস্তেনৈব বিক্রান্তয়ঃ ॥ ৫২ ॥

pīḍābhir nava-kāla-kūṭa-kaṭutā-garvasya nirvāsano
nisyandena mudāṁ sudhā-madhurimāhaṅkāra-saṅkocanaḥ
premā sundari nanda-nandana-paro jāgarti yasyāntare
jñāyante sphuṭam asya vakra-madhurās tenaiva vikrāntayaḥ

SYNONYMS

pīḍābhiḥ—by the sufferings; *nava*—fresh; *kāla-kūṭa*—of poison; *kaṭutā*—of the severity; *garvasya*—of pride; *nirvāsanaḥ*—banishment; *nisyandena*—by pouring down; *mudām*—happiness; *sudhā*—of nectar; *madhurimā*—of the sweetness; *ahaṅkāra*—the pride; *saṅkocanaḥ*—minimizing; *premā*—love; *sundari*—beautiful friend; *nanda-nandana-paraḥ*—fixed upon the son of Mahārāja Nanda; *jāgarti*—develops; *yasya*—of whom; *antare*—in the heart; *jñāyante*—are perceived; *sphuṭam*—explicitly; *asya*—of that; *vakra*—crooked; *madhurāḥ*—and sweet; *tena*—by him; *eva*—alone; *vikrāntayaḥ*—the influences.

TRANSLATION

Lord Caitanya Mahāprabhu spoke: " 'My dear beautiful friend, if one develops love of Godhead, love of Kṛṣṇa, the son of Nanda Mahārāja, all the bitter and sweet influences of this love will manifest in one's heart. Such love of Godhead acts in two ways. The poisonous effects of love of Godhead defeat the severe and fresh poison of the serpent. Yet there is simultaneously transcendental bliss, which pours down and defeats the pride of nectar and diminishes its value. In other words, love of Kṛṣṇa is so powerful that it simultaneously defeats the poisonous effects of a snake, as well as the happiness derived from pouring nectar on one's head. It is perceived as doubly effective, simultaneously poisonous and nectarean.' "

PURPORT

This verse is spoken by Paurṇamāsī to Nāndīmukhī in the *Vidagdha-mādhava* (2.18) of Śrīla Rūpa Gosvāmī.

TEXT 53

যে কালে দেখে জগন্নাথ- শ্রীরাম-সুভদ্রা-সাথ,
তবে জানে—আইলাম কুরুক্ষেত্র।
সফল হৈল জীবন, দেখিলুঁ পদ্মলোচন,
জুড়াইল তনু-মন-নেত্র ॥ ৫৩ ॥

ye kāle dekhe jagannātha- śrīrāma-subhadrā-sātha,
tabe jāne——āilāma kurukṣetra
saphala haila jīvana, dekhiluṅ padma-locana,
juḍāila tanu-mana-netra

SYNONYMS

ye kāle—at that time when; *dekhe*—He sees; *jagannātha*—Lord Jagannātha; *śrī-rāma*—Balarāma; *subhadrā*—Subhadrā; *sātha*—with; *tabe*—at that time; *jāne*—knows; *āilāma*—I have come; *kuru-kṣetra*—to the pilgrimage site known as Kurukṣetra; *sa-phala*—successful; *haila*—has become; *jīvana*—life; *dekhiluṅ*—I have seen; *padma-locana*—the lotus eyes; *juḍāila*—pacified; *tanu*—body; *mana*—mind; *netra*—eyes.

TRANSLATION

When Śrī Caitanya Mahāprabhu would see Jagannātha along with Balarāma and Subhadrā, He would immediately think that He had reached Kurukṣetra, where all of Them had come. He would think that His life was successful because He had seen the lotus-eyed one, whom, if seen, pacifies the body, mind and eyes.

TEXT 54

গরুড়ের সন্নিধানে, রহি' করে দরশনে,
সে আনন্দের কি কহিব ব'লে ।
গরুড়-স্তম্ভের তলে, আছে এক নিম্ন খালে,
সে খাল ভরিল অশ্রুজলে ॥ ৫৪ ॥

garuḍera sannidhāne, rahi' kare daraśane,
se ānandera ki kahiba ba'le
garuḍa-stambhera tale, āche eka nimna khāle,
se khāla bharila aśru-jale

SYNONYMS

garuḍera—Garuḍa; *sannidhāne*—near; *rahi'*—staying; *kare*—does; *daraśane*—seeing; *se ānandera*—of that bliss; *ki*—what; *kahiba*—I shall say; *ba'le*—on the strength; *garuḍa*—of the statue of Garuḍa; *stambhera*—of the column; *tale*—underneath; *āche*—there is; *eka*—one; *nimna*—low; *khāle*—ditch; *se khāla*—that ditch; *bharila*—became filled; *aśru-jale*—with the water of tears.

TRANSLATION

Staying near the Garuḍa-stambha, the Lord would look upon Lord Jagannātha. What can be said about the strength of that love? On the

ground beneath the column of the Garuḍa-stambha was a deep ditch, and that ditch was filled with the water of His tears.

PURPORT

In front of the temple of Jagannātha is a column on which the statue of Garuḍa is situated. It is called the Garuḍa-stambha. Behind that column is a ditch, and that ditch was filled with the tears of the Lord.

TEXT 55

তাহাঁ হৈতে ঘরে আসি' মাটীর উপরে বসি',
নখে করে পৃথিবী লিখন ।
হা-হা কাহাঁ বৃন্দাবন, কাহাঁ গোপেন্দ্রনন্দন,
কাহাঁ সেই বংশীবদন ॥ ৫৫ ॥

tāhāṅ haite ghare āsi', māṭīra upare vasi',
nakhe kare pṛthivī likhana
hā-hā kāhāṅ vṛndāvana, kāhāṅ gopendra-nandana,
kāhāṅ sei vaṁśī-vadana

SYNONYMS

tāhāṅ haite—from there; *ghare āsi'*—coming back home; *māṭīra*—the ground; *upare*—upon; *vasi'*—sitting; *nakhe*—by the nails; *kare*—does; *pṛthivī*—on the surface of the earth; *likhana*—marking; *hā-hā*—alas; *kāhāṅ*—where is; *vṛndāvana*—Vṛndāvana; *kāhāṅ*—where; *gopa-indra-nandana*—the son of the King of the cowherd men; *kāhāṅ*—where; *sei*—that; *vaṁśī-vadana*—the person with the flute.

TRANSLATION

When coming from the Jagannātha temple to return to His house, Śrī Caitanya Mahāprabhu used to sit on the ground and mark it with His nails. At such times He would be greatly morose and would cry, "Alas, where is Vṛndāvana? Where is Kṛṣṇa, the son of the King of the cowherd men? Where is that person who plays the flute?"

TEXT 56

কাহাঁ সে ত্রিভঙ্গঠাম, কাহাঁ সেই বেণুগান,
কাহাঁ সেই যমুনা-পুলিন ।

কাহাঁ সে রাসবিলাস, কাহাঁ নৃত্যগীত-হাস,
কাহাঁ প্রভু মদনমোহন ॥ ৫৬ ॥

kāhāṅ se tri-bhaṅga-ṭhāma, kāhāṅ sei veṇu-gāna,
kāhāṅ sei yamunā-pulina
kāhāṅ se rāsa-vilāsa, kāhāṅ nṛtya-gīta-hāsa,
kāhāṅ prabhu madana-mohana

SYNONYMS

kāhāṅ—where; *se*—that; *tri-bhaṅga-ṭhāma*—figure curved in three places; *kāhāṅ*—where; *sei*—that; *veṇu-gāna*—sweet song of the flute; *kāhāṅ*—where; *sei*—that; *yamunā-pulina*—bank of the Yamunā River; *kāhāṅ*—where; *se*—that; *rāsa-vilāsa*—*rāsa* dance; *kāhāṅ*—where; *nṛtya-gīta-hāsa*—dancing, music and laughing; *kāhāṅ*—where; *prabhu*—My Lord; *madana-mohana*—the enchanter of Madana (Cupid).

TRANSLATION

Śrī Caitanya Mahāprabhu used to lament by saying: "Where is Śrī Kṛṣṇa, whose form is curved in three places? Where is the sweet song of His flute, and where is the bank of the Yamunā? Where is the rāsa dance? Where is that dancing, singing, and laughing? Where is My Lord, Madana-mohana, the enchanter of Cupid?"

TEXT 57

উঠিল নানা ভাবাবেগ, মনে হৈল উদ্বেগ,
ক্ষণমাত্র নারে গোঙাইতে ।
প্রবল বিরহানলে, ধৈর্য হৈল টলমলে,
নানা শ্লোক লাগিলা পড়িতে ॥ ৫৭ ॥

uṭhila nānā bhāvāvega, mane haila udvega,
kṣaṇa-mātra nāre goṅāite
prabala virahānale, dhairya haila ṭalamale,
nānā śloka lāgilā paḍite

SYNONYMS

uṭhila—arose; *nānā*—various; *bhāva-āvega*—forces of emotion; *mane*—in the mind; *haila*—there was; *udvega*—anxiety; *kṣaṇa-mātra*—even for a moment; *nāre*—not able; *goṅāite*—to pass; *prabala*—powerful; *viraha-anale*—in the fire of separation; *dhairya*—patience; *haila*—became; *ṭalamale*—tottering; *nānā*—various; *śloka*—verses; *lāgilā*—began; *paḍite*—to recite.

TRANSLATION

In this way various ecstatic emotions evolved, and the Lord's mind filled with anxiety. He could not escape even for a moment. In this way, because of fierce feelings of separation, His patience began to totter, and He began to recite various verses.

TEXT 58

অমূন্যধন্যানি দিনান্তরাণি হরে ত্বদালোকনমন্তরেণ ।
অনাথবন্ধো করুণৈকসিন্ধো হা হন্ত হা হন্ত কথং নয়ামি ॥

amūny adhanyāni dināntarāṇi
hare tvad-ālokanam antareṇa
anātha-bandho karuṇaika-sindho
hā hanta hā hanta kathaṁ nayāmi

SYNONYMS

amūni—all those; *adhanyāni*—inauspicious; *dina-antarāṇi*—other days; *hare*—O My Lord; *tvat*—of You; *ālokanam*—seeing; *antareṇa*—without; *anātha-bandho*—O friend of the helpless; *karuṇā-eka-sindho*—O only ocean of mercy; *hā hanta*—alas; *hā hanta*—alas; *katham*—how; *nayāmi*—shall I pass.

TRANSLATION

" 'O My Lord, O Supreme Personality of Godhead, O friend of the helpless! You are the only ocean of mercy! Because I have not met You, My inauspicious days and nights have become unbearable. I do not know how I shall pass the time.'

PURPORT

This is a verse from *Kṛṣṇa-karṇāmṛta* (41) by Bilvamaṅgala Ṭhākura.

TEXT 59

তোমার দর্শন-বিনে, অধন্য এ রাত্রি-দিনে,
এই কাল না যায় কাটন ।

তুমি অনাথের বন্ধু, অপার করুণা-সিন্ধু,
কৃপা করি' দেহ দরশন ॥ ৫৯ ॥

tomāra darśana-vine, adhanya e rātri-dine,
ei kāla nā yāya kāṭana
tumi anāthera bandhu, apāra karuṇā-sindhu,
kṛpā kari' deha daraśana

SYNONYMS

tomāra—Your; *darśana*—audience; *vine*—without; *adhanya*—inauspicious; *e*—this; *rātri-dine*—night and day; *ei kāla*—this time; *nā yāya*—does not go; *kāṭana*—passing; *tumi*—You; *anāthera bandhu*—friend of the helpless; *apāra*—unlimited; *karuṇā-sindhu*—ocean of mercy; *kṛpā kari'*—showing mercy; *deha*—kindly give; *daraśana*—audience.

TRANSLATION

"All these inauspicious days and nights are not passing, for I have not met You. It is difficult to know how to pass all this time. But You are the friend of the helpless and an ocean of mercy. Kindly give Me Your audience, for I am in a precarious position."

TEXT 60

উঠিল ভাব-চাপল, মন হইল চঞ্চল,
ভাবের গতি বুঝন না যায়।
অদর্শনে পোড়ে মন, কেমনে পাব দরশন,
কৃষ্ণ-ঠাঞি পুছেন উপায় ॥ ৬০ ॥

uṭhila bhāva-cāpala, mana ha-ila cañcala,
bhāvera gati bujhana nā yāya
adarśane poḍe mana, kemane pāba daraśana,
kṛṣṇa-ṭhāñi puchena upāya

SYNONYMS

uṭhila—arose; *bhāva-cāpala*—restlessness of ecstatic emotion; *mana*—mind; *ha-ila*—became; *cañcala*—agitated; *bhāvera*—of ecstatic emotion; *gati*—the course; *bujhana*—understanding; *nā yāya*—not possible; *adar-*

śane—without seeing; *poḍe*—burns; *mana*—the mind; *kemane*—how; *pāba*—I shall get; *daraśana*—audience; *kṛṣṇa-ṭhāñi*—from Kṛṣṇa; *puchena*—inquires; *upāya*—the means.

TRANSLATION

In this way, the Lord's restlessness was awakened by ecstatic feelings, and His mind became agitated. No one could understand what course such ecstasy would take. Not being able to meet the Supreme Personality of Godhead, Kṛṣṇa, Lord Caitanya's mind burned. He began to ask Kṛṣṇa of the means by which He could reach Him.

TEXT 61

ত্বচ্ছৈশবং ত্রিভুবনাদ্ভুতমিত্যবেহি
মচ্চাপলঞ্চ তব বা মম বাধিগম্যম্ ।
তৎ কিং করোমি বিরলং মুরলীবিলাসি
মুগ্ধং মুখাম্বুজমুদীক্ষিতুমীক্ষণাভ্যাম্ ॥ ৬১ ॥

tvac-chaiśavaṁ tri-bhuvanādbhutam ity avehi
mac-cāpalaṁ ca tava vā mama vādhigamyam
tat kiṁ karomi viralaṁ muralī-vilāsi
mugdhaṁ mukhāmbujam udīkṣitum īkṣaṇābhyām

SYNONYMS

tvat—Your; *śaiśavam*—early age; *tri-bhuvana*—within the three worlds; *adbhutam*—wonderful; *iti*—thus; *avehi*—know; *mat-cāpalam*—My unsteadiness; *ca*—and; *tava*—of You; *vā*—or; *mama*—of Me; *vā*—or; *adhigamyam*—to be understood; *tat*—that; *kim*—what; *karomi*—I do; *viralam*—in solitude; *muralī-vilāsi*—O player of the flute; *mugdham*—attractive; *mukha-ambujam*—lotuslike face; *udīkṣitum*—to see sufficiently; *īkṣaṇābhyām*—by the eyes.

TRANSLATION

" 'O Kṛṣṇa, O flute-player, the sweetness of Your early age is wonderful within these three worlds. You know My unsteadiness, and I know Yours. No one else knows about this. I want to see Your beautiful attractive face somewhere in a solitary place, but how can this be accomplished?'

PURPORT

This is another quote from the *Kṛṣṇa-karṇāmṛta* (32) of Bilvamaṅgala Ṭhākura.

TEXT 62

তোমার মাধুরী-বল, তাতে মোর চাপল,
এই দুই, তুমি আমি জানি।
কাহাঁ করোঁ কাহাঁ যাঙ, কাহাঁ গেলে তোমা পাঙ,
তাহা মোরে কহ ত' আপনি ॥ ৬২ ॥

tomāra mādhurī-bala, tāte mora cāpala,
ei dui, tumi āmi jāni
kāhāṅ karoṅ kāhāṅ yāṅ, kāhāṅ gele tomā pāṅ,
tāhā more kaha ta' āpani

SYNONYMS

tomāra—Your; *mādhurī-bala*—strength of sweetness; *tāte*—in that; *mora*—My; *cāpala*—impotence; *ei*—these; *dui*—two; *tumi*—You; *āmi*—I; *jāni*—know; *kāhāṅ*—where; *karoṅ*—I do; *kāhāṅ*—where; *yāṅ*—I go; *kāhāṅ*—where; *gele*—by going; *tomā*—You; *pāṅ*—I can get; *tāhā*—that; *more*—unto Me; *kaha*—please speak; *ta' āpani*—You.

TRANSLATION

"My dear Kṛṣṇa, only You and I know the strength of Your beautiful features and, because of them, My unsteadiness. Now, this is My position; I do not know what to do or where to go. Where can I find You? I am asking You to give directions."

TEXT 63

নানা-ভাবের প্রাবল্য, হৈল সন্ধি-শাবল্য,
ভাবে-ভাবে হৈল মহারণ।
ঔৎসুক্য, চাপল্য, দৈন্য, রোষামর্ষ আদি সৈন্য,
প্রেমোন্মাদ—সবার কারণ ॥ ৬৩ ॥

nānā-bhāvera prābalya, haila sandhi-śābalya,
bhāve-bhāve haila mahā-raṇa

autsukya, cāpalya, dainya, roṣāmarṣa ādi sainya,
premonmāda——sabāra kāraṇa

SYNONYMS

nānā—various; *bhāvera*—of ecstasies; *prābalya*—the force; *haila*—there was; *sandhi*—meeting; *śābalya*—contradiction; *bhāve-bhāve*—between ecstasies; *haila*—there was; *mahā-raṇa*—a great fight; *autsukya*—eagerness; *cāpalya*—impotence; *dainya*—humility; *roṣa-amarṣa*—anger and impatience; *ādi*—all these; *sainya*—soldiers; *prema-unmāda*—madness in love; *sabāra*—of all; *kāraṇa*—the cause.

TRANSLATION

Because of the various kinds of ecstasy, contradictory states of mind occurred, and this resulted in a great fight between different types of ecstasy. Anxiety, impotence, humility, anger and impatience were all like soldiers fighting, and the madness of love of Godhead was the cause.

PURPORT

In *Bhakti-rasāmṛta-sindhu* it is stated that when similar ecstasies from separate causes meet, they are called *svarūpa-sandhi.* When opposing elements meet, whether they arise from a common cause or different causes, their conjunction is called *bhinna-rūpa-sandhi,* the meeting of contradictory ecstasies. The simultaneous joining of different ecstasies—fear and happiness, regret and happiness—is called meeting (*sandhi*). The word *śābalya* refers to different types of ecstatic symptoms combined together, like pride, despondency, humility, remembrance, doubt, impatience caused by insult, fear, disappointment, patience and eagerness. The friction that occurs when these combine is called *śābalya.* Similarly, when the desire to see the object is very prominent, or when one is unable to tolerate any delay in seeing the desired object, the incapability is called *autsukya,* or eagerness. If such eagerness is present, one's mouth dries up, and he becomes restless. He also becomes full of anxiety, and hard breathing and patience are observed. Similarly, the lightness of heart caused by strong attachment and strong agitation of the mind is called impotence (*cāpalya*). Failure of judgment, misuse of words, and obstinate activities devoid of anxiety are observed. Similarly, when one becomes too angry at the other party, offensive and abominable speech occurs, and this anger is called *roṣa.* When one becomes impatient due to being scolded or insulted, the resultant state of mind is called *amarṣa.* In this state of mind, one perspires, acquires a headache, fades in bodily color and experiences anxiety and an urge to search out the remedy. The bearing of a grudge, aversion and chastisement are all visible symptoms.

TEXT 64

মত্তগজ ভাবগণ, প্রভুর দেহ—ইক্ষুবন,
গজ-যুদ্ধে বনের দলন ।
প্রভুর হৈল দিব্যোন্মাদ, তনুমনের অবসাদ,
ভাবাবেশে করে সম্বোধন ॥ ৬৪ ॥

matta-gaja bhāva-gaṇa, prabhura deha——ikṣu-vana,
gaja-yuddhe vanera dalana
prabhura haila divyonmāda, tanu-manera avasāda,
bhāvāveśe kare sambodhana

SYNONYMS

matta-gaja—mad elephant; *bhāva-gaṇa*—symptoms of ecstasy; *prabhura*—of the Lord; *deha*—body; *ikṣu-vana*—sugarcane forest; *gaja-yuddhe*—in the fight of the elephants; *vanera*—of the forest; *dalana*—trampling; *prabhura*—of the Lord; *haila*—was; *divya-unmāda*—transcendental madness; *tanu-manera*—of the mind and body; *avasāda*—despondency; *bhāva-āveśe*—on account of absorption in ecstasy; *kare*—does; *sambodhana*—addressing.

TRANSLATION

The body of the Lord was just like a field of sugarcane into which the mad elephants of ecstasy entered. There was a fight amongst the elephants, and in the process the entire field of sugarcane was destroyed. Thus transcendental madness was awakened in the body of the Lord, and He experienced despondency in mind and body. In this ecstatic condition, He began to speak as follows.

TEXT 65

হে দেব হে দয়িত হে ভুবনৈকবন্ধো
হে কৃষ্ণ হে চপল হে করুণৈকসিন্ধো ।
হে নাথ হে রমণ হে নয়নাভিরাম
হা হা কদা নু ভবিতাসি পদং দৃশোর্মে ॥ ৬৫ ॥

he deva he dayita he bhuvanaika-bandho
he kṛṣṇa he capala he karuṇaika-sindho
he nātha he ramaṇa he nayanābhirāma
hā hā kadā nu bhavitāsi padaṁ dṛśor me

SYNONYMS

he deva—O Lord; *he dayita*—O most dear; *he bhuvana-eka-bandho*—O only friend of the universe; *he kṛṣṇa*—O Lord Kṛṣṇa; *he capala*—O restless one; *he karuṇa-eka-sindho*—O ocean of mercy; *he nātha*—O My Lord; *he ramaṇa*—O My enjoyer; *he nayana-abhirāma*—O most beautiful to My eyes; *hā hā*—alas; *kadā*—when; *nu*—certainly; *bhavitāsi*—will You be; *padam*—the dwelling place; *dṛśoḥ me*—of My vision.

TRANSLATION

" 'O My Lord! O dearest one! O only friend of the universe! O Kṛṣṇa, O restless one, O ocean of mercy! O My Lord, O My enjoyer, O beloved to My eyes! Alas, when will You again be visible to Me?' "

PURPORT

This is Text 40 of *Kṛṣṇa-karṇāmṛta*.

TEXT 66

উন্মাদের লক্ষণ, করায় কৃষ্ণ-স্ফুরণ,
ভাবাবেশে উঠে প্রণয় মান ।
সোল্লুণ্ঠ-বচন-রীতি, মান, গর্ব্ব, ব্যাজ-স্তুতি,
কভু নিন্দা, কভু বা সম্মান ॥ ৬৬ ॥

unmādera lakṣaṇa, karāya kṛṣṇa-sphuraṇa,
bhāvāveśe uṭhe praṇaya māna
solluṇṭha-vacana-rīti, māna, garva, vyāja-stuti,
kabhu nindā, kabhu vā sammāna

SYNONYMS

unmādera lakṣaṇa—the symptoms of madness; *karāya*—causes; *kṛṣṇa*—Lord Kṛṣṇa; *sphuraṇa*—impetus; *bhāva-āveśe*—in an ecstatic condition; *uṭhe*—awakens; *praṇaya*—love; *māna*—disdain; *solluṇṭha-vacana*—of disrespect by sweet words; *rīti*—the way; *māna*—honor; *garva*—pride; *vyāja-*

stuti—indirect prayer; *kabhu*—sometimes; *nindā*—blasphemy; *kabhu*—sometimes; *vā*—or; *sammāna*—honor.

TRANSLATION

The symptoms of madness served as an impetus for remembering Kṛṣṇa. The mood of ecstasy awoke love, disdain, defamation by words, pride, honor and indirect prayer. Thus Śrī Kṛṣṇa was sometimes blasphemed and sometimes honored.

PURPORT

The word *unmāda* is explained in *Bhakti-rasāmṛta-sindhu* as extreme joy, misfortune and bewilderment in the heart due to separation. Symptoms of *unmāda* are laughing like a madman, dancing, singing, performing ineffectual activities, talking nonsense, running, shouting and sometimes working in contradictory ways. The word *praṇaya* is explained thus: When there is a possibility to receive direct honor, but it is avoided, that love is called *praṇaya*. Śrīla Rūpa Gosvāmī, in his *Ujjvala-nīlamaṇi,* explains the word *māna* thus: When the lover feels novel sweetness by exchanging hearty loving words but wishes to hide his feelings by crooked means, *māna* is experienced.

TEXT 67

তুমি দেব—ক্রীড়া-রত, ভুবনের নারী যত,
তাহে কর অভীষ্ট ক্রীড়ন ।
তুমি মোর দয়িত, মোতে বৈসে তোমার চিত,
মোর ভাগ্যে কৈলে আগমন ॥ ৬৭ ॥

tumi deva——krīḍā-rata, bhuvanera nārī yata,
tāhe kara abhīṣṭa krīḍana
tumi mora dayita, mote vaise tomāra cita,
mora bhāgye kaile āgamana

SYNONYMS

tumi—You; *deva*—the Supreme Lord; *krīḍā-rata*—engaged in Your pastimes; *bhuvanera*—of all the universes; *nārī*—women; *yata*—all; *tāhe*—in those pastimes; *kara*—You do; *abhīṣṭa*—desired; *krīḍana*—acting; *tumi*—You; *mora*—My; *dayita*—merciful; *mote*—to Me; *vaise*—rest; *tomāra*—Your; *cita*—mind; *mora*—My; *bhāgye*—by fortune; *kaile*—You have made; *āgamana*—appearance.

TRANSLATION

"My dear Lord, You are engaged in Your pastimes, and You utilize all the women in the universe according to Your desire. You are so kind to Me. Please divert Your attention to Me, for by fortune You have appeared before Me.

TEXT 68

ভুবনের নারীগণ, সবা' কর আকর্ষণ,
তাহাঁ কর সব সমাধান।
তুমি কৃষ্ণ—চিত্তহর, ঐছে কোন পামর,
তোমারে বা কেবা করে মান॥ ৬৮॥

bhuvanera nārī-gaṇa, sabā' kara ākarṣaṇa,
tāhāṅ kara saba samādhāna
tumi kṛṣṇa——citta-hara, aiche kona pāmara,
tomāre vā kebā kare māna

SYNONYMS

bhuvanera—of all the universe; *nārī-gaṇa*—women; *sabā'*—all; *kara*—You do; *ākarṣaṇa*—attraction; *tāhāṅ*—there; *kara*—You made; *saba*—all; *samādhāna*—adjustment; *tumi*—You; *kṛṣṇa*—Lord Kṛṣṇa; *citta-hara*—the enchanter of the mind; *aiche*—in that way; *kona*—some; *pāmara*—debauchee; *tomāre*—You; *vā*—or; *kebā*—who; *kare*—does; *māna*—honor.

TRANSLATION

"My dear Lord, You attract all the women of the universe, and You make adjustments for all of them when they appear. You are Lord Kṛṣṇa, and You can enchant everyone, but on the whole, You are nothing but a debauchee. Who can honor You?

TEXT 69

তোমার চপল-মতি, একত্র না হয় স্থিতি,
তা'তে তোমার নাহি কিছু দোষ।
তুমি ত' করুণাসিন্ধু, আমার পরাণ-বন্ধু,
তোমায় নাহি মোর কভু রোষ॥ ৬৯॥

tomāra capala-mati, ekatra nā haya sthiti,
tā'te tomāra nāhi kichu doṣa
tumi ta' karuṇā-sindhu, āmāra parāṇa-bandhu,
tomāya nāhi mora kabhu roṣa

SYNONYMS

tomāra—Your; *capala-mati*—restless mind; *ekatra*—in one place; *nā*—never; *haya*—is; *sthiti*—established; *tā'te*—in that; *tomāra*—Your; *nāhi*—there is not; *kichu*—any; *doṣa*—fault; *tumi*—You are; *ta'*—certainly; *karuṇā-sindhu*—the ocean of mercy; *āmāra*—My; *parāṇa-bandhu*—friend of the heart; *tomāya*—toward You; *nāhi*—there is not; *mora*—My; *kabhu*—any time; *roṣa*—anger.

TRANSLATION

"My dear Kṛṣṇa, Your mind is always restless. You cannot remain in one place, but You are not at fault for this. You are actually the ocean of mercy, the friend of My heart. Therefore I have no reason to be angry with You.

TEXT 70

তুমি নাথ—ব্রজপ্রাণ, ব্রজের কর পরিত্রাণ,
বহু কার্যে নাহি অবকাশ ।
তুমি আমার রমণ, সুখ দিতে আগমন,
এ তোমার বৈদগ্ধ্য-বিলাস ॥ ৭০ ॥

tumi nātha——vraja-prāṇa, vrajera kara paritrāṇa,
bahu kārye nāhi avakāśa
tumi āmāra ramaṇa, sukha dite āgamana,
e tomāra vaidagdhya-vilāsa

SYNONYMS

tumi—You; *nātha*—the master; *vraja-prāṇa*—the life of Vrajabhūmi (Vṛndāvana); *vrajera*—of Vraja; *kara*—do; *paritrāṇa*—deliverance; *bahu*—many; *kārye*—in activities; *nāhi*—there is not; *avakāśa*—rest; *tumi*—You; *āmāra*—My; *ramaṇa*—enjoyer; *sukha*—happiness; *dite*—to give; *āgamana*—appearing; *e*—this; *tomāra*—Your; *vaidagdhya-vilāsa*—activities of expert transactions.

TRANSLATION

"My dear Lord, You are the master and the life and soul of Vṛndāvana. Kindly arrange for the deliverance of Vṛndāvana. We have no leisure hours away from our many activities. Actually, You are My enjoyer. You have appeared just to give Me happiness, and this is one of Your expert activities.

PURPORT

The word *vaidagdhya* means that one must be very expert, learned, humorous, cunning, beautiful and expert in manifesting caricatures.

TEXT 71

মোর বাক্য নিন্দা মানি, কৃষ্ণ ছাড়ি' গেলা জানি,
শুন, মোর এ স্তুতি-বচন।
নয়নের অভিরাম, তুমি মোর ধন-প্রাণ,
হাহা পুনঃ দেহ দরশন ॥ ৭১ ॥

mora vākya nindā māni, kṛṣṇa chāḍi' gelā jāni,
śuna, mora e stuti-vacana
nayanera abhirāma, tumi mora dhana-prāṇa,
hā-hā punaḥ deha daraśana

SYNONYMS

mora—My; *vākya*—words; *nindā*—blasphemy; *māni*—accepting; *kṛṣṇa*—Lord Kṛṣṇa; *chāḍi'*—giving up; *gelā*—went away; *jāni*—I know; *śuna*—hear; *mora*—My; *e*—this; *stuti-vacana*—words of praise; *nayanera*—of the eyes; *abhirāma*—the satisfaction; *tumi*—You are; *mora*—My; *dhana-prāṇa*—wealth and life; *hā-hā*—alas; *punaḥ*—again; *deha*—give Me; *daraśana*—audience.

TRANSLATION

"Taking My words as defamation, Lord Kṛṣṇa has left Me. I know that He is gone, but kindly hear My prayers in praise. You are the satisfaction of My eyes. You are My wealth and My life. Alas, please give Me your audience once again."

TEXT 72

স্তম্ভ, কম্প, প্রস্বেদ, বৈবর্ণ্য, অশ্রু, স্বরভেদ,
দেহ হৈল পুলকে ব্যাপিত ।
হাসে, কান্দে, নাচে, গায়, উঠি' ইতি উতি ধায়,
ক্ষণে ভূমে পড়িয়া মূর্চ্ছিত ॥ ৭২ ॥

stambha, kampa, prasveda, vaivarṇya, aśru, svara-bheda,
deha haila pulake vyāpita
hāse, kānde, nāce, gāya, uṭhi' iti uti dhāya,
kṣaṇe bhūme paḍiyā mūrcchita

SYNONYMS

stambha—being stunned; *kampa*—trembling; *prasveda*—perspiration; *vaivarṇya*—fading away of the color; *aśru*—tears; *svara-bheda*—choking of the voice; *deha*—body; *haila*—was; *pulake*—in joy; *vyāpita*—pervaded; *hāse*—laughs; *kānde*—cries; *nāce*—dances; *gāya*—sings; *uṭhi'*—getting up; *iti uti*—here and there; *dhāya*—runs; *kṣaṇe*—sometimes; *bhūme*—on the ground; *paḍiyā*—falling down; *mūrcchita*—unconscious.

TRANSLATION

There were different transformations of the body of Lord Caitanya Mahāprabhu: being stunned, trembling, perspiring, fading away of color, weeping and choking. In this way His whole body was pervaded by transcendental joy. As a result, sometimes Caitanya Mahāprabhu would laugh, sometimes cry, sometimes dance and sometimes sing. Sometimes He would get up and run here and there, and sometimes fall on the ground and lose consciousness.

PURPORT

In *Bhakti-rasāmṛta-sindhu,* eight kinds of transcendental change taking place in the body are described. *Stambha,* being stunned, refers to the mind's becoming transcendentally absorbed. In that state, the peaceful mind is placed on the life air, and different bodily transformations are manifest. These symptoms are visible in the body of an advanced devotee. When life becomes almost inactive, it is called "stunned." The emotions resulting from this condition are joy, fear, astonishment, moroseness and anger. In this condition, the power of speech is lost, and there is no movement in the hands and legs.

Otherwise, being stunned is a mental condition. Many other symptoms are visible on the entire body in the beginning. These are very subtle, but gradually they become very apparent. When one cannot speak, naturally one's active senses are arrested, and the knowledge-acquiring senses are rendered inoperative. *Kampa,* trembling of the body, is mentioned in *Bhakti-rasāmṛta-sindhu* as a result of a special kind of fear, anger and joy. This is called *vepathu,* or *kampa.* When the body begins to perspire because of joy, fear and anger combined, this is called *sveda. Vaivarṇya* is described as a change in the bodily color. It is caused by a combination of moroseness, anger and fear. When these emotions are experienced, the complexion turns pale, and the body becomes lean and thin. *Aśru* is explained in *Bhakti-rasāmṛta-sindhu* as a combination of joy, anger and moroseness that causes water to flow from the eyes without effort. When there is joy and there are tears in the eyes, the temperature of the tears is cold, but when there is anger, the tears are hot. In both cases, the eyes are restless, the eyeballs are red and there is itching. These are all symptoms of *aśru.* When there is a combination of moroseness, astonishment, anger, joy and fear, there is a choking in the voice. This choking is called *gadgada.* Śrī Caitanya Mahāprabhu refers to *gadgada-ruddhayā girā,* or "a faltering voice." In *Bhakti-rasāmṛta-sindhu, pulaka* is described as joy, encouragement and fear. When these combine, the hairs on the body stand on end, and this bodily state is called *pulaka.*

TEXT 73

মূর্চ্ছায় হৈল সাক্ষাৎকার, উঠি' করে হুহুঙ্কার,
কহে—এই আইলা মহাশয়।
কৃষ্ণের মাধুরী-গুণে, নানা ভ্রম হয় মনে,
শ্লোক পড়ি' করয়ে নিশ্চয় ॥ ৭৩ ॥

mūrcchāya haila sākṣātkāra, uṭhi' kare huhuṅkāra,
kahe——ei āilā mahāśaya
kṛṣṇera mādhurī-guṇe, nānā bhrama haya mane,
śloka paḍi' karaye niścaya

SYNONYMS

mūrcchāya—in the swoon; *haila*—there was; *sākṣātkāra*—direct meeting; *uṭhi'*—getting up; *kare*—does; *hu-huṅkāra*—tumultuous sound; *kahe*—says; *ei*—thus; *āilā*—He has come; *mahā-āśaya*—the great personality; *kṛṣṇera*—

of Lord Kṛṣṇa; *mādhurī*—sweetness; *guṇe*—by qualities; *nānā*—various; *bhrama*—mistakes; *haya*—are; *mane*—in the mind; *śloka*—the verse; *paḍi'*—reading; *karaye*—does; *niścaya*—ascertainment.

TRANSLATION

When Śrī Caitanya Mahāprabhu was thus unconscious, He happened to meet the Supreme Personality of Godhead. Consequently He got up and immediately made a tumultuous sound, very loudly declaring, "Now Kṛṣṇa, the great personality, is present." In this way, because of Kṛṣṇa's sweet qualities, Caitanya Mahāprabhu made different types of mistakes in His mind. Thus by reading the following verse, He ascertained the presence of Lord Kṛṣṇa.

TEXT 74

মারঃ স্বয়ং নু মধুরদ্যুতিমণ্ডলং নু
মাধুর্যমেব নু মনোনয়নামৃতং নু ।
বেণীমৃজো নু মম জীবিতবল্লভো নু
কৃষ্ণোঽয়মভ্যুদয়তে মম লোচনায় ॥ ৭৪ ॥

māraḥ svayaṁ nu madhura-dyuti-maṇḍalaṁ nu
mādhuryam eva nu mano-nayanāmṛtaṁ nu
veṇī-mṛjo nu mama jīvita-vallabho nu
kṛṣṇo 'yam abhyudayate mama locanāya

SYNONYMS

māraḥ—Cupid; *svayam*—personally; *nu*—whether; *madhura*—sweet; *dyuti*—of effulgence; *maṇḍalam*—encirclement; *nu*—whether; *mādhuryam*—sweetness; *eva*—even; *nu*—certainly; *manaḥ-nayana-amṛtam*—nectar for the mind and eyes; *nu*—whether; *veṇī-mṛjaḥ*—loosening of the hair; *nu*—whether; *mama*—My; *jīvita-vallabhaḥ*—the pleasure of the life and soul; *nu*—whether; *kṛṣṇaḥ*—Lord Kṛṣṇa; *ayam*—this; *abhyudayate*—manifests; *mama*—My; *locanāya*—for the eyes.

TRANSLATION

In the attitude of Rādhārāṇī, Śrī Caitanya Mahāprabhu addressed the gopīs: " 'My dear friends, where is that Kṛṣṇa, Cupid personified, who has the effulgence of a kadamba flower, who is sweetness itself, the nectar of

My eyes and mind, He who loosens the hair of the gopīs, who is the supreme source of transcendental bliss and My life and soul? Has He come before My eyes again?' "

PURPORT

This is another verse from *Kṛṣṇa-karṇāmṛta* (68).

TEXT 75

কিবা এই সাক্ষাৎ কাম, দ্যুতিবিম্ব মূর্তিমান্,
কি মাধুর্য স্বয়ং মূর্তিমন্ত ।
কিবা মনো-নেত্রোৎসব, কিবা প্রাণবল্লভ,
সত্য কৃষ্ণ আইলা নেত্রানন্দ ॥ ৭৫ ॥

kibā ei sākṣāt kāma, dyuti-bimba mūrtimān,
ki mādhurya svayaṁ mūrtimanta
kibā mano-netrotsava, kibā prāṇa-vallabha,
satya kṛṣṇa āilā netrānanda

SYNONYMS

kibā—whether; *ei*—this; *sākṣāt*—directly; *kāma*—Cupid; *dyuti-bimba*—reflection of the effulgence; *mūrtimān*—personified; *ki*—whether; *mādhurya*—sweetness; *svayam*—personally; *mūrtimanta*—personified; *kibā*—whether; *manaḥ-netra-utsava*—festival of the mind and eyes; *kibā*—whether; *prāṇa-vallabha*—My life and soul; *satya*—truly; *kṛṣṇa*—Lord Kṛṣṇa; *āilā*—has come; *netra-ānanda*—the pleasure of My eyes.

TRANSLATION

Śrī Caitanya Mahāprabhu then would begin to talk like this: "Is Cupid personified present with the effulgence and reflection of the kadamba tree? Is He the same person, personified sweetness, who is the pleasure of My eyes and mind, who is My life and soul? Has Kṛṣṇa actually come before My eyes?"

TEXT 76

গুরু—নানা ভাবগণ, শিষ্য—প্রভুর তনু-মন,
নানা রীতে সতত নাচায় ।

নির্বেদ, বিষাদ, দৈন্য, চাপল্য, হর্ষ, ধৈর্য, মন্যু,
এই নৃত্যে প্রভুর কাল যায় ॥ ৭৬ ॥

guru——nānā bhāva-gaṇa, śiṣya——prabhura tanu-mana,
nānā rīte satata nācāya
nirveda, viṣāda, dainya, cāpalya, harṣa, dhairya, manyu,
ei nṛtye prabhura kāla yāya

SYNONYMS

guru—the teacher; *nānā*—various; *bhāva-gaṇa*—ecstasies; *śiṣya*—disciples; *prabhura*—of Lord Caitanya; *tanu-mana*—body and mind; *nānā*—various; *rīte*—in ways; *satata*—always; *nācāya*—causes to dance; *nirveda*—despondency; *viṣāda*—moroseness; *dainya*—humility; *cāpalya*—restlessness; *harṣa*—joy; *dhairya*—endurance; *manyu*—anger; *ei*—this; *nṛtye*—in dancing; *prabhura*—of the Lord; *kāla*—time; *yāya*—passes.

TRANSLATION

As the spiritual master chastises the disciple and teaches him the art of devotional service, so all the ecstatic symptoms of Lord Caitanya Mahāprabhu—including despondency, moroseness, humility, restlessness, joy, endurance and anger—all instructed His body and mind. In this way, Śrī Caitanya Mahāprabhu passed His time.

TEXT 77

চণ্ডীদাস, বিদ্যাপতি, রায়ের নাটক-গীতি,
কর্ণামৃত, শ্রীগীতগোবিন্দ ।
স্বরূপ-রামানন্দ-সনে, মহাপ্রভু রাত্রি-দিনে,
গায়, শুনে—পরম আনন্দ ॥ ৭৭ ॥

caṇḍīdāsa, vidyāpati, rāyera nāṭaka-gīti,
karṇāmṛta, śrī-gīta-govinda
svarūpa-rāmānanda-sane, mahāprabhu rātri-dine,
gāya, śune——parama ānanda

SYNONYMS

caṇḍī-dāsa—the poet Caṇḍīdāsa; *vidyā-pati*—the poet Vidyāpati; *rāyera*—of the poet Rāya Rāmānanda; *nāṭaka*—the *Jagannātha-vallabha-*

nāṭaka; gīti—songs; *karṇāmṛta*—the *Kṛṣṇa-karṇāmṛta* of Bilvamaṅgala Ṭhākura; *śrī-gīta-govinda*—the *Gīta-govinda* of Jayadeva Gosvāmī; *sva-rūpa*—Svarūpa Dāmodara; *rāmānanda-sane*—with Rāya Rāmānanda; *mahā-prabhu*—Lord Caitanya Mahāprabhu; *rātri-dine*—day and night; *gāya*—sings; *śune*—hears; *parama ānanda*—with great pleasure.

TRANSLATION

He also passed His time reading the books and singing the songs of Caṇḍīdāsa and Vidyāpati, and listening to quotations from the Jagannātha-vallabha-nāṭaka, Kṛṣṇa-karṇāmṛta and Gīta-govinda. Thus in the association of Svarūpa Dāmodara and Rāya Rāmānanda, Śrī Caitanya Mahāprabhu passed His days and nights chanting and hearing with great pleasure.

TEXT 78

পুরীর বাৎসল্য মুখ্য, রামানন্দের শুদ্ধসখ্য,
গোবিন্দাদ্যের শুদ্ধদাস্যরস ।
গদাধর, জগদানন্দ, স্বরূপের মুখ্য রসানন্দ,
এই চারি ভাবে প্রভু বশ ॥ ৭৮ ॥

purīra vātsalya mukhya, rāmānandera śuddha-sakhya,
govindādyera śuddha-dāsya-rasa
gadādhara, jagadānanda, svarūpera mukhya rasānanda,
ei cāri bhāve prabhu vaśa

SYNONYMS

purīra—of Paramānanda Purī; *vātsalya*—paternal affection; *mukhya*—chiefly; *rāmānandera*—of Rāya Rāmānanda; *śuddha-sakhya*—pure fraternity; *govinda-ādyera*—of Govinda and others; *śuddha-dāsya-rasa*—the pure and unalloyed mellow of service; *gadā-dhara*—Gadādhara Paṇḍita; *jagad-ānanda*—Jagadānanda Paṇḍita; *sva-rūpera*—of Svarūpa Dāmodara; *mukhya*—chiefly; *rasa-ānanda*—tasting the pleasure of conjugal love; *ei*—these; *cāri*—in four; *bhāve*—ecstatic conditions; *prabhu*—the Lord; *vaśa*—became obliged.

TRANSLATION

Among His associates, Lord Caitanya Mahāprabhu enjoyed paternal loving affection with Paramānanda Purī, friendly affection with

Rāmānanda Rāya, unalloyed service from Govinda and others, and humors of conjugal love with Gadādhara, Jagadānanda and Svarūpa Dāmodara. Śrī Caitanya Mahāprabhu enjoyed all these four mellows, and thus He remained obliged to His devotees.

PURPORT

Paramānanda Purī is said to have been Uddhava in Vṛndāvana. His affections with Śrī Caitanya Mahāprabhu were on the platform of paternal love. This was because Paramānanda Purī happened to be the Godbrother of the spiritual master of Śrī Caitanya Mahāprabhu. Similarly, Rāmānanda Rāya, who is considered an incarnation of Arjuna and by some an incarnation of Viśākhādevī, enjoyed unalloyed fraternal love with the Lord. Unalloyed personal service was enjoyed by Govinda and others. In the presence of His most confidential devotees like Gadādhara Paṇḍita, Jagadānanda and Svarūpa Dāmodara, Caitanya Mahāprabhu enjoyed the ecstatic conditions of Śrīmatī Rādhārāṇī in Her conjugal relationship with Kṛṣṇa. Absorbed in these four transcendental mellows, Śrī Caitanya Mahāprabhu resided in Jagannātha Purī, feeling very much obliged to His devotees.

TEXT 79

লীলাশুক মর্ত্যজন, তাঁর হয় ভাবোদ্গম,
ঈশ্বরে সে—কি ইহা বিস্ময়।
তাহে মুখ্য-রসাশ্রয়, হইয়াছেন মহাশয়,
তাতে হয় সর্বভাবোদয় ॥ ৭৯ ॥

līlāśuka martya-jana, tāṅra haya bhāvodgama,
īśvare se——ki ihā vismaya
tāhe mukhya-rasāśraya, ha-iyāchena mahāśaya,
tāte haya sarva-bhāvodaya

SYNONYMS

līlā-śuka—Bilvamaṅgala Ṭhākura; *martya-jana*—a person of this world; *tāṅra*—of him; *haya*—there is; *bhāva-udgama*—manifestation of different ecstasies; *īśvare*—in the Supreme Lord; *se*—that; *ki*—what; *ihā*—here; *vismaya*—astonishing; *tāhe*—in that; *mukhya*—chief; *rasa-āśraya*—mellows; *ha-iyāchena*—has become; *mahā-āśaya*—the great personality Śrī Caitanya Mahāprabhu; *tāte*—therefore; *haya*—there is; *sarva-bhāva-udaya*—a manifestation of all ecstasies.

TRANSLATION

Līlāśuka [Bilvamaṅgala Ṭhākura] was an ordinary human being, yet he developed many ecstatic symptoms in his body. What, then, is so astonishing about these symptoms' being manifest in the body of the Supreme Personality of Godhead? In the ecstatic mood of conjugal love, Śrī Caitanya Mahāprabhu was on the highest platform; therefore, all the exuberant ecstasies were naturally visible in His body.

PURPORT

Līlāśuka is Bilvamaṅgala Ṭhākura Gosvāmī. He was a south Indian, a *brāhmaṇa,* and his former name was Śilhana Miśra. When he was a householder, he became attracted to a prostitute named Cintāmaṇi, but eventually he took her advice and became renounced. Thus he wrote one book, *Śānti-śataka,* and later, by the mercy of Lord Kṛṣṇa and the Vaiṣṇavas, he became a great devotee. Thus he became famous as Bilvamaṅgala Ṭhākura Gosvāmī. On that elevated platform, he wrote a book named *Kṛṣṇa-karṇāmṛta,* which is very famous amongst Vaiṣṇavas. Since he exhibited so many ecstatic symptoms, people used to call him Līlāśuka.

TEXT 80

পূর্বে ব্রজবিলাসে, যেই তিন অভিলাষে,
যত্নেহ আস্বাদ না হৈল ।
শ্রীরাধার ভাবসার, আপনে করি' অঙ্গীকার,
সেই তিন বস্তু আস্বাদিল ॥ ৮০ ॥

pūrve vraja-vilāse, yei tina abhilāṣe,
yatneha āsvāda nā haila
śrī-rādhāra bhāva-sāra, āpane kari' aṅgīkāra,
sei tina vastu āsvādila

SYNONYMS

pūrve—formerly; *vraja-vilāse*—in the pastimes of Vṛndāvana; *yei tina*—those three; *abhilāṣe*—in desires; *yatneha*—by great endeavor; *āsvāda*—taste; *nā haila*—there was not; *śrī-rādhāra*—of Śrīmatī Rādhārāṇī; *bhāva-sāra*—the essence of the ecstasy; *āpane*—personally; *kari'*—making; *aṅgīkāra*—acceptance; *sei*—those; *tina vastu*—three subjects; *āsvādila*—tasted.

TRANSLATION

During His previous pastimes in Vṛndāvana, Lord Kṛṣṇa desired to enjoy the three different types of ecstasy, but despite great endeavor, He could not taste them. Such ecstasies are the monopoly of Śrīmatī Rādhārāṇī. Therefore, in order to taste them, Śrī Kṛṣṇa accepted the position of Śrīmatī Rādhārāṇī in the form of Śrī Caitanya Mahāprabhu.

TEXT 81

আপনে করি' আস্বাদনে, শিখাইল ভক্তগণে,
প্রেমচিন্তামণির প্রভু ধনী ।
নাহি জানে স্থানাস্থান, যারে তারে কৈল দান,
মহাপ্রভু—দাতা-শিরোমণি ॥ ৮১ ॥

āpane kari' āsvādane, śikhāila bhakta-gaṇe,
prema-cintāmaṇira prabhu dhanī
nāhi jāne sthānāsthāna, yāre tāre kaila dāna,
mahāprabhu——dātā-śiromaṇi

SYNONYMS

āpane—personally; *kari'*—doing; *āsvādane*—tasting; *śikhāila*—He taught; *bhakta-gaṇe*—to His direct disciples; *prema-cintāmaṇira*—of the touchstone of love of Godhead; *prabhu*—the Lord; *dhanī*—capitalist; *nāhi*—does not; *jāne*—know; *sthāna-asthāna*—the proper place or improper place; *yāre*—to whomever; *tāre*—to him; *kaila*—made; *dāna*—charity; *mahā-prabhu*—Śrī Caitanya Mahāprabhu; *dātā-śiromaṇi*—the most munificent personality.

TRANSLATION

By personally tasting the mellows of love of Godhead, Caitanya Mahāprabhu taught His direct disciples the process. Śrī Caitanya Mahāprabhu is the most munificent incarnation of the touchstone of love of God. He does not consider whether one is a proper or improper recipient, but gives His treasure to anyone and everyone. Thus He is the most munificent.

PURPORT

Śrī Caitanya Mahāprabhu's capital is the touchstone of love of Godhead, and consequently He is a great owner of that transcendental treasure. After making unlimited amounts of gold, the touchstone remains the same. Similarly, Śrī Caitanya Mahāprabhu, although distributing love of Godhead unlimitedly, still remained the supreme owner of this transcendental opulence. His devotees, who learned it from Him, also had to distribute it munificently all over the world. This Kṛṣṇa consciousness movement, following in the footsteps of Śrī Caitanya Mahāprabhu and His confidential devotees, is also trying to distribute love of Godhead all over the world through the chanting of the holy names of the Lord——Hare Kṛṣṇa, Hare Kṛṣṇa, Kṛṣṇa Kṛṣṇa, Hare Hare/ Hare Rāma, Hare Rāma, Rāma Rāma, Hare Hare.

TEXT 82

এই গুপ্ত ভাব-সিন্ধু, ব্রহ্মা না পায় এক বিন্দু,
হেন ধন বিলাইল সংসারে ।
ঐছে দয়ালু অবতার, ঐছে দাতা নাহি আর,
গুণ কেহ নারে বর্ণিবারে ॥ ৮২ ॥

ei gupta bhāva-sindhu, brahmā nā pāya eka bindu,
hena dhana vilāila saṁsāre
aiche dayālu avatāra, aiche dātā nāhi āra,
guṇa keha nāre varṇibāre

SYNONYMS

ei—this; *gupta*—confidential; *bhāva-sindhu*—ocean of ecstasies; *brahmā*—Lord Brahmā; *nā*—does not; *pāya*—get; *eka*—one; *bindu*—drop; *hena*—such; *dhana*—wealth; *vilāila*—distributed; *saṁsāre*—all over the world; *aiche*—such; *dayālu*—merciful; *avatāra*—incarnation; *aiche*—such; *dātā*—charitable donor; *nāhi*—there is not; *āra*—anyone else; *guṇa*—this quality; *keha*—anyone; *nāre*—not able; *varṇibāre*—to describe.

TRANSLATION

No one, not even Lord Brahmā, can ascertain or even taste a drop of this confidential ocean of ecstasy, but Śrī Caitanya Mahāprabhu, out of His causeless mercy, has distributed this love of Godhead all over the world. Thus there cannot be any incarnation more munificent than Śrī Caitanya Mahāprabhu. There is no greater donor. Who can describe His transcendental qualities?

TEXT 83

কহিবার কথা নহে, কহিলে কেহ না বুঝয়ে,
ঐছে চিত্র চৈতন্যের রঙ্গ ।
সেই সে বুঝিতে পারে, চৈতন্যের কৃপা যাঁরে,
হয় তাঁর দাসানুদাস-সঙ্গ ॥ ৮৩ ॥

kahibāra kathā nahe, kahile keha nā bujhaye,
aiche citra caitanyera raṅga
sei se bujhite pāre, caitanyera kṛpā yāṅre,
haya tāṅra dāsānudāsa-saṅga

SYNONYMS

kahibāra kathā nahe—not a subject matter to describe freely; *kahile*—if spoken; *keha*—someone; *nā bujhaye*—not understands; *aiche*—in that way; *citra*—wonderful; *caitanyera*—of Śrī Caitanya Mahāprabhu; *raṅga*—pastimes; *sei se*—whoever; *bujhite*—to understand; *pāre*—is able; *caitanyera*—of Lord Śrī Caitanya Mahāprabhu; *kṛpā*—the mercy; *yāṅre*—unto whom; *haya*—becomes; *tāṅra*—His; *dāsa-anudāsa-saṅga*—association with the servant of the servant.

TRANSLATION

Such topics are not to be discussed freely because if they are, no one will understand them. Such are the wonderful pastimes of Śrī Caitanya Mahāprabhu. Unto one who is able to understand, Śrī Caitanya Mahāprabhu has shown mercy by giving him the association of the servant of His own servant.

PURPORT

An ordinary person cannot understand the transcendental ecstasies in the mode of Śrīmatī Rādhārāṇī. Unfit persons who utilize them are perverted into the *sahajiyā, bāula* and other *sampradāyas.* Thus the teachings are perverted. Even learned scholars in the academic field cannot understand the transcendental bliss and ecstasy exhibited by Śrī Caitanya Mahāprabhu and His pure devotees. One must be fit to understand the purport of Śrī Caitanya Mahāprabhu's activities.

TEXT 84

চৈতন্যলীলা-রত্ন-সার, স্বরূপের ভাণ্ডার,
তেঁহো থুইলা রঘুনাথের কণ্ঠে ।
তাহাঁ কিছু যে শুনিলুঁ, তাহা ইহাঁ বিস্তারিলুঁ,
ভক্তগণে দিলুঁ এই ভেটে ॥ ৮৪ ॥

caitanya-līlā-ratna-sāra, svarūpera bhāṇḍāra,
teṅho thuilā raghunāthera kaṇṭhe
tāhāṅ kichu ye śuniluṅ, tāhā ihāṅ vistāriluṅ,
bhakta-gaṇe diluṅ ei bheṭe

SYNONYMS

caitanya-līlā—the pastimes of Lord Caitanya; *ratna-sāra*—the topmost jewel; *sva-rūpera*—of Svarūpa Dāmodara; *bhāṇḍāra*—of the storehouse; *teṅho*—he; *thuilā*—kept; *raghu-nāthera kaṇṭhe*—in the throat of Raghunātha dāsa Gosvāmī; *tāhāṅ*—there; *kichu ye*—whatever little; *śuniluṅ*—I have heard; *tāhā*—that only; *ihāṅ*—in this book; *vistāriluṅ*—I have described; *bhakta-gaṇe*—to the pure devotees; *diluṅ*—I gave; *ei*—this; *bheṭe*—presentation.

TRANSLATION

The pastimes of Śrī Caitanya Mahāprabhu are the topmost of jewels. They have been kept in the storehouse of Svarūpa Dāmodara Gosvāmī, who has explained them to Raghunātha dāsa Gosvāmī, who has repeated them to me. Whatever little I have heard from Raghunātha dāsa Gosvāmī I have described in this book, which is presented to all devotees.

PURPORT

All the activities of Śrī Caitanya Mahāprabhu were noted by His personal secretary Svarūpa Dāmodara and repeated to Raghunātha dāsa Gosvāmī, who memorized them. Whatever Kṛṣṇadāsa Kavirāja Gosvāmī heard is recorded in *Śrī Caitanya-caritāmṛta*. This is called the *paramparā* system, from Śrī Caitanya Mahāprabhu to Svarūpa Dāmodara to Raghunātha dāsa Gosvāmī to Kavirāja Gosvāmī. Kṛṣṇadāsa Kavirāja Gosvāmī has distributed this information in his book *Caitanya-caritāmṛta*. In other words, *Caitanya-caritāmṛta* is the essence of the instruction given through the *paramparā* system of the disciplic succession stemming from Śrī Caitanya Mahāprabhu.

TEXT 85

যদি কেহ হেন কয়, গ্রন্থ কৈল শ্লোকময়,
ইতর জনে নারিবে বুঝিতে ।
প্রভুর যেই আচরণ, সেই করি বর্ণন,
সর্ব-চিত্ত নারি আরাধিতে ॥ ৮৫ ॥

yadi keha hena kaya, grantha kaila śloka-maya,
itara jane nāribe bujhite
prabhura yei ācaraṇa, sei kari varṇana,
sarva-citta nāri ārādhite

SYNONYMS

yadi—if; *keha*—someone; *hena*—thus; *kaya*—says; *grantha*—this book; *kaila*—is made; *śloka-maya*—with various Sanskrit verses; *itara*—ordinary; *jane*—persons; *nāribe bujhite*—will not be able to understand; *prabhura*—of Lord Śrī Caitanya Mahāprabhu; *yei*—whatever; *ācaraṇa*—activities; *sei*—that; *kari*—I do; *varṇana*—description; *sarva-citta*—all hearts; *nāri*—I am unable; *ārādhite*—to please.

TRANSLATION

If one says that Śrī Caitanya-caritāmṛta is full of Sanskrit verses and therefore not understandable by a common man, I reply that what I have described are the pastimes of Śrī Caitanya Mahāprabhu and that for me to satisfy everyone is not possible.

PURPORT

Śrīla Kavirāja Gosvāmī and one who follows in his footsteps do not have to cater to the public. Their business is simply to satisfy the previous *ācāryas* and describe the pastimes of the Lord. One who is able to understand can relish this exalted transcendental literature, which is actually not meant for ordinary persons like scholars and literary men. Generally, Śrī Caitanya Mahāprabhu's pastimes recorded in *Caitanya-caritāmṛta* are studied in universities and scholastic circles from a literary and historical point of view, but actually *Caitanya-caritāmṛta* is not a subject matter for research workers or literary scholars. It is simply meant for those devotees who have dedicated their lives to the service of Śrī Caitanya Mahāprabhu.

TEXT 86

নাহি কাহাঁ সবিরোধ, নাহি কাহাঁ অনুরোধ,
সহজ বস্তু করি বিবরণ ।
যদি হয় রাগোদ্দেশ, তাহাঁ হয়ে আবেশ,
সহজ বস্তু না যায় লিখন ॥ ৮৬ ॥

nāhi kāhāṅ savirodha, nāhi kāhāṅ anurodha,
sahaja vastu kari vivaraṇa
yadi haya rāgoddeśa, tāhāṅ haye āveśa,
sahaja vastu nā yāya likhana

SYNONYMS

nāhi—there is not; *kāhāṅ*—anywhere; *sa-virodha*—opposing element; *nāhi*—there is not; *kāhāṅ*—anywhere; *anurodha*—acceptance of someone's opinion; *sahaja*—simple; *vastu*—substance; *kari*—I do; *vivaraṇa*—description; *yadi*—if; *haya*—there is; *rāga-uddeśa*—someone's attraction or obstruction; *tāhāṅ*—there; *haye*—becoming; *āveśa*—involved; *sahaja*—simple; *vastu*—substance; *nā yāya*—is not possible; *likhana*—the writing.

TRANSLATION

In this Caitanya-caritāmṛta there is no contradictory conclusion, nor is anyone else's opinion accepted. I have written this book to describe the simple substance as I have heard it from superiors. If I become involved in someone's likes and dislikes, I cannot possibly write the simple truth.

PURPORT

The simplest thing for human beings is to follow their predecessors. Judgment according to mundane senses is not a very easy process. Whatever is awakened by attachment to one's predecessor is the way of devotional service as indicated by Śrī Caitanya Mahāprabhu. The author says, however, that he cannot consider the opinions of those who become attracted or repelled by such things, because one cannot write impartially in that way. In other words, the author is stating that he did not inject personal opinion in *Caitanya-caritāmṛta*. He has simply described his spontaneous understanding from superiors. If he had been carried away by someone's likes and dislikes, he could not have written of such a sublime subject matter in such an easy way. The actual facts are understandable to real devotees. When these facts are recorded, they are very congenial to the devotees, but one who is not a devotee cannot understand. Such is the subject matter for realization. Mundane scholarship and its concomitant attachments and detachments cannot arouse spontaneous love of Godhead. Such love cannot be described by a mundane scholar.

TEXT 87

যেবা নাহি বুঝে কেহ, শুনিতে শুনিতে সেহ,
কি অদ্ভুত চৈতন্যচরিত ।
কৃষ্ণে উপজিবে প্রীতি, জানিবে রসের রীতি,
শুনিলেই বড় হয় হিত ॥ ৮৭ ॥

yebā nāhi bujhe keha, śunite śunite seha,
ki adbhuta caitanya-carita
kṛṣṇe upajibe prīti, jānibe rasera rīti,
śunilei baḍa haya hita

SYNONYMS

yebā—whoever; *nāhi*—does not; *bujhe*—understand; *keha*—someone; *śunite śunite*—hearing and hearing; *seha*—he; *ki*—what; *adbhuta*—wonderful; *caitanya-carita*—pastimes of Lord Śrī Caitanya Mahāprabhu; *kṛṣṇe*—unto Kṛṣṇa; *upajibe*—will develop; *prīti*—love; *jānibe*—he will understand; *rasera*—of transcendental mellows; *rīti*—the ways; *śunilei*—simply by hearing; *baḍa*—great; *haya*—there is; *hita*—benefit.

TRANSLATION

If one does not understand in the beginning but continues to hear again and again, the wonderful effects of Lord Caitanya's pastimes will bring love for Kṛṣṇa. Gradually one will come to understand the loving affairs between Kṛṣṇa and the gopīs and other associates of Vṛndāvana. Everyone is advised to continue to hear over and over again in order to greatly benefit.

TEXT 88

ভাগবত—শ্লোকময়, টীকা তার সংস্কৃত হয়,
তবু কৈছে বুঝে ত্রিভুবন ।

ইহাঁ শ্লোক দুই চারি, তার ব্যাখ্যা ভাষা করি,
কেনে না বুঝিবে সর্বজন ॥ ৮৮ ॥

bhāgavata——śloka-maya, ṭīkā tāra saṁskṛta haya,
tabu kaiche bujhe tri-bhuvana
ihāṅ śloka dui cāri, tāra vyākhyā bhāṣā kari,
kene nā bujhibe sarva-jana

SYNONYMS

bhāgavata—the *Śrīmad-Bhāgavatam*; *śloka-maya*—full of Sanskrit verses; *ṭīkā*—commentaries; *tāra*—of that; *saṁskṛta*—Sanskrit language; *haya*—there are; *tabu*—still; *kaiche*—how; *bujhe*—understands; *tri-bhuvana*—the whole world; *ihāṅ*—in this; *śloka*—verses; *dui cāri*—a few; *tāra*—of them; *vyākhyā*—explanation; *bhāṣā*—in simple language; *kari*—I do; *kene*—why; *nā*—not; *bujhibe*—will understand; *sarva-jana*—all people.

TRANSLATION

In reply to those critics who say that Śrī Caitanya-caritāmṛta is full of Sanskrit verses, it can be said that Śrīmad-Bhāgavatam is also full of Sanskrit verses, as are the commentaries on Śrīmad-Bhāgavatam. Nonetheless, Śrīmad-Bhāgavatam can be understood by everyone, as well as by advanced devotees who study the Sanskrit commentaries. Why, then, will people not understand Caitanya-caritāmṛta? There are only a few Sanskrit verses, and these have been explained in the Bengali vernacular. What is the difficulty in understanding?

TEXT 89

শেষ-লীলার সূত্রগণ, কৈলুঁ কিছু বিবরণ,
ইহাঁ বিস্তারিতে চিত্ত হয়।
থাকে যদি আয়ুঃ-শেষ, বিস্তারিব লীলা-শেষ,
যদি মহাপ্রভুর কৃপা হয় ॥ ৮৯ ॥

śeṣa-līlāra sūtra-gaṇa, kailuṅ kichu vivaraṇa,
ihāṅ vistārite citta haya
thāke yadi āyuḥ-śeṣa, vistāriba līlā-śeṣa,
yadi mahāprabhura kṛpā haya

SYNONYMS

śeṣa-līlāra—of the pastimes at the end; *sūtra-gaṇa*—the codes; *kailuṅ*—I have done; *kichu*—some; *vivaraṇa*—description; *ihāṅ*—here; *vistārite*—to expand more and more; *citta haya*—there is a desire; *thāke*—remains; *yadi*—if; *āyuḥ-śeṣa*—the end of life; *vistāriba*—I shall describe; *līlā*—pastimes; *śeṣa*—at the end; *yadi*—if; *mahā-prabhura*—of Śrī Caitanya Mahāprabhu; *kṛpā*—mercy; *haya*—there is.

TRANSLATION

I have already given in codes all the facts and figures of Lord Śrī Caitanya Mahāprabhu's last pastimes, and I have a desire to describe them elaborately. If I remain longer and am fortunate enough to receive the mercy of Lord Śrī Caitanya Mahāprabhu, I shall try to describe them again more elaborately.

TEXT 90

আমি বৃদ্ধ জরাতুর, লিখিতে কাঁপয়ে কর,
মনে কিছু স্মরণ না হয় ।
না দেখিয়ে নয়নে, না শুনিয়ে শ্রবণে,
তবু লিখি'—এ বড় বিস্ময় ॥ ৯০ ॥

āmi vṛddha jarātura, likhite kāṅpaye kara,
mane kichu smaraṇa nā haya
nā dekhiye nayane, nā śuniye śravaṇe,
tabu likhi'——e baḍa vismaya

SYNONYMS

āmi—I; *vṛddha*—old man; *jarā-ātura*—disturbed by invalidity; *likhite*—to write; *kāṅpaye*—trembles; *kara*—the hand; *mane*—in the mind; *kichu*—any; *smaraṇa*—remembrance; *nā haya*—there is not; *nā dekhiye*—I cannot see; *nayane*—by the eyes; *nā śuniye*—I cannot hear; *śravaṇe*—with the ears; *tabu*—still; *likhi'*—writing; *e*—this; *baḍa vismaya*—a great wonder.

TRANSLATION

I have now become too old and disturbed by invalidity. While writing, my hands tremble. I cannot remember anything, nor can I see or hear properly. Still I write, and this is a great wonder.

TEXT 91

এই অন্ত্যলীলা-সার, সূত্রমধ্যে বিস্তার,
করি' কিছু করিলুঁ বর্ণন।
ইহা-মধ্যে মরি যবে, বর্ণিতে না পারি তবে,
এই লীলা ভক্তগণ-ধন ॥ ৯১ ॥

ei antya-līlā-sāra, sūtra-madhye vistāra,
kari' kichu kariluṅ varṇana
ihā-madhye mari yabe, varṇite nā pāri tabe,
ei līlā bhakta-gaṇa-dhana

SYNONYMS

ei antya-līlā-sāra—the essence of the *antya-līlā* (Lord Caitanya's pastimes at the end); *sūtra-madhye*—in the codes; *vistāra*—expansion; *kari'*—doing; *kichu*—something; *kariluṅ varṇana*—have described; *ihā-madhye*—in the meantime; *mari*—I die; *yabe*—when; *varṇite*—to describe; *nā pāri*—not able; *tabe*—then; *ei līlā*—these pastimes; *bhakta-gaṇa-dhana*—the treasure of the devotees.

TRANSLATION

In this chapter I have to some extent described the essence of the pastimes of Lord Caitanya at the end. If I die in the meantime and cannot describe them in detail, at least the devotees will have this transcendental treasure.

TEXT 92

সংক্ষেপে এই সূত্র কৈল, যেই ইহাঁ না লিখিল,
আগে তাহা করিব বিস্তার।
যদি তত দিন জিয়ে, মহাপ্রভুর কৃপা হয়ে,
ইচ্ছা ভরি' করিব বিচার ॥ ৯২ ॥

saṅkṣepe ei sūtra kaila, yei ihāṅ nā likhila,
āge tāhā kariba vistāra
yadi tata dina jiye, mahāprabhura kṛpā haye,
icchā bhari' kariba vicāra

SYNONYMS

saṅkṣepe—in brief; *ei sūtra*—these codes; *kaila*—I have made; *yei*—whatever; *ihāṅ*—in this; *nā likhila*—I could not write; *āge*—in the future; *tāhā*—that; *kariba*—I shall make; *vistāra*—expansion; *yadi*—if; *tata*—so many; *dina*—days; *jiye*—I live; *mahā-prabhura*—of Śrī Caitanya Mahāprabhu; *kṛpā*—the mercy; *haye*—there is; *icchā bhari'*—satisfying the desire; *kariba*—I shall do; *vicāra*—consideration.

TRANSLATION

In this chapter I have briefly described the codes. Whatever I have not described I shall describe extensively in the future. If, by Śrī Caitanya Mahāprabhu's mercy, I live for so many days that I can fulfill my desires, I will give full consideration to these pastimes.

TEXT 93

ছোট বড় ভক্তগণ, বন্দোঁ সবার শ্রীচরণ,
সবে মোরে করহ সন্তোষ।
স্বরূপ-গোসাঞির মত, রূপ-রঘুনাথ জানে যত,
তাই লিখি' নাহি মোর দোষ ॥ ৯৩ ॥

choṭa baḍa bhakta-gaṇa, vandoṅ sabāra śrī-caraṇa,
sabe more karaha santoṣa
svarūpa-gosāñira mata, rūpa-raghunātha jāne yata,
tāi likhi' nāhi mora doṣa

SYNONYMS

choṭa—small; *baḍa*—great; *bhakta-gaṇa*—devotees; *vandoṅ*—I worship; *sabāra*—all of them; *śrī-caraṇa*—the lotus feet; *sabe*—all of you; *more*—unto me; *karaha*—please do; *santoṣa*—satisfaction; *sva-rūpa-gosāñira mata*—the view of Svarūpa Dāmodara Gosvāmī; *rūpa-raghu-nātha*—Rūpa and Raghunātha; *jāne*—know; *yata*—all; *tāi*—that; *likhi'*—writing; *nāhi*—there is not; *mora*—my; *doṣa*—fault.

TRANSLATION

I worship herewith the lotus feet of all kinds of devotees, both advanced and neophyte. I request all of them to be satisfied with me. I am faultless because I have written herein whatever I have understood from

Svarūpa Dāmodara Gosvāmī and Rūpa and Raghunātha dāsa Gosvāmīs. I have neither added nor subtracted from their version.

PURPORT

According to Śrīla Bhaktisiddhānta Sarasvatī Ṭhākura, there are three kinds of devotees, known as *bhajana-vijña* (experts in devotional service), *bhajana-śīla* (devotees engaged in devotional service), and *kṛṣṇa-nāme dīkṣita kṛṣṇa-nāmakārī* (initiated devotees engaged in chanting). The author of *Caitanya-caritāmṛta* begs the mercy of all these devotees and asks them to be pleased with him. He says, "Let the neophyte devotees—the devotees who are very expert in arguing though they have no sense of advanced devotional service, who think themselves very advanced because they imitate some *smārta-brāhmaṇa*—let such devotees not be displeased with me, thinking that I have committed errors in this regard. I beg their pardon with great humility, but I am submitting that I personally have no desire to add or subtract anything. I have only written what I have heard in the disciplic succession because I am dedicated to the lotus feet of previous *ācāryas* like Svarūpa Dāmodara, Raghunātha dāsa Gosvāmī and Rūpa Gosvāmī. I have only written what I have learned from them."

TEXT 94

শ্রীচৈতন্য, নিত্যানন্দ, অদ্বৈতাদি ভক্তবৃন্দ,
শিরে ধরি সবার চরণ ।
স্বরূপ, রূপ, সনাতন, রঘুনাথের শ্রীচরণ,
ধূলি করোঁ মস্তকে ভূষণ ॥ ৯৪ ॥

śrī-caitanya, nityānanda, advaitādi bhakta-vṛnda,
śire dhari sabāra caraṇa
svarūpa, rūpa, sanātana, raghunāthera śrī-caraṇa,
dhūli karoṅ mastake bhūṣaṇa

SYNONYMS

śrī-caitanya—Śrī Caitanya Mahāprabhu; *nityānanda*—Lord Nityānanda Prabhu; *advaita-ādi bhakta-vṛnda*—as well as personalities like Advaita Ācārya and all the devotees; *śire*—on my head; *dhari*—taking; *sabāra*—of all; *caraṇa*—the lotus feet; *sva-rūpa*—Śrīla Svarūpa Dāmodara Gosvāmī; *rūpa*—Śrīla Rūpa Gosvāmī; *sanātana*—Śrīla Sanātana Gosvāmī; *raghu-nāthera*—of

Śrīla Raghunātha Gosvāmī; *śrī-caraṇa*—the lotus feet; *dhūli*—dust; *karoṅ*—I do; *mastake*—on my head; *bhūṣaṇa*—decoration.

TRANSLATION

According to the paramparā system, I wish to take the dust from the lotus feet of Śrī Caitanya Mahāprabhu, Nityānanda Prabhu, Advaita Prabhu, and all the associates of Śrī Caitanya Mahāprabhu like Svarūpa Dāmodara, Rūpa Gosvāmī and Sanātana Gosvāmī and Raghunātha dāsa Gosvāmī. I wish to take the dust of their lotus feet upon my head. In this way I wish to be blessed with their mercy.

TEXT 95

পাঞা যাঁর আজ্ঞা-ধন, ব্রজের বৈষ্ণবগণ,
বন্দোঁ তাঁর মুখ্য হরিদাস।
চৈতন্যবিলাস-সিন্ধু- কল্লোলের এক বিন্দু,
তার কণা কহে কৃষ্ণদাস ॥ ৯৫ ॥

pāñā yāṅra ājñā-dhana, vrajera vaiṣṇava-gaṇa,
vandoṅ tāṅra mukhya haridāsa
caitanya-vilāsa-sindhu- kallolera eka bindu,
tāra kaṇā kahe kṛṣṇadāsa

SYNONYMS

pāñā—getting; *yāṅra*—whose; *ājñā-dhana*—order; *vrajera*—of Vṛndāvana; *vaiṣṇava-gaṇa*—all the Vaiṣṇavas; *vandoṅ*—I worship; *tāṅra*—of them; *mukhya*—the chief; *hari-dāsa*—Haridāsa; *caitanya-vilāsa-sindhu*—of the ocean of the pastimes of Lord Caitanya; *kallolera eka bindu*—one drop of one wave; *tāra*—of it; *kaṇā*—a particle only; *kahe*—describes; *kṛṣṇa-dāsa*—Kṛṣṇadāsa Kavirāja Gosvāmī.

TRANSLATION

Receiving orders from the above authorities and the Vaiṣṇavas of Vṛndāvana, especially from Haridāsa, the priest of Govindajī, I, Kṛṣṇadāsa Kavirāja Gosvāmī, have tried to describe one small particle of one drop of one wave of the ocean of the pastimes of Śrī Caitanya Mahāprabhu.

Thus end the Bhaktivedanta purports to the Śrī Caitanya-caritāmṛta, Madhya-līlā, *Second Chapter, describing the ecstatic manifestations of Lord Caitanya Mahāprabhu.*

CHAPTER 3

Lord Śrī Caitanya Mahāprabhu's Stay at the House of Advaita Ācārya

In his *Amṛta-pravāha-bhāṣya,* Śrīla Bhaktivinoda Ṭhākura gives the following summary study of the Third Chapter. After accepting the *sannyāsa* order at Katwa, Śrī Caitanya Mahāprabhu traveled continuously for three days in the Rāḍha-deśa and, by the trick of Nityānanda Prabhu, eventually came to the western side of Śāntipura. Śrī Caitanya Mahāprabhu was induced to believe that the River Ganges was the Yamunā. When He was worshiping the sacred river, Advaita Prabhu appeared with a boat. Advaita Prabhu asked Him to take His bath in the Ganges and took Him to His own house. There, at the house of Advaita Prabhu, all the Navadvīpa devotees, along with mother Śacīdevī, came to see Śrī Caitanya Mahāprabhu. This house was located at Śāntipura. Mother Śacīdevī cooked for Śrī Caitanya Mahāprabhu and Nityānanda Prabhu, and at that time there were many joking exchanges between Advaita Prabhu and Nityānanda Prabhu. In the evening there was a mass *saṅkīrtana* at the house of Advaita Prabhu, and mother Śacīdevī gave Śrī Caitanya Mahāprabhu permission to leave. She requested Him to make Jagannātha Purī, Nīlācala, His headquarters. Śrī Caitanya Mahāprabhu granted His mother's request and, followed by Nityānanda, Mukunda, Jagadānanda and Dāmodara, left Śāntipura. Bidding farewell to mother Śacīdevī, they all proceeded toward Jagannātha Purī, following the path of Chatrabhoga.

TEXT 1

ন্যাসং বিধায়োৎপ্রণয়োঽথ গৌরো
বৃন্দাবনং গন্তুমনা ভ্রমাদ্ যঃ ।
রাঢ়ে ভ্রমন্ শান্তিপুরীময়িত্বা
ললাস ভক্তৈরিহ তং নতোঽস্মি ॥ ১ ॥

nyāsaṁ vidhāyotpraṇayo 'tha gauro
vṛndāvanaṁ gantu-manā bhramād yaḥ
rāḍhe bhraman śānti-purīm ayitvā
lalāsa bhaktair iha taṁ nato 'smi

SYNONYMS

nyāsam—the regular ritualistic ceremonies of the *sannyāsa* order; *vidhāya*—after accepting; *utpraṇayaḥ*—arousal of intense love for Kṛṣṇa; *atha*—thus; *gauraḥ*—Śrī Caitanya Mahāprabhu; *vṛndāvanam*—to Vṛndāvana; *gantu-manāḥ*—thinking of going; *bhramāt*—apparently by mistake; *yaḥ*—who; *rāḍhe*—in the tract of land known as Rāḍha; *bhraman*—wandering; *śānti-purīm*—to Śāntipura; *ayitvā*—going; *lalāsa*—enjoyed; *bhaktaiḥ*—with the devotees; *iha*—here; *tam*—unto Him; *nataḥ asmi*—I offer my respectful obeisances.

TRANSLATION

After accepting the sannyāsa order of life, Lord Caitanya Mahāprabhu, out of intense love for Kṛṣṇa, wanted to go to Vṛndāvana, but apparently by mistake He wandered in the Rāḍha-deśa. Later He arrived at Śāntipura and enjoyed Himself there with His devotees. I offer my respectful obeisances to Śrī Caitanya Mahāprabhu.

TEXT 2

জয় জয় শ্রীচৈতন্য জয় নিত্যানন্দ ।
জয়াদ্বৈতচন্দ্র জয় গৌরভক্তবৃন্দ ॥ ২ ॥

jaya jaya śrī-caitanya jaya nityānanda
jayādvaitacandra jaya gaura-bhakta-vṛnda

SYNONYMS

jaya jaya—all glories; *śrī-caitanya*—to Lord Śrī Caitanya Mahāprabhu; *jaya*—all glories; *nityānanda*—to Lord Nityānanda Prabhu; *jaya*—all glories; *advaita-candra*—to Śrī Advaita Gosāñi; *jaya*—all glories; *gaura-bhakta-vṛnda*—to the devotees of Lord Caitanya.

TRANSLATION

All glories to Śrī Caitanya Mahāprabhu! All glories to Nityānanda! All glories to Advaita Prabhu! And all glories to the devotees of Lord Caitanya, headed by Śrīvāsa!

TEXT 3

চব্বিশ বৎসর-শেষ যেই মাঘ-মাস ।
তার শুক্লপক্ষে প্রভু করিলা সন্ন্যাস ॥ ৩ ॥

cabbiśa vatsara-śeṣa yei māgha-māsa
tāra śukla-pakṣe prabhu karilā sannyāsa

SYNONYMS

cabbiśa—twenty-fourth; *vatsara*—of the year; *śeṣa*—at the end; *yei*—that; *māgha-māsa*—the month of Māgha (January and February); *tāra*—of that; *śukla-pakṣe*—in the waxing period of the moon; *prabhu*—the Lord; *karilā*—accepted; *sannyāsa*—the *sannyāsa* order of life.

TRANSLATION

At the end of His twenty-fourth year, in the month of Māgha, Śrī Caitanya Mahāprabhu accepted the sannyāsa order during the waxing period of the moon.

TEXT 4

সন্ন্যাস করি' প্রেমাবেশে চলিলা বৃন্দাবন ।
রাঢ়-দেশে তিন দিন করিলা ভ্রমণ ॥ ৪ ॥

sannyāsa kari' premāveśe calilā vṛndāvana
rāḍha-deśe tina dina karilā bhramaṇa

SYNONYMS

sannyāsa kari'—after accepting the *sannyāsa* order; *prema-āveśe*—in intense love for Kṛṣṇa; *calilā*—proceeded; *vṛndāvana*—toward Vṛndāvana-dhāma; *rāḍha-deśe*—in the tract of land known as Rāḍha; *tina dina*—continuously for three days; *karilā*—did; *bhramaṇa*—wandering.

TRANSLATION

After accepting the sannyāsa order, Caitanya Mahāprabhu, out of intense love for Kṛṣṇa, started for Vṛndāvana. However, He mistakenly wandered about in a trance continuously for three days in the tract of land known as Rāḍha-deśa.

PURPORT

The word Rāḍha-deśa comes from the word *rāṣṭra,* or "state." From *rāṣṭra* the perverted word *rāḍha* has come. The part of Bengal on the western side of the Ganges is known as Rāḍha-deśa. Another name is Pauṇḍra-deśa. The word *pauṇḍra* is a perverted form of the word *peṅḍo.* It appears that the capital of Rāṣṭra-deśa was situated in that part of Bengal.

TEXT 5

এই শ্লোক পড়ি' প্রভু ভাবের আবেশে ।
ভ্রমিতে পবিত্র কৈল সব রাঢ়-দেশে ॥ ৫ ॥

ei śloka paḍi' prabhu bhāvera āveśe
bhramite pavitra kaila saba rāḍha-deśe

SYNONYMS

ei śloka—this verse; *paḍi'*—reciting; *prabhu*—the Lord; *bhāvera*—of ecstasy; *āveśe*—in a condition; *bhramite*—wandering; *pavitra*—purified; *kaila*—did; *saba rāḍha-deśe*—all of the tract of land known as Rāḍha-deśa.

TRANSLATION

Passing through the tract of land known as Rāḍha-deśa, Śrī Caitanya Mahāprabhu recited the following verse in ecstasy.

TEXT 6

এতাং স আস্থায় পরাত্মনিষ্ঠামধ্যাসিতাং পূর্বতমৈর্মহদ্ভিঃ।
অহং তরিষ্যামি দুরন্তপারং তমো মুকুন্দাঙ্ঘ্রিনিষেবয়ৈব ॥৬॥

etāṁ sa āsthāya parātma-niṣṭhām
adhyāsitāṁ pūrvatamair mahadbhiḥ
ahaṁ tariṣyāmi duranta-pāraṁ
tamo mukundāṅghri-niṣevayaiva

SYNONYMS

etām—this; *saḥ*—such; *āsthāya*—being completely fixed in; *para-ātma-niṣṭhām*—devotion to the Supreme Person, Kṛṣṇa; *adhyāsitām*—worshiped; *pūrvatamaiḥ*—by previous; *mahadbhiḥ*—*ācāryas;* *aham*—I; *tariṣyāmi*—shall cross over; *duranta-pāram*—the insurmountable; *tamaḥ*—the ocean of nescience; *mukunda-aṅghri*—of the lotus feet of Mukunda; *niṣevayā*—by worship; *eva*—certainly.

TRANSLATION

[As a brāhmaṇa from Avantī-deśa said:] "I shall cross over the insurmountable ocean of nescience by being firmly fixed in the service of the lotus feet of Kṛṣṇa. This was approved by the previous ācāryas, who were

fixed in firm devotion to the Lord, Paramātmā, the Supreme Personality of Godhead."

PURPORT

In connection with this verse, which is a quotation from *Śrīmad-Bhāgavatam* (11.23.58), Śrīla Bhaktisiddhānta Sarasvatī Ṭhākura says that of the sixty-four items required for rendering devotional service, acceptance of the symbolic marks of *sannyāsa* is a regulative principle. If one accepts the *sannyāsa* order, his main business is to devote his life completely to the service of Mukunda, Kṛṣṇa. If one does not completely devote his mind and body to the service of the Lord, he does not actually become a *sannyāsī*. It is not simply a matter of changing dress. In *Bhagavad-gītā* (6.1) it is also stated, *anāśritaḥ karma-phalaṁ kāryaṁ karma karoti yaḥ/sa sannyāsī ca yogī ca:* one who works devotedly for the satisfaction of Kṛṣṇa is a *sannyāsī*. The dress is not *sannyāsa,* but the attitude of service to Kṛṣṇa is.

The word *parātma-niṣṭhā* means being a devotee of Lord Kṛṣṇa. *Parātmā,* the Supreme Person, is Kṛṣṇa. *Īśvaraḥ paramaḥ kṛṣṇaḥ sac-cid-ānanda-vigrahaḥ*. Those who are completely dedicated to the lotus feet of Kṛṣṇa in service are actually *sannyāsīs*. As a matter of formality, the devotee accepts the *sannyāsa* dress as previous *ācāryas* did. He also accepts the three *daṇḍas*. Later Viṣṇusvāmī considered that accepting the dress of a *tri-daṇḍī* was *parātma-niṣṭhā*. Therefore sincere devotees add another *daṇḍa,* the *jīva-daṇḍa,* to the three existing *daṇḍas*. The Vaiṣṇava *sannyāsī* is known as a *tridaṇḍi-sannyāsī*. The Māyāvādī *sannyāsī* accepts only one *daṇḍa,* not understanding the purpose of *tri-daṇḍa*. Later, many persons in the community of Śiva Svāmī gave up the *ātma-niṣṭhā* (devotional service) of the Lord and followed the path of Śaṅkarācārya. Instead of accepting 108 names, those in the Śiva Svāmī-sampradāya follow the path of Śaṅkarācārya and accept the ten names of *sannyāsa*. Although Śrī Caitanya Mahāprabhu accepted the then-existing order of *sannyāsa* (namely *eka-daṇḍa*), He still recited a verse from *Śrīmad-Bhāgavatam* about the *tridaṇḍa-sannyāsa* accepted by the *brāhmaṇa* of Avantīpura. Indirectly He declared that within that *eka-daṇḍa,* one *daṇḍa,* four *daṇḍas* existed as one. Accepting *ekadaṇḍa-sannyāsa* without *parātma-niṣṭhā* (devotional service to Lord Kṛṣṇa) is not acceptable to Śrī Caitanya Mahāprabhu. In addition, according to the exact regulative principles, one should add the *jīva-daṇḍa* to the *tri-daṇḍa*. These four *daṇḍas,* bound together as one, are symbolic of unalloyed devotional service to the Lord. Because the *ekadaṇḍi-sannyāsīs* of the Māyāvāda school are not devoted to the service of Kṛṣṇa, they try to merge into the Brahman effulgence, which is a marginal position between material and spiritual existence. They accept this impersonal position as liberation. Māyāvādī *sannyāsīs,* not knowing that Śrī Caitanya Mahāprabhu was a *tri-daṇḍī,* think of Caitanya Mahāprabhu as an *ekadaṇḍi-sannyāsī.* This is due to their *vivarta,* bewilderment. In *Śrīmad-Bhāgavatam* there is no such thing as an *ekadaṇḍi-sannyāsī;* indeed, the *tri-daṇḍi-sannyāsī* is accepted as the symbolic representation of the *sannyāsa* order. By citing this verse from *Śrīmad-Bhāgavatam,* Śrī Caitanya Mahāprabhu accepted the *sannyāsa* order recommended in *Śrīmad-Bhāgavatam.* The Māyāvādī *sannyāsīs,* who are enamored of the external energy of the Lord, cannot understand the mind of Śrī Caitanya Mahāprabhu.

To date, all the devotees of Śrī Caitanya Mahāprabhu, following in His footsteps, accept the *sannyāsa* order and keep the sacred thread and tuft of unshaved hair. The *ekadaṇḍi-sannyāsīs* of the Māyāvādī school give up the sacred thread and do not keep any tuft of hair. Therefore they are unable to understand the purport of *tridaṇḍa-sannyāsa,* and as such they are not inclined to dedicate their lives to the service of Mukunda. They simply think of merging into the existence of Brahman because of their disgust with material existence. The *ācāryas* who advocate the *daiva-varṇāśrama* (the social order of *cātur-varṇyam* mentioned in *Bhagavad-gītā)* do not accept the proposition of *āsura-varṇāśrama,* which maintains that the social order of *varṇa* is indicated by birth.

The most intimate devotee of Śrī Caitanya Mahāprabhu, namely Gadādhara Paṇḍita, accepted *tridaṇḍa-sannyāsa* and also accepted Mādhava Upādhyāya as his *tridaṇḍi-sannyāsī* disciple. It is said that from this Mādhavācārya the *sampradāya* known in western India as the Vallabhācārya-sampradāya has begun. Śrīla Gopāla Bhaṭṭa Bose, who is known as a *smṛty-ācārya* in the Gauḍīya-Vaiṣṇava-sampradāya, later accepted the *tridaṇḍa-sannyāsa* order from Tridaṇḍipāda Prabodhānanda Sarasvatī. Although acceptance of *tridaṇḍa-sannyāsa* is not distinctly mentioned in the Gauḍīya Vaiṣṇava literature, the first verse of Śrīla Rūpa Gosvāmī's *Upadeśāmṛta* advocates that one should accept the *tridaṇḍa-sannyāsa* order by controlling the six forces:

vāco vegaṁ manasaḥ krodha-vegaṁ
jihvā-vegam udaropastha-vegam
etān vegān yo viṣaheta dhīraḥ
sarvām apīmāṁ pṛthivīṁ sa śiṣyāt

"One who can control the forces of speech, mind, anger, belly, tongue and genitals is known as a *gosvāmī* and is competent to accept disciples all over the world." The followers of Śrī Caitanya Mahāprabhu never accepted the Māyāvāda order of *sannyāsa,* and for this they cannot be blamed. Śrī Caitanya

Mahāprabhu accepted Śrīdhara Svāmī, who was a *tridaṇḍi-sannyāsī,* but the Māyāvādī *sannyāsīs,* not understanding Śrīdhara Svāmī, sometimes think that Śrīdhara Svāmī belonged to the Māyāvāda *ekadaṇḍa-sannyāsa* community. Actually this was not the case.

TEXT 7

প্রভু কহে,—সাধু এই ভিক্ষুর বচন ।
মুকুন্দ সেবন-ব্রত কৈল নির্ধারণ ॥ ৭ ॥

prabhu kahe,——sādhu ei bhikṣura vacana
mukunda sevana-vrata kaila nirdhāraṇa

SYNONYMS

prabhu kahe—the Lord said; *sādhu*—very much purified; *ei*—this; *bhikṣura*—of the mendicant; *vacana*—words; *mukunda*—Lord Kṛṣṇa; *sevana-vrata*—decision to serve; *kaila*—made; *nirdhāraṇa*—indication.

TRANSLATION

Śrī Caitanya Mahāprabhu approved the purport of this verse on account of the determination of the mendicant devotee to engage in the service of Lord Mukunda. He gave His approval of this verse, indicating that it was very good.

TEXT 8

পরাত্মনিষ্ঠা-মাত্র বেষ-ধারণ ।
মুকুন্দ-সেবায় হয় সংসার-তারণ ॥ ৮ ॥

parātma-niṣṭhā-mātra veṣa-dhāraṇa
mukunda-sevāya haya saṁsāra-tāraṇa

SYNONYMS

para-ātma-niṣṭhā-mātra—only for the determination to serve Kṛṣṇa; *veṣa-dhāraṇa*—changing the dress; *mukunda-sevāya*—by serving Mukunda; *haya*—there is; *saṁsāra-tāraṇa*—liberation from this material bondage.

TRANSLATION

The real purpose of accepting sannyāsa is to dedicate oneself to the service of Mukunda. By serving Mukunda, one can actually be liberated from the bondage of material existence.

PURPORT

In this connection, Śrīla Bhaktivinoda Ṭhākura says that Śrī Caitanya Mahāprabhu accepted the *sannyāsa* order and recommended the determination of the Avantīpura *bhikṣu* to engage in the service of Mukunda. He accepted the *brāhmaṇa's* version due to his determination to serve Mukunda. The *sannyāsī* dress is actually an attraction for material formality. Śrī Caitanya Mahāprabhu did not like such formality, but He wanted the essence of it—service to Mukunda. Such determination in any condition is *parātma-niṣṭhā*. That is required. The conclusion is that the *sannyāsa* order depends not on the dress but the determination to serve Mukunda.

TEXT 9

সেই বেষ কৈল, এবে বৃন্দাবন গিয়া ।
কৃষ্ণনিষেবণ করি নিভৃতে বসিয়া ॥ ৯ ॥

sei veṣa kaila, ebe vṛndāvana giyā
kṛṣṇa-niṣevaṇa kari nibhṛte vasiyā

SYNONYMS

sei—that; *veṣa*—dress; *kaila*—accepted; *ebe*—now; *vṛndāvana*—to Vṛndāvana-dhāma; *giyā*—going; *kṛṣṇa-niṣevaṇa*—service to the Lord; *kari*—I shall execute; *nibhṛte*—in a solitary place; *vasiyā*—sitting.

TRANSLATION

After accepting the sannyāsa order, Śrī Caitanya Mahāprabhu decided to go to Vṛndāvana and engage Himself wholly and solely in the service of Mukunda in a solitary place.

TEXT 10

এত বলি' চলে প্রভু, প্রেমোন্মাদের চিহ্ন ।
দিক্-বিদিক্-জ্ঞান নাহি, কিবা রাত্রি-দিন ॥ ১০ ॥

eta bali' cale prabhu, premonmādera cihna
dik-vidik-jñāna nāhi, kibā rātri-dina

SYNONYMS

eta bali'—saying this; *cale prabhu*—the Lord began to proceed; *prema-unmādera cihna*—the symptoms of ecstatic love; *dik-vidik-jñāna*—knowledge of the right direction or wrong direction; *nāhi*—there is not; *kibā*—whether; *rātri-dina*—night or day.

TRANSLATION

As Śrī Caitanya Mahāprabhu was en route to Vṛndāvana, all the ecstatic symptoms became manifest, and He did not know in which direction He was going, nor did He know whether it was day or night.

TEXT 11

নিত্যানন্দ, আচার্যরত্ন, মুকুন্দ,—তিন জন ।
প্রভু-পাছে-পাছে তিনে করেন গমন ॥ ১১ ॥

nityānanda, ācāryaratna, mukunda,——tina jana
prabhu-pāche-pāche tine karena gamana

SYNONYMS

nityānanda—Nityānanda Prabhu; *ācārya-ratna*—Candraśekhara; *mukunda*—and Mukunda; *tina jana*—three persons; *prabhu-pāche-pāche*—following the Lord; *tine*—all three of them; *karena gamana*—go.

TRANSLATION

When Śrī Caitanya Mahāprabhu went toward Vṛndāvana, Nityānanda Prabhu, Candraśekhara and Prabhu Mukunda followed Him.

TEXT 12

যেই যেই প্রভু দেখে, সেই সেই লোক ।
প্রেমাবেশে 'হরি' বলে, খণ্ডে দুঃখ-শোক ॥ ১২ ॥

yei yei prabhu dekhe, sei sei loka
premāveśe 'hari' bale, khaṇḍe duḥkha-śoka

SYNONYMS

yei yei—whoever; *prabhu*—the Lord; *dekhe*—sees; *sei sei loka*—those persons; *prema-āveśe*—in the ecstasy of love; *hari bale*—exclaim "Hari"; *khaṇḍe*—pass over; *duḥkha-śoka*—all kinds of material unhappiness and lamentation.

TRANSLATION

When Śrī Caitanya Mahāprabhu passed through the Rāḍha-deśa, whoever saw Him in ecstasy exclaimed, "Hari! Hari!" As they chanted this with the Lord, all the unhappiness of material existence diminished.

TEXT 13

গোপ-বালক সব প্রভুকে দেখিয়া ।
'হরি' 'হরি' বলি' ডাকে উচ্চ করিয়া ॥ ১৩ ॥

gopa-bālaka saba prabhuke dekhiyā
'hari' 'hari' bali' ḍāke ucca kariyā

SYNONYMS

gopa-bālaka saba—all the cowherd boys; *prabhuke dekhiyā*—seeing the Lord; *hari hari bali'*—vibrating the sounds "Hari Hari"; *ḍāke*—shout; *ucca kariyā*—loudly.

TRANSLATION

All the cowherd boys who saw Śrī Caitanya Mahāprabhu passing joined with Him and began to shout loudly, "Hari! Hari!"

TEXT 14

শুনি' তা-সবার নিকট গেলা গৌরহরি ।
'বল' 'বল' বলে সবার শিরে হস্ত ধরি' ॥ ১৪ ॥

śuni' tā-sabāra nikaṭa gelā gaurahari
'bala' 'bala' bale sabāra śire hasta dhari'

SYNONYMS

śuni'—hearing; *tā-sabāra*—of all of them; *nikaṭa*—near; *gelā*—went; *gaura-hari*—Śrī Caitanya Mahāprabhu; *bala bala*—go on speaking, go on speaking; *bale*—He said; *sabāra*—of all of them; *śire hasta dhari'*—keeping His hand on their heads.

TRANSLATION

When He heard all the cowherd boys also chanting "Hari! Hari!" Śrī Caitanya Mahāprabhu was very pleased. He approached them, put His hand on their heads and said, "Go on chanting like that."

TEXT 15

তা'-সবার স্তুতি করে,--তোমরা ভাগ্যবান্।
কৃতার্থ করিলে মোরে শুনাঞা হরিনাম ॥ ১৫ ॥

tā'-sabāra stuti kare,——tomarā bhāgyavān
kṛtārtha karile more śunāñā hari-nāma

SYNONYMS

tā'-sabāra—of all of them; *stuti kare*—Lord Caitanya Mahāprabhu praised the behavior; *tomarā*—you; *bhāgyavān*—fortunate; *kṛta-artha*—successful; *karile*—you have made; *more*—to Me; *śunāñā*—by chanting; *hari-nāma*—the holy name of Lord Hari.

TRANSLATION

Śrī Caitanya Mahāprabhu thus blessed them all, saying that they were all fortunate. In this way He praised them, and He felt very successful because they chanted the holy name of Lord Hari.

TEXT 16

গুপ্তে তা-সবাকে আনি' ঠাকুর নিত্যানন্দ।
শিখাইলা সবাকারে করিয়া প্রবন্ধ ॥ ১৬ ॥

gupte tā-sabāke āni' ṭhākura nityānanda
śikhāilā sabākāre kariyā prabandha

SYNONYMS

gupte—in confidence; *tā-sabāke*—unto all the cowherd boys; *āni'*—taking them; *ṭhākura nityānanda*—Nityānanda Ṭhākura; *śikhāilā*—instructed; *sabākāre*—all of them; *kariyā prabandha*—by making a reasonable story.

TRANSLATION

Calling all the boys in confidence and telling a reasonable story, Nityānanda Prabhu instructed them as follows.

TEXT 17

বৃন্দাবনপথ প্রভু পুছেন তোমারে।
গঙ্গাতীর-পথ তবে দেখাইহ তাঁরে ॥ ১৭ ॥

vṛndāvana-patha prabhu puchena tomāre
gaṅgā-tīra-patha tabe dekhāiha tāṅre

SYNONYMS

vṛndāvana-patha—the path to Vṛndāvana; *prabhu*—the Lord; *puchena*—inquires; *tomāre*—from you; *gaṅgā-tīra-patha*—the path on the bank of the Ganges; *tabe*—at that time; *dekhāiha*—please show; *tāṅre*—Him.

TRANSLATION

"If Śrī Caitanya Mahāprabhu asks you about the path to Vṛndāvana, please show Him the path on the bank of the Ganges instead."

TEXTS 18-19

তবে প্রভু পুছিলেন,—'শুন, শিশুগণ ।
কহ দেখি, কোন্ পথে যাব বৃন্দাবন' ॥ ১৮ ॥
শিশু সব গঙ্গাতীরপথ দেখাইল ।
সেই পথে আবেশে প্রভু গমন করিল ॥ ১৯ ॥

tabe prabhu puchilena,—'śuna, śiśu-gaṇa
kaha dekhi, kon pathe yāba vṛndāvana'

śiśu saba gaṅgā-tīra-patha dekhāila
sei pathe āveśe prabhu gamana karila

SYNONYMS

tabe—thereafter; *prabhu*—the Lord; *puchilena*—inquired; *śuna*—hear; *śiśu-gaṇa*—O boys; *kaha dekhi*—please tell Me; *kon pathe*—in which way; *yāba*—I shall go; *vṛndāvana*—to Vṛndāvana; *śiśu*—the boys; *saba*—all; *gaṅgā-tīra-patha*—the path on the bank of the Ganges; *dekhāila*—showed; *sei*—that; *pathe*—on the path; *āveśe*—in ecstasy; *prabhu*—the Lord; *gamana karila*—went.

TRANSLATION

When the cowherd boys were questioned by Lord Caitanya Mahāprabhu about the path to Vṛndāvana, the boys showed Him the path on the bank of the Ganges, and the Lord went that way in ecstasy.

TEXT 20

আচার্যরত্নেরে কহে নিত্যানন্দ-গোসাঞি ।
শীঘ্র যাহ তুমি অদ্বৈত-আচার্যের ঠাঞি ॥ ২০ ॥

ācāryaratnere kahe nityānanda-gosāñi
śīghra yāha tumi advaita-ācāryera ṭhāñi

SYNONYMS

ācārya-ratnere—to Candraśekhara Ācārya; *kahe*—said; *nityānanda-gosāñi*—Lord Nityānanda Prabhu; *śīghra*—immediately; *yāha*—go; *tumi*—you; *advaita-ācāryera ṭhāñi*—to the place of Advaita Ācārya.

TRANSLATION

As the Lord proceeded along the bank of the Ganges, Śrī Nityānanda Prabhu requested Ācāryaratna [Candraśekhara Ācārya] to go immediately to the house of Advaita Ācārya.

TEXT 21

প্রভু লয়ে যাব আমি তাঁহার মন্দিরে ।
সাবধানে রহেন যেন নৌকা লঞা তীরে ॥ ২১॥

prabhu laye yāba āmi tāṅhāra mandire
sāvadhāne rahena yena naukā lañā tīre

SYNONYMS

prabhu laye—taking the Lord; *yāba*—shall go; *āmi*—I; *tāṅhāra*—of Him; *mandire*—to the house; *sāvadhāne*—very carefully; *rahena*—let Him stay; *yena*—there; *naukā*—boat; *lañā*—taking; *tīre*—on the bank.

TRANSLATION

Śrī Nityānanda Gosvāmī told him: "I shall take Śrī Caitanya Mahāprabhu to the bank of the Ganges at Śāntipura, and Advaita Ācārya should carefully stay there on shore with a boat.

TEXT 22

তবে নবদ্বীপে তুমি করিহ গমন ।
শচী-সহ লঞা আইস সব ভক্তগণ ॥ ২২ ॥

tabe navadvīpe tumi kariha gamana
śacī-saha lañā āisa saba bhakta-gaṇa

SYNONYMS

tabe—thereafter; *nava-dvīpe*—to Navadvīpa; *tumi*—you; *kariha*—should do; *gamana*—going; *śacī-saha*—mother Śacī; *lañā*—taking along; *āisa*—come back; *saba bhakta-gaṇa*—all the devotees.

TRANSLATION

"After that," Nityānanda Prabhu continued, "I shall go to Advaita Ācārya's house, and you should go to Navadvīpa and return with mother Śacī and all the other devotees."

TEXT 23

তাঁরে পাঠাইয়া নিত্যানন্দ মহাশয়।
মহাপ্রভুর আগে আসি' দিল পরিচয়॥ ২৩॥

tāṅre pāṭhāiyā nityānanda mahāśaya
mahāprabhura āge āsi' dila paricaya

SYNONYMS

tāṅre—him; *pāṭhāiyā*—sending; *nityānanda*—Lord Nityānanda; *mahā-āśaya*—the great personality; *mahā-prabhura*—of Śrī Caitanya Mahāprabhu; *āge*—in front; *āsi'*—coming; *dila*—gave; *paricaya*—introduction.

TRANSLATION

After sending Ācāryaratna to the house of Advaita Ācārya, Śrī Nityānanda Prabhu went before Lord Caitanya Mahāprabhu and gave notice of His coming.

TEXT 24

প্রভু কহে,—শ্রীপাদ, তোমার কোথাকে গমন।
শ্রীপাদ কহে, তোমার সঙ্গে যাব বৃন্দাবন॥ ২৪॥

prabhu kahe,——śrīpāda, tomāra kothāke gamana
śrīpāda kahe, tomāra saṅge yāba vṛndāvana

SYNONYMS

prabhu kahe—the Lord inquired; *śrī-pāda*—sir; *tomāra*—of You; *kothāke*—where; *gamana*—going; *śrī-pāda kahe*—Nityānanda Prabhu replied; *tomāra*—You; *saṅge*—with; *yāba*—I shall go; *vṛndāvana*—toward Vṛndāvana.

TRANSLATION

Śrī Caitanya Mahāprabhu was in ecstasy, and He asked where Nityānanda Prabhu was going. Nityānanda replied that He was going with Him toward Vṛndāvana.

TEXT 25

প্রভু কহে,—কত দূরে আছে বৃন্দাবন।
তেঁহো কহেন,—কর এই যমুনা দরশন ॥ ২৫ ॥

prabhu kahe,——kata dūre āche vṛndāvana
teṅho kahena,——kara ei yamunā daraśana

SYNONYMS

prabhu kahe—the Lord replied; *kata dūre*—how far; *āche*—there is; *vṛndāvana*—Vṛndāvana-dhāma; *teṅho kahena*—He replied; *kara*—just do; *ei*—this; *yamunā*— Yamunā River; *daraśana*—seeing.

TRANSLATION

When the Lord asked Nityānanda Prabhu how far it was to Vṛndāvana, Nityānanda replied, "Just see! Here is the River Yamunā."

TEXT 26

এত বলি' আনিল তাঁরে গঙ্গা-সন্নিধানে।
আবেশে প্রভুর হৈল গঙ্গারে যমুনা-জ্ঞানে ॥ ২৬ ॥

eta bali' ānila tāṅre gaṅgā-sannidhāne
āveśe prabhura haila gaṅgāre yamunā-jñāne

SYNONYMS

eta bali'—saying this; *ānila*—He brought; *tāṅre*—Him; *gaṅgā-sannidhāne*—near the Ganges; *āveśe*—in ecstasy; *prabhura*—of the Lord;

haila—there was; *gaṅgāre*—of the River Ganges; *yamunā-jñāne*—acceptance as the River Yamunā.

TRANSLATION

Saying this, Nityānanda Prabhu took Caitanya Mahāprabhu near the Ganges, and the Lord, in His ecstasy, accepted the River Ganges as the River Yamunā.

TEXT 27

অহো ভাগ্য, যমুনারে পাইলুঁ দরশন ।
এত বলি' যমুনার করেন স্তবন ॥ ২৭ ॥

aho bhāgya, yamunāre pāiluṅ daraśana
eta bali' yamunāra karena stavana

SYNONYMS

aho bhāgya—oh, My great fortune; *yamunāre*—of the River Yamunā; *pāiluṅ*—I have gotten; *daraśana*—vision; *eta bali'*—after saying this; *yamunāra*—of the River Yamunā; *karena*—does; *stavana*—praising.

TRANSLATION

The Lord said: "Oh, what good fortune! Now I have seen the River Yamunā." Thus thinking the Ganges to be the River Yamunā, Caitanya Mahāprabhu began to offer prayers to it.

TEXT 28

চিদানন্দভানোঃ সদা নন্দসূনোঃ
পরপ্রেমপাত্রী দ্রবব্রহ্মগাত্রী ।
অঘানাং লবিত্রী জগৎক্ষেমধাত্রী
পবিত্রীক্রিয়ান্নো বপুর্মিত্রপুত্রী ॥ ২৮ ॥

cid-ānanda-bhānoḥ sadā nanda-sūnoḥ
para-prema-pātrī drava-brahma-gātrī
aghānāṁ lavitrī jagat-kṣema-dhātrī
pavitrī-kriyān no vapur mitra-putrī

SYNONYMS

cit-ānanda-bhānoḥ—of the direct manifestation of spiritual energy and bliss; *sadā*—always; *nanda-sūnoḥ*—of the son of Mahārāja Nanda; *para-prema-pātrī*—the giver of the highest love; *drava-brahma-gātrī*—composed of the water of the spiritual world; *aghānām*—of all sins and offenses; *lavitrī*—the destroyer; *jagat-kṣema-dhātrī*—the performer of everything auspicious for the world; *pavitrī-kriyāt*—kindly purify; *naḥ*—our; *vapuḥ*—existence; *mitra-putrī*—O daughter of the sun-god.

TRANSLATION

"O River Yamunā, you are the blissful spiritual water that gives love to the son of Nanda Mahārāja. You are the same as the water of the spiritual world, for you can vanquish all our offenses and the sinful reactions incurred in life. You are the creator of all auspicious things for the world. O daughter of the son-god, kindly purify us by your pious activities."

PURPORT

This verse is recorded in the *Caitanya-candrodaya-nāṭaka* (5.13) by Kavi-karṇapura.

TEXT 29

এত বলি' নমস্করি' কৈল গঙ্গাস্নান ।
এক কৌপীন, নাহি দ্বিতীয় পরিধান ॥ ২৯ ॥

eta bali' namaskari' kaila gaṅgā-snāna
eka kaupīna, nāhi dvitīya paridhāna

SYNONYMS

eta bali'—saying this; *namaskari'*—offering obeisances; *kaila*—did; *gaṅgā-snāna*—bathing in the Ganges; *eka kaupīna*—only one piece of underwear; *nāhi*—there was not; *dvitīya*—second; *paridhāna*—garment.

TRANSLATION

After reciting this mantra, Śrī Caitanya Mahāprabhu offered obeisances and took His bath in the Ganges. At that time He had on only one piece of underwear, for there was no second garment.

TEXT 30

হেন কালে আচার্য-গোসাঞি নৌকাতে চড়িঞা ।
আইল নূতন কৌপীন-বহির্বাস লঞা ॥ ৩০ ॥

hena kāle ācārya-gosāñi naukāte caḍiñā
āila nūtana kaupīna-bahirvāsa lañā

SYNONYMS

hena kāle—at that time; *ācārya-gosāñi*—Advaita Ācārya Prabhu; *naukāte caḍiñā*—on board a boat; *āila*—reached there; *nūtana*—new; *kaupīna*—underwear; *bahiḥ-vāsa*—outer garments; *lañā*—bringing.

TRANSLATION

While Śrī Caitanya Mahāprabhu was standing there without a second garment, Śrī Advaita Ācārya arrived on a boat, bringing with Him new underwear and external garments.

TEXT 31

আগে আচার্য আসি' রহিলা নমস্কার করি' ।
আচার্য দেখি' বলে প্রভু মনে সংশয় করি' ॥ ৩১ ॥

āge ācārya āsi' rahilā namaskāra kari'
ācārya dekhi' bale prabhu mane saṁśaya kari'

SYNONYMS

āge—in front; *ācārya*—Advaita Ācārya; *āsi'*—coming; *rahilā*—stood; *namaskāra kari'*—making obeisances; *ācārya dekhi'*—seeing Advaita Ācārya; *bale*—says; *prabhu*—the Lord; *mane*—within His mind; *saṁśaya kari'*—doubting.

TRANSLATION

When Advaita Ācārya arrived, He stood before the Lord and offered His obeisances. After seeing Him, the Lord began to wonder about the entire situation.

TEXT 32

তুমি ত' আচার্য-গোসাঞি, এথা কেনে আইলা ।
আমি বৃন্দাবনে, তুমি কেমতে জানিলা ॥ ৩২ ॥

tumi ta' ācārya-gosāñi, ethā kene āilā
āmi vṛndāvane, tumi ke-mate jānilā

SYNONYMS

tumi—You are; *ta'*—certainly; *ācārya-gosāñi*—Advaita Ācārya; *ethā*—here; *kene*—why; *āilā*—You have come; *āmi*—I; *vṛndāvane*—in Vṛndāvana; *tumi*—You; *ke-mate*—how; *jānilā*—knew.

TRANSLATION

Still in His ecstasy, the Lord began asking Advaita Ācārya, "Why did You come here? How did You know that I was in Vṛndāvana?"

TEXT 33

আচার্য কহে,—তুমি যাহাঁ, সেই বৃন্দাবন ।
মোর ভাগ্যে গঙ্গাতীরে তোমার আগমন ॥ ৩৩ ॥

ācārya kahe,—tumi yāhāṅ, sei vṛndāvana
mora bhāgye gaṅgā-tīre tomāra āgamana

SYNONYMS

ācārya kahe—Ācārya replied; *tumi yāhāṅ*—wherever You are; *sei*—that; *vṛndāvana*—Vṛndāvana; *mora bhāgye*—by My great fortune; *gaṅgā-tīre*—on the bank of the Ganges; *tomāra āgamana*—Your appearance.

TRANSLATION

Advaita Ācārya disclosed the whole situation, telling Śrī Caitanya Mahāprabhu, "Wherever You are, that is Vṛndāvana. Now it is My great fortune that You have come to the bank of the Ganges."

TEXT 34

প্রভু কহে,—নিত্যানন্দ আমারে বঞ্চিলা ।
গঙ্গাকে আনিয়া মোরে যমুনা কহিলা ॥ ৩৪ ॥

prabhu kahe,——nityānanda āmāre vañcilā
gaṅgāke āniyā more yamunā kahilā

SYNONYMS

prabhu kahe—the Lord replied; *nityānanda*—Lord Nityānanda; *āmāre*—Me; *vañcilā*—has cheated; *gaṅgāke*—to the bank of the Ganges; *āniyā*—bringing; *more*—Me; *yamunā*—the River Yamunā; *kahilā*—informed.

TRANSLATION

Śrī Caitanya Mahāprabhu then said, "Nityānanda has cheated Me. He has brought Me to the bank of the Ganges and told Me that it was the Yamunā."

TEXT 35

আচার্য কহে, মিথ্যা নহে শ্রীপাদ-বচন ।
যমুনাতে স্নান তুমি করিলা এখন ॥ ৩৫ ॥

ācārya kahe, mithyā nahe śrīpāda-vacana
yamunāte snāna tumi karilā ekhana

SYNONYMS

ācārya kahe—Advaita Ācārya replied; *mithyā nahe*—this is not untrue; *śrī-pāda-vacana*—the words of Śrī Nityānanda Prabhu; *yamunāte*—in the River Yamunā; *snāna*—bathing; *tumi*—You; *karilā*—did; *ekhana*—just now.

TRANSLATION

When Śrī Caitanya Mahāprabhu accused Nityānanda of cheating Him, Śrīla Advaita Ācārya said, "Whatever Nityānanda Prabhu has told You is not false. You have indeed just now taken Your bath in the River Yamunā."

TEXT 36

গঙ্গায় যমুনা বহে হঞা একধার ।
পশ্চিমে যমুনা বহে, পূর্বে গঙ্গাধার ॥ ৩৬ ॥

gaṅgāya yamunā vahe hañā eka-dhāra
paścime yamunā vahe, pūrve gaṅgā-dhāra

SYNONYMS

gaṅgāya—with the River Ganges; *yamunā*—the River Yamunā; *vahe*—flows; *hañā*—becoming; *eka-dhāra*—one stream; *paścime*—on the western side; *yamunā*—the River Yamunā; *vahe*—flows; *pūrve*—on the eastern side; *gaṅgā-dhāra*—the flow of the Ganges.

TRANSLATION

Advaita Ācārya then explained that at that spot both the Ganges and Yamunā flow together. On the western side was the Yamunā, and on the eastern side was the Ganges.

PURPORT

The Ganges and Yamunā mix at the confluence at Allahabad (Prayāga). The Yamunā flows from the western side and the Ganges from the eastern, and they merge. Since Caitanya Mahāprabhu bathed on the western side, He actually took His bath in the River Yamunā.

TEXT 37

পশ্চিমধারে যমুনা বহে, তাহাঁ কৈলে স্নান।
আর্দ্র কৌপীন ছাড়ি' শুষ্ক কর পরিধান ॥ ৩৭ ॥

paścima-dhāre yamunā vahe, tāhāṅ kaile snāna
ārdra kaupīna chāḍi' śuṣka kara paridhāna

SYNONYMS

paścima-dhāre—in the western flow; *yamunā*—the River Yamunā; *vahe*—flows; *tāhāṅ*—there; *kaile*—You did; *snāna*—bathing; *ārdra*—wet; *kaupīna*—underwear; *chāḍi'*—giving up; *śuṣka*—dry; *kara*—do; *paridhāna*—putting on.

TRANSLATION

Advaita Ācārya then suggested that since Caitanya Mahāprabhu had taken His bath in the River Yamunā and His underwear was now wet, the Lord should change His underwear for dry garments.

TEXT 38

প্রেমাবেশে তিন দিন আছ উপবাস।
আজি মোর ঘরে ভিক্ষা, চল মোর বাস ॥ ৩৮ ॥

premāveśe tina dina ācha upavāsa
āji mora ghare bhikṣā, cala mora vāsa

SYNONYMS

prema-āveśe—in the ecstasy of love; *tina dina*—three days; *ācha*—You are; *upavāsa*—fasting; *āji*—today; *mora*—My; *ghare*—at the house; *bhikṣā*—alms; *cala*—kindly come; *mora vāsa*—to My residence.

TRANSLATION

Advaita Ācārya said: "You have been fasting continuously for three days in Your ecstasy of love for Kṛṣṇa. I therefore invite You to My home, where You may kindly take Your alms. Come with Me to My residence."

TEXT 39

একমুষ্টি অন্ন মুঞি করিয়াছোঁ পাক ।
শুখারুখা ব্যঞ্জন কৈলুঁ, সূপ আর শাক ॥ ৩৯ ॥

eka-muṣṭi anna muñi kariyāchoṅ pāka
śukhārukhā vyañjana kailuṅ, sūpa āra śāka

SYNONYMS

eka-muṣṭi—one palmful; *anna*—rice; *muñi*—I; *kariyāchoṅ*—have done; *pāka*—cooking; *śukhārukhā*—not very luxurious; *vyañjana*—vegetables; *kailuṅ*—I have done; *sūpa*—liquid vegetables; *āra*—and; *śāka*—spinach.

TRANSLATION

Advaita Prabhu continued: "At My home I have just cooked one palmful of rice. The vetetables are always very simple. There is no luxurious cooking—simply a little liquid vegetable and spinach."

TEXT 40

এত বলি' নৌকায় চড়াঞা নিল নিজ-ঘর ।
পাদপ্রক্ষালন কৈল আনন্দ-অন্তর ॥ ৪০ ॥

eta bali' naukāya caḍāñā nila nija-ghara
pāda-prakṣālana kaila ānanda-antara

SYNONYMS

eta bali'—saying this; *naukāya caḍāñā*—making Him board the small boat; *nila*—took; *nija-ghara*—to His own residence; *pāda-prakṣālana*—washing the feet; *kaila*—did; *ānanda-antara*—very happy within Himself.

TRANSLATION

Saying this, Śrī Advaita Ācārya took the Lord into the boat and brought the Lord to His residence. There Advaita Ācārya washed the feet of the Lord and was consequently very happy within.

TEXT 41

প্রথমে পাক করিয়াছেন আচার্যাণী ।
বিষ্ণু-সমর্পণ কৈল আচার্য আপনি ॥ ৪১ ॥

prathame pāka kariyāchena ācāryāṇī
viṣṇu-samarpaṇa kaila ācārya āpani

SYNONYMS

prathame—first; *pāka*—cooking; *kariyāchena*—performed; *ācāryāṇī*—the wife of Advaita Ācārya; *viṣṇu-samarpaṇa*—offering to Lord Viṣṇu; *kaila*—did; *ācārya*—Advaita Ācārya; *āpani*—Himself.

TRANSLATION

All the eatables were first cooked by the wife of Advaita Ācārya. Then Śrīla Advaita Ācārya personally offered everything to Lord Viṣṇu.

PURPORT

This is the ideal householder's life. The husband and wife live together, and the husband works very hard to secure paraphernalia for worshiping Lord Viṣṇu. The wife at home cooks a variety of foodstuffs for Lord Viṣṇu, and the husband offers it to the Deity. After that, *ārati* is performed, and the *prasāda* is distributed amongst family members and guests. According to the Vedic principles, there must always be a guest in the householder's house. In my childhood I have actually seen my father receive not less than four guests every day, and in those days my father's income was not very great. Nonetheless, there was no difficulty in offering *prasāda* to at least four guests every day. According to Vedic principles, a householder, before taking lunch, should go outside and shout very loudly to see if there is anyone without food. In this way he invites people to take *prasāda*. If someone comes, the householder offers him *prasāda,* and if there is not much left, he should offer his own portion to the guest. If no one responds to his call, the householder can accept his own lunch. Thus the householder's life is also a kind of austerity. Because of this, the householder's life is called the *gṛhastha-āśrama*. Although a person may live with his wife and children happily in Kṛṣṇa consciousness, he also observes the regulative principles followed in any temple. If there is no Kṛṣṇa consciousness, the householder's abode is called a *gṛhamedhī's* house. Householders in Kṛṣṇa consciousness are actually *gṛhasthas*—that is, those living in the *āśrama* with their families and children. Śrī Advaita Prabhu was an ideal *gṛhastha,* and His house was the ideal *gṛhastha-āśrama.*

TEXT 42

তিন ঠাঞি ভোগ বাড়াইল সম করি' ।
কৃষ্ণের ভোগ বাড়াইল ধাতু-পাত্রোপরি ॥ ৪২ ॥

tina ṭhāñi bhoga bāḍāila sama kari'
kṛṣṇera bhoga bāḍāila dhātu-pātropari

SYNONYMS

tina ṭhāñi—in three places; *bhoga*—cooked foodstuffs; *bāḍāila*—distributed; *sama*—equal; *kari'*—making; *kṛṣṇera bhoga*—the foodstuff offered to Kṛṣṇa; *bāḍāila*—was arranged; *dhātu-pātra upari*—on a metal plate.

TRANSLATION

All the prepared foods were divided into three equal parts. One part was arranged on a metal plate for offering to Lord Kṛṣṇa.

PURPORT

The word *bāḍāila,* meaning "increased," is very significant in this verse. It is a sophisticated word used by the *gṛhasthas* in Bengal. Whenever food is prepared and we take away a portion, the food is actually decreased. But here it is the system to say *bāḍāila,* or "increased." If food is prepared for Kṛṣṇa and offered to Him and the Vaiṣṇavas, the stock is increased, never decreased.

TEXT 43

বত্তিশা-আঠিয়া-কলার আঙ্গটিয়া পাতে ।
দুই ঠাঞি ভোগ বাড়াইল ভাল মতে ॥ ৪৩ ॥

battiśā-āṭhiyā-kalāra āṅgaṭiyā pāte
dui ṭhāñi bhoga bāḍāila bhāla mate

SYNONYMS

battiśā-āṭhiyā—producing thirty-two bunches; *kalāra*—of a banana tree; *āṅgaṭiyā*—undivided; *pāte*—on leaves; *dui ṭhāñi*—in two places; *bhoga*—the eatables; *bāḍāila*—arranged; *bhāla mate*—very nicely.

TRANSLATION

Of the three divisions, one was arranged on a metal plate, and the other two were arranged on plantain leaves. These leaves were not bifurcated, and they were taken from a banana tree that held at least thirty-two bunches of bananas. The two plates were filled very nicely with the kinds of food described below.

TEXT 44

মধ্যে পীত-ঘৃতসিক্ত শাল্যন্নের স্তূপ ।
চারিদিকে ব্যঞ্জন-ডোঙ্গা, আর মুদ্গসূপ ॥ ৪৪ ॥

madhye pīta-ghṛta-sikta śālyannera stūpa
cāri-dike vyañjana-ḍoṅgā, āra mudga-sūpa

SYNONYMS

madhye—in the middle; *pīta*—yellow; *ghṛta-sikta*—wet with clarified butter; *śālyannera*—of very fine cooked rice; *stūpa*—a mound; *cāri-dike*—surrounding the mound of rice; *vyañjana-ḍoṅgā*—vegetable pots; *āra*—and; *mudga-sūpa*—dahl made of split mung.

TRANSLATION

The cooked rice was a stack of very fine grains nicely cooked, and in the middle was yellow butter clarified from the milk of cows. Surrounding the stack of rice were pots made of the skins of banana trees, and in these pots were varieties of vegetables and mung dahl.

TEXT 45

সার্দ্রক, বাস্তুক-শাক বিবিধ প্রকার ।
পটোল, কুষ্মাণ্ড-বড়ি, মানকচু আর ॥ ৪৫ ॥

sārdraka, vāstuka-śāka vividha prakāra
paṭola, kuṣmāṇḍa-baḍi, mānakacu āra

SYNONYMS

sārdraka—pots with ginger dishes; *vāstuka-śāka*—spinach; *vividha*—various; *prakāra*—kinds; *paṭola*—a kind of fruit; *kuṣmāṇḍa*—squash; *baḍi*—with split dahl; *mānakacu*—the root of a vegetable tree called *kacu; āra*—and.

TRANSLATION

Among the cooked vegetables were paṭolas, squash, mānakacu, and a salad made with pieces of ginger and various types of spinach.

TEXT 46

চই-মরিচ-সুখ্‌ত দিয়া সব ফল-মূলে ।
অমৃতনিন্দক পঞ্চবিধ তিক্ত-ঝালে ॥ ৪৬ ॥

ca-i-marica-sukhta diyā saba phala-mūle
amṛta-nindaka pañca-vidha tikta-jhāle

SYNONYMS

ca-i-marica—with black pepper and *ca-i* (a kind of spice); *sukhta*—vegetables made bitter; *diyā*—giving; *saba*—all; *phala-mūle*—various kinds of fruits and roots; *amṛta-nindaka*—defying nectar; *pañca-vidha*—five kinds of; *tikta*—bitter; *jhāle*—and pungent.

TRANSLATION

There was sukhta, bitter melon mixed with all kinds of vegetables, defying the taste of nectar. There were five types of bitter and pungent sukhtas.

TEXT 47

কোমল নিম্বপত্র সহ ভাজা বার্তাকী ।
পটোল-ফুলবড়ি-ভাজা, কুষ্মাণ্ড-মানচাকি ॥ ৪৭ ॥

komala nimba-patra saha bhājā vārtākī
paṭola-phula-baḍi-bhājā, kuṣmāṇḍa-mānacāki

SYNONYMS

komala—newly grown; *nimba-patra*—*nimba* leaves; *saha*—with; *bhājā*—fried; *vārtākī*—eggplant; *paṭola*—with *paṭola* fruit; *phula-baḍi*—a preparation of dahl; *bhājā*—fried; *kuṣmāṇḍa*—squashes; *mānacāki*—the foodstuff called *mānacāki.*

TRANSLATION

Amongst the various vegetables were newly grown leaves of nimba trees fried with eggplant. The fruit known as paṭola was fried with phula-baḍi, a kind of dahl preparation first mashed and then dried in the sun. There was also a preparation known as kuṣmāṇḍa-mānacāki.

PURPORT

We request our editors of cookbooks to add all these nice preparations described by the experienced author Śrīla Kavirāja Gosvāmī.

TEXT 48

নারিকেল-শস্য, ছানা, শর্করা মধুর ।
মোছাঘণ্ট, দুগ্ধকুষ্মাণ্ড, সকল প্রচুর ॥ ৪৮ ॥

nārikela-śasya, chānā, śarkarā madhura
mochā-ghaṇṭa, dugdha-kuṣmāṇḍa, sakala pracura

SYNONYMS

nārikela-śasya—the pulp of coconut; *chānā*—curd; *śarkarā*—fruit sugar; *madhura*—very sweet; *mochā-ghaṇṭa*—a semisolid preparation made with banana flowers; *dugdha-kuṣmāṇḍa*—newly grown squash cut into pieces and boiled in milk; *sakala*—all; *pracura*—plentiful.

TRANSLATION

The preparation made with coconut pulp mixed with curd and rock candy was very sweet. There was a curry made of banana flowers and squash boiled in milk, all in great quantity.

TEXT 49

মধুরাম্লবড়া, অম্লাদি পাঁচ-ছয়।
সকল ব্যঞ্জন কৈল লোকে যত হয়॥ ৪৯॥

madhurāmla-baḍā, amlādi pāṅca-chaya
sakala vyañjana kaila loke yata haya

SYNONYMS

madhura-amla-baḍā—sweet and sour cakes; *amla-ādi*—sour preparations; *pāṅca-chaya*—five or six; *sakala vyañjana*—all vegetables; *kaila*—made; *loke*—for the people; *yata haya*—as many as there were.

TRANSLATION

There were small cakes in sweet and sour sauce and five or six kinds of sour preparations. All the vegetables were so made that everyone present could take prasāda.

TEXT 50

মুদ্গবড়া, কলাবড়া, মাষবড়া, মিষ্ট।
ক্ষীরপুলী, নারিকেল, যত পিঠা ইষ্ট॥ ৫০॥

mudga-baḍā, kalā-baḍā, māṣa-baḍā, miṣṭa
kṣīra-pulī, nārikela, yata piṭhā iṣṭa

SYNONYMS

mudga-baḍā—soft cake made with mung; *kalā-baḍā*—soft cake made with fried banana; *māṣa-baḍā*—soft cake made with urd dahl; *miṣṭa*—various kinds of sweets; *kṣīra-pulī*—condensed milk mixed with rice cakes; *nārikela*—a preparation of coconut; *yata*—all kinds of; *piṭhā*—cakes; *iṣṭa*—desirable.

TRANSLATION

There were soft cakes made with mung dahl, soft cakes made with ripe bananas, and soft cakes made with urd dahl. There were various kinds of sweetmeats, and condensed milk mixed with rice cakes, a coconut preparation and every kind of cake desirable.

TEXT 51

বত্তিশা-আঠিয়া কলার ডোঙ্গা বড় বড় ।
চলে হালে নাহি,—ডোঙ্গা অতি বড় দড় ॥৫১ ॥

battiśā-āṭhiyā kalāra ḍoṅgā baḍa baḍa
cale hāle nāhi,——ḍoṅgā ati baḍa daḍa

SYNONYMS

battiśā-āṭhiyā—producing thirty-two bunches of bananas; *kalāra*—of the banana tree; *doṅgā*—pots made of leaves; *baḍa baḍa*—big; *cale hāle nāhi*—they did not tilt or totter; *doṅgā*—pots; *ati*—very; *baḍa*—big; *daḍa*—strong.

TRANSLATION

All the vegetables were served in pots made of banana leaves taken from trees producing at least thirty-two bunches of bananas. These pots were very strong and big and did not tilt or totter.

TEXT 52

পঞ্চাশ পঞ্চাশ ডোঙ্গা ব্যঞ্জনে পূরিঞা ।
তিন ভোগের আশে পাশে রাখিল ধরিঞা ॥ ৫২ ॥

pañcāśa pañcāśa ḍoṅgā vyañjane pūriñā
tina bhogera āśe pāśe rākhila dhariñā

SYNONYMS

pañcāśa pañcāśa—fifty and fifty; *ḍoṅgā*—pots; *vyañjane*—with vegetables; *pūriñā*—filling; *tina*—three; *bhogera*—of eating places; *āśe pāśe*—all around; *rākhila*—kept; *dhariñā*—fixing.

TRANSLATION

All around the three eating places were a hundred pots filled with various kinds of vegetables.

TEXT 53

সঘৃত-পায়স নব-মৃৎকুণ্ডিকা ভরিঞা ।
তিন পাত্রে ঘনাবর্ত-দুগ্ধ রাখেত ধরিঞা ॥ ৫৩ ॥

saghṛta-pāyasa nava-mṛt-kuṇḍikā bhariñā
tina pātre ghanāvarta-dugdha rākheta dhariñā

SYNONYMS

sa-ghṛta-pāyasa—sweet rice mixed with ghee; *nava-mṛt-kuṇḍikā*—new earthen pots; *bhariñā*—filling; *tina pātre*—in three pots; *ghanāvarta-dugdha*—finely condensed milk; *rākheta*—were kept; *dhariñā*—fixing.

TRANSLATION

Along with the various vegetables was sweet rice mixed with ghee. This was kept in new earthen pots. Earthen pots filled with highly condensed milk were placed in three places.

TEXT 54

দুগ্ধ-চিড়া-কলা আর দুগ্ধ-লক্লকী ।
যতেক করিল' তাহা কহিতে না শকি ॥ ৫৪ ॥

dugdha-ciḍā-kalā āra dugdha-laklakī
yateka karila' tāhā kahite nā śaki

SYNONYMS

dugdha-ciḍā—chipped rice made with milk; *kalā*—mixed with bananas; *āra*—and; *dugdha-laklakī*—a kind of squash known as *lāu,* boiled with milk; *yateka*—all that; *karila'*—was prepared; *tāhā*—that; *kahite*—to describe; *nā*—not; *śaki*—I am able.

TRANSLATION

Besides the other preparations, there were chipped rice, made with milk and mixed with bananas, and white squash boiled in milk. Indeed, it is not possible to describe all the preparations that were made.

TEXT 55

দুই পাশে ধরিল সব মৃৎকুণ্ডিকা ভরি' ।
চাঁপাকলা-দধি-সন্দেশ কহিতে না পারি ॥ ৫৫ ॥

dui pāśe dharila saba mṛt-kuṇḍikā bhari'
cāṅpākalā-dadhi-sandeśa kahite nā pāri

SYNONYMS

dui pāśe—on two sides; *dharila*—kept; *saba*—all; *mṛt-kuṇḍikā*—earthen pots; *bhari'*—filling; *cāṅpākalā*—a kind of banana known as *cāṅpākalā; dadhi-sandeśa*—mixed with yogurt and *sandeśa*; *kahite*—to say; *nā*—not; *pāri*—I am able.

TRANSLATION

In two places there were earthen pots filled with another preparation made with yogurt, sandeśa [a sweetmeat made with curd] and banana. I am unable to describe it all.

TEXT 56

অন্ন-ব্যঞ্জন-উপরি দিল তুলসীমঞ্জরী ।
তিন জলপাত্রে সুবাসিত জল ভরি' ॥ ৫৬ ॥

anna-vyañjana-upari dila tulasī-mañjarī
tina jala-pātre suvāsita jala bhari'

SYNONYMS

anna-vyañjana-upari—on top of the boiled rice and vegetables; *dila*—placed; *tulasī-mañjarī*—flowers of *tulasī*; *tina*—three; *jala-pātre*—waterpots; *su-vāsita*—scented; *jala*—water; *bhari'*—filling.

TRANSLATION

Upon the stack of boiled rice and all the vegetables were flowers of the tulasī trees. There were also pots filled with scented rosewater.

TEXT 57

তিন শুভ্রপীঠ, তার উপরি বসন ।
এইরূপে সাক্ষাৎ কৃষ্ণে করাইল ভোজন ॥ ৫৭ ॥

tina śubhra-pīṭha, tāra upari vasana
ei-rūpe sākṣāt kṛṣṇe karāila bhojana

SYNONYMS

tina—three; *śubhra-pīṭha*—white sitting places; *tāra*—of them; *upari*—on top; *vasana*—soft cloth; *ei-rūpe*—in this way; *sākṣāt*—directly; *kṛṣṇe*—unto Kṛṣṇa; *karāila*—made to do; *bhojana*—eating.

TRANSLATION

There were three sitting places where soft cloths were placed. Thus Lord Kṛṣṇa was offered all the foodstuff, and the Lord took it very pleasantly.

TEXT 58

আরতির কালে দুই প্রভু বোলাইল।
প্রভু-সঙ্গে সবে আসি' আরতি দেখিল ॥ ৫৮ ॥

āratira kāle dui prabhu bolāila
prabhu-saṅge sabe āsi' ārati dekhila

SYNONYMS

āratira kāle—during the time of *ārati*; *dui prabhu*—Lord Nityānanda and Śrī Caitanya Mahāprabhu; *bolāila*—He called; *prabhu-saṅge*—with the Lords; *sabe*—all other people; *āsi'*—coming there; *ārati*—the *ārati* ceremony; *dekhila*—observed.

TRANSLATION

It is the system, after offering food, to perform bhoga-ārati. Advaita Prabhu asked the two brothers, Lord Caitanya Mahāprabhu and Nityānanda Prabhu, to come see the ārati. The two Lords and all others present went to see the ārati ceremony.

TEXT 59

আরতি করিয়া কৃষ্ণে করা'ল শয়ন।
আচার্য আসি' প্রভুরে তবে কৈলা নিবেদন ৫৯ ॥

ārati kariyā kṛṣṇe karā'la śayana
ācārya āsi' prabhure tabe kailā nivedana

SYNONYMS

ārati kariyā—after finishing the *ārati*; *kṛṣṇe*—Lord Kṛṣṇa; *karā'la*—made to do; *śayana*—lying down to rest; *ācārya*—Advaita Ācārya; *āsi'*—coming; *prabhure*—unto Lord Caitanya Mahāprabhu; *tabe*—then; *kailā*—made; *nivedana*—submission.

TRANSLATION

After ārati was performed for the Deities in the temple, Lord Kṛṣṇa was made to lie down to rest. Advaita Ācārya then came out to submit something to Lord Caitanya Mahāprabhu.

TEXT 60

গৃহের ভিতরে প্রভু করুন গমন ।
দুই ভাই আইলা তবে করিতে ভোজন ॥ ৬০ ॥

gṛhera bhitare prabhu karuna gamana
dui bhāi āilā tabe karite bhojana

SYNONYMS

gṛhera bhitare—within the room; *prabhu*—Caitanya Mahāprabhu; *karuna*—kindly do; *gamana*—entering; *dui bhāi*—the two brothers, Caitanya Mahāprabhu and Nityānanda Prabhu; *āilā*—came; *tabe*—then; *karite bhojana*—to partake of the *prasāda.*

TRANSLATION

Śrī Advaita Prabhu said: "My dear Lords, kindly enter this room." The two brothers, Caitanya Mahāprabhu and Nityānanda Prabhu, then came forward to take the prasāda.

TEXT 61

মুকুন্দ, হরিদাস,—দুই প্রভু বোলাইল ।
যোড়হাতে দুইজন কহিতে লাগিল ॥ ৬১ ॥

mukunda, haridāsa,——dui prabhu bolāila
yoḍa-hāte dui-jana kahite lāgila

SYNONYMS

mukunda—Mukunda; *hari-dāsa*—Haridāsa; *dui prabhu*—the two Lords; *bolāila*—called for; *yoḍa-hāte*—with folded hands; *dui-jana*—two persons; *kahite lāgila*—began to say.

TRANSLATION

When Lord Śrī Caitanya Mahāprabhu and Nityānanda Prabhu went to accept the prasāda, They both called Mukunda and Haridāsa to come with Them. However, Mukunda and Haridāsa, both with folded hands, spoke as follows.

TEXT 62

মুকুন্দ কহে—মোর কিছু কৃত্য নাহি সরে।
পাছে মুঞি প্রসাদ পামু, তুমি যাহ ঘরে ॥ ৬২ ॥

mukunda kahe——mora kichu kṛtya nāhi sare
pāche muñi prasāda pāmu, tumi yāha ghare

SYNONYMS

mukunda kahe—Mukunda said; *mora*—of me; *kichu*—something; *kṛtya*—to perform; *nāhi sare*—not yet finished; *pāche*—later; *muñi*—I; *prasāda*—*prasāda*; *pāmu*—shall accept; *tumi yāha ghare*—You both kindly enter the room.

TRANSLATION

When Mukunda was called for, he submitted, "My dear sir, I have something to do that is not yet finished. Later I shall accept the prasāda, so You two Prabhus should now please enter the room."

TEXT 63

হরিদাস কহে—মুঞি পাপিষ্ঠ অধম।
বাহিরে এক মুষ্টি পাছে করিমু ভোজন ॥ ৬৩ ॥

haridāsa kahe——muñi pāpiṣṭha adhama
bāhire eka muṣṭi pāche karimu bhojana

SYNONYMS

hari-dāsa kahe—Haridāsa said; *muñi*—I; *pāpiṣṭha*—sinful; *adhama*—the lowest of men; *bāhire*—outside; *eka*—one; *muṣṭi*—palmful; *pāche*—later; *karimu*—I shall do; *bhojana*—eating.

TRANSLATION

Haridāsa Ṭhākura said: "I am the most sinful and lowest among men. Later I shall eat one palmful of prasāda while waiting outside."

PURPORT

Although the Hindus and Muslims lived together in a very friendly manner, still there were distinctions between them. The Mohammedans were considered *yavanas,* or low-born, and whenever a Mohammedan was invited, he would be fed outside of the house. Although personally called by Śrī Caitanya Mahāprabhu and Nityānanda Prabhu to take *prasāda* with Them, still, out of great humility, Haridāsa Ṭhākura submitted, "I shall take the *prasāda* outside of the house." Although Haridāsa Ṭhākura was an exalted Vaiṣṇava accepted by Advaita Ācārya, Nityānanda Prabhu and Śrī Caitanya Mahāprabhu, nonetheless, in order not to disturb social tranquility, he humbly kept himself in the position of a Mohammedan, outside the jurisdiction of the Hindu community. Therefore he proposed to take *prasāda* outside the house. Although he was in an exalted position and equal to other great Vaiṣṇavas, he considered himself a *pāpiṣṭha,* a most sinful man, and *adhama,* the lowest among men. Although a Vaiṣṇava may be very much advanced spiritually, he keeps himself externally humble and submissive.

TEXT 64

দুই প্রভু লঞা আচার্য গেলা ভিতর ঘরে ।
প্রসাদ দেখিয়া প্রভুর আনন্দ অন্তরে ॥ ৬৪ ॥

dui prabhu lañā ācārya gelā bhitara ghare
prasāda dekhiyā prabhura ānanda antare

SYNONYMS

dui prabhu—the two *prabhus* (Caitanya Mahāprabhu and Nityānanda Prabhu); *lañā*—with; *ācārya*—Advaita Ācārya; *gelā*—went; *bhitara*—within; *ghare*—the room; *prasāda*—the *prasāda*; *dekhiyā*—seeing; *prabhura*—of Caitanya Mahāprabhu; *ānanda antare*—was very pleased within Himself.

TRANSLATION

Advaita Ācārya took Lord Nityānanda Prabhu and Lord Caitanya Mahāprabhu within the room, and the two Lords saw the arrangement of the prasāda. Śrī Caitanya Mahāprabhu was especially very much pleased.

PURPORT

Śrī Caitanya Mahāprabhu was pleased because He saw how nicely so many varieties of food were prepared for Kṛṣṇa. Actually all kinds of *prasāda* are prepared for Kṛṣṇa, not for the people, but the devotees partake of *prasāda* with great pleasure.

TEXT 65

ঐছে অন্ন যে কৃষ্ণকে করায় ভোজন।
জন্মে জন্মে শিরে ধরোঁ তাঁহার চরণ ॥ ৬৫ ॥

aiche anna ye kṛṣṇake karāya bhojana
janme janme śire dharoṅ tāṅhāra caraṇa

SYNONYMS

aiche—in this way; *anna*—the eatables; *ye*—anyone who; *kṛṣṇake*—unto Kṛṣṇa; *karāya*—made to do; *bhojana*—eating; *janme janme*—birth after birth; *śire*—on My head; *dharoṅ*—I keep; *tāṅhāra*—his; *caraṇa*—lotus feet.

TRANSLATION

Śrī Caitanya Mahāprabhu approved of all the methods employed in cooking and offering food to Kṛṣṇa. Indeed, He was so pleased that He said, "Frankly, I will personally take the lotus feet of anyone who can offer Kṛṣṇa such nice food and place those lotus feet on My head birth after birth."

TEXT 66

প্রভু জানে তিন ভোগ—কৃষ্ণের নৈবেদ্য।
আচার্যের মনঃকথা নহে প্রভুর বেদ্য ॥ ৬৬॥

prabhu jāne tina bhoga——kṛṣṇera naivedya
ācāryera manaḥ-kathā nahe prabhura vedya

SYNONYMS

prabhu jāne—the Lord knows; *tina bhoga*—three divisions of *bhoga*; *kṛṣṇera naivedya*—offerings to Lord Kṛṣṇa; *ācāryera*—of Advaita Ācārya; *manaḥ-kathā*—the intentions; *nahe*—not; *prabhura*—to the Lord; *vedya*—understandable.

TRANSLATION

When Śrī Caitanya Mahāprabhu entered the room, He saw three divisions of food, and He knew that all of these were meant for Kṛṣṇa. However, He did not understand the intentions of Advaita Ācārya.

PURPORT

Śrīla Bhaktisiddhānta Sarasvatī Ṭhākura states that one of these servings was offered in a metal dish and was meant for Kṛṣṇa, whereas the other two were placed on big banana leaves. The offering on the metal plate was personally offered by Advaita Ācārya to Kṛṣṇa. The other two servings, on banana leaves, were to be accepted by Śrī Caitanya Mahāprabhu and Lord Nityānanda. That was Advaita Ācārya's intention, but He did not disclose this to Śrī Caitanya Mahāprabhu. Thus when Śrī Caitanya Mahāprabhu saw the foodstuff offered in three places, He thought that all of it was meant for Kṛṣṇa.

TEXT 67

প্রভু বলে—বৈস তিনে করিয়ে ভোজন ।
আচার্য কহে—আমি করিব পরিবেশন ॥ ৬৭ ॥

prabhu bale——vaisa tine kariye bhojana
ācārya kahe——āmi kariba pariveśana

SYNONYMS

prabhu bale—Lord Caitanya Mahāprabhu said; *vaisa*—sit down; *tine*—in the three places; *kariye*—do; *bhojana*—eating; *ācārya kahe*—Advaita Ācārya replied; *āmi kariba pariveśana*—I shall distribute.

TRANSLATION

Śrī Caitanya Mahāprabhu said: "Let Us sit down in these three places, and We shall take prasāda." However, Advaita Ācārya said, "I shall distribute the prasāda."

TEXT 68

কোন্ স্থানে বসিব, আর আন দুই পাত ।
অল্প করি' আনি' তাহে দেহ ব্যঞ্জন ভাত ॥ ৬৮ ॥

kon sthāne vasiba, āra āna dui pāta
alpa kari' āni' tāhe deha vyañjana bhāta

SYNONYMS

kon sthāne vasiba—where shall We sit down; *āra*—other; *āna*—bring; *dui pāta*—two leaves; *alpa kari'*—making a small quantity; *āni'*—bringing; *tāhe*—on that; *deha*—give; *vyañjana*—vegetables; *bhāta*—and boiled rice.

TRANSLATION

Śrī Caitanya Mahāprabhu thought that all three servings were meant for distribution; therefore He asked for another two banana leaves, saying, "Let Us have a very little quantity of vegetable and rice."

TEXT 69

আচার্য কহে—বৈস দোঁহে পিঁড়ির উপরে ।
এত বলি' হাতে ধরি' বসাইল দুঁহারে ॥ ৬৯ ॥

ācārya kahe——vaisa doṅhe piṅḍira upare
eta bali' hāte dhari' vasāila duṅhāre

SYNONYMS

ācārya kahe—Advaita Ācārya said; *vaisa*—sit down; *doṅhe*—You two; *piṅḍira upare*—on the planks of wood; *eta bali'*—saying this; *hāte dhari'*—catching Their hands; *vasāila duṅhāre*—sat the two Lords down.

TRANSLATION

Advaita Ācārya said: "Just sit down here on these seats." Catching Their hands, He sat Them both down.

TEXT 70

প্রভু কহে—সন্ন্যাসীর ভক্ষ্য নহে উপকরণ ।
ইহা খাইলে কৈছে হয় ইন্দ্রিয় বারণ ॥ ৭০ ॥

prabhu kahe——sannyāsīra bhakṣya nahe upakaraṇa
ihā khāile kaiche haya indriya vāraṇa

SYNONYMS

prabhu kahe—the Lord said; *sannyāsīra*—by a *sannyāsī*; *bhakṣya*—to be eaten; *nahe*—this is not; *upakaraṇa*—varieties of food; *ihā*—this; *khāile*—if eating; *kaiche*—how; *haya*—there is; *indriya*—senses; *vāraṇa*—controlling.

TRANSLATION

Śrī Caitanya Mahāprabhu said: "It is not proper for a sannyāsī to eat such a variety of foodstuff. If he does, how can he control his senses?"

PURPORT

The word *upakaraṇa* indicates a variety of foodstuffs, such as dahl, vegetables and other varieties of possible dishes that one can eat very nicely with rice. It is not proper, however, for a *sannyāsī* to eat such palatable dishes. If he did so, he would not be able to control his senses. Śrī Caitanya Mahāprabhu did not encourage *sannyāsīs* to eat very palatable dishes, for the whole Vaiṣṇava cult is *vairāgya-vidyā,* as renounced as possible. Caitanya Mahāprabhu also advised Raghunātha dāsa Gosvāmī not to eat very palatable dishes, wear very nice garments or talk on mundane subjects. These things are all prohibited for those in the renounced order. A devotee does not accept anything to eat that is not first offered to Kṛṣṇa. All the rich foodstuffs offered to Kṛṣṇa are given to the *gṛhasthas,* the householders. There are many nice things offered to Kṛṣṇa—garlands, bedsteads, nice ornaments, nice food, and even nicely prepared pan, betel nuts—but a humble Vaiṣṇava, thinking his body material and nasty, does not accept such preparations for himself. He thinks that by accepting such things he will offend the lotus feet of the Lord. Those who are *sahajiyās* cannot understand what Śrī Caitanya Mahāprabhu meant when He asked Advaita Ācārya to bring two separate leaves and give a small quantity of the *prasāda* to Him.

TEXT 71

আচার্য কহে—ছাড় তুমি আপনার চুরি ।
আমি সব জানি তোমার সন্ন্যাসের ভারিভুরি ॥৭১॥

ācārya kahe——chāḍa tumi āpanāra curi
āmi saba jāni tomāra sannyāsera bhāri-bhuri

SYNONYMS

ācārya kahe—Advaita Ācārya replied; *chāḍa*—give up; *tumi*—You; *āpanāra*—of Yourself; *curi*—the concealment; *āmi*—I; *saba*—all; *jāni*—know; *tomāra*—of You; *sannyāsera*—of the acceptance of the renounced order; *bhāri-bhuri*—the confidential meaning.

TRANSLATION

When Śrī Caitanya Mahāprabhu did not accept the food that had already been served, Advaita Ācārya said, "Please give up Your concealment. I know what You are, and I know the confidential meaning of Your accepting the sannyāsa order."

TEXT 72

ভোজন করহ, ছাড় বচন-চাতুরী ।
প্রভু কহে—এত অন্ন খাইতে না পারি ॥ ৭২ ॥

bhojana karaha, chāḍa vacana-cāturī
prabhu kahe——eta anna khāite nā pāri

SYNONYMS

bhojana karaha—kindly accept this *prasāda*; *chāḍa*—give up; *vacana-cāturī*—jugglery of words; *prabhu kahe*—the Lord said; *eta*—so much; *anna*—foodstuffs; *khāite*—to eat; *nā pāri*—I am not able.

TRANSLATION

Advaita Ācārya thus requested Śrī Caitanya Mahāprabhu to eat and give up juggling words. The Lord replied, "I certainly cannot eat so much food."

TEXT 73

আচার্য বলে—অকপটে করহ আহার ।
যদি খাইতে না পার পাতে রহিবেক আর ॥ ৭৩ ॥

ācārya bale——akapaṭe karaha āhāra
yadi khāite nā pāra pāte rahibeka āra

SYNONYMS

ācārya bale—Advaita Ācārya says; *akapaṭe*—without pretense; *karaha*—kindly do; *āhāra*—eating; *yadi*—if; *khāite*—to eat; *nā pāra*—You are not able; *pāte*—on the leaf; *rahibeka āra*—let the balance remain.

TRANSLATION

Advaita Ācārya then requested the Lord to simply accept the prasāda, without pretense. If He could not eat it all, the balance could be left on the plate.

TEXT 74

প্রভু বলে—এত অন্ন নারিব খাইতে ।
সন্ন্যাসীর ধর্ম নহে উচ্ছিষ্ট রাখিতে ॥ ৭৪ ॥

prabhu bale——eta anna nāriba khāite
sannyāsīra dharma nahe ucchiṣṭa rākhite

SYNONYMS

prabhu bale—the Lord said; *eta*—so much; *anna*—eatables; *nāriba*—I will not be able; *khāite*—to eat; *sannyāsīra*—of a *sannyāsī*; *dharma nahe*—it is not the duty; *ucchiṣṭa*—remnants of foodstuff; *rākhite*—to keep.

TRANSLATION

Śrī Caitanya Mahāprabhu said, "I will not be able to eat so much food, and it is not the duty of a sannyāsī to leave remnants."

PURPORT

According to *Śrīmad-Bhāgavatam* (11.18.19):

bahir jalāśayaṁ gatvā
tatropaspṛśya vāg-yataḥ
vibhajya pāvitaṁ śeṣaṁ
bhuñjītāśeṣam āhṛtam

"Whatever a *sannyāsī* gets that is edible from a householder's house, he should take outside near some lake or river, and, after offering it to Viṣṇu, Brahmā and the sun (three divisions), he should eat the entire offering and should not leave anything for others to eat." This is an injunction for *sannyāsīs* given in *Śrīmad-Bhāgavatam.*

TEXT 75

আচার্য বলে—নীলাচলে খাও চৌয়ান্নবার ।
একবারে অন্ন খাও শত শত ভার ॥ ৭৫ ॥

ācārya bale——nīlācale khāo cauyānna-bāra
eka-bāre anna khāo śata śata bhāra

SYNONYMS

ācārya bale—Advaita Ācārya replies; *nīlācale*—at Jagannātha Purī; *khāo*—You eat; *cauyānna-bāra*—fifty-four times; *eka-bāre*—at one time; *anna*—eatables; *khāo*—You eat; *śata śata bhāra*—hundreds of pots.

TRANSLATION

In this connection Advaita Ācārya referred to Caitanya Mahāprabhu's eating at Jagannātha Purī. Lord Jagannātha and Śrī Caitanya Mahāprabhu are identical. Advaita Ācārya pointed out that at Jagannātha Purī Caitanya Mahāprabhu ate fifty-four times, and each time He ate many hundreds of pots of food.

TEXT 76

তিন জনার ভক্ষ্যপিণ্ড—তোমার এক গ্রাস ।
তার লেখায় এই অন্ন নহে পঞ্চগ্রাস ॥ ৭৬ ॥

tina janāra bhakṣya-piṇḍa——tomāra eka grāsa
tāra lekhāya ei anna nahe pañca-grāsa

SYNONYMS

tina janāra—of three persons; *bhakṣya-piṇḍa*—the stack of eatables; *tomāra*—of You; *eka grāsa*—one morsel; *tāra*—to that; *lekhāya*—in proportion; *ei anna*—this foodstuff; *nahe*—is not; *pañca-grāsa*—five morsels.

TRANSLATION

Śrī Advaita Ācārya said, "The amount of food that three people can eat does not constitute even a morsel for You. In proportion to that, these edibles are not even five morsels of food for You."

TEXT 77

মোর ভাগ্যে, মোর ঘরে, তোমার আগমন ।
ছাড়হ চাতুরী, প্রভু, করহ ভোজন ॥ ৭৭ ॥

mora bhāgye, mora ghare, tomāra āgamana
chāḍaha cāturī, prabhu, karaha bhojana

SYNONYMS

mora bhāgye—by My fortune; *mora ghare*—at My home; *tomāra*—Your; *āgamana*—appearance; *chāḍaha*—please give up; *cāturī*—all this jugglery; *prabhu*—My Lord; *karaha*—just do; *bhojana*—eating.

TRANSLATION

Advaita Ācārya continued: "By my great fortune You have just come to My home. Please do not juggle words. Just begin eating and do not talk."

TEXT 78

এত বলি' জল দিল দুই গোসাঞির হাতে।
হাসিয়া লাগিলা দুঁহে ভোজন করিতে ॥ ৭৮ ॥

eta bali' jala dila dui gosāñira hāte
hāsiyā lāgilā duṅhe bhojana karite

SYNONYMS

eta bali'—saying this; *jala dila*—supplied water; *dui gosāñira*—of Lord Caitanya Mahāprabhu and Lord Nityānanda; *hāte*—on the hands; *hāsiyā*—smiling; *lāgilā*—began; *duṅhe*—both of Them; *bhojana karite*—to eat.

TRANSLATION

Upon saying this, Advaita Ācārya supplied water to the two Lords so that They could wash Their hands. The two Lords then sat down and, smiling, began to eat the prasāda.

TEXT 79

নিত্যানন্দ কহে—কৈলুঁ তিন উপবাস।
আজি পারণা করিতে ছিল বড় আশ ॥ ৭৯ ॥

nityānanda kahe——kailuṅ tina upavāsa
āji pāraṇā karite chila baḍa āśa

SYNONYMS

nityānanda kahe—Lord Nityānanda said; *kailuṅ*—I have undergone; *tina*—three; *upavāsa*—fasting days; *āji*—today; *pāraṇā*—breaking the fast; *karite*—to do; *chila*—there was; *baḍa*—great; *āśa*—hope.

TRANSLATION

Nityānanda Prabhu said, "I have undergone fasting for three days continuously. Today I hoped to break My fast."

TEXT 80

আজি উপবাস হৈল আচার্য-নিমন্ত্রণে।
অর্ধপেট না ভরিবে এই গ্রাসেক অন্নে ॥ ৮০ ॥

āji upavāsa haila ācārya-nimantraṇe
ardha-peṭa nā bharibe ei grāseka anne

SYNONYMS

āji—today also; *upavāsa*—fasting; *haila*—there was; *ācārya-nimantraṇe*—by the invitation of Advaita Ācārya; *ardha-peṭa*—half My belly; *nā*—not; *bharibe*—will fill; *ei*—this; *grāseka anne*—one morsel of food.

TRANSLATION

Although Śrī Caitanya Mahāprabhu was thinking that the quantity of food was enormous, Nityānanda Prabhu, on the contrary, thought it not even a morsel. He had been fasting for three days and had greatly hoped to break fast on that day. Indeed, He said, "Although I am invited to eat by Advaita Ācārya, today also is a fast. So small a quantity of foodstuffs will not even fill half of My belly."

TEXT 81

আচার্য কহে—তুমি হও তৈর্থিক সন্ন্যাসী।
কভু ফল-মূল খাও, কভু উপবাসী ॥ ৮১ ॥

ācārya kahe——tumi hao tairthika sannyāsī
kabhu phala-mūla khāo, kabhu upavāsī

SYNONYMS

ācārya kahe—Advaita Ācārya replied to Nityānanda Prabhu; *tumi*—You; *hao*—are; *tairthika sannyāsī*—a mendicant wandering on pilgrimages; *kabhu*—sometimes; *phala-mūla*—fruits and roots; *khāo*—You eat; *kabhu upavāsī*—sometimes fasting.

TRANSLATION

Advaita Ācārya replied, "Sir, You are a mendicant traveling on pilgrimages. Sometimes You eat fruits and roots, and sometimes You simply go on fasting.

TEXT 82

**দরিদ্র-ব্রাহ্মণ-ঘরে যে পাইলা মুষ্ট্যেক অন্ন ।
ইহাতে সন্তুষ্ট হও, ছাড় লোভ-মন ॥ ৮২ ॥**

*daridra-brāhmaṇa-ghare ye pāilā muṣṭy-eka anna
ihāte santuṣṭa hao, chāḍa lobha-mana*

SYNONYMS

daridra-brāhmaṇa—of a poor *brāhmaṇa;* *ghare*—at the home; *ye*—whatever; *pāilā*—You have gotten; *muṣṭi-eka*—one handful; *anna*—food; *ihāte*—in this; *santuṣṭa hao*—please be satisfied; *chāḍa*—give up; *lobha-mana*—Your greedy mentality.

TRANSLATION

"I am a poor brāhmaṇa, and You have come to My home. Please be satisfied with whatever little foodstuffs You have received, and give up Your greedy mentality."

TEXT 83

**নিত্যানন্দ বলে—যবে কৈলে নিমন্ত্রণ ।
তত দিতে চাহ, যত করিয়ে ভোজন ॥ ৮৩ ॥**

*nityānanda bale——yabe kaile nimantraṇa
tata dite cāha, yata kariye bhojana*

SYNONYMS

nityānanda bale—Lord Nityānanda said; *yabe*—when; *kaile*—You have done; *nimantraṇa*—invitation; *tata*—so much; *dite cāha*—You must supply; *yata*—as much as; *kariye bhojana*—I can eat.

TRANSLATION

Lord Nityānanda Prabhu replied, "Whatever I may be, You have invited Me. Therefore you must supply as much as I want to eat."

TEXT 84

**শুনি' নিত্যানন্দের কথা ঠাকুর অদ্বৈত ।
কহেন তাঁহারে কিছু পাইয়া পিরীত ॥ ৮৪ ॥**

śuni' nityānandera kathā ṭhākura advaita
kahena tāṅhāre kichu pāiyā pirīta

SYNONYMS

śuni'—hearing; *nityānandera*—of Lord Nityānanda Prabhu; *kathā*—words; *ṭhākura*—His Divine Grace; *advaita*—Advaita Ācārya; *kahena*—spoke; *tāṅhāre*—unto Nityānanda Prabhu; *kichu*—something; *pāiyā*—taking the opportunity; *pirīta*—pleasing words.

TRANSLATION

His Divine Grace Advaita Ācārya, after hearing the statement of Nityānanda Prabhu, took the opportunity presented by the joking words and spoke to Him as follows.

TEXT 85

"ভ্রষ্ট অবধূত তুমি, উদর ভরিতে।
সন্ন্যাস লইয়াছ, বুঝি, ব্রাহ্মণ দণ্ডিতে ॥ ৮৫ ॥

bhraṣṭa avadhūta tumi, udara bharite
sannyāsa la-iyācha, bujhi, brāhmaṇa daṇḍite

SYNONYMS

bhraṣṭa avadhūta—reject *paramahaṁsa*; *tumi*—You; *udara bharite*—to fill Your belly; *sannyāsa la-iyācha*—You have accepted the renounced order of life; *bujhi*—I understand; *brāhmaṇa daṇḍite*—to give trouble to a *brāhmaṇa*.

TRANSLATION

Advaita Ācārya said: "You are a reject paramahaṁsa, and You have accepted the renounced order of life just to fill up Your belly. I can understand that Your business is to give trouble to brāhmaṇas."

PURPORT

There is always a difference of opinion between a *smārta-brāhmaṇa* and a Vaiṣṇava *gosvāmī*. There are even *smārta* opinions and Vaiṣṇava *gosvāmī* opinions available in astrological and astronomical calculations. By calling Nityānanda Prabhu a *bhraṣṭa avadhūta* (a rejected *paramahaṁsa*), Advaita Ācārya Prabhu in a sense accepted Nityānanda Prabhu as a *paramahaṁsa*. In other words, Nityānanda Prabhu had nothing to do with the rules governing *smārta-brāhmaṇas*. Thus under pretense of condemning Him, Advaita Ācārya was actually praising Him. In the *avadhūta* stage, the *paramahaṁsa* stage, which is the supermost stage, one may appear to be *viṣayī*, on the platform of sense gratification, but in actuality he has nothing to do with sense gratification. At that stage, a person sometimes accepts the symptoms and dress of a *sannyāsī* and sometimes does not. Sometimes he dresses like a householder. We should know, however, that these are all joking words between Advaita Ācārya and Nityānanda Prabhu. They are not to be taken as insults.

In Khaḍadaha, sometimes people misunderstood Nityānanda Prabhu to belong to the *śākta-sampradāya*, whose philosophy is *antaḥ śāktaḥ bahiḥ śaivaḥ sabhāyāṁ vaiṣṇavo mataḥ*. According to the *śākta-sampradāya*, a person called *kaulāvadhūta* thinks materially while externally appearing to be a great devotee of Lord Śiva. When such a person is in an assembly of Vaiṣṇavas, he appears like a Vaiṣṇava. Actually Nityānanda Prabhu did not belong to such a community. Nityānanda Prabhu was always a *brahmacārī* of a *sannyāsī* of the *vaidika* order. Actually He was a *paramahaṁsa*. Sometimes He is accepted to be a disciple of Lakṣmīpati Tīrtha. If He is so accepted, Nityānanda Prabhu belonged to the Madhva-sampradāya. He did not belong to the *tāntrika-sampradāya* of Bengal.

TEXT 86

তুমি খেতে পার দশ-বিশ মানের অন্ন ।
আমি তাহা কাঁহা পাব দরিদ্র ব্রাহ্মণ ॥ ৮৬ ॥

tumi khete pāra daśa-viśa mānera anna
āmi tāhā kāṅhā pāba daridra brāhmaṇa

SYNONYMS

tumi—You; *khete*—to eat; *pāra*—able; *daśa-viśa*—ten or twenty; *mānera*—of the measurement of a *māna*; *anna*—rice; *āmi*—I; *tāhā*—that; *kāṅhā*—where; *pāba*—shall get; *daridra*—poverty-stricken; *brāhmaṇa*—*brāhmaṇa*.

TRANSLATION

Advaita Ācārya accused Nityānanda Prabhu, saying, "You can eat ten to twenty mānas of rice. I am a poor brāhmaṇa. How shall I get so much rice?

PURPORT

A *māna* is a measurement containing about four kilos.

TEXT 87

যে পাঞাছ মুষ্ট্যেক অন্ন, তাহা খাঞা উঠ।
পাগলামি না করিহ, না ছড়াইও ঝুঠ ॥ ৮৭ ॥

ye pāñācha muṣṭy-eka anna, tāhā khāñā uṭha
pāgalāmi nā kariha, nā chaḍāio jhuṭha

SYNONYMS

ye pāñācha—whatever You have; *muṣṭi-eka*—one handful; *anna*—rice; *tāhā*—that; *khāñā*—eating; *uṭha*—please get up; *pāgalāmi*—madness; *nā*—do not; *kariha*—do; *nā*—do not; *chaḍāio*—strew; *jhuṭha*—remnants of foodstuff.

TRANSLATION

"Whatever You have, though it be a palmful of rice, please eat it and get up. Don't show Your madness and strew the remnants of food here and there."

TEXT 88

এই মত হাস্যরসে করেন ভোজন।
অর্ধ-অর্ধ খাঞা প্রভু ছাড়েন ব্যঞ্জন ॥ ৮৮ ॥

ei mata hāsya-rase karena bhojana
ardha-ardha khāñā prabhu chāḍena vyañjana

SYNONYMS

ei mata—in this way; *hāsya-rase*—jokingly; *karena*—does; *bhojana*—eating; *ardha-ardha*—half and half; *khāñā*—after eating; *prabhu*—the Lord; *chāḍena*—gives up; *vyañjana*—all the vegetables.

TRANSLATION

In this way, Nityānanda Prabhu and Lord Caitanya Mahāprabhu ate and talked with Advaita Ācārya jokingly. After eating half of each vegetable preparation given to Him, Śrī Caitanya Mahāprabhu abandoned it and went on to the next.

TEXT 89

সেই ব্যঞ্জন আচার্য পুনঃ করেন পূরণ ।
এই মত পুনঃ পুনঃ পরিবেশে ব্যঞ্জন ॥ ৮৯ ॥

sei vyañjana ācārya punaḥ karena pūraṇa
ei mata punaḥ punaḥ pariveśe vyañjana

SYNONYMS

sei vyañjana—that half-finished vegetable; *ācārya*—Advaita Ācārya; *punaḥ*—again; *karena*—does; *pūraṇa*—filling; *ei mata*—in this way; *punaḥ punaḥ*—again and again; *pariveśe*—distributes; *vyañjana*—vegetables.

TRANSLATION

As soon as half of the vegetable in the pot was finished, Advaita Ācārya filled it up again. In this way, as the Lord finished half of a preparation, Advaita Ācārya again and again filled it up.

TEXT 90

দোনা ব্যঞ্জনে ভরি' করেন প্রার্থন ।
প্রভু বলেন—আর কত করিব ভোজন ॥ ৯০ ॥

donā vyañjane bhari' karena prārthana
prabhu balena——āra kata kariba bhojana

SYNONYMS

donā—the pot; *vyañjane*—with vegetables; *bhari'*—filling; *karena*—makes; *prārthana*—request; *prabhu balena*—Lord Caitanya Mahāprabhu says; *āra*—more; *kata*—how much; *kariba*—can I do; *bhojana*—eating.

TRANSLATION

After filling a pot with vegetables, Advaita Ācārya requested Them to eat more, and Caitanya Mahāprabhu said, "How much more can I go on eating?"

TEXT 91

আচার্য কহে—যে দিয়াছি, তাহা না ছাড়িবা ।
এখন যে দিয়ে, তার অর্ধেক খাইবা ॥ ৯১ ॥

ācārya kahe——ye diyāchi, tāhā nā chāḍibā
ekhana ye diye, tāra ardheka khāibā

SYNONYMS

ācārya kahe—Advaita Ācārya said; *ye diyāchi*—whatever I have given; *tāhā nā chāḍibā*—please do not give it up; *ekhana*—now; *ye*—whatever; *diye*—I am giving; *tāra ardheka*—half of it; *khāibā*—You will eat.

TRANSLATION

Advaita Ācārya said, "Please do not give up whatever I have already given You. Now, whatever I am giving, You may eat half and leave half."

TEXT 92

নানা যত্ন-দৈন্যে প্রভুরে করাইল ভোজন ।
আচার্যের ইচ্ছা প্রভু করিল পূরণ ॥ ৯২ ॥

nānā yatna-dainye prabhure karāila bhojana
ācāryera icchā prabhu karila pūraṇa

SYNONYMS

nānā yatna-dainye—in this way, by various efforts and by humility; *prabhure*—Lord Caitanya Mahāprabhu; *karāila*—caused; *bhojana*—eating; *ācāryera icchā*—the wish of Advaita Ācārya; *prabhu*—Lord Caitanya Mahāprabhu; *karila*—did; *pūraṇa*—fulfillment.

TRANSLATION

In this way, by submitting various humble requests, Advaita Ācārya made Śrī Caitanya Mahāprabhu and Lord Nityānanda eat. Thus Caitanya Mahāprabhu fulfilled all the desires of Advaita Ācārya.

TEXT 93

নিত্যানন্দ কহে—আমার পেট না ভরিল ।
লঞা যাহ, তোর অন্ন কিছু না খাইল ॥ ৯৩ ॥

nityānanda kahe—āmāra peṭa nā bharila
lañā yāha, tora anna kichu nā khāila

SYNONYMS

nityānanda kahe—Nityānanda Prabhu said; *āmāra*—My; *peṭa*—belly; *nā*—not; *bharila*—filled; *lañā*—taking away; *yāha*—go; *tora*—Your; *anna*—food; *kichu nā khāila*—I have not eaten anything.

TRANSLATION

Again Nityānanda Prabhu jokingly said, "My belly is not yet filled up. Please take away Your foodstuff. I have not taken the least of it."

TEXT 94

এত বলি' একগ্রাস ভাত হাতে লঞা ।
উঝালি' ফেলিল আগে যেন ক্রুদ্ধ হঞা ॥ ৯৪ ॥

eta bali' eka-grāsa bhāta hāte lañā
ujhāli' phelila āge yena kruddha hañā

SYNONYMS

eta bali'—saying this; *eka-grāsa*—one palmful; *bhāta*—rice; *hāte*—in the hand; *lañā*—taking; *ujhāli'*—releasing; *phelila*—threw; *āge*—in front; *yena*—as if; *kruddha hañā*—becoming angry.

TRANSLATION

After saying this, Nityānanda Prabhu took a handful of rice and threw it on the floor in front of Him, as if He were angry.

TEXT 95

ভাত দুই-চারি লাগে আচার্যের অঙ্গে ।
ভাত অঙ্গে লঞা আচার্য নাচে বহুরঙ্গে ॥ ৯৫ ॥

bhāta dui-cāri lāge ācāryera aṅge
bhāta aṅge lañā ācārya nāce bahu-raṅge

SYNONYMS

bhāta dui-cāri—two or four pieces of the thrown rice; *lāge*—touch; *ācāryera aṅge*—the body of Advaita Ācārya; *bhāta*—the rice; *aṅge*—on His body; *lañā*—with; *ācārya nāce*—the Ācārya began to dance; *bahu-raṅge*—in many ways.

TRANSLATION

When two or four pieces of the thrown rice touched His body, Advaita Ācārya began to dance in various ways with the rice still stuck to His body.

TEXT 96

অবধূতের ঝুঠা লাগিল মোর অঙ্গে ।
পরম পবিত্র মোরে কৈল এই ঢঙ্গে ॥ ৯৬ ॥

avadhūtera jhuṭhā lāgila mora aṅge
parama pavitra more kaila ei ḍhaṅge

SYNONYMS

avadhūtera jhuṭhā—the remnants of the food of the *avadhūta; lāgila*—touched; *mora*—My; *aṅge*—on the body; *parama pavitra*—perfectly purified; *more*—Me; *kaila*—made; *ei*—this; *ḍhaṅge*—behavior.

TRANSLATION

When the rice thrown by Nityānanda Prabhu touched His body, Advaita Ācārya thought Himself purified by the touch of remnants thrown by paramahaṁsa Nityānanda. Therefore He began dancing.

PURPORT

The word *avadhūta* refers to one above all rules and regulations. Sometimes, not observing all the rules and regulations of a *sannyāsī,* Nityānanda Prabhu exhibited the behavior of a mad *avadhūta.* He threw the remnants of food on the ground, and some of these remnants touched the body of Advaita Ācārya. Advaita Ācārya accepted this happily because He presented Himself as a member of the community of *smārta-brāhmaṇas.* By touching the remnants of food thrown by Nityānanda Prabhu, Advaita Ācārya immediately felt Himself purified of all *smārta* contamination. The remnants of food left by a pure Vaiṣṇava are called *mahā-mahā-prasāda.* This is completely spiritual and is identified with Lord Viṣṇu. Such remnants are not ordinary. The spiritual master is to be considered on the stage of *paramahaṁsa* and beyond the jurisdiction of the *varṇāśrama* institution. The remnants of food left by the spiritual master and similar *paramahaṁsas* or pure Vaiṣṇavas are purifying. When an ordinary person touches such *prasāda,* his mind is purified, and his mind is raised to the status of a pure *brāhmaṇa.* The behavior and statements of Advaita Ācārya are meant for the understanding of ordinary people who are unaware of the strength of spiritual values, not knowing the potency of foodstuffs left by the bona fide spiritual master and pure Vaiṣṇavas.

TEXT 97

তোরে নিমন্ত্রণ করি' পাইনু তার ফল ।
তোর জাতি-কুল নাহি, সহজে পাগল ॥ ৯৭ ॥

tore nimantraṇa kari' pāinu tāra phala
tora jāti-kula nāhi, sahaje pāgala

SYNONYMS

tore—You; *nimantraṇa*—invitation; *kari'*—making; *pāinu*—I have gotten in return; *tāra*—of that; *phala*—the result; *tora*—Your; *jāti-kula nāhi*—there is no indication of Your caste and family; *sahaje*—by nature; *pāgala*—You are a madman.

TRANSLATION

Advaita Ācārya jokingly said: "My dear Nityānanda, I invited You, and indeed I have received the results. You have no fixed caste or dynasty. By nature You are a madman.

PURPORT

The words *sahaje pāgala* ("by nature a madman") indicate that Nityānanda Prabhu was transcendentally situated on the *paramahaṁsa* stage. Because He always remembered Rādhā-Kṛṣṇa and Their service, this was transcendental madness. Śrī Advaita Ācārya was pointing out this fact.

TEXT 98

আপনার সম মোরে করিবার তরে ।
ঝুঠা দিলে, বিপ্র বলি' ভয় না করিলে ॥ ৯৮ ॥

āpanāra sama more karibāra tare
jhuṭhā dile, vipra bali' bhaya nā karile

SYNONYMS

āpanāra sama—like You; *more*—Me; *karibāra tare*—for making; *jhuṭhā*—remnants of foodstuffs; *dile*—You have given; *vipra bali'*—considering as a *brāhmaṇa*; *bhaya*—fear; *nā karile*—You did not do.

TRANSLATION

"To make Me a madman like Yourself, You have thrown the remnants of Your food at Me. You did not even fear the fact that I am a brāhmaṇa."

PURPORT

The words *āpanāra sama* indicate that Advaita Ācārya considered Himself to belong to the *smārta-brāhmaṇas,* and He considered Nityānanda Prabhu to be on the transcendental stage with pure Vaiṣṇavas. Lord Nityānanda gave Advaita Ācārya His remnants to situate Him on the same platform and make Him a pure unalloyed Vaiṣṇava or *paramahaṁsa*. Advaita Ācārya's statement indicates that a *paramahaṁsa* Vaiṣṇava is transcendentally situated. A pure Vaiṣṇava is not subject to the rules and regulations of the *smārta-brāhmaṇas.* That was the reason for Advaita Ācārya's stating, *āpanāra sama more karibāra tare*: "To raise Me to Your own standard." A pure Vaiṣṇava or a person on the *paramahaṁsa* stage accepts the remnants of food (*mahā-prasāda*) as spiritual. He does not consider it to be material or sense gratificatory. He accepts *mahā-prasāda* not as ordinary dahl and rice but as spiritual substance. To say nothing of the remnants of food left by a pure Vaiṣṇava, *prasāda* is never polluted even if it is touched by the mouth of a *caṇḍāla*. Indeed, it retains its spiritual value. Therefore by eating or touching such *mahā-prasāda,* a *brāhmaṇa* is not degraded. There is no question of being polluted by touching the remnants of such food. Actually, by eating such *mahā-prasāda,* one is freed from all the contaminations of the material condition. That is the verdict of the *śāstra.*

TEXT 99

নিত্যানন্দ বলে,—এই কৃষ্ণের প্রসাদ।
ইহাকে 'ঝুঠা' কহিলে, তুমি কৈলে অপরাধ॥ ৯৯॥

nityānanda bale,——ei kṛṣṇera prasāda
ihāke 'jhuṭhā' kahile, tumi kaile aparādha

SYNONYMS

nityānanda bale—Lord Nityānanda said; *ei*—this; *kṛṣṇera prasāda*—*mahā-prasāda* of Lord Kṛṣṇa; *ihāke*—unto it; *jhuṭhā*—remnants of foodstuff; *kahile*—if You say; *tumi*—You; *kaile*—have made; *aparādha*—offense.

TRANSLATION

Nityānanda Prabhu replied: "These are the remnants of food left by Lord Kṛṣṇa. If You take them to be ordinary remnants, You have committed an offense."

PURPORT

In the *Bṛhad-viṣṇu Purāṇa* it is stated that one who considers *mahā-prasāda* to be equal to ordinary rice and dahl certainly commits a great offense. Ordinary edibles are touchable and untouchable, but there are no such dualistic considerations where *prasāda* is concerned. *Prasāda* is transcendental, and there are no transformations or contaminations, just as there are no contaminations or transformations in the body of Lord Viṣṇu Himself. Thus even if one is a *brāhmaṇa* he is certain to be attacked by leprosy and bereft of all family members if he makes such dualistic considerations. Such an offender goes to hell, never to return. This is the injunction of the *Bṛhad-viṣṇu Purāṇa*.

TEXT 100

শতেক সন্ন্যাসী যদি করাহ ভোজন ।
তবে এই অপরাধ হইবে খণ্ডন ॥ ১০০ ॥

śateka sannyāsī yadi karāha bhojana
tabe ei aparādha ha-ibe khaṇḍana

SYNONYMS

śateka sannyāsī—one hundred *sannyāsīs*; *yadi*—if; *karāha*—You make; *bhojana*—the eating; *tabe*—then; *ei*—this; *aparādha*—offense; *ha-ibe*—there will be; *khaṇḍana*—nullification.

TRANSLATION

Śrīla Nityānanda Prabhu continued: "If you invite at least one hundred sannyāsīs to Your home and feed them sumptuously, Your offense will be nullified."

TEXT 101

আচার্য কহে—না করিব সন্ন্যাসি-নিমন্ত্রণ ।
সন্ন্যাসী নাশিল মোর সব স্মৃতি-ধর্ম ॥ ১০১ ॥

ācārya kahe——nā kariba sannyāsi-nimantraṇa
sannyāsī nāśila mora saba smṛti-dharma

SYNONYMS

ācārya kahe—Advaita Ācārya said; *nā kariba*—I shall never do; *sannyāsi-nimantraṇa*—invitation to the *sannyāsīs*; *sannyāsī*—a *sannyāsī*; *nāśila*—has spoiled; *mora*—My; *saba*—all; *smṛti-dharma*—regulative principles of the *smṛti-śāstra.*

TRANSLATION

Advaita Ācārya replied: "I shall never again invite another sannyāsī, for it is a sannyāsī who has spoiled all My brahminical smṛti regulations."

TEXT 102

এত বলি' দুই জনে করাইল আচমন ।
উত্তম শয্যাতে লইয়া করাইল শয়ন ॥ ১০২ ॥

eta bali' dui jane karāila ācamana
uttama śayyāte la-iyā karāila śayana

SYNONYMS

eta bali'—saying this; *dui jane*—unto the two personalities; *karāila ācamana*—washed Their hands and mouth; *uttama*—very nice; *śayyāte*—on a bed; *la-iyā*—taking; *karāila*—made Them do; *śayana*—lying down.

TRANSLATION

After this, Advaita Ācārya made the Lords wash Their hands and mouths. He then took Them to a nice bed and made Them lie down to take rest.

TEXT 103

লবঙ্গ এলাচী-বীজ—উত্তম রসবাস ।
তুলসী-মঞ্জরী সহ দিল মুখবাস ॥ ১০৩ ॥

lavaṅga elācī-bīja——uttama rasa-vāsa
tulasī-mañjarī saha dila mukha-vāsa

SYNONYMS

lavaṅga—cloves; *elācī*—cardamom; *bīja*—seeds; *uttama*—very nice; *rasa-vāsa*—tasteful spices; *tulasī-mañjarī*—the flowers of *tulasī*; *saha*—with; *dila*—gave; *mukha-vāsa*—perfume of the mouth.

TRANSLATION

Śrī Advaita Ācārya fed the two Lords cloves and cardamom mixed with tulasī flowers. Thus there was a good flavor within Their mouths.

TEXT 104

সুগন্ধি চন্দনে লিপ্ত কৈল কলেবর ।
সুগন্ধি পুষ্পমালা আনি' দিল হৃদয়-উপর ॥ ১০৪ ॥

sugandhi candane lipta kaila kalevara
sugandhi puṣpa-mālā āni' dila hṛdaya-upara

SYNONYMS

su-gandhi—fragrant; *candane*—in sandalwood; *lipta*—smeared; *kaila*—made; *kalevara*—the bodies; *su-gandhi*—very fragrant; *puṣpa-mālā*—flower garlands; *āni'*—bringing; *dila*—gave; *hṛdaya-upara*—on the chests.

TRANSLATION

Śrī Advaita Ācārya then smeared the bodies of the Lords with sandalwood pulp and then placed very fragrant flower garlands on Their chests.

TEXT 105

আচার্য করিতে চাহে পাদ-সম্বাহন ।
সঙ্কুচিত হঞা প্রভু বলেন বচন ॥ ১০৫ ॥

ācārya karite cāhe pāda-saṁvāhana
saṅkucita hañā prabhu balena vacana

SYNONYMS

ācārya—Advaita Ācārya; *karite*—to do; *cāhe*—wants; *pāda-saṁvāhana*—massaging the feet; *saṅkucita*—hesitant; *hañā*—becoming; *prabhu*—the Lord; *balena*—says; *vacana*—the words.

TRANSLATION

When the Lord lay down on the bed, Advaita Ācārya wanted to massage His legs, but the Lord was very hesitant and spoke as follows to Advaita Ācārya.

TEXT 106

বহুত নাচাইলে তুমি, ছাড় নাচান ।
মুকুন্দ-হরিদাস লইয়া করহ ভোজন ॥ ১০৬ ॥

bahuta nācāile tumi, chāḍa nācāna
mukunda-haridāsa la-iyā karaha bhojana

SYNONYMS

bahuta—in various ways; *nācāile*—have made Me dance; *tumi*—You; *chāḍa*—give up; *nācāna*—dancing; *mukunda*—Mukunda; *hari-dāsa*—Haridāsa; *la-iyā*—with; *karaha*—do; *bhojana*—eating.

TRANSLATION

Śrī Caitanya Mahāprabhu said: "Advaita Ācārya, You have made Me dance in various ways. Now give up this practice. Go with Mukunda and Haridāsa and accept Your lunch."

PURPORT

Śrī Caitanya Mahāprabhu is here telling Advaita Ācārya that it is not befitting for a *sannyāsī* to accept nice beds to lie on or to chew cloves and cardamom and have his body smeared with sandalwood pulp. Nor is it befitting for him to accept fragrant garlands and have his legs massaged by a pure Vaiṣṇava. "You have already made Me dance according to your vow," Caitanya Mahāprabhu said. "Now please stop it. You can go and take Your lunch with Mukunda and Haridāsa."

TEXT 107

তবে ত' আচার্য সঙ্গে লঞা দুই জনে ।
করিল ইচ্ছায় ভোজন, যে আছিল মনে ॥ ১০৭ ॥

tabe ta' ācārya saṅge lañā dui jane
karila icchāya bhojana, ye āchila mane

SYNONYMS

tabe ta'—thereafter; *ācārya*—Advaita Ācārya; *saṅge*—with; *lañā*—taking; *dui jane*—the two persons, namely Mukunda and Haridāsa; *karila*—did; *icchāya*—according to desire; *bhojana*—eating; *ye āchila mane*—whatever there was in mind.

TRANSLATION

Thereupon Advaita Ācārya took prasāda with Mukunda and Haridāsa, and they all wholeheartedly ate as much as they desired.

TEXT 108

শান্তিপুরের লোক শুনি' প্রভুর আগমন।
দেখিতে আইলা লোক প্রভুর চরণ ॥ ১০৮ ॥

śāntipurera loka śuni' prabhura āgamana
dekhite āilā loka prabhura caraṇa

SYNONYMS

śānti-purera loka—all the people of Śāntipura; *śuni'*—hearing; *prabhura āgamana*—the arrival of Śrī Caitanya Mahāprabhu; *dekhite āilā*—came to see; *loka*—all the people; *prabhura caraṇa*—the lotus feet of the Lord.

TRANSLATION

When the people of Śāntipura heard that Lord Śrī Caitanya Mahāprabhu was staying there, they all immediately came to see His lotus feet.

TEXT 109

'হরি' 'হরি' বলে লোক আনন্দিত হঞা।
চমৎকার পাইল প্রভুর সৌন্দর্য দেখিঞা ॥ ১০৯ ॥

'hari' 'hari' bale loka ānandita hañā
camatkāra pāila prabhura saundarya dekhiñā

SYNONYMS

hari hari—the holy name of the Lord; *bale*—say; *loka*—all the people; *ānandita*—pleased; *hañā*—being; *camatkāra*—wonder; *pāila*—got; *prabhura*—of the Lord; *saundarya*—the beauty; *dekhiñā*—by seeing.

TRANSLATION

Being very pleased, all the people loudly began to shout the holy name of the Lord, "Hari! Hari!" Indeed, they became struck with wonder upon seeing the beauty of the Lord.

TEXT 110

গৌর-দেহ-কান্তি সূর্য জিনিয়া উজ্জ্বল ।
অরুণ-বস্ত্রকান্তি তাহে করে ঝলমল ॥ ১১০ ॥

gaura-deha-kānti sūrya jiniyā ujjvala
aruṇa-vastra-kānti tāhe kare jhala-mala

SYNONYMS

gaura—fair-complexioned; *deha*—of the body; *kānti*—the luster; *sūrya*—the sun; *jiniyā*—conquering; *ujjvala*—bright; *aruṇa*—reddish; *vastra-kānti*—the beauty of the garments; *tāhe*—in that; *kare*—does; *jhala-mala*—glittering.

TRANSLATION

They saw Śrī Caitanya Mahāprabhu's very fair-complexioned body and its bright luster, which conquered the brilliance of the sun. Over and above this was the beauty of the saffron garments that glittered upon His body.

TEXT 111

আইসে যায় লোক হর্ষে, নাহি সমাধান ।
লোকের সঙ্ঘট্টে দিন হৈল অবসান ॥ ১১১ ॥

āise yāya loka harṣe, nāhi samādhāna
lokera saṅghaṭṭe dina haila avasāna

SYNONYMS

āise—come; *yāya*—go; *loka*—all people; *harṣe*—in great pleasure; *nāhi*—there is not; *samādhāna*—calculation; *lokera*—of the people; *saṅghaṭṭe*—in crowds; *dina*—the day; *haila*—there was; *avasāna*—the end.

TRANSLATION

People came and went with great pleasure. There was no calculating how many people assembled there before the day was over.

TEXT 112

সন্ধ্যাতে আচার্য আরম্ভিল সঙ্কীর্তন ।
আচার্য নাচেন, প্রভু করেন দর্শন ॥ ১১২ ॥

sandhyāte ācārya ārambhila saṅkīrtana
ācārya nācena, prabhu karena darśana

SYNONYMS

sandhyāte—in the evening; *ācārya*—Advaita Ācārya; *ārambhila*—began; *saṅkīrtana*—congregational chanting; *ācārya*—Advaita Ācārya; *nācena*—dances; *prabhu*—the Lord; *karena*—does; *darśana*—seeing.

TRANSLATION

As soon as it was evening, Advaita Ācārya began the congregational chanting. He even began to dance Himself, and the Lord saw the performance.

TEXT 113

নিত্যানন্দ গোসাঞি বুলে আচার্য ধরিঞা ।
হরিদাস পাছে নাচে হরষিত হঞা ॥ ১১৩ ॥

nityānanda gosāñi bule ācārya dhariñā
haridāsa pāche nāce harașita hañā

SYNONYMS

nityānanda gosāñi—Lord Nityānanda Prabhu; *bule*—began to move, dancing; *ācārya dhariñā*—following Advaita Ācārya; *hari-dāsa*—Haridāsa Ṭhākura; *pāche*—behind; *nāce*—dances; *harașita hañā*—being pleased.

TRANSLATION

When Advaita Ācārya began to dance, Nityānanda Prabhu began dancing behind Him. Haridāsa Ṭhākura, being very pleased, also began dancing behind Him.

TEXT 114

কি কহিব রে সখি আজুক আনন্দ ওর ।
চিরদিনে মাধব মন্দিরে মোর ॥ ১১৪ ॥ ধ্রু ॥

ki kahiba re sakhi ājuka ānanda ora
cira-dine mādhava mandire mora

SYNONYMS

ki—what; *kahiba*—shall I say; *re*—O; *sakhi*—My dear friends; *ājuka*—today; *ānanda*—pleasure; *ora*—the limit; *cira-dine*—after many days; *mādhava*—Lord Kṛṣṇa; *mandire*—in the temple; *mora*—My.

TRANSLATION

Advaita Ācārya said: " 'My dear friends, what shall I say? Today I have received the highest transcendental pleasure. After many, many days, Lord Kṛṣṇa is in My house.' "

PURPORT

This is a song composed by Vidyāpati. Sometimes the word *mādhava* is misunderstood to refer to Mādhavendra Purī. Advaita Ācārya was a disciple of Mādhavendra Purī, and consequently some people think that He was referring to Mādhavendra Purī by using the word *mādhava.* But actually this is not the fact. This song was composed to commemorate the separation of Kṛṣṇa from Rādhārāṇī during Kṛṣṇa's absence in Mathurā. This song was supposed to be sung by Śrīmatī Rādhārāṇī when Kṛṣṇa returned. It is technically called *Mathurā-viraha.*

TEXT 115

এই পদ গাওয়াইয়া হর্ষে করেন নর্তন ।
স্বেদ-কম্প-পুলকাশ্রু-হুঙ্কার-গর্জন ॥ ১১৫ ॥

ei pada gāoyāiyā harṣe karena nartana
sveda-kampa-pulakāśru-huṅkāra-garjana

SYNONYMS

ei pada—this verse; *gāoyāiyā*—causing to be sung; *harṣe*—in pleasure; *karena*—does; *nartana*—dancing; *sveda*—perspiration; *kampa*—shivering; *pulaka*—standing of hairs; *aśru*—tears on account of pleasure; *huṅkāra*—thundering; *garjana*—bellowing.

TRANSLATION

Advaita Ācārya led the saṅkīrtana party, and with great pleasure He sang this verse. There was a manifestation of ecstatic perspiration,

shivering, raised hairs, tears in the eyes, and sometimes thundering and bellowing.

TEXT 116

ফিরি' ফিরি' কভু প্রভুর ধরেন চরণ ।
চরণে ধরিয়া প্রভুরে বলেন বচন ॥ ১১৬ ॥

phiri' phiri' kabhu prabhura dharena caraṇa
caraṇe dhariyā prabhure balena vacana

SYNONYMS

phiri' phiri'—turning and turning; *kabhu*—sometimes; *prabhura*—of the Lord; *dharena*—catches; *caraṇa*—the lotus feet; *caraṇe dhariyā*—catching the lotus feet; *prabhure*—unto the Lord; *balena*—says; *vacana*—words.

TRANSLATION

While dancing, Advaita Ācārya would sometimes turn around and around and catch the lotus feet of Śrī Caitanya Mahāprabhu. He then began to speak to Him as follows.

TEXT 117

অনেক দিন তুমি মোরে বেড়াইলে ভাণ্ডিয়া ।
ঘরেতে পাঞাছি, এবে রাখিব বান্ধিয়া ॥ ১১৭ ॥

aneka dina tumi more beḍāile bhāṇḍiyā
gharete pāñāchi, ebe rākhiba bāndhiyā

SYNONYMS

aneka dina—many days; *tumi*—You; *more*—Me; *beḍāile*—escaped; *bhāṇḍiyā*—cheating or bluffing; *gharete*—at My home; *pāñāchi*—I have gotten; *ebe*—now; *rākhiba*—I shall keep; *bāndhiyā*—binding up.

TRANSLATION

Śrī Advaita Ācārya would say: "Many days You escaped Me by bluffing. Now I have You in my home, and I will keep You bound up."

TEXT 118

এত বলি' আচার্য আনন্দে করেন নর্তন।
প্রহরেক-রাত্রি আচার্য কৈল সংকীর্তন ॥ ১১৮ ॥

eta bali' ācārya ānande karena nartana
prahareka-rātri ācārya kaila saṅkīrtana

SYNONYMS

eta bali'—saying this; *ācārya*—Advaita Ācārya; *ānande*—in pleasure; *karena*—does; *nartana*—dancing; *prahar-eka*—about three hours; *rātri*—at night; *ācārya*—Śrī Advaita Ācārya; *kaila saṅkīrtana*—performed *saṅkīrtana,* or congregational chanting.

TRANSLATION

So speaking, Advaita Ācārya performed congregational chanting with great pleasure for three hours that night and danced all the time.

TEXT 119

প্রেমের উৎকণ্ঠা,—প্রভুর নাহি কৃষ্ণ-সঙ্গ।
বিরহে বাড়িল প্রেমজ্বালার তরঙ্গ ॥ ১১৯ ॥

premera utkaṇṭhā,——prabhura nāhi kṛṣṇa-saṅga
virahe bāḍila prema-jvālāra taraṅga

SYNONYMS

premera utkaṇṭhā—the ecstasy of the love; *prabhura*—of the Lord; *nāhi*—there is not; *kṛṣṇa-saṅga*—meeting with Lord Kṛṣṇa; *virahe*—in separation; *bāḍila*—increased; *prema-jvālāra*—of flames of love; *taraṅga*—waves.

TRANSLATION

When Advaita Ācārya danced in that way, Lord Caitanya felt ecstatic love for Kṛṣṇa, and because of His separation, the waves and flames of love increased.

TEXT 120

ব্যাকুল হঞা প্রভু ভূমিতে পড়িলা।
গোসাঞি দেখিয়া আচার্য নৃত্য সম্বরিলা ॥ ১২০ ॥

vyākula hañā prabhu bhūmite paḍilā
gosāñi dekhiyā ācārya nṛtya sambarilā

SYNONYMS

vyākula hañā—being too much agitated; *prabhu*—the Lord; *bhūmite*—on the ground; *paḍilā*—fell; *gosāñi*—the Lord; *dekhiyā*—seeing; *ācārya*—Advaita Ācārya; *nṛtya*—the dancing; *sambarilā*—checked.

TRANSLATION

Being agitated by the ecstasy, Śrī Caitanya Mahāprabhu suddenly fell on the ground. Seeing this, Advaita Ācārya stopped dancing.

TEXT 121

প্রভুর অন্তর মুকুন্দ জানে ভালমতে ।
ভাবের সদৃশ পদ লাগিলা গাইতে ॥ ১২১ ॥

prabhura antara mukunda jāne bhāla-mate
bhāvera sadṛśa pada lāgilā gāite

SYNONYMS

prabhura—of the Lord; *antara*—the heart; *mukunda*—Mukunda; *jāne*—knows; *bhāla-mate*—very well; *bhāvera*—to the ecstatic mood; *sadṛśa*—suitable; *pada*—verses; *lāgilā gāite*—began to sing.

TRANSLATION

When Mukunda saw the ecstasy of Śrī Caitanya Mahāprabhu, he understood the feelings of the Lord and began to sing many stanzas augmenting the force of the Lord's ecstasy.

TEXT 122

আচার্য উঠাইল প্রভুকে করিতে নর্তন ।
পদ শুনি' প্রভুর অঙ্গ না যায় ধারণ ॥ ১২২ ॥

ācārya uṭhāila prabhuke karite nartana
pada śuni' prabhura aṅga nā yāya dhāraṇa

SYNONYMS

ācārya—Advaita Ācārya; *uṭhāila*—raised; *prabhuke*—the Lord; *karite*—to do; *nartana*—dancing; *pada śuni'*—by hearing the stanzas; *prabhura*—of the Lord; *aṅga*—the body; *nā*—not; *yāya*—possible; *dhāraṇa*—to hold.

TRANSLATION

Advaita Ācārya raised the body of Śrī Caitanya Mahāprabhu to help Him dance, but the Lord, after hearing the stanzas sung by Mukunda, could not be held due to His bodily symptoms.

TEXT 123

অশ্রু, কম্প, পুলক, স্বেদ, গদ্গদ বচন ।
ক্ষণে উঠে, ক্ষণে পড়ে, ক্ষণেক রোদন ॥ ১২৩ ॥

aśru, kampa, pulaka, sveda, gadgada vacana
kṣaṇe uṭhe, kṣaṇe paḍe, kṣaṇeka rodana

SYNONYMS

aśru—tears; *kampa*—trembling; *pulaka*—standing of hairs in ecstasy; *sveda*—perspiration; *gadgada*—faltering; *vacana*—words; *kṣaṇe*—sometimes; *uṭhe*—stands; *kṣaṇe*—sometimes; *paḍe*—falls down; *kṣaṇeka*—sometimes; *rodana*—crying.

TRANSLATION

Tears fell from His eyes, and His whole body trembled. His hair stood on end, He perspired heavily, and His words faltered. Sometimes He stood, and sometimes He fell. And sometimes He cried.

TEXT 124

হা হা প্রাণপ্রিয়সখি, কি না হৈল মোরে ।
কানুপ্রেমবিষে মোর তনু-মন জরে ॥ ১২৪ ॥ ধ্রু ॥

hā hā prāṇa-priya-sakhi, ki nā haila more
kānu-prema-viṣe mora tanu-mana jare

SYNONYMS

hā hā—O; *prāṇa-priya-sakhi*—my dear friend; *ki nā haila more*—what has not happened to me; *kānu-prema-viṣe*—the poison of love of Kṛṣṇa; *mora*—my; *tanu*—body; *mana*—mind; *jare*—afflicts.

TRANSLATION

Mukunda sang: " 'My dear intimate friend! What has not happened to me! Due to the effects of the poison of love for Kṛṣṇa, my body and mind have been severely afflicted.

PURPORT

When Mukunda saw that Caitanya Mahāprabhu was feeling ecstatic pain and manifesting ecstatic bodily symptoms, all due to feelings of separation from Kṛṣṇa, he sang songs about meeting with Kṛṣṇa. Advaita Ācārya also stopped dancing.

TEXT 125

রাত্রি-দিনে পোড়ে মন সোয়াস্তি না পাঙ।
যাহাঁ গেলে কানু পাঙ, তাহাঁ উড়ি' যাঙ ॥ ১২৫ ॥

rātri-dine poḍe mana soyāsti nā pāṅ
yāhāṅ gele kānu pāṅ, tāhāṅ uḍi' yāṅ

SYNONYMS

rātri-dine—day and night; *poḍe*—burns; *mana*—mind; *soyāsti*—rest; *nā*—not; *pāṅ*—I get; *yāhāṅ*—where; *gele*—if going; *kānu pāṅ*—I can get Kṛṣṇa; *tāhāṅ*—there; *uḍi'*—flying; *yāṅ*—I go.

TRANSLATION

" 'My feeling is like this: My mind burns day and night, and I can get no rest. If there were someplace I could go to meet Kṛṣṇa, I would immediately fly there.' "

TEXT 126

এই পদ গায় মুকুন্দ মধুর সুস্বরে।
শুনিয়া প্রভুর চিত্ত অন্তরে বিদরে ॥ ১২৬ ॥

ei pada gāya mukunda madhura susvare
śuniyā prabhura citta antare vidare

SYNONYMS

ei pada—this stanza; *gāya*—sings; *mukunda*—Mukunda; *madhura*—sweet; *su-svare*—in a voice; *śuniyā*—hearing; *prabhura*—of the Lord; *citta*—mind; *antare*—within; *vidare*—splits into pieces.

TRANSLATION

This stanza was sung by Mukunda in a very sweet voice, but as soon as Caitanya Mahāprabhu heard this stanza, His mind went to pieces.

TEXT 127

নির্বেদ, বিষাদ হর্ষ, চাপল্য, গর্ব, দৈন্য ।
প্রভুর সহিত যুদ্ধ করে ভাব-সৈন্য ॥ ১২৭ ॥

nirveda, viṣāda, harṣa, cāpalya, garva, dainya
prabhura sahita yuddha kare bhāva-sainya

SYNONYMS

nirveda—disappointment; *viṣāda*—moroseness; *harṣa*—pleasure; *cāpalya*—restlessness; *garva*—pride; *dainya*—humility; *prabhura*—the Lord; *sahita*—with; *yuddha*—fight; *kare*—do; *bhāva*—of ecstatic feelings; *sainya*—soldiers.

TRANSLATION

The transcendental ecstatic symptoms (disappointment, moroseness, pleasure, restlessness, pride and humility) all began to fight like soldiers within the Lord.

PURPORT

Harṣa is described in *Bhakti-rasāmṛta-sindhu. Harṣa* is experienced when one finally attains the desired goal of life and consequently becomes very glad. When *harṣa* is present, the body shivers, and one's hairs stand on end. There are perspiration, tears and an outburst of passion and madness. The mouth becomes swollen, and one experiences inertia and illusion. When a person attains his desired object and feels very fortunate, the luster of his body increases. Because of his own qualities and feelings of greatness, he does not care for anyone else, and this is called *garva,* or pride. In this condition one utters prayers and does not reply to others' inquiries. Seeing one's own body, concealing one's desires and not heeding the words of others are symptoms visible in the ecstasy of *garva*.

TEXT 128

জর-জর হৈল প্রভু ভাবের প্রহারে ।
ভূমিতে পড়িল, শ্বাস নাহিক শরীরে ॥ ১২৮ ॥

jara-jara haila prabhu bhāvera prahāre
bhūmite paḍila, śvāsa nāhika śarīre

SYNONYMS

jara-jara—tottering; *haila*—there was; *prabhu*—the Lord; *bhāvera*—of the ecstatic moods; *prahāre*—in the onslaught; *bhūmite*—on the ground; *paḍila*—fell; *śvāsa*—breathing; *nāhika*—there was not; *śarīre*—in the body.

TRANSLATION

The entire body of Lord Śrī Caitanya Mahāprabhu began to totter due to the onslaught of various ecstatic symptoms. As a result, He immediately fell on the ground, and His breathing almost stopped.

TEXT 129

দেখিয়া চিন্তিত হৈলা যত ভক্তগণ ।
আচম্বিতে উঠে প্রভু করিয়া গর্জন ॥ ১২৯ ॥

dekhiyā cintita hailā yata bhakta-gaṇa
ācambite uṭhe prabhu kariyā garjana

SYNONYMS

dekhiyā—seeing; *cintita*—anxious; *hailā*—became; *yata*—all; *bhakta-gaṇa*—devotees; *ācambite*—all of a sudden; *uṭhe*—rises; *prabhu*—the Lord; *kariyā*—making; *garjana*—thundering.

TRANSLATION

Upon seeing the condition of the Lord, all the devotees became very anxious. Then, suddenly, the Lord got up and began to make thundering sounds.

TEXT 130

'বল্' 'বল্' বলে, নাচে, আনন্দে বিহ্বল ।
বুঝন না যায় ভাব-তরঙ্গ প্রবল ॥ ১৩০ ॥

'bal' 'bal' bale, nāce, ānande vihvala
bujhana nā yāya bhāva-taraṅga prabala

SYNONYMS

bal bal—speak, speak; *bale*—the Lord says; *nāce*—dances; *ānande*—in pleasure; *vihvala*—overwhelmed; *bujhana*—understanding; *nā yāya*—not possible; *bhāva-taraṅga*—the waves of ecstasy; *prabala*—powerful.

TRANSLATION

Upon standing up, the Lord said: "Go on speaking! Go on speaking!" Thus He began to dance, overwhelmed with pleasure. No one could understand the strong waves of this ecstasy.

TEXT 131

নিত্যানন্দ সঙ্গে বুলে প্রভুকে ধরিঞা ।
আচার্য, হরিদাস বুলে পাছে ত, নাচিঞা ॥ ১৩১ ॥

nityānanda saṅge bule prabhuke dhariñā
ācārya, haridāsa bule pāche ta, nāciñā

SYNONYMS

nityānanda—Nityānanda Prabhu; *saṅge*—with; *bule*—walks; *prabhuke*—the Lord; *dhariñā*—catching; *ācārya*—Advaita Ācārya; *hari-dāsa*—Ṭhākura Haridāsa; *bule*—walk; *pāche*—behind; *ta*—certainly; *nāciñā*—dancing.

TRANSLATION

Lord Nityānanda began to walk with Caitanya Mahāprabhu to see that He would not fall, and Advaita Ācārya and Haridāsa Ṭhākura followed Them, dancing.

TEXT 132

এই মত প্রহরেক নাচে প্রভু রঙ্গে ।
কভু হর্ষ, কভু বিষাদ, ভাবের তরঙ্গে ॥ ১৩২ ॥

ei mata prahar-eka nāce prabhu raṅge
kabhu harṣa, kabhu viṣāda, bhāvera taraṅge

SYNONYMS

ei mata—in this way; *prahar-eka*—for about three hours; *nāce*—dances; *prabhu*—Lord Caitanya Mahāprabhu; *raṅge*—in great ecstasy; *kabhu*—sometimes; *harṣa*—pleasure; *kabhu*—sometimes; *viṣāda*—moroseness; *bhāvera*—of ecstasy; *taraṅge*—in the waves.

TRANSLATION

In this way the Lord danced for at least three hours. Sometimes the symptoms of ecstasy were visible, including pleasure, moroseness and many other waves of ecstatic emotional love.

TEXT 133

তিন দিন উপবাসে করিয়া ভোজন ।
উদ্দণ্ড-নৃত্যেতে প্রভুর হৈল পরিশ্রম ॥ ১৩৩ ॥

tina dina upavāse kariyā bhojana
uddaṇḍa-nṛtyete prabhura haila pariśrama

SYNONYMS

tina dina—three days; *upavāse*—in fasting; *kariyā*—doing; *bhojana*—eating; *uddaṇḍa*—jumping high; *nṛtyete*—in dancing; *prabhura*—of the Lord; *haila*—there was; *pariśrama*—fatigue.

TRANSLATION

The Lord had been fasting for three days, and after that period He took eatables sumptuously. Thus when He danced and jumped high, He became a little fatigued.

TEXT 134

তবু ত' না জানে শ্রম প্রেমাবিষ্ট হঞা ।
নিত্যানন্দ মহাপ্রভুকে রাখিল ধরিঞা ॥ ১৩৪ ॥

tabu ta' nā jāne śrama premāviṣṭa hañā
nityānanda mahāprabhuke rākhila dhariñā

SYNONYMS

tabu—still; *ta'*—certainly; *nā jāne*—does not know; *śrama*—fatigue; *prema-āviṣṭa*—absorbed in love; *hañā*—being; *nityānanda*—Lord Nityānanda; *mahā-prabhuke*—Lord Caitanya Mahāprabhu; *rākhila*—stopped; *dhariñā*—catching.

TRANSLATION

Being fully absorbed in love of Godhead, He would not understand His fatigue. But Nityānanda Prabhu, catching Him, stopped His dancing.

TEXT 135

আচার্য্য-গোসাঞি তবে রাখিল কীর্তন ।
নানা সেবা করি' প্রভুকে করাইল শয়ন ॥ ১৩৫ ॥

ācārya-gosāñi tabe rākhila kīrtana
nānā sevā kari' prabhuke karāila śayana

SYNONYMS

ācārya-gosāñi—Advaita Ācārya; *tabe*—then; *rākhila*—suspended; *kīrtana*—the chanting; *nānā*—various; *sevā*—service; *kari'*—performing; *prabhuke*—unto the Lord; *karāila*—made to do; *śayana*—lying down.

TRANSLATION

Although the Lord was fatigued, Nityānanda Prabhu kept Him steady by holding Him. At that time, Advaita Ācārya suspended the chanting and, by rendering various services to the Lord, made Him lie down to take rest.

TEXT 136

এইমত দশদিন ভোজন-কীর্তন ।
একরূপে করি' করে প্রভুর সেবন ॥ ১৩৬ ॥

ei-mata daśa-dina bhojana-kīrtana
eka-rūpe kari' kare prabhura sevana

SYNONYMS

ei-mata—in this way; *daśa-dina*—continuously for ten days; *bhojana-kīrtana*—eating and chanting; *eka-rūpe*—without change; *kari'*—doing; *kare*—does; *prabhura*—of the Lord; *sevana*—service.

TRANSLATION

For ten continuous days Advaita Ācārya held feasting and chanting in the evening. He served the Lord in this way without any change.

TEXT 137

প্রভাতে আচার্যরত্ন দোলায় চড়াঞা।
ভক্তগণ-সঙ্গে আইলা শচীমাতা লঞা ॥ ১৩৭ ॥

prabhāte ācāryaratna dolāya caḍāñā
bhakta-gaṇa-saṅge āilā śacīmātā lañā

SYNONYMS

prabhāte—in the morning; *ācārya-ratna*—Candraśekhara; *dolāya*—in a palanquin; *caḍāñā*—seating; *bhakta-gaṇa-saṅge*—with devotees; *āilā*—came; *śacī-mātā*—mother Śacī; *lañā*—bringing.

TRANSLATION

In the morning Candraśekhara brought Śacīmātā from her house with many devotees, and he seated her in a palanquin.

TEXT 138

নদীয়া-নগরের লোক—স্ত্রী-বালক-বৃদ্ধ।
সব লোক আইলা, হৈল সংঘট্ট সমৃদ্ধ ॥ ১৩৮ ॥

nadīyā-nagarera loka——strī-bālaka-vṛddha
saba loka āilā, haila saṅghaṭṭa samṛddha

SYNONYMS

nadīyā—known as Nadia; *nagarera*—of the city; *loka*—the people; *strī*—women; *bālaka*—boys; *vṛddha*—old men; *saba loka*—all people; *āilā*—came; *haila*—was; *saṅghaṭṭa*—crowd; *samṛddha*—increased.

TRANSLATION

In this way, all the people of the town of Nadia—including all women, boys and old men—came there. Thus the crowd increased.

TEXT 139

প্রাতঃকৃত্য করি' করে নাম-সংকীর্তন ।
শচীমাতা লঞা আইলা অদ্বৈত-ভবন ॥ ১৩৯ ॥

prātaḥ-kṛtya kari' kare nāma-saṅkīrtana
śacīmātā lañā āilā advaita-bhavana

SYNONYMS

prātaḥ-kṛtya—the morning duties; *kari'*—finishing; *kare*—does; *nāma-saṅkīrtana*—chanting the Hare Kṛṣṇa *mantra;* *śacī-mātā*—mother Śacī; *lañā*—with; *āilā*—came; *advaita-bhavana*—at the house of Advaita Ācārya.

TRANSLATION

In the morning, after regular duties were completed and the Lord was chanting the Hare Kṛṣṇa mahā-mantra, the people accompanied Śacīmātā to the house of Advaita Ācārya.

TEXT 140

শচী-আগে পড়িলা প্রভু দণ্ডবৎ হঞা ।
কান্দিতে লাগিলা শচী কোলে উঠাইঞা ॥ ১৪০ ॥

śacī-āge paḍilā prabhu daṇḍavat hañā
kāndite lāgilā śacī kole uṭhāiñā

SYNONYMS

śacī-āge—in front of mother Śacī; *paḍilā*—fell down; *prabhu*—the Lord; *daṇḍa-vat*—like a stick; *hañā*—becoming; *kāndite*—to cry; *lāgilā*—began; *śacī*—mother Śacī; *kole*—on the lap; *uṭhāiñā*—taking.

TRANSLATION

As soon as mother Śacī appeared on the scene, Caitanya Mahāprabhu fell before her like a stick. Mother Śacī began to cry, taking the Lord on her lap.

TEXT 141

দোঁহার দর্শনে দুঁহে হইলা বিহ্বল ।
কেশ না দেখিয়া শচী হইলা বিকল ॥ ১৪১ ॥

doṅhāra darśane duṅhe ha-ilā vihvala
keśa nā dekhiyā śacī ha-ilā vikala

SYNONYMS

doṅhāra darśane—in seeing one another; *duṅhe*—both of them; *ha-ilā*—became; *vihvala*—overwhelmed; *keśa*—hair; *nā*—not; *dekhiyā*—seeing; *śacī*—mother Śacī; *ha-ila*—became; *vikala*—agitated.

TRANSLATION

Upon seeing one another, they both became overwhelmed. Seeing the Lord's head without hair, mother Śacī became greatly agitated.

TEXT 142

অঙ্গ মুছে, মুখ চুম্বে, করে নিরীক্ষণ ।
দেখিতে না পায়,—অশ্রু ভরিল নয়ন ॥ ১৪২ ॥

aṅga muche, mukha cumbe, kare nirīkṣaṇa
dekhite nā pāya,——aśru bharila nayana

SYNONYMS

aṅga—the body; *muche*—smears; *mukha*—face; *cumbe*—kisses; *kare*—does; *nirīkṣaṇa*—observing; *dekhite*—to see; *nā pāya*—not able; *aśru*—tears; *bharila*—filled; *nayana*—the eyes.

TRANSLATION

She began to smear the body of the Lord with kisses. Sometimes she kissed His face and tried to observe Him carefully, but because her eyes were filled with tears, she could not see.

TEXT 143

কান্দিয়া কহেন শচী, বাছারে নিমাঞি ।
বিশ্বরূপ-সম না করিহ নিঠুরাই ॥ ১৪৩ ॥

kāndiyā kahena śacī, bāchāre nimāñi
viśvarūpa-sama nā kariha niṭhurāi

SYNONYMS

kāndiyā—crying; *kahena*—says; *śacī*—mother Śacī; *bāchāre*—my darling; *nimāñi*—O Nimāi; *viśva-rūpa*—Viśvarūpa; *sama*—like; *nā kariha*—do not do; *niṭhurāi*—cruelty.

TRANSLATION

Understanding that Lord Caitanya had accepted the renounced order of life, Śacīmātā, crying, said to the Lord, "My darling Nimāi, do not be cruel like Viśvarūpa, Your elder brother."

TEXT 144

সন্ন্যাসী হইয়া পুনঃ না দিল দরশন।
তুমি তৈছে কৈলে মোর হইবে মরণ ॥ ১৪৪ ॥

sannyāsī ha-iyā punaḥ nā dila daraśana
tumi taiche kaile mora ha-ibe maraṇa

SYNONYMS

sannyāsī—a member of the renounced order; *ha-iyā*—after becoming; *punaḥ*—again; *nā*—not; *dila*—gave; *daraśana*—visit; *tumi*—You; *taiche*—like that; *kaile*—if doing; *mora*—my; *ha-ibe*—there will be; *maraṇa*—death.

TRANSLATION

Mother Śacī continued: "After accepting the renounced order, Viśvarūpa never again gave me audience. If You do like Him, that will certainly be the death of Me."

TEXT 145

কান্দিয়া বলেন প্রভু – শুন, মোর আই।
তোমার শরীর এই, মোর কিছু নাই ॥ ১৪৫ ॥

kāndiyā balena prabhu——śuna, mora āi
tomāra śarīra ei, mora kichu nāi

SYNONYMS

kāndiyā—crying; *balena*—says; *prabhu*—the Lord; *śuna*—hear; *mora*—My; *āi*—mother; *tomāra*—your; *śarīra*—body; *ei*—this; *mora*—My; *kichu*—anything; *nāi*—is not.

TRANSLATION

The Lord replied, "My dear mother, please hear. This body belongs to you. I do not possess anything.

TEXT 146

তোমার পালিত দেহ, জন্ম তোমা হৈতে ।
কোটি জন্মে তোমার ঋণ না পারি শোধিতে ॥১৪৬॥

tomāra pālita deha, janma tomā haite
koṭi janme tomāra ṛṇa nā pāri śodhite

SYNONYMS

tomāra—your; *pālita*—raised; *deha*—body; *janma*—birth; *tomā*—you; *haite*—from; *koṭi*—millions; *janme*—in births; *tomāra*—your; *ṛṇa*—debt; *nā*—not; *pāri*—I am able; *śodhite*—to repay.

TRANSLATION

"This body was raised by you, and it comes from you. I cannot repay this debt even in millions of births.

TEXT 147

জানি' বা না জানি' কৈল যদ্যপি সন্ন্যাস ।
তথাপি তোমারে কভু নহিব উদাস ॥ ১৪৭ ॥

jāni' vā nā jāni' kaila yadyapi sannyāsa
tathāpi tomāre kabhu nahiba udāsa

SYNONYMS

jāni'—knowing; *vā*—or; *nā*—not; *jāni'*—knowing; *kaila*—accepted; *yadyapi*—although; *sannyāsa*—the renounced order; *tathāpi*—still; *tomāre*—unto you; *kabhu*—at any time; *nahiba*—shall not become; *udāsa*—indifferent.

TRANSLATION

"Knowingly or unknowingly I have accepted this renounced order. Still, I shall never be indifferent to you.

TEXT 148

তুমি যাহাঁ কহ, আমি তাহাঁই রহিব ।
তুমি যেই আজ্ঞা কর, সেই ত' করিব ॥ ১৪৮ ॥

tumi yāhāṅ kaha, āmi tāhāṅi rahiba
tumi yei ājñā kara, sei ta' kariba

SYNONYMS

tumi—you; *yāhāṅ*—wherever; *kaha*—ask; *āmi*—I; *tāhāṅi*—there; *rahiba*—shall stay; *tumi*—you; *yei*—whatever; *ājñā*—order; *kara*—give; *sei*—that; *ta'*—certainly; *kariba*—I shall execute.

TRANSLATION

"My dear mother, wherever you ask Me to stay I shall stay, and whatever you order I shall execute."

TEXT 149

এত বলি' পুনঃ পুনঃ করে নমস্কার ।
তুষ্ট হঞা আই কোলে করে বার বার ॥ ১৪৯ ॥

eta bali' punaḥ punaḥ kare namaskāra
tuṣṭa hañā āi kole kare bāra bāra

SYNONYMS

eta bali'—saying this; *punaḥ punaḥ*—again and again; *kare*—offers; *namaskāra*—obeisances; *tuṣṭa hañā*—being pleased; *āi*—mother Śacī; *kole*—on the lap; *kare*—takes; *bāra bāra*—again and again.

TRANSLATION

Saying this, the Lord offered obeisances to His mother again and again, and mother Śacī, being pleased, took Him again and again on her lap.

TEXT 150

তবে আই লঞা আচার্য গেলা অভ্যন্তর ।
ভক্তগণ মিলিতে প্রভু হইলা সত্বর ॥ ১৫০ ॥

tabe āi lañā ācārya gelā abhyantara
bhakta-gaṇa milite prabhu ha-ilā satvara

SYNONYMS

tabe—thereafter; *āi*—the mother; *lañā*—taking; *ācārya*—Advaita Ācārya; *gelā*—entered; *abhyantara*—within the house; *bhakta-gaṇa*—all the devotees; *milite*—to meet; *prabhu*—the Lord; *ha-ilā*—became; *satvara*—immediately.

TRANSLATION

Then Advaita Ācārya took mother Śacī within the house. The Lord was immediately ready to meet all the devotees.

TEXT 151

একে একে মিলিল প্রভু সব ভক্তগণ ।
সবার মুখ দেখি' করে দৃঢ় আলিঙ্গন ॥ ১৫১ ॥

eke eke milila prabhu saba bhakta-gaṇa
sabāra mukha dekhi' kare dṛḍha āliṅgana

SYNONYMS

eke eke—one after another; *milila*—met; *prabhu*—the Lord; *saba*—all; *bhakta-gaṇa*—the devotees; *sabāra*—of everyone; *mukha*—face; *dekhi'*—seeing; *kare*—does; *dṛḍha*—tightly; *āliṅgana*—embracing.

TRANSLATION

The Lord met all the devotees one after the other, and looking at everyone's face individually, He embraced them tightly.

TEXT 152

কেশ না দেখিয়া ভক্ত যদ্যপি পায় দুঃখ ।
সৌন্দর্য দেখিতে তবু পায় মহাসুখ ॥ ১৫২ ॥

keśa nā dekhiyā bhakta yadyapi pāya duḥkha
saundarya dekhite tabu pāya mahā-sukha

SYNONYMS

keśa—hair; *nā dekhiyā*—not seeing; *bhakta*—the devotees; *yadyapi*—although; *pāya*—get; *duḥkha*—unhappiness; *saundarya*—the beautiful posture; *dekhite*—to see; *tabu*—still; *pāya*—get; *mahā-sukha*—great happiness.

TRANSLATION

Although the devotees were unhappy at not seeing the Lord's hair, they nonetheless derived great happiness from seeing His beauty.

TEXTS 153-155

শ্রীবাস, রামাই, বিদ্যানিধি, গদাধর ।
গঙ্গাদাস, বক্রেশ্বর, মুরারি, শুক্লাম্বর ॥ ১৫৩ ॥
বুদ্ধিমন্ত খাঁন, নন্দন, শ্রীধর, বিজয় ।
বাসুদেব, দামোদর, মুকুন্দ, সঞ্জয় ॥ ১৫৪ ॥
কত নাম লইব যত নবদ্বীপবাসী ।
সবারে মিলিলা প্রভু কৃপাদৃষ্ট্যে হাসি' ॥ ১৫৫ ॥

śrīvāsa, rāmāi, vidyānidhi, gadādhara
gaṅgādāsa, vakreśvara, murāri, śuklāmbara

buddhimanta khāṅ, nandana, śrīdhara, vijaya
vāsudeva, dāmodara, mukunda, sañjaya

kata nāma la-iba yata navadvīpa-vāsī
sabāre mililā prabhu kṛpā-dṛṣṭye hāsi'

SYNONYMS

śrī-vāsa—Śrīvāsa; *rāmāi*—Rāmāi; *vidyā-nidhi*—Vidyānidhi; *gadā-dhara*—Gadādhara; *gaṅgā-dāsa*—Gaṅgādāsa; *vakreśvara*—Vakreśvara; *murāri*—Murāri; *śuklāmbara*—Śuklāmbara; *buddhimanta khāṅ*—Buddhimanta Khāṅ; *nandana*—Nandana; *śrī-dhara*—Śrīdhara; *vijaya*—Vijaya; *vāsu-deva*—Vāsudeva; *dāmodara*—Dāmodara; *mukunda*—Mukunda; *sañjaya*—Sañjaya; *kata nāma*—how many names; *la-iba*—I shall mention; *yata*—all; *nava-dvīpa-vāsī*—the inhabitants of Navadvīpa; *sabāre*—all of them; *mililā*—met; *prabhu*—the Lord; *kṛpā-dṛṣṭye*—with merciful glances; *hāsi'*—smiling.

TRANSLATION

Śrīvāsa, Rāmāi, Vidyānidhi, Gadādhara, Gaṅgādāsa, Vakreśvara, Murāri, Śuklāmbara, Buddhimanta Khāṅ, Nandana, Śrīdhara, Vijaya, Vāsudeva, Dāmodara, Mukunda, Sañjaya and all the others, however many I can mention—indeed, all the inhabitants of Navadvīpa—arrived there, and the Lord met them with smiles and glances of mercy.

TEXT 156

আনন্দে নাচয়ে সবে বলি' 'হরি' 'হরি'।
আচার্য-মন্দির হৈল শ্রীবৈকুণ্ঠপুরী ॥ ১৫৬ ॥

ānande nācaye sabe bali' 'hari' 'hari'
ācārya-mandira haila śrī-vaikuṇṭha-purī

SYNONYMS

ānande—in pleasure; *nācaye*—dance; *sabe*—all; *bali'*—saying; *hari hari*—the holy name of the Lord; *ācārya-mandira*—the house of Advaita Ācārya; *haila*—became; *śrī-vaikuṇṭha-purī*—a spiritual Vaikuṇṭha planet.

TRANSLATION

Everyone was dancing and chanting the holy names of Hari. In this way the domicile of Advaita Ācārya was converted into Śrī Vaikuṇṭha Purī.

TEXT 157

যত লোক আইল মহাপ্রভুকে দেখিতে।
নানা-গ্রাম হৈতে, আর নবদ্বীপ হৈতে ॥ ১৫৭ ॥

yata loka āila mahāprabhuke dekhite
nānā-grāma haite, āra navadvīpa haite

SYNONYMS

yata loka—all the people; *āila*—came; *mahā-prabhuke*—Śrī Caitanya Mahāprabhu; *dekhite*—to see; *nānā-grāma haite*—from various villages; *āra*—and; *nava-dvīpa haite*—from Navadvīpa.

TRANSLATION

People came to see Śrī Caitanya Mahāprabhu from various other villages nearby, as well as Navadvīpa.

TEXT 158

সবাকারে বাসা দিল—ভক্ষ্য, অন্নপান ।
বহুদিন আচার্য-গোসাঞি কৈল সমাধান ॥ ১৫৮ ॥

sabākāre vāsā dila——bhakṣya, anna-pāna
bahu-dina ācārya-gosāñi kaila samādhāna

SYNONYMS

sabākāre—to all of them; *vāsā dila*—gave residential quarters; *bhakṣya*—eatables; *anna-pāna*—food and drink; *bahu-dina*—for many days; *ācārya-gosāñi*—Advaita Ācārya; *kaila*—did; *samādhāna*—adjustment.

TRANSLATION

To everyone who came to see the Lord from villages nearby, especially from Navadvīpa, Advaita Ācārya gave residential quarters, as well as all kinds of eatables, for many days. Indeed, He properly adjusted everything.

TEXT 159

আচার্য-গোসাঞির ভাণ্ডার— অক্ষয়, অব্যয় ।
যত দ্রব্য ব্যয় করে তত দ্রব্য হয় ॥ ১৫৯ ॥

ācārya-gosāñira bhāṇḍāra——akṣaya, avyaya
yata dravya vyaya kare tata dravya haya

SYNONYMS

ācārya-gosāñira—of Advaita Ācārya; *bhāṇḍāra*—storehouse; *akṣaya*—inexhaustible; *avyaya*—indestructible; *yata*—all; *dravya*—commodities; *vyaya*—expenditure; *kare*—does; *tata*—so much; *dravya*—commodity; *haya*—becomes filled.

TRANSLATION

The supplies of Advaita Ācārya were inexhaustible and indestructible. As many goods and commodities as He used, just as many again appeared.

TEXT 160

সেই দিন হৈতে শচী করেন রন্ধন ।
ভক্তগণ লঞা প্রভু করেন ভোজন ॥ ১৬০ ॥

sei dina haite śacī karena randhana
bhakta-gaṇa lañā prabhu karena bhojana

SYNONYMS

sei dina haite—from that date; *śacī*—mother Śacī; *karena*—does; *randhana*—cooking; *bhakta-gaṇa*—all the devotees; *lañā*—accompanied by; *prabhu*—Lord Caitanya Mahāprabhu; *karena*—does; *bhojana*—dining.

TRANSLATION

From the day Śacīmātā arrived at the house of Advaita Ācārya, she took charge of the cooking, and Śrī Caitanya Mahāprabhu dined in the company of all the devotees.

TEXT 161

দিনে আচার্যের প্রীতি—প্রভুর দর্শন ।
রাত্রে লোক দেখে প্রভুর নর্তন-কীর্তন ॥ ১৬১ ॥

dine ācāryera prīti——prabhura darśana
rātre loka dekhe prabhura nartana-kīrtana

SYNONYMS

dine—during the daytime; *ācāryera prīti*—the loving affairs of Advaita Ācārya; *prabhura darśana*—the sight of Lord Caitanya Mahāprabhu; *rātre*—at night; *loka*—all the people; *dekhe*—see; *prabhura*—of the Lord; *nartana-kīrtana*—dancing and chanting.

TRANSLATION

All the people who came there during the day saw Lord Caitanya Mahāprabhu and the friendly behavior of Advaita Ācārya. At night they had the opportunity to see the Lord's dancing and hear His chanting.

TEXT 162

কীর্তন করিতে প্রভুর সর্বভাবোদয় ।
স্তম্ভ, কম্প, পুলকাশ্রু, গদ্গদ, প্রলয় ॥ ১৬২ ॥

kīrtana karite prabhura sarva-bhāvodaya
stambha, kampa, pulakāśru, gadgada, pralaya

SYNONYMS

kīrtana karite—while performing chanting; *prabhura*—of the Lord; *sarva*—all; *bhāva-udaya*—manifestations of ecstatic symptoms; *stambha*—being stunned; *kampa*—trembling; *pulaka*—standing of the hair; *aśru*—tears; *gadgada*—faltering of the voice; *pralaya*—devastation.

TRANSLATION

When the Lord performed kīrtana, He manifested all kinds of transcendental symptoms. He appeared stunned and trembling, His hair stood on end, and His voice faltered. There were tears and devastation.

PURPORT

Devastation is described in *Bhakti-rasāmṛta-sindhu* as a combination of happiness and distress that becomes conspicuous by an absence of any sense of them. In this condition, a devotee falls to the ground, and the subsequent symptoms in the body ensue. These symptoms are mentioned above, and when they become prominent in the body, a state called *pralaya* (devastation) is manifest.

TEXT 163

ক্ষণে ক্ষণে পড়ে প্রভু আছাড় খাঞা ।
দেখি' শচীমাতা কহে রোদন করিয়া ॥ ১৬৩ ॥

kṣaṇe kṣaṇe paḍe prabhu āchāḍa khāñā
dekhi' śacīmātā kahe rodana kariyā

SYNONYMS

kṣaṇe kṣaṇe—very frequently; *paḍe*—falls; *prabhu*—the Lord; *āchāḍa khāñā*—tumbling down; *dekhi'*—seeing; *śacī-mātā*—mother Śacī; *kahe*—says; *rodana kariyā*—crying.

TRANSLATION

Frequently the Lord would tumble to the ground. Seeing this, mother Śacī would cry.

TEXT 164

চূর্ণ হৈল, হেন বাসোঁ নিমাঞি-কলেবর ।
হাহা করি' বিষ্ণু-পাশে মাগে এই বর ॥ ১৬৪ ॥

cūrṇa haila, hena vāsoṅ nimāñi-kalevara
hā-hā kari' viṣṇu-pāśe māge ei vara

SYNONYMS

cūrṇa—smashed; *haila*—has become; *hena*—thus; *vāsoṅ*—I think; *nimāñi-kalevara*—the body of Nimāi; *hā-hā kari'*—crying loudly; *viṣṇu-pāśe*—Lord Viṣṇu; *māge*—begs; *ei*—this; *vara*—benediction.

TRANSLATION

Śrīmatī Śacīmātā thought that the body of Nimāi was being smashed when He fell down so. She cried, "Alas!" and petitioned Lord Viṣṇu.

TEXT 165

বাল্যকাল হৈতে তোমার যে কৈলুঁ সেবন ।
তার এই ফল মোরে দেহ নারায়ণ ॥ ১৬৫ ॥

bālya-kāla haite tomāra ye kailuṅ sevana
tāra ei phala more deha nārāyaṇa

SYNONYMS

bālya-kāla haite—from my childhood; *tomāra*—Your; *ye*—whatever; *kailuṅ*—I have done; *sevana*—service; *tāra*—of that; *ei phala*—this result; *more*—unto me; *deha*—kindly award; *nārāyaṇa*—O Supreme Lord.

TRANSLATION

"My dear Lord, kindly bestow this benediction as a result of whatever service I have rendered unto You from my childhood.

TEXT 166

যে কালে নিমাঞি পড়ে ধরণী-উপরে ।
ব্যথা যেন নাহি লাগে নিমাঞি-শরীরে ॥ ১৬৬ ॥

ye kāle nimāñi paḍe dharaṇī-upare
vyathā yena nāhi lāge nimāñi-śarīre

SYNONYMS

ye kāle—whenever; *nimāñi*—my son Nimāi; *paḍe*—falls down; *dharaṇī-upare*—on the surface of the earth; *vyathā*—pain; *yena*—as if; *nāhi*—not; *lāge*—touch; *nimāñi-śarīre*—the body of my son Nimāi.

TRANSLATION

"Whenever Nimāi falls to the surface of the earth, please do not let Him feel any pain."

TEXT 167

এইমত শচীদেবী বাৎসল্যে বিহ্বল ।
হর্ষ-ভয়-দৈন্যভাবে হইল বিকল ॥ ১৬৭ ॥

ei-mata śacīdevī vātsalye vihvala
harṣa-bhaya-dainya-bhāve ha-ila vikala

SYNONYMS

ei-mata—in this way; *śacī-devī*—mother Śacī; *vātsalye*—in parental affection; *vihvala*—overwhelmed; *harṣa*—happiness; *bhaya*—fear; *dainya-bhāve*—and in humility; *ha-ila*—became; *vikala*—transformed.

TRANSLATION

When mother Śacī was thus overwhelmed in paternal love for Lord Caitanya Mahāprabhu, she became transformed with happiness, fear and humility, as well as bodily symptoms.

PURPORT

These verses indicate that mother Śacī, born in the family of Nīlāmbara Cakravartī, used to worship Lord Viṣṇu even before her marriage. As stated in *Bhagavad-gītā* (6:41):

prāpya puṇya-kṛtāṁ lokān
uṣitvā śāśvatīḥ samāḥ
śucīnāṁ śrīmatāṁ gehe
yoga-bhraṣṭo 'bhijāyate

"The unsuccessful *yogī,* after many, many years of enjoyment on the planets of the pious living entities, is born into a family of righteous people, or into a family of rich aristocracy." Mother Śacī, a *nitya-siddha* living entity, is an incarnation of mother Yaśodā. She appeared in the house of Nīlāmbara Cakravartī and was everlastingly engaged in the service of Lord Viṣṇu. Later she directly had as her child Lord Viṣṇu, Śrī Caitanya Mahāprabhu, and she served Him from the day of His appearance. This is the position of *nitya-siddha* associates. Śrī Narottama dāsa Ṭhākura therefore sings: *gaurāṅgera saṅgi-gaṇe nitya-siddha kari māne.* Every devotee should know that all the associates of Śrī Caitanya Mahāprabhu—His family members, friends and other associates—were all *nitya-siddhas.* A *nitya-siddha* never forgets the service of the Lord. He is always engaged, even from childhood, in worshiping the Supreme Personality of Godhead.

TEXT 168

শ্রীবাসাদি যত প্রভুর বিপ্র ভক্তগণ ।
প্রভুকে ভিক্ষা দিতে হৈল সবাকার মন ॥ ১৬৮ ॥

śrīvāsādi yata prabhura vipra bhakta-gaṇa
prabhuke bhikṣā dite haila sabākāra mana

SYNONYMS

śrī-vāsa-ādi—the devotees, headed by Śrīvāsa Ṭhākura; *yata*—all; *prabhura*—of the Lord; *vipra*—especially the *brāhmaṇas;* *bhakta-gaṇa*—devotees; *prabhuke*—unto the Lord; *bhikṣā*—lunch; *dite*—to give; *haila*—there was; *sabākāra*—of all of them; *mana*—the mind.

TRANSLATION

Since Advaita Ācārya was giving alms and food to Lord Caitanya Mahāprabhu, the other devotees, headed by Śrīvāsa Ṭhākura, also desired to give Him alms and invite Him for lunch.

PURPORT

It is the duty of all *gṛhasthas* to invite a *sannyāsī* to their homes if he happens to be in the neighborhood or village. This very system is still current in India. If a *sannyāsī* is in the neighborhood of a village, he is invited by all householders, one after another. As long as a *sannyāsī* remains in the village, he enlightens the inhabitants in spiritual understanding. In other words, a *san-*

nyāsī has no housing or food problems even when he travels extensively. Even though Advaita Ācārya was supplying Caitanya Mahāprabhu with *prasāda,* the other devotees from Navadvīpa and Śāntipura also desired to offer Him *prasāda.*

TEXT 169

শুনি' শচী সবাকারে করিল মিনতি ।
নিমাঞির দরশন আর মুঞি পাব কতি ॥ ১৬৯ ॥

śuni' śacī sabākāre karila minati
nimāñira daraśana āra muñi pāba kati

SYNONYMS

śuni'—hearing of this; *śacī*—mother Śacī; *sabākāre*—unto all of them; *karila*—made; *minati*—submission; *nimāñira*—of Nimāi, Śrī Caitanya Mahāprabhu; *daraśana*—visit; *āra*—any more; *muñi*—I; *pāba*—shall get; *kati*—where or how many times.

TRANSLATION

Hearing these proposals made by other devotees of the Lord, mother Śacī said to the devotees: "How many times shall I get the chance to see Nimāi again?"

TEXT 170

তোমা-সবা-সনে হবে অন্যত্র মিলন ।
মুঞি অভাগিনীর মাত্র এই দরশন ॥ ১৭০ ॥

tomā-sabā-sane habe anyatra milana
muñi abhāginīra mātra ei daraśana

SYNONYMS

tomā-sabā-sane—with all of you; *habe*—there will be; *anyatra*—in another place; *milana*—meeting; *muñi*—I; *abhāginīra*—of one who is unfortunate; *mātra*—only; *ei*—this; *daraśana*—meeting.

TRANSLATION

Śacīmātā submitted: "As far as you are concerned, you can meet Nimāi, Śrī Caitanya Mahāprabhu, many times somewhere else, but what is the

possibility of my ever meeting Him again? I shall have to remain at home. A sannyāsī never returns to his home."

TEXT 171

যাবৎ আচার্যগৃহে নিমাঞির অবস্থান ।
মুঞি ভিক্ষা দিমু, সবাকারে মাগোঁ দান ॥ ১৭১ ॥

yāvat ācārya-gṛhe nimāñira avasthāna
muñi bhikṣā dimu, sabākāre māgoṅ dāna

SYNONYMS

yāvat—as long as; *ācārya-gṛhe*—in the house of Advaita Ācārya; *nimāñira*—of Śrī Caitanya Mahāprabhu; *avasthāna*—the stay; *muñi*—I; *bhikṣā dimu*—shall supply the food; *sabākāre*—everyone; *māgoṅ*—I beg; *dāna*—this charity.

TRANSLATION

Mother Śacī appealed to all the devotees to give her this charity: As long as Śrī Caitanya Mahāprabhu remained at the house of Advaita Ācārya, only she would supply Him food.

TEXT 172

শুনি' ভক্তগণ কহে করি' নমস্কার ।
মাতার যে ইচ্ছা সেই সম্মত সবার ॥ ১৭২ ॥

śuni' bhakta-gaṇa kahe kari' namaskāra
mātāra ye icchā sei sammata sabāra

SYNONYMS

śuni'—hearing this; *bhakta-gaṇa*—all the devotees; *kahe*—say; *kari'*—offering; *namaskāra*—obeisances; *mātāra*—of mother Śacīdevī; *ye icchā*—whatever desire; *sei*—that; *sammata*—agreeable; *sabāra*—to all the devotees.

TRANSLATION

Hearing this appeal from mother Śacī, all the devotees offered obeisances and said, "We all agree to whatever mother Śacī desires."

TEXT 173

মাতার ব্যগ্রতা দেখি' প্রভুর ব্যগ্র মন ।
ভক্তগণ একত্র করি' বলিলা বচন ॥ ১৭৩ ॥

mātāra vyagratā dekhi' prabhura vyagra mana
bhakta-gaṇa ekatra kari' balilā vacana

SYNONYMS

mātāra—of the mother; *vyagratā*—eagerness; *dekhi'*—seeing; *prabhura*—of Śrī Caitanya Mahāprabhu; *vyagra*—agitated; *mana*—mind; *bhakta-gaṇa*—all the devotees; *ekatra kari'*—assembling together; *balilā*—said; *vacana*—words.

TRANSLATION

When Śrī Caitanya Mahāprabhu saw His mother's great eagerness, He became a little agitated. He therefore assembled all the devotees present and spoke to them.

TEXT 174

তোমা-সবার আজ্ঞা বিনা চলিলাম বৃন্দাবন ।
যাইতে নারিল, বিঘ্ন কৈল নিবর্তন ॥ ১৭৪ ॥

tomā-sabāra ājñā vinā calilāma vṛndāvana
yāite nārila, vighna kaila nivartana

SYNONYMS

tomā-sabāra—of all of you; *ājñā*—order; *vinā*—without; *calilāma*—I started; *vṛndāvana*—for Vṛndāvana; *yāite nārila*—not able to go; *vighna*—some obstruction; *kaila*—did; *nivartana*—made to return.

TRANSLATION

Śrī Caitanya Mahāprabhu informed them all: "Without your order, I tried to go to Vṛndāvana. There was some obstacle, however, and I had to return.

TEXT 175

যত্তপি সহসা আমি করিয়াছি সন্ন্যাস ।
তথাপি তোমা-সবা হৈতে নহিব উদাস ॥ ১৭৫ ॥

yadyapi sahasā āmi kariyāchi sannyāsa
tathāpi tomā-sabā haite nahiba udāsa

SYNONYMS

yadyapi—although; *sahasā*—all of a sudden; *āmi*—I; *kariyāchi sannyāsa*—accepted *sannyāsa;* *tathāpi*—still; *tomā-sabā*—all of you; *haite*—from; *nahiba*—I shall never be; *udāsa*—indifferent.

TRANSLATION

"My dear friends, although I have suddenly accepted this renounced order, I still know that I shall never be indifferent to you.

TEXT 176

তোমা-সব না ছাড়িব, যাবৎ আমি জীব' ।
মাতারে তাবৎ আমি ছাড়িতে নারিব ॥ ১৭৬ ॥

tomā-saba nā chāḍiba, yāvat āmi jība'
mātāre tāvat āmi chāḍite nāriba

SYNONYMS

tomā-saba—all of you; *nā*—not; *chāḍiba*—I shall give up; *yāvat*—as long as; *āmi*—I; *jība*—shall live or shall remain manifest; *mātāre*—mother; *tāvat*—that long; *āmi*—I; *chāḍite*—to give up; *nāriba*—shall be unable.

TRANSLATION

"My dear friends, as long as I remain manifest, I shall never give you up. Nor shall I be able to give up My mother.

TEXT 177

সন্ন্যাসীর ধর্ম নহে—সন্ন্যাস করিঞা ।
নিজ জন্মস্থানে রহে কুটুম্ব লঞা ॥ ১৭৭ ॥

sannyāsīra dharma nahe——sannyāsa kariñā
nija janma-sthāne rahe kuṭumba lañā

SYNONYMS

sannyāsīra—of a *sannyāsī; dharma*—duty; *nahe*—it is not; *sannyāsa*—*sannyāsa; kariñā*—accepting; *nija*—own; *janma-sthāne*—at the birthplace; *rahe*—remains; *kuṭumba*—relatives; *lañā*—with.

TRANSLATION

"After accepting sannyāsa, it is not the duty of a sannyāsī to remain at his birthplace, encircled by relatives.

TEXT 178

কেহ যেন এই বলি' না করে নিন্দন।
সেই যুক্তি কহ, যাতে রহে দুই ধর্ম ॥ ১৭৮ ॥

keha yena ei bali' nā kare nindana
sei yukti kaha, yāte rahe dui dharma

SYNONYMS

keha—anyone; *yena*—so that; *ei*—this; *bali'*—saying; *nā kare*—does not do; *nindana*—blasphemy; *sei*—that; *yukti*—consideration; *kaha*—tell Me; *yāte*—by which; *rahe*—remain; *dui*—two; *dharma*—duties.

TRANSLATION

"Make some arrangement so that I may not leave you and at the same time people may not blame Me for remaining with relatives after taking sannyāsa."

TEXT 179

শুনিয়া প্রভুর এই মধুর বচন।
শচীপাশ আচার্যাদি করিল গমন ॥ ১৭৯ ॥

śuniyā prabhura ei madhura vacana
śacī-pāśa ācāryādi karila gamana

SYNONYMS

śuniyā—hearing this; *prabhura*—of the Lord; *ei*—this; *madhura*—sweet; *vacana*—statement; *śacī-pāśa*—before mother Śacī; *ācārya-ādi*—Advaita Ācārya and other devotees; *karila*—did; *gamana*—going.

TRANSLATION

After hearing Lord Caitanya's statement, all the devotees, headed by Advaita Ācārya, approached mother Śacī.

TEXT 180

প্রভুর নিবেদন তাঁরে সকল কহিল ।
শুনি' শচী জগন্মাতা কহিতে লাগিল ॥ ১৮০ ॥

prabhura nivedana tāṅre sakala kahila
śuni' śacī jagan-mātā kahite lāgila

SYNONYMS

prabhura—of the Lord; *nivedana*—submission; *tāṅre*—unto her; *sakala*—all; *kahila*—told; *śuni'*—hearing this; *śacī*—mother Śacī; *jagat-mātā*—the mother of the universe; *kahite*—to say; *lāgila*—began.

TRANSLATION

When they submitted Lord Caitanya's statement, mother Śacī, who is the mother of the universe, began to speak.

TEXT 181

তেঁহো যদি ইহাঁ রহে, তবে মোর সুখ ।
তাঁ'র নিন্দা হয় যদি, সেহ মোর দুঃখ ॥ ১৮১ ॥

teṅho yadi ihāṅ rahe, tabe mora sukha
tāṅ'ra nindā haya yadi, seha mora duḥkha

SYNONYMS

teṅho—Lord Caitanya; *yadi*—if; *ihāṅ*—here; *rahe*—stays; *tabe*—then; *mora*—my; *sukha*—happiness; *tāṅ'ra nindā*—blasphemy of Him; *haya*—there is; *yadi*—if; *seha*—that also; *mora*—my; *duḥkha*—unhappiness.

TRANSLATION

Śacīmātā said: "It will be a great happiness for me if Nimāi, Śrī Caitanya Mahāprabhu, stays here. But at the same time, if someone blames Him, it will be my great unhappiness."

PURPORT

It is a great happiness for a mother if her son does not leave home to search out Kṛṣṇa but remains with her. At the same time, if a son does not search after Kṛṣṇa but simply remains at home, he is certainly blamed by experienced saintly persons. Such blame certainly causes great unhappiness for a mother. If a real mother wants her son to progress spiritually, she had better allow him to go out searching for Kṛṣṇa. The mother naturally desires the welfare of the son. If a mother does not allow her son to search for Kṛṣṇa, she is called *mā,* which indicates *māyā.* By allowing her son to go as a *sannyāsī* and search for Kṛṣṇa, Śacīmātā instructs all mothers of the world. She indicates that all sons should become real devotees of Kṛṣṇa and should not stay at home under the care of an affectionate mother. This is supported by *Śrīmad-Bhāgavatam* (5.5.18):

gurur na sa syāt sva-jano na sa syāt
pitā na sa syāj jananī na sā syāt
daivaṁ na tat syān na patiś ca sa syān
na mocayed yaḥ samupeta-mṛtyum

"No one should become a spiritual master—nor a relative, father, mother, worshipable Deity or husband—if he cannot help a person escape the imminent path of death." Every living entity is wandering within the universe, subjected to the law of *karma* and transmigrating from one body to another and from one planet to another. Therefore the whole Vedic process is meant to save the wandering living entities from the clutches of *māyā*—birth, death, disease and old age. This means stopping the cycle of birth and death. This cycle can be stopped only if one worships Kṛṣṇa. As the Lord says in *Bhagavad-gītā* (4.9):

janma karma ca me divyam
evaṁ yo vetti tattvataḥ
tyaktvā dehaṁ punar janma
naiti mām eti so 'rjuna

"One who knows the transcendental nature of My appearance and activities does not, upon leaving the body, take his birth again in this material world, but attains My eternal abode, O Arjuna.

To stop the cycle of birth and death, one has to understand Kṛṣṇa as He is. Simply by knowing Kṛṣṇa, one can stop the process of rebirth into this material world. By acting in Kṛṣṇa consciousness, one can return to Godhead. The highest perfection of life is for a father, mother, spiritual master, husband or any other family member to help others return home, back to Godhead. That is the most preferred welfare activity for the benefit of relatives. Therefore, Śacīmātā, although the mother of Nimāi Paṇḍita, Śrī Caitanya Mahāprabhu, considered all the facts and decided to allow her son to go out and search for Kṛṣṇa. At the same time, she made some arrangements in order that she might get news of all the activities of Śrī Caitanya Mahāprabhu.

TEXT 182

তাতে এই যুক্তি ভাল, মোর মনে লয়।
নীলাচলে রহে যদি, দুই কার্য হয়॥ ১৮২ ॥

tāte ei yukti bhāla, mora mane laya
nīlācale rahe yadi, dui kārya haya

SYNONYMS

tāte—therefore; *ei*—this; *yukti*—consideration; *bhāla*—as good; *mora*—my; *mane*—mind; *laya*—takes; *nīlācale*—in Jagannātha Purī; *rahe*—He stays; *yadi*—if; *dui*—two; *kārya*—purposes; *haya*—are achieved.

TRANSLATION

Mother Śacī said: "This consideration is good. In my opinion, if Nimāi remains at Jagannātha Purī, He may not leave any one of us and at the same time can remain aloof as a sannyāsī. Thus both purposes are fulfilled.

TEXT 183

নীলাচলে নবদ্বীপে যেন দুই ঘর।
লোক-গতাগতি-বার্তা পাব নিরন্তর॥ ১৮৩ ॥

nīlācale navadvīpe yena dui ghara
loka-gatāgati-vārtā pāba nirantara

SYNONYMS

nīlācale—at Jagannātha Purī; *nava-dvīpe*—as well as Navadvīpa; *yena*—as if; *dui*—two; *ghara*—rooms; *loka*—people; *gatāgati*—come and go; *vārtā*—news; *pāba*—I shall get; *nirantara*—always.

TRANSLATION

"Since Jagannātha Purī and Navadvīpa are intimately related—as if they were two rooms in the same house—people from Navadvīpa generally go to Jagannātha Purī, and those in Jagannātha Purī go to Navadvīpa. This going and coming will help carry news of Lord Caitanya. In this way I will be able to get news of Him.

TEXT 184

তুমি সব করিতে পার গমনাগমন ।
গঙ্গাস্নানে কভু হবে তাঁর আগমন ॥ ১৮৪ ॥

tumi saba karite pāra gamanāgamana
gaṅgā-snāne kabhu habe tāṅra āgamana

SYNONYMS

tumi—you; *saba*—all; *karite*—to do; *pāra*—are able; *gamana-āgamana*—going and coming; *gaṅgā-snāne*—for bathing in the Ganges; *kabhu*—sometimes; *habe*—it will be possible; *tāṅra*—His; *āgamana*—coming here.

TRANSLATION

"All you devotees will be able to come and go, and sometimes He may also come to take His bath in the Ganges.

TEXT 185

আপনার দুঃখ-সুখ তাহাঁ নাহি গণি ।
তাঁর যেই সুখ, তাহা নিজ-সুখ মানি ॥ ১৮৫ ॥

āpanāra duḥkha-sukha tāhāṅ nāhi gaṇi
tāṅra yei sukha, tāhā nija-sukha māni

SYNONYMS

āpanāra—of my own; *duḥkha-sukha*—unhappiness and happiness; *tāhāṅ*—there; *nāhi*—not; *gaṇi*—I count; *tāṅra*—His; *yei*—whatever; *sukha*—happiness; *tāhā*—that; *nija*—my own; *sukha*—happiness; *māni*—I accept.

TRANSLATION

"I do not care for my personal happiness or unhappiness, but only for His happiness. Indeed, I accept His happiness as my happiness."

TEXT 186

শুনি' ভক্তগণ তাঁরে করিল স্তবন ।
বেদ-আজ্ঞা যৈছে, মাতা, তোমার বচন ॥ ১৮৬ ॥

śuni' bhakta-gaṇa tāṅre karila stavana
veda-ājñā yaiche, mātā, tomāra vacana

SYNONYMS

śuni'—hearing this; *bhakta-gaṇa*—all the devotees; *tāṅre*—to her; *karila*—did; *stavana*—praying; *veda-ājñā*—an injunction of the *Vedas*; *yaiche*—like; *mātā*—my dear mother; *tomāra vacana*—your word.

TRANSLATION

After hearing Śacīmātā, all the devotees offered her prayers and assured her that her order, like a Vedic injunction, could not be violated.

TEXT 187

ভক্তগণ প্রভু-আগে আসিয়া কহিল ।
শুনিয়া প্রভুর মনে আনন্দ হইল ॥ ১৮৭ ॥

bhakta-gaṇa prabhu-āge āsiyā kahila
śuniyā prabhura mane ānanda ha-ila

SYNONYMS

bhakta-gaṇa—the devotees; *prabhu*—Śrī Caitanya Mahāprabhu; *āge*—before; *āsiyā*—coming; *kahila*—informed; *śuniyā*—hearing; *prabhura*—of Lord Caitanya; *mane*—in the mind; *ānanda*—pleasure; *ha-ila*—there was.

TRANSLATION

All the devotees informed Lord Caitanya of Śacīmātā's decision. Hearing it, the Lord became very pleased.

TEXT 188

নবদ্বীপ-বাসী আদি যত ভক্তগণ ।
সবারে সম্মান করি' বলিলা বচন ॥ ১৮৮ ॥

navadvīpa-vāsī ādi yata bhakta-gaṇa
sabāre sammāna kari' balilā vacana

SYNONYMS

nava-dvīpa-vāsī—all the inhabitants of Navadvīpa; *ādi*—primarily; *yata*—all; *bhakta-gaṇa*—devotees; *sabāre*—to all of them; *sammāna*—respect; *kari'*—showing; *balilā*—said; *vacana*—these words.

TRANSLATION

Lord Śrī Caitanya Mahāprabhu offered respects to all the devotees present from Navadvīpa and other towns, speaking to them as follows.

TEXT 189

তুমি-সব লোক—মোর পরম বান্ধব ।
এই ভিক্ষা মাগোঁ,—মোরে দেহ তুমি সব ॥ ১৮৯ ॥

tumi-saba loka——mora parama bāndhava
ei bhikṣā māgoṅ,——more deha tumi saba

SYNONYMS

tumi-saba loka—all of you people; *mora*—My; *parama bāndhava*—intimate friends; *ei bhikṣā māgoṅ*—I beg one favor; *more*—unto Me; *deha*—kindly give; *tumi*—you; *saba*—all.

TRANSLATION

"My dear friends, you are all My intimate friends. Now I am begging a favor of you. Please give it to Me."

TEXT 190

ঘরে যাঞা কর সদা কৃষ্ণসংকীর্তন ।
কৃষ্ণনাম, কৃষ্ণকথা, কৃষ্ণ আরাধন ॥ ১৯০ ॥

ghare yāñā kara sadā kṛṣṇa-saṅkīrtana
kṛṣṇa-nāma, kṛṣṇa-kathā, kṛṣṇa ārādhana

SYNONYMS

ghare yāñā—returning home; *kara*—kindly do; *sadā*—always; *kṛṣṇa-saṅkīrtana*—chanting of the holy name of the Lord; *kṛṣṇa-nāma*—the holy name of the Lord; *kṛṣṇa-kathā*—discussion of Kṛṣṇa's pastimes; *kṛṣṇa*—of Lord Kṛṣṇa; *ārādhana*—worshiping.

TRANSLATION

Lord Caitanya Mahāprabhu requested them all to return home and begin chanting the holy name congregationally. He also requested them to worship Kṛṣṇa, chant His holy name and discuss His holy pastimes.

PURPORT

The cult of Śrī Caitanya Mahāprabhu, the Hare Kṛṣṇa movement, is very nicely explained by Lord Caitanya Mahāprabhu authoritatively. It is not that everyone has to take *sannyāsa* like Śrī Caitanya Mahāprabhu. Everyone can execute the cult of Kṛṣṇa consciousness at home, as ordered by the Lord. Everyone can congregationally chant the holy name of Kṛṣṇa, the Hare Kṛṣṇa *mahā-mantra*. One can also discuss the subject matter of *Bhagavad-gītā* and *Śrīmad-Bhāgavatam* and install Deities of Rādhā-Kṛṣṇa or Gaura-Nitāi or both and worship them very carefully in one's own home. It is not that we have to open different centers all over the world. Whoever cares for the Kṛṣṇa consciousness movement can install Deities at home and, under superior guidance, worship the Deity regularly, chanting the *mahā-mantra* and discussing *Bhagavad-gītā* and *Śrīmad-Bhāgavatam*. We are actually teaching in our classes how to go about this. One who feels that he is not yet ready to live in a temple or undergo strict regulative principles in the temple—especially householders who live with wife and children—can start a center at home by installing the Deity, worshiping the Lord morning and evening, chanting Hare Kṛṣṇa and discussing *Bhagavad-gītā* and *Śrīmad-Bhāgavatam*. Anyone can do this at home without difficulty, and Śrī Caitanya Mahāprabhu requested all the devotees present there to do so.

TEXT 191

আজ্ঞা দেহ নীলাচলে করিয়ে গমন ।
মধ্যে মধ্যে আসি' তোমায় দিব দরশন ॥ ১৯১ ॥

ājñā deha nīlācale kariye gamana
madhye madhye āsi' tomāya diba daraśana

SYNONYMS

ājñā deha—give permission; *nīlācale*—to Jagannātha Purī; *kariye*—I do; *gamana*—going; *madhye madhye*—sometimes; *āsi'*—coming here; *tomāya*—to all of you; *diba*—I shall give; *daraśana*—audience.

TRANSLATION

After thus instructing the devotees, the Lord asked their permission to go to Jagannātha Purī. He assured them that at intervals He would come there and meet them again and again.

TEXT 192

এত বলি' সবাকারে ঈষৎ হাসিঞা ।
বিদায় করিল প্রভু সম্মান করিঞা ॥ ১৯২ ॥

eta bali' sabākāre īṣat hāsiñā
vidāya karila prabhu sammāna kariñā

SYNONYMS

eta bali'—saying this; *sabākāre*—to all the devotees; *īṣat hāsiñā*—smiling very mildly; *vidāya karila*—bid them farewell; *prabhu*—the Lord; *sammāna kariñā*—showing all respect.

TRANSLATION

In this way, Śrī Caitanya Mahāprabhu, offering due respects to all the devotees and smiling very mildly, bid them farewell.

TEXT 193

সবা বিদায় দিয়া প্রভু চলিতে কৈল মন ।
হরিদাস কান্দি' কহে করুণ বচন ॥ ১৯৩ ॥

sabā vidāya diyā prabhu calite kaila mana
haridāsa kāndi' kahe karuṇa vacana

SYNONYMS

sabā vidāya diyā—asking everyone to return home; *prabhu*—the Lord; *calite*—to go; *kaila*—decided; *mana*—the mind; *hari-dāsa kāndi'*—Haridāsa Ṭhākura began to cry; *kahe*—says; *karuṇa*—pathetic; *vacana*—words.

TRANSLATION

After requesting all the devotees to return home, the Lord decided to go to Jagannātha Purī. At that time Haridāsa Ṭhākura began to cry and speak some pathetic words.

TEXT 194

নীলাচলে যাবে তুমি, মোর কোন্ গতি।
নীলাচলে যাইতে মোর নাহিক শকতি॥ ১৯৪॥

nīlācale yābe tumi, mora kon gati
nīlācale yāite mora nāhika śakati

SYNONYMS

nīlācale yābe tumi—You will go to Jagannātha Purī; *mora*—my; *kon*—what; *gati*—destination; *nīlācale*—to Jagannātha Purī; *yāite*—to go; *mora*—my; *nāhika*—there is not; *śakati*—strength.

TRANSLATION

Haridāsa Ṭhākura said: "You are going to Jagannātha Purī, and that is all right, but what will be my destination? I am not able to go to Jagannātha Purī."

PURPORT

Although Śrīla Haridāsa Ṭhākura was born in a Mohameddan family, he was accepted as a properly initiated *brāhmaṇa.* As such, he had every right to enter the temple of Jagannātha Purī, but because there were some rules and regulations stipulating that only *brāhmaṇas, kṣatriyas, vaiśyas* and *śūdras* (members of the *varṇāśrama-dharma* system) could enter, Haridāsa Ṭhākura, out of his great humility, did not want to violate these existing rules. He therefore said that he did not have the strength to enter into the temple, and he pointed out that if Lord Śrī Caitanya Mahāprabhu lived within the temple, there would be no way for Haridāsa Ṭhākura to see Him. Later, when Haridāsa

Ṭhākura went to Jagannātha Purī, he lived outside the temple on the beach by the sea. A monastery has now been erected there, known as Siddha-bakula Maṭha. People go there to see the tomb of Haridāsa Ṭhākura.

TEXT 195

মুঞি অধম তোমার না পাব দরশন ।
কেমতে ধরিব এই পাপিষ্ঠ জীবন ॥ ১৯৫ ॥

muñi adhama tomāra nā pāba daraśana
kemate dhariba ei pāpiṣṭha jīvana

SYNONYMS

muñi—I; *adhama*—the lowest of men; *tomāra*—Your; *nā*—not; *pāba*—will get; *daraśana*—seeing; *kemate*—how; *dhariba*—shall I maintain; *ei*—this; *pāpiṣṭha*—sinful; *jīvana*—life.

TRANSLATION

"Because I am the lowest among men, I shall not be able to see You. How shall I maintain my sinful life?"

TEXT 196

প্রভু কহে,—কর তুমি দৈন্য সম্বরণ ।
তোমার দৈন্যেতে মোর ব্যাকুল হয় মন ॥ ১৯৬ ॥

prabhu kahe,——kara tumi dainya saṁvaraṇa
tomāra dainyete mora vyākula haya mana

SYNONYMS

prabhu kahe—the Lord replied; *kara*—do; *tumi*—you; *dainya*—humility; *saṁvaraṇa*—checking; *tomāra*—your; *dainyete*—by humility; *mora*—My; *vyākula*—agitated; *haya*—becomes; *mana*—the mind.

TRANSLATION

The Lord replied to Haridāsa Ṭhākura: "Please check your humility. Just by seeing your humility, my mind becomes very much agitated."

TEXT 197

তোমা লাগি' জগন্নাথে করিব নিবেদন ।
তোমা-লঞা যাব আমি শ্রীপুরুষোত্তম ॥ ১৯৭ ॥

tomā lāgi' jagannāthe kariba nivedana
tomā-lañā yāba āmi śrī-puruṣottama

SYNONYMS

tomā lāgi'—for you; *jagannāthe*—unto Lord Jagannātha; *kariba*—I shall do; *nivedana*—petition; *tomā-lañā*—taking you; *yāba*—shall go; *āmi*—I; *śrī-puruṣottama*—to Jagannātha Purī.

TRANSLATION

Lord Caitanya Mahāprabhu assured Haridāsa Ṭhākura that He would place a petition before Lord Jagannātha and that He would certainly take him there to Jagannātha Purī.

TEXT 198

তবে ত' আচার্য কহে বিনয় করিঞা ।
দিন দুই-চারি রহ কৃপা ত' করিঞা ॥ ১৯৮ ॥

tabe ta' ācārya kahe vinaya kariñā
dina dui-cāri raha kṛpā ta' kariñā

SYNONYMS

tabe—thereafter; *ta'*—certainly; *ācārya kahe*—Advaita Ācārya says; *vinaya kariñā*—offering all respect; *dina dui-cāri*—another two or four days; *raha*—kindly remain; *kṛpā*—mercy; *ta'*—certainly; *kariñā*—showing.

TRANSLATION

After that, Advaita Ācārya respectfully requested Lord Caitanya Mahāprabhu to show Him mercy by remaining another two or four days.

TEXT 199

আচার্যের বাক্য প্রভু না করে লঙ্ঘন ।
রহিলা অদ্বৈত-গৃহে, না কৈল গমন ॥ ১৯৯ ॥

ācāryera vākya prabhu nā kare laṅghana
rahilā advaita-gṛhe, nā kaila gamana

SYNONYMS

ācāryera vākya—the words of Śrī Advaita Ācārya; *prabhu*—the Lord; *nā kare laṅghana*—does not deny; *rahilā*—remained; *advaita-gṛhe*—at the house of Advaita Ācārya; *nā kaila gamana*—did not go immediately.

TRANSLATION

Caitanya Mahāprabhu never violated the request of Advaita Ācārya; therefore He remained at His home and did not leave immediately for Jagannātha Purī.

TEXT 200

আনন্দিত হৈল আচার্য, শচী, ভক্ত, সব ।
প্রতিদিন করে আচার্য মহা-মহোৎসব ॥ ২০০ ॥

ānandita haila ācārya, śacī, bhakta, saba
prati-dina kare ācārya mahā-mahotsava

SYNONYMS

ānandita haila—became pleased; *ācārya*—Advaita Ācārya; *śacī*—mother Śacīdevī; *bhakta*—the devotees; *saba*—all; *prati-dina*—every day; *kare*—does; *ācārya*—Advaita Ācārya; *mahā-mahā-utsava*—great festival.

TRANSLATION

Lord Caitanya's decision was received very happily by Advaita Ācārya, mother Śacī and all the devotees. Advaita Ācārya celebrated every day with a great festival.

TEXT 201

দিনে কৃষ্ণ-কথা-রস ভক্তগণ-সঙ্গে ।
রাত্রে মহা-মহোৎসব সংকীর্তন-রঙ্গে ॥ ২০১ ॥

dine kṛṣṇa-kathā-rasa bhakta-gaṇa-saṅge
rātre mahā-mahotsava saṅkīrtana-raṅge

SYNONYMS

dine—during daytime; *kṛṣṇa-kathā-rasa*—discussion on Kṛṣṇa; *bhakta-gaṇa-saṅge*—with the devotees; *rātre*—at night; *mahā-mahā-utsava*—a great festival; *saṅkīrtana-raṅge*—in the matter of congregational chanting.

TRANSLATION

During the day the devotees discussed subject matters concerning Kṛṣṇa, and at night there was a great festival of congregational chanting at the house of Advaita Ācārya.

TEXT 202

আনন্দিত হঞা শচী করেন রন্ধন ।
সুখে ভোজন করে প্রভু লঞা ভক্তগণ ॥ ২০২ ॥

ānandita hañā śacī karena randhana
sukhe bhojana kare prabhu lañā bhakta-gaṇa

SYNONYMS

ānandita hañā—being pleased; *śacī*—mother Śacī; *karena*—does; *randhana*—cooking; *sukhe*—in happiness; *bhojana*—eating; *kare*—does; *prabhu*—Lord Caitanya Mahāprabhu; *lañā*—accompanied by; *bhakta-gaṇa*—all the devotees.

TRANSLATION

Mother Śacī cooked with great pleasure, and Śrī Caitanya Mahāprabhu, along with the devotees, accepted the prasāda with great pleasure.

TEXT 203

আচার্যের শ্রদ্ধা-ভক্তি-গৃহ-সম্পদ-ধনে ।
সকল সফল হৈল প্রভুর আরাধনে ॥ ২০৩ ॥

ācāryera śraddhā-bhakti-gṛha-sampada-dhane
sakala saphala haila prabhura ārādhane

SYNONYMS

ācāryera—of Advaita Ācārya; *śraddhā*—faith; *bhakti*—devotion; *gṛha*—home; *sampada*—opulence; *dhane*—the wealth; *sakala*—all; *saphala*—successful; *haila*—became; *prabhura*—of Lord Caitanya Mahāprabhu; *ārādhane*—in the worship.

TRANSLATION

In this way all the opulences of Advaita Ācārya—His faith, devotion, home, riches and everything else—were successfully utilized in the worship of Lord Caitanya Mahāprabhu.

PURPORT

Advaita Ācārya set an ideal example for all householder devotees in His receiving of Lord Caitanya Mahāprabhu and His devotees and in His execution of a daily festival at His home. If one has the proper means and wealth, he should occasionally invite the devotees of Lord Caitanya, who are engaged in preaching all over the world, and hold a festival at home simply by distributing *prasāda* and talking about Kṛṣṇa during the day and holding congregational chanting for at least three hours in the evening. This procedure must be adopted in all centers of the Kṛṣṇa consciousness movement. Thus they will daily perform *saṅkīrtana-yajña*. In *Śrīmad-Bhāgavatam* (11.5.32) the daily performance of *saṅkīrtana-yajña* is recommended for this age (*yajñaiḥ saṅkīrtana-prāyair yajanti hi sumedhasaḥ*). One should worship Lord Caitanya Mahāprabhu and His four associates, the Pañca-tattva, by distributing *prasāda* and holding congregational chanting. Indeed, that *yajña* or sacrifice is most recommended in this age of Kali. In this age, other *yajñas* are not possible to perform, but this *yajña* can be performed everywhere and anywhere without difficulty.

TEXT 204

শচীর আনন্দ বাড়ে দেখি' পুত্রমুখ ।
ভোজন করাঞা পূর্ণ কৈল নিজসুখ ॥ ২০৪ ॥

śacīra ānanda bāḍe dekhi' putra-mukha
bhojana karāñā pūrṇa kaila nija-sukha

SYNONYMS

śacīra—of Śacīmātā; *ānanda bāḍe*—pleasure increases; *dekhi'*—seeing; *putra-mukha*—the face of her son; *bhojana karāñā*—feeding; *pūrṇa*—full; *kaila*—made; *nija-sukha*—her own happiness.

TRANSLATION

As mother Śacī constantly saw the face of her son and fed Him, her own happiness increased and was indeed complete.

TEXT 205

এইমত অদ্বৈত-গৃহে ভক্তগণ মিলে ।
বঞ্চিলা কতকদিন মহা-কুতুহলে ॥ ২০৫ ॥

ei-mata advaita-gṛhe bhakta-gaṇa mile
vañcilā kataka-dina mahā-kutūhale

SYNONYMS

ei-mate—in this way; *advaita-gṛhe*—at the home of Advaita Ācārya; *bhakta-gaṇa*—all the devotees; *mile*—meet together; *vañcilā*—passed; *kataka-dina*—some days; *mahā-kutūhale*—in a greatly festive mood.

TRANSLATION

In this way, at Advaita Ācārya's house all the devotees met and passed some days together in a greatly festive mood.

TEXT 206

আর দিন প্রভু কহে সব ভক্তগণে ।
নিজ-নিজ-গৃহে সবে করহ গমনে ॥ ২০৬ ॥

āra dina prabhu kahe saba bhakta-gaṇe
nija-nija-gṛhe sabe karaha gamane

SYNONYMS

āra dina—the next day; *prabhu*—the Lord; *kahe*—says; *saba*—all; *bhakta-gaṇe*—to the devotees; *nija-nija-gṛhe*—to your respective homes; *sabe*—all; *karaha*—do; *gamane*—returning.

TRANSLATION

The next day, Lord Caitanya Mahāprabhu requested all the devotees to return to their respective homes.

TEXT 207

ঘরে গিয়া কর সবে কৃষ্ণসংকীর্তন ।
পুনরপি আমা-সঙ্গে হইবে মিলন ॥ ২০৭ ॥

ghare giyā kara sabe kṛṣṇa-saṅkīrtana
punarapi āmā-saṅge ha-ibe milana

SYNONYMS

ghare giyā—returning home; *kara*—do; *sabe*—all; *kṛṣṇa-saṅkīrtana*—congregational chanting of the *mahā-mantra*; *punarapi*—again; *āmā-saṅge*—with Me; *ha-ibe*—there will be; *milana*—meeting.

TRANSLATION

Śrī Caitanya Mahāprabhu also asked them to execute the congregational chanting of the holy name of the Lord at their homes, and He assured them that they would be able to meet Him again.

TEXT 208

কভু বা তোমরা করিবে নীলাদ্রি গমন ।
কভু বা আসিব আমি করিতে গঙ্গাস্নান ॥ ২০৮ ॥

kabhu vā tomarā karibe nīlādri gamana
kabhu vā āsiba āmi karite gaṅgā-snāna

SYNONYMS

kabhu—sometimes; *vā*—either; *tomarā*—you; *karibe*—will do; *nīlādri*—to Jagannātha Purī; *gamana*—going; *kabhu*—sometimes; *vā*—or; *āsiba*—shall come; *āmi*—I; *karite*—to do; *gaṅgā-snāna*—bathing in the Ganges.

TRANSLATION

Śrī Caitanya Mahāprabhu told them: "Sometimes you will come to Jagannātha Purī, and sometimes I shall come bathe in the Ganges."

TEXTS 209-210

নিত্যানন্দ-গোসাঞি, পণ্ডিত জগদানন্দ ।
দামোদর পণ্ডিত, আর দত্ত মুকুন্দ ॥ ২০৯ ॥

এই চারিজন আচার্য দিল প্রভু সনে।
জননী প্রবোধ করি' বন্দিল চরণে ॥ ২১০ ॥

nityānanda-gosāñi, paṇḍita jagadānanda
dāmodara paṇḍita, āra datta mukunda

ei cāri-jana ācārya dila prabhu sane
jananī prabodha kari' vandila caraṇe

SYNONYMS

nityānanda gosāñi—Lord Nityānanda Prabhu; *paṇḍita jagadānanda*—Jagadānanda Paṇḍita; *dāmodara paṇḍita*—Dāmodara Paṇḍita; *āra datta mukunda*—and Mukunda Datta; *ei cāri-jana*—these four persons; *ācārya*—Advaita Ācārya; *dila*—gave; *prabhu sane*—with Śrī Caitanya Mahāprabhu; *jananī*—mother Śacī; *prabodha kari'*—pacifying; *vandila caraṇe*—offered prayers at her lotus feet.

TRANSLATION

Śrī Advaita Ācārya sent four persons—Nityānanda Gosāñi, Jagadānanda Paṇḍita, Dāmodara Paṇḍita and Mukunda Datta—to accompany the Lord. After pacifying His mother, Śacīmātā, Śrī Caitanya Mahāprabhu submitted prayers to her lotus feet.

TEXT 211

তাঁরে প্রদক্ষিণ করি' করিল গমন।
এথা আচার্যের ঘরে উঠিল ক্রন্দন ॥ ২১১ ॥

tāṅre pradakṣiṇa kari' karila gamana
ethā ācāryera ghare uṭhila krandana

SYNONYMS

tāṅre—mother Śacī; *pradakṣiṇa kari'*—circumambulating; *karila*—did; *gamana*—going; *ethā*—there; *ācāryera*—of Advaita Ācārya; *ghare*—in the house; *uṭhila*—there arose; *krandana*—crying.

TRANSLATION

When everything was arranged, Lord Caitanya Mahāprabhu circumambulated His mother and then started for Jagannātha Purī. In the house of Advaita Ācārya there arose tumultuous crying.

TEXT 212

নিরপেক্ষ হঞা প্রভু শীঘ্র চলিলা ।
কান্দিতে কন্দিতে আচার্য পশ্চাৎ চলিলা ॥ ২১২ ॥

nirapekṣa hañā prabhu śīghra calilā
kāndite kandite ācārya paścāt calilā

SYNONYMS

nirapekṣa—indifferent; *hañā*—becoming; *prabhu*—the Lord; *śīghra*—very quickly; *calilā*—went; *kāndite kandite*—crying and crying; *ācārya*—Advaita Ācārya; *paścāt*—behind; *calilā*—went.

TRANSLATION

Śrī Caitanya Mahāprabhu was unaffected. He left swiftly, and Advaita Ācārya followed Him weeping.

PURPORT

As Śrīla Bhaktisiddhānta Sarasvatī Ṭhākura explains, the word *nirapekṣa* means not being affected by anything material and remaining fixed in the service of the Lord. Śrī Caitanya Mahāprabhu did not very much care for the roaring tumult and cry at the house of Advaita Ācārya, which He heard when starting for Jagannātha Purī. Worldly moralists may criticize Śrī Caitanya Mahāprabhu for being very cruel, but the Lord did not care for such criticism. As the world teacher of this Kṛṣṇa consciousness movement, He actually showed that a person seriously engaged in Kṛṣṇa consciousness should not be affected by worldly affection. The best course is to engage in rendering service to the Lord and to become callous to material objectives. Externally everyone is attached to material things, but if one becomes entangled in such things, he cannot make progress in Kṛṣṇa consciousness. Therefore those who are engaged in Kṛṣṇa consciousness should not care for the so-called morality of the material world if that morality opposes the service of the Lord. As Lord Caitanya Mahāprabhu has personally shown, one cannot properly execute Kṛṣṇa consciousness without being neutral.

TEXT 213

কত দূর গিয়া প্রভু করি' যোড় হাত ।
আচার্যে প্রবোধি' কহে কিছু মিষ্ট বাত ॥ ২১৩ ॥

kata dūra giyā prabhu kari' yoḍa hāta
ācārye prabodhi' kahe kichu miṣṭa vāta

SYNONYMS

kata dūra giyā—after going some distance; *prabhu*—the Lord; *kari'*—making; *yoḍa hāta*—folded hands; *ācārye*—Advaita Ācārya; *prabodhi'*—pacifying; *kahe*—says; *kichu*—something; *miṣṭa vāta*—sweet words.

TRANSLATION

After He had followed Śrī Caitanya Mahāprabhu for some distance, Advaita Ācārya was petitioned by Śrī Caitanya Mahāprabhu with folded hands. The Lord spoke the following sweet words.

TEXT 214

জননী প্রবোধি' কর ভক্ত সমাধান ।
তুমি ব্যগ্র হৈলে কারো না রহিবে প্রাণ ॥ ২১৪ ॥

jananī prabodhi' kara bhakta samādhāna
tumi vyagra haile kāro nā rahibe prāṇa

SYNONYMS

jananī prabodhi'—pacifying the mother; *kara*—make; *bhakta*—devotees; *samādhāna*—adjustments; *tumi*—You; *vyagra haile*—if becoming agitated; *kāro*—anyone's; *nā rahibe*—will not remain; *prāṇa*—the life.

TRANSLATION

Śrī Caitanya Mahāprabhu said: "Please pacify all the devotees and My mother. If you become agitated, no one will be able to continue to exist."

TEXT 215

এত বলি' প্রভু তাঁরে করি' আলিঙ্গন ।
নিবৃত্তি করিয়া কৈল স্বচ্ছন্দ গমন ॥ ২১৫ ॥

eta bali' prabhu tāṅre kari' āliṅgana
nivṛtti kariyā kaila svacchanda gamana

SYNONYMS

eta bali'—saying this; *prabhu*—the Lord; *tāṅre*—unto Him; *kari'*—doing; *āliṅgana*—embracing; *nivṛtti*—stop; *kariyā*—making; *kaila*—did; *svacchanda*—without anxiety; *gamana*—going toward Jagannātha Purī.

TRANSLATION

Saying this, Śrī Caitanya Mahāprabhu embraced Advaita Ācārya and stopped Him from following any further. Then, without anxiety, He proceeded to Jagannātha Purī.

TEXT 216

গঙ্গাতীরে-তীরে প্রভু চারিজন-সাথে।
নীলাদ্রি চলিলা প্রভু ছত্রভোগ-পথে ॥ ২১৬ ॥

gaṅgā-tīre-tīre prabhu cāri-jana-sāthe
nīlādri calilā prabhu chatrabhoga-pathe

SYNONYMS

gaṅgā-tīre-tīre—on the banks of the Ganges; *prabhu*—the Lord; *cāri-jana-sāthe*—with the other four persons; *nīlādri*—to Jagannātha Purī; *calilā*—proceeded; *prabhu*—the Lord; *chatra-bhoga-pathe*—on the path of Chatrabhoga.

TRANSLATION

The Lord, with the other four persons, went along the banks of the Ganges through the path of Chatrabhoga toward Nīlādri, Jagannātha Purī.

PURPORT

In the southern section of the eastern railway, in the district of twenty-four *parganās,* is a station named Magrāhāṭa. If one goes to the southeastern side of that station for some fourteen miles, there is a place called Jayanagara. About six miles south of this Jayanagara station is a village named Chatrabhoga. Sometimes this village is called Khāḍi. In this village is a Deity of Lord Śiva known as Vaijurkānātha. A festival takes place there every year during the months of March and April. The festival is known as Nandā-melā. At the present moment the Ganges does not flow there. On the same railway line is another station, known as Bāruipura, and near this station is another place, called Āṭisārā. Formerly this village was also situated on the banks of the Ganges. One can go from this village to Pāṇihāṭī and from there to Varāha-nagara, north of Calcutta. In those days the Ganges flowed to the south of Calcutta through Kālī-ghāṭa, which is still known as *ādi-gaṅgā*. From Bāruipura, the Ganges branched out and flowed through Diamond Harbor near the Mathurāpura police station. It is to be noted that Śrī Caitanya Mahāprabhu passed through all these places on His way to Jagannātha Purī.

TEXT 217

'চৈতন্যমঙ্গলে' প্রভুর নীলাদ্রি-গমন ।
বিস্তারি বর্ণিয়াছেন দাস-বৃন্দাবন ॥ ২১৭ ॥

'caitanya-maṅgale' prabhura nīlādri-gamana
vistāri varṇiyāchena dāsa-vṛndāvana

SYNONYMS

caitanya-maṅgale—in the book named *Caitanya-maṅgala*; *prabhura*—of the Lord; *nīlādri-gamana*—going to Jagannātha Purī; *vistāri*—elaborating; *varṇiyāchena*—has described; *dāsa-vṛndāvana*—Vṛndāvana dāsa Ṭhākura.

TRANSLATION

In his book known as Caitanya-maṅgala [Caitanya-bhāgavata] Vṛndāvana dāsa Ṭhākura has elaborately described the Lord's passage to Jagannātha Purī.

PURPORT

Śrīla Bhaktisiddhānta Sarasvatī Ṭhākura states that while Śrī Caitanya Mahāprabhu passed through Bengal, He passed through Āṭisārā-grāma, Varāha-grāma and Chatrabhoga. He then reached the Orissa province, where he passed through Prayāga-ghāṭa, Suvarṇarekhā, Remuṇā, Yājapura, Vaitaraṇī, Daśāśvamedha-ghāṭa, Kaṭaka, Mahānadī, Bhuvaneśvara (where there is a big lake known as Bindu-sarovara), Kamalapura and Āthāranālā. In this way, passing through all these and other places, He reached Jagannātha Purī.

TEXT 218

অদ্বৈত-গৃহে প্রভুর বিলাস শুনে যেই জন ।
অচিরে মিলয়ে তাঁরে কৃষ্ণপ্রেম-ধন ॥ ২১৮ ॥

advaita-gṛhe prabhura vilāsa śune yei jana
acire milaye tāṅre kṛṣṇa-prema-dhana

SYNONYMS

advaita-gṛhe—at the house of Advaita Ācārya; *prabhura*—of the Lord; *vilāsa*—the pastimes; *śune*—hears; *yei*—one who; *jana*—person; *acire*—very soon; *milaye*—meets; *tāṅre*—him; *kṛṣṇa-prema-dhana*—the riches of love of Godhead.

TRANSLATION

If one hears the activities of the Lord at the house of Advaita Ācārya, he will certainly very soon attain the riches of love of Kṛṣṇa.

TEXT 219

শ্রীরূপ-রঘুনাথ-পদে যার আশ ।
চৈতন্যচরিতামৃত কহে কৃষ্ণদাস ॥ ২১৯ ॥

śrī-rūpa-raghunātha-pade yāra āśa
caitanya-caritāmṛta kahe kṛṣṇadāsa

SYNONYMS

śrī-rūpa—Śrīla Rūpa Gosvāmī; *raghu-nātha*—Śrīla Raghunātha dāsa Gosvāmī; *pade*—at their lotus feet; *yāra*—whose; *āśa*—expectation; *caitanya-caritāmṛta*—the book named *Caitanya-caritāmṛta; kahe*—describes; *kṛṣṇa-dāsa*—Śrīla Kṛṣṇadāsa Kavirāja Gosvāmī.

TRANSLATION

Praying at the lotus feet of Śrī Rūpa and Śrī Raghunātha, always desiring their mercy, I, Kṛṣṇadāsa, narrate Śrī Caitanya-caritāmṛta, following in their footsteps.

Thus end the Bhaktivedanta purports to the Śrī Caitanya-caritāmṛta, Madhya-līlā, *Third Chapter, describing Lord Caitanya Mahāprabhu's stay at the house of Advaita Ācārya, His acceptance of the* sannyāsa *order and observation of daily festivals at Advaita Ācārya's house, His congregationally chanting the holy name of the Lord and His feasting with all the devotees.*

References

The statements of *Śrī Caitanya-caritāmṛta* are all confirmed by standard Vedic authorities. The following authentic scriptures are quoted in this book on the pages listed. Numerals in bold type refer the reader to *Śrī Caitanya-caritāmṛta's* translations. Numerals in regular type are references to its purports.

Amṛta-pravāha-bhāṣya (Bhaktivinoda Ṭhākura), 239

Anubhāṣya, (Bhaktisiddhānta Sarasvatī), 31-33, 54

Bhagavad-gītā, 18, 97, 107, 243, 324-327, 332

Bhakti-rasāmṛta-sindhu (Rūpa Gosvāmī), 60, **113,** 173, 190-191, 211-212, 214 218 219, 306-307, 322

Bhakti-ratnākara (Narahari Cakravartī), 19,112

Bṛhad-viṣṇu Purāṇa, 293

Caitanya-candrodaya-nāṭaka (Prabhodhānanda Sarasvatī), 255

Caitanya-maṅgala (Vṛndāvana dāsa Ṭhākura), **7, 351**

Gīta-govinda (Jayadeva Gosvāmī), **223**

Jagannātha-vallabha-nāṭaka (Rāmānanda Rāya), **176-177, 191-192**

Kṛṣṇa-karṇāmṛta (Bilvamaṅgala Ṭhākura), **207, 209, 213**

Kūrma Purāṇa, **75**

Lalita-mādhava (Rūpa Gosvāmī), **56**

Padma Purāṇa, 125

Padyāvalī (Rūpa Gosvāmī), **41,** 51

Śrīmad-Bhāgavatam, 18, 39, **53-54,** 112, 119-120, 186-188, **242-243,** 279, 332, 344

Stotra-ratna (Yamunācārya), **122, 124**

Glossary

A

Adhama—the lowest among men.
Ādi-līlā—the first twenty-four years of Lord Caitanya's pastimes.
Ahaṅgrahopāsanā—self-worship.
Antya-līlā—the last eighteen years of Lord Caitanya's pastimes.
Anubhāva—bodily symptoms manifested by a devotee in ecstatic love for Kṛṣṇa.
Avadhūta—one who is above all rules and regulations.

B

Bhakti—purified service of the senses of the Lord by one's own senses.
Bhakti-rasa—the mellow derived from devotional service.
Bhaya—fear.
Bhinna-rūpa-sandhi—the meeting of contradictory ecstasies.

D

Daṇḍavat—falling down like a rod before one's superior.

G

Gaura—of fair complexion.
Gṛhamedhī—envious householder who lives only for sense gratification.
Gṛhastha—a God-conscious householder.
Guru-pūjā—worship of the spiritual master.

J

Jñāna-kāṇḍa—philosophical speculation with the intention of being delivered from material entanglement.

K

Kāma—lusty desire.
Karma-tyāga—the giving of the results of *karma* to the Supreme Lord.
Kīrtana—glorification of the Supreme Lord.

Krodha—anger.
Kṛṣṇa-kathā—topics spoken by or about Kṛṣṇa.
Ku-viṣaya—sense gratificatory activities performed under sinful conditions.

L

Līlā-avatāras—incarnations who descend to display spiritual pastimes in the material world.

M

Madana-mohana—Kṛṣṇa, the enchanter of Cupid.
Madhya-līlā—the pastimes of Lord Caitanya performed while He was traveling all over India.
Mahā-bhāgavata—a great devotee of the Lord.
Mahābhāva—the highest stage of love of God.
Mahā-mahā-prasāda—the remnants of food left by a pure Vaiṣṇava.
Mālā—chanting with beads.
Mantra—a sound vibration which liberates the mind.
Mleccha—a meat-eater.
Mukti—liberation.

N

Nitya-siddha—eternally liberated.

P

Puruṣāvatāras—incarnations of the Lord who create, maintain and destroy the material universes.

R

Rāgānugā-bhakti—spontaneous love of Godhead.

S

Śālagrāma-śilā—a Deity of Nārāyaṇa in the form of a small stone.
Sālokya—liberation in which one goes to the Lord's abode.
Sāmīpya—liberation in which one becomes an associate of the Lord.

Saṁskāra—Vedic reformatory rituals.
Saṅkīrtana—congregational chanting of the Lord's holy names.
Śānta—the neutral stage of love of God.
Sārūpya—liberation in which one obtains a body like the Lord's.
Śāstras—Vedic literatures.
Sāttvika—symptoms of ecstatic love coming from the transcendental platform.
Śeṣa-līlā—the last twenty-four years of Lord Caitanya's pastimes.
Śuddha-sattva—the spiritual platform of pure goodness.
Su-viṣaya—regulated sense gratification according to the *Vedas.*
Svāṁśa—Kṛṣṇa's plenary portions.
Svarūpa-sandhi—the meeting of similar ecstasies from separate causes.

T

Tilaka—symbols of the Lord on a devotee's body.

V

Vaikuṇṭha-jagat—the spiritual world.
Vibhāva—the cause or basis for relishing transcendental mellow.
Vibhinnāṁśa—the minute living entities, who are part and parcel of the Supreme Lord.
Viṣaya—entanglement in the laws of nature by sense gratification.

Y

Yavana—one who has deviated from Vedic culture.

Bengali Pronunciation Guide

BENGALI DIACRITICAL EQUIVALENTS AND PRONUNCIATION

Vowels

অ a আ ā ই i ঈ ī উ u ঊ ū ঋ ṛ

ৠ ṝ এ e ঐ ai ও o ঔ au

ং ṁ *(anusvāra)* ঁ ṅ *(candra-bindu)* ঃ ḥ *(visarga)*

Consonants

Gutturals:	ক ka	খ kha	গ ga	ঘ gha	ঙ ṅa
Palatals:	চ ca	ছ cha	জ ja	ঝ jha	ঞ ña
Cerebrals:	ট ṭa	ঠ ṭha	ড ḍa	ঢ ḍha	ণ ṇa
Dentals:	ত ta	থ tha	দ da	ধ dha	ন na
Labials:	প pa	ফ pha	ব ba	ভ bha	ম ma
Semivowels:	য ya	র ra	ল la	ব va	
Sibilants:	শ śa	ষ ṣa	স sa	হ ha	

Vowel Symbols

The vowels are written as follows after a consonant:

া ā ি i ী ī ু u ূ ū ৃ ṛ ৄ ṝ ে e ৈ ai ো o ৌ au

For example: কা kā কি ki কী kī কু ku কূ kū কৃ kṛ

কৄ kṝ কে ke কৈ kai কো ko কৌ kau

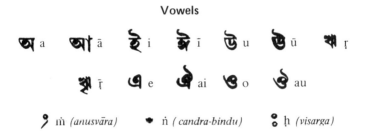

The letter *a* is implied after a consonant with no vowel symbol.

The symbol *virāma* (্) indicates that there is no final vowel. ক্ k

The letters above should be pronounced as follows:

a –like the *o* in h*o*t; sometimes like the *o* in go; final *a* is usually silent.
ā –like the *a* in f*a*r.
i, ī –like the *ee* in m*ee*t.
u, ū –like the *u* in r*u*le.
ṛ –like the *ri* in *ri*m.
ṝ –like the *ree* in *ree*d.
e –like the *ai* in p*ai*n; rarely like *e* in b*e*t.
ai –like the *oi* in b*oi*l.
o –like the *o* in g*o*.
au –like the *ow* in *ow*l.
ṁ –*(anusvāra)* like the *ng* in so*ng*.
ḥ –*(visarga)* a final *h* sound like in Ah.
ṅ – *(candra-bindu)* a nasal *n* sound like in the French word *bon*.
k –like the *k* in *k*ite.
kh –like the *kh* in Ec*kh*art.
g –like the *g* in *g*ot.
gh –like the *gh* in bi*g-h*ouse.
ṅ –like the *n* in ba*n*k.
c –like the *ch* in *ch*alk.
ch –like the *chh* in mu*ch-h*aste.
j –like the *j* in *j*oy.
jh –like the *geh* in colle*ge-h*all.
ñ –like the *n* in bu*n*ch.
ṭ –like the *t* in *t*alk.
ṭh –like the *th* in ho*t-h*ouse.
ḍ –like the *d* in *d*awn.
ḍh –like the *dh* in goo*d-h*ouse.
ṇ –like the *n* in *gn*aw.
t–as in *t*alk but with the tongue against the the teeth.
th–as in ho*t-h*ouse but with the tongue against the teeth.
d–as in *d*awn but with the tongue against the teeth.
dh–as in goo*d-h*ouse but with the tongue against the teeth.
n–as in *n*or but with the tongue against the teeth.
p –like the *p* in *p*ine.
ph –like the *ph* in *ph*ilosopher.
b –like the *b* in *b*ird.
bh –like the *bh* in ru*b-h*ard.
m –like the *m* in *m*other.
y –like the *j* in *j*aw. য
y –like the *y* in *y*ear. য়
r –like the *r* in *r*un.
l –like the *l* in *l*aw.
v –like the *b* in *b*ird or like the *w* in d*w*arf.
ś, ṣ –like the *sh* in *sh*op.
s –like the *s* in *s*un.
h–like the *h* in *h*ome.

This is a general guide to Bengali pronunciation. The Bengali transliterations in this book accurately show the original Bengali spelling of the text. One should note, however, that in Bengali, as in English, spelling is not always a true indication of how a word is pronounced. Tape recordings of His Divine Grace A.C. Bhaktivedanta Swami Prabhupāda chanting the original Bengali verses are available from the International Society for Krishna Consciousness, 3959 Landmark St., Culver City, California 90230.

Index of Bengali and Sanskrit Verses

This index constitutes a complete alphabetical listing of the first and third lines of each Bengali verse and all the lines of each Sanskrit verse in *Śrī Caitanya-caritāmṛta*. In the first column the transliteration is given, and in the second and third columns respectively the chapter-verse references and page number for each verse are to be found.

B

L

M

N

R

U

General Index

Numerals in bold type indicate references to *Śrī Caitanya-caritāmṛta's* verses. Numerals in regular type are references to its purports.

A

Ācāryaratna
as name of Candraśekhara, **251**
Advaita Ācārya
all His opulences used to worship Lord, **344**
as ideal *gṛhastha,* 262
brought devotees to Jagannātha Purī, **85**
Caitanya ate at house of, **62**
Caitanya fulfilled all desires of, **288**
Caitanya stayed at house of, **138**
danced with Nityānanda and Haridāsa, **299**
house of converted into Vaikuṇṭha, **319**
joking words between Nityānanda and, **282-286**
Lord fed by hands of, **152**
visited Lord at Purī, **149**
Ahovala-nṛsiṁha
temple of visited by Caitanya, **69**
Ālālanātha
visited by Caitanya, **77**-78
Allahabad (Prayāga)
Ganges and Yamunā mix at, 259
Amṛta-pravāha-bhāṣya
summary study of Third Chapter in, 239
Anantadeva
Caitanya visited temple of, **73**
Anāsaktasya viṣayān
verses quoted, 60
Anāśritaḥ karma-phalaṁ
quoted, 243
Anubhāṣya
information about *Gopāla-campū* in, 31-33
quoted on service of *gopīs,* 54
Arjuna
Rāmānanda Rāya as incarnation of, 224
Āyur harati vai puṁsām
verses quoted, 186

B

Bahir jalāśayaṁ gatvā
verses quoted, 279
Balabhadra Bhaṭṭācārya
accompanied Caitanya to Jagannātha Purī, **140**
Balārama
Nityānanda as, 15
Bali
killed by Rāmacandra, 74
Barhāyite te nayane narāṇāṁ
verses quoted, 187
Benares
Caitanya bestowed mercy on Māyāvādīs in, **144**
Caitanya stayed at, **141**
Bengal
Nityānanda sent to, **13,152**
Bhadraka
as city visited by Caitanya, **91**
Bhagavad-gītā
quoted on appearance of Lord, 332
quoted on essence of Vedic knowledge, 18
quoted on fate of unsuccessful *yogī,* 324-325
quoted on Lord as supreme proprietor, 107
quoted on offering to Lord with love, 97
quoted on real *sannyāsī,* 243
Bhagavān
resided with Lord at Jagannātha Purī, **148**
Bhāgavatāmṛta
as book compiled by Sanātana Gosvāmī, **19**
Bhāgavata-sandarbha
contents of described, **28**-31
Bhagavat-sandarbha
as division of *Bhāgavata-sandarbha,* 28

H

I

T